DO371761

Advance praise for Jill Filipovic's *The H-Spot*

"*The H-Spot* is the feminist book we've all been waiting for. Filipovic is a brilliant and engaging writer, and offers a necessary new way to think about gender, politics, and happiness. In the current political moment, *The H-Spot* couldn't be better timed."   —JESSICA VALENTI, author of *Sex Object*

"What if, instead of relying on women to self-sacrifice and man-please, society valued women's happiness? What would have to change—in our social and political arrangements, at work, at home, in bed? Widely known for her shrewd and searching journalism on contemporary feminist issues, Jill Filipovic is the perfect writer to raise these provocative questions—and point the way to some answers."
   —KATHA POLLITT, author of *Pro: Reclaiming Abortion Rights*

"Jill Fillipovic consistently captures the modern zeitgeist and I rely on her fresh perspective. Read her book; she will give us hope for the future like no one else can."   —SALLY KOHN

"This is a damn good book that is filling in blank spots I didn't know I had about sex, about women, about history, and about how much better our lives, relationships, and societies could be if we opened up our imaginations as Jill has so courageously, generously, and effectively done. Men, women, and everyone on the spectrum in between should read and talk about this book."   —BARATUNDE THURSTON, author of *How to Be Black*

"Sexism and misogyny may be humankind's primary flaws, and Jill Filipovic offers a searing and sanguine look at how they block the happiness of women and men alike. Her debut is a guide to better living through an emancipatory mindset. If you thought feminism's goal was gender equality alone, *The H-Spot* demands that we expect more."
   —JAMIL SMITH, journalist and cultural critic

"Jill's book is a much-needed examination of the intersection of two issues we rarely see discussed together: feminism and happiness. For too long, critics of feminism have used the happiness argument to belittle the importance of the cause and argue that female emancipation somehow makes women unhappy. It couldn't be further from the truth. Empowered women are happier women. We should all have a right to happiness and for far too long, women have been excluded from that pursuit. In her book, Jill makes an eloquent case for women's right to be truly happy. It's about damn time someone said it, women deserve and have earned their happiness, and they are going to take it!"   —LIZ PLANK, senior correspondent, Vox

"By politicizing the question 'What makes women happy?' Jill Filipovic turns us away from the world of self-help and self-improvement to focus on the systems that deny women the right to fulfillment. *The H-Spot* is a deeply researched and cogently argued book that demands a radical reimagining of policy to ensure not only an end to gender oppression, but the establishment of new systems where women's happiness is not sidelined or ignored, and is instead central to our understanding of freedom."
   —MYCHAL DENZEL SMITH, author of *Invisible Man,*
      Got the Whole World Watching

"Women have come a long way, but the idea that women deserve to feel pleasure is still a third rail in American society. Jill Filipovic asks, instead, what if we stopped talking about women solely as wives, mothers, and workers, and started to think of women as people who have a right to pursue happiness—for themselves. The idea makes many people squirm, but the result would be a better society, for everyone."
   —AMANDA MARCOTTE, author of *It's a Jungle Out There*

"A sound analysis of what really makes women happy. . . . An assertive, eye-opening investigation of women's happiness. [Filipovic's] research and analysis are spot-on, and she provides readers with plenty of useful information to drive deep and necessary discussions for years to come. A timely, enlightening exploration of what American women truly want and need to live purposeful, fulfilling, happy lives."   —*Kirkus Reviews*

THE H-SPOT

The

H-SPOT

The Feminist Pursuit *of* Happiness

JILL FILIPOVIC

NATION
BOOKS
New York

Published by Nation Books, an imprint of Perseus Books, LLC, a subsidiary of Hachette Book Group, Inc.
116 East 16th Street, 8th Floor
New York, NY 10003

Nation Books is a co-publishing venture of the Nation Institute and the Perseus Books Group.

Books published by Nation Books are available at special discounts for bulk purchases in the United States by corporations, institutions, and other organizations. For more information, please contact the Special Markets Department at the Perseus Books Group, 2300 Chestnut Street, Suite 200, Philadelphia, PA 19103, or call (800) 810-4145, ext. 5000, or e-mail special.markets@perseusbooks.com.

Designed by Jeff Williams

Library of Congress Cataloging-in-Publication Data

Names: Filipovic, Jill.
Title: The H-spot : the feminist pursuit of happiness / Jill Filipovic.
Description: New York : Nation Books, 2017. | Includes bibliographical
    references.
Identifiers: LCCN 2016050782 | ISBN 9781568585475 (hardback) | ISBN
9781568585482 (ebook)
Subjects: LCSH: Women—Psychology. | Happiness. | BISAC: SOCIAL SCIENCE/
    Women's Studies. | POLITICAL SCIENCE / Public Policy / Social Policy. |
    SOCIAL SCIENCE / Feminism & Feminist Theory.
Classification: LCC HQ1206 F4628 2017 | DDC 155.3/33242—dc23 LC record
available at https://lccn.loc.gov/2016050782

10 9 8 7 6 5 4 3 2 1

For Mom.
I hope this makes up for the fourth grade.

Contents

Introduction

> Ultimately the greatest service a woman can do to her
> community is to be happy; the degree of revolt and
> irresponsibility which she must manifest to acquire
> happiness is the only sure indication of the way things
> must change if there is to be any point in continuing
> to be a woman at all.
>
> —*Germaine Greer*

FOR THREE YEARS of my midtwenties, the happiest I felt was in the backseat of a car, late at night, driving down the FDR on the east side of Manhattan. I would look out the window across the river at the lit-up Pepsi-Cola sign in Queens, then the Domino Sugar factory in Williamsburg, and finally the three bridges—Williamsburg, Manhattan, Brooklyn—the last of which would take me home. I took that drive probably a hundred times. It was usually dark, maybe 11 p.m., maybe 3 a.m.; maybe the sun was already peeking up. I would slump back, gaze out, and silently calculate how long I had to sleep before I had to be back in midtown Manhattan. But in those nighttime hours speeding down the East Side, I would look at the outer borough lights and the imposing bridges and this impossibly bright city and remind myself to grasp at the one thing that made me happy: *at least you're here.*

Up until that point, I had spent most of my life doing things right. I was a good student in high school, went to college, and then chose a path to an upper-middle-class life that is well worn by risk-averse overachievers: law school. All around me in New York City it seemed people were doing dynamic, fascinating things, but I had no idea how to be one of them, no knowledge of how to balance my desire for an interesting life with the need for stability. And growing up with parents who were the first in their families to elbow their way into the middle class, I understood instinctively that stability mattered most. So, more than $200,000 in debt from law school, I took a job at a Manhattan law firm, clicking like a Clydesdale in cushion-soled heels through the front doors of a big Midtown building every morning, feeling very grown up.

It's one of the least sympathetic and most clichéd stories of modern American life: Young corporate lawyer is overworked and trapped (in the romantic comedy version of this story, she's also undersexed and wears her hair in a very severe bun). She makes six figures, but her tasteful apartment and designer clothes don't bring her happiness (in the real-life version of this story, most of that money goes to her law school loans and she lives with a roommate in Brooklyn).

The story doesn't end with me leaning in harder and opening my own firm, or leaning all the way out and moving to Bali to do yoga, or meeting someone handsome who works with his hands and moving to a farmhouse where I find purpose making artisanal jams. It doesn't end at all, and definitely not with a self-help book or some sort of manifesto about how to find personal happiness. The book in your hands is, thankfully, not about another young lawyer who quit her job and found herself.

It is instead about all of the ways in which Americans carry, and our institutions reflect, a profound and abiding antipathy toward women's day-to-day enjoyment and our broader fulfillment. At twenty-seven, physically ill and emotionally depleted, I made the decision to seek happiness elsewhere—I left practicing law and began writing full time, and I remain lucky (and extraordinarily happy) to have a job that doesn't feel like one. Still, when people ask me what I write about, I often joke, darkly, that I'm on "the rape and abortion beat." That's what I find myself writing about again and again: stigma, trauma, pain, the moments in women's lives that are often some of the hardest, that are routinely made more difficult by American law, culture, and pervasive inequality.

In writing about the same topics from different angles—the social and often sexual punishment of women who are perceived to have misbehaved, the lashing out at powerful women, the uneasiness with which the general public interacts with women who have power or money or influence or some combination of all three, the political opposition to women having sex for fun—it became clear, quickly, that a lot of the problems feminists continue to take on are rooted in a deep hostility toward and suspicion of unfettered female pleasure, happiness, and independence.

As I rounded the corner into my thirties as a member of one of the most privileged groups of people in human history—college-educated white professionals living in a major First World metropolis—I was looking out from a bubble where feminism and progressivism were fairly standard but where, still, so many of the women I knew were butting up against barriers we assumed had been largely dismantled. We were trying to figure out which parts of the old model of femininity to keep and which ones were worth discarding—and what social costs we would bear for both.

I watched the men I know reckon with exactly none of this.

As a journalist, I talked to a lot of women outside this bubble of New York City privilege, around the United States and outside of it. What I heard is that, although the details are all different and the struggles often more pronounced, their overarching questions were similar to mine: What does it mean to be a woman when there are more ways to be female than ever before but when the choices in front of us feel at once overwhelmingly wide and impossibly restrictive? How do I reconcile what I want with the options I have—and how do I even know what I want or what my options are when so many paths seem to lead to closed doors? I've done the things I was supposed to do; why do I feel so cheated?

The challenges, too, may differ in the specifics, but there are through lines: too much work and not enough time; pressure to be a perfect wife or mother or daughter or girlfriend; anxiety at having bad sex or not enough sex or the wrong kind of sex; not enough money and not enough resources. Across the board, women are on a gerbil wheel, running to catch up—to their own expectations, to outside ideals, to men—and never quite making it.

Well before I began this book, it was clear to me that we have a problem with female pleasure and that it is holding women back. Our political and cultural priorities aren't about making life more enjoyable but about getting ahead, attaining bigger and better things, "having it all." But the system is rigged: Men have long been able to "have it all" because of free female labor. As women have achieved more highly in the workplace and gained greater social, political, and economic freedoms, the bar of success has gotten higher—never before have we had to work so much at every level, whether it's to be an accomplished white-collar professional or just to make ends meet; never before have the requirements for being a good mother been so extreme.

At the same time, political debates rage around the very policies that would make it easier for women to succeed. Women today live in a world of unfinished feminism, where we're told we're equal but see our basic rights up for grabs, where we're told to just push harder at work, or recognize we can't have it all, or marry Mr. Good Enough.

The feminist movement's answer to pervasive inequality has been simple: make women equal to men. That's a laudable goal, especially in the early stages of any movement for social equality: Get laws on the books that put two disparate groups on equal footing and enforce them. Get members of the disempowered group into positions of power, roughly proportional to their share of the population. Shift policy priorities to reflect the needs of the disempowered group so that that group may become more equal to the powerful one.

In the second wave of the feminist movement, roughly in the 1960s and '70s, there was a sometimes complementary and sometimes competing vision for the movement's priorities: appreciate women's work more, rather than pushing women to work like men. Proposals included everything from valuing more highly pink-collar care work (that is, low-skilled work dominated by women, like nursing and child care) to paying women for their at-home labor (compensating women for cleaning the house and caring for their own kids). There have been a handful of successes: unionizing domestic workers, requiring minimum wage and basic labor protections for some workers whose job sites are in private homes. But traditional "women's work" remains undervalued and underpaid. The idea that women should get paid for being stay-at-home moms is laughable, and isn't much discussed within feminist circles today, at least outside of academic settings.

Instead, we talk more about "balance" and sharing at-home work with a presumably heterosexual partner. As feminist discourse becomes increasingly mainstream, feminists continue to debate how best to achieve gender equality (some feminists debate whether gender equality is even the ultimate goal); we debate what equality looks like, what it means, and who is making themselves equal to whom. Does gender equality start with making individual adjustments to better our professional prospects—each of us climbing the corporate ladder, and giving the women below a hand up, until we break the glass ceiling? Or is the feminist project about undoing entire systems, challenging capitalist norms, and trying to improve conditions for the masses—recognizing, as feminist writer Audre Lorde put it, that the master's tools can never dismantle the master's house? Can it be both?

The more I interviewed women and wrote about reproduction and sex and work and family, the more I became convinced we were getting inadequate results because we were asking the wrong questions. No amount of trying to catch up or insisting women's work had value was going to fix the fundamental problem: we're operating in a system created by men, for men, according to their whims and desires. Of course women can't flourish in a system that needs us as support pillars for someone else's building. We're here to prop it up, not to live in it. This is not a place that was built for us to thrive.

The answer isn't then to simply value more highly what women actually do—lots of women do what they do because it makes men's lives easier. The answer isn't to simply try to be better at the limited tasks set before us. The answer is to ask, What would we make if we had all the tools? What do we want?

That's a more complicated proposition than it sounds, mostly because people are terrible at predicting what will make them happy and what they actually desire, and there are all kinds of social benefits for women who say that what they want is, conveniently, the same thing men want for them. Figuring out what works for women means talking to women and observing our lives, while also folding in the increasingly large body of social science on what makes us happy, what keeps us healthy, and what helps us to prosper. Increased gender equality is one of those things, and feminism has undoubtedly improved conditions for both women and men across the United States. What could topple the most stubborn roadblocks is a feminism and a politics that reorient themselves away from simple equality and toward happiness and pleasure.

There is no question that the women's rights movement in the United States has been a success, if one that came in fits and starts. Less than one hundred years after women gained the right to vote, we're now graduating from college at higher rates than men; we're getting married later, having fewer children, living longer. The rights to abortion and contraception have allowed many American women to delay child-bearing until we're ready, opening up new opportunities and improving the health of women and our children. Women are making inroads into traditionally male careers, from law and medicine to sports and blue-collar labor. Millennial women are some of the most feminist in history. Little girls grow up hearing that they can be whatever they want.

But that promise remains unfulfilled because, still, we haven't caught up. Men make more money for the same work in nearly every profession and across age ranges. That wage gap is exacerbated when you compare white men to women of color, and it gets worse with age, especially when women have kids. Poverty remains feminized, and many of the women living in poverty are single moms who are unsupported and socially stigmatized. Women hitting retirement are finding that a lifelong wage gap coupled with social security programs that don't consider at-home work to be real work means less to live on as they age, which translates into greater financial instability and, often, reliance on their children (and caretakers for elderly parents are more likely to be daughters than sons, often pulling those younger women out of the paid workforce and perpetuating a cycle of financial vulnerability).

The problems aren't just economic. Decades after the advent of hormonal birth control, women in the United States still struggle for the right to make basic reproductive decisions without political interference. The "sexual revolution" made sex more present in the public sphere than ever before, but sexual pleasure—which is different from using visual representations of sex to sell stuff—is remarkably absent. Women's sexuality remains understood primarily in relation to men's, and women's bodies still serve as physical stand-ins for sex itself, with sexy women selling everything from hamburgers to car parts to Internet service. At the same time, we punish women who are actually sexual or who cross some always-shifting external boundary of sexual propriety. Our identities are too often defined by our relationships to other people—wife, mother, daughter—and prominent politicians defend women's rights by describing us relationally to men. Even many "egalitarian" hetero sexual relationships still involve the female partner putting her career second and doing the majority of the care work, whether that's for her husband, their children, or an aging parent.

Often, you'll see this billed as "choice" or as women pursuing personal happiness because the language of feminism has been neatly co-opted by a strain of peculiarly American individualism. If you're an American woman today, you have almost certainly come across outlets promising paths to happiness and to its distorted sibling, "empowerment." Mostly, those paths involve buying something: a chain restaurant meal, a SoulCycle class, a chocolate bar, a self-help book that tells you to have more collections or own less stuff or quit your job. Happiness is now a concept you find in magazines selling women regressive ideas repackaged for an Instagram photo.

The American pursuit of happiness has morphed from a political promise made in the very declaration of our independent nation into a thoroughly capitalist endeavor, packaged and sold to individuals with the promise that if you just get this thing—if you just choose to pay for this thing—you'll be fulfilled. We are aspirational and pleasure saturated, yet still happiness deficient.

We're learning more and more about what actually benefits women and how that fits with what women say we want for our lives—and how what women say shifts as our opportunities do. The idea that women are entitled not just to equality but to pleasure—to that term specifically, with its connotations of sex and hedonism and selfishness—remains taboo in political discourse. We're programmed to assume the best women can do is to just get by—or if we are remarkably privileged, embark on expensive quests of personal self-betterment.

What if, instead, the goal were happiness? Not at an individual level, with more yoga or self-care or Pinterest-perfect hobbies, but a political one: What would the world look like if our laws and policies prioritized feeling good?

When it comes to pleasure, our political forces run the gamut from indifference to outright hostility, either ignoring any interest in feeling good or writing off pleasure as immoral, hedonistic, even lazy. That American law and policy should keep citizens healthy and safe is controversial enough; that it should strive to make us happy seems laughable.

Even in the absence of institutional and structural forces promoting female happiness, most women still try, however imperfectly and with mixed results, to maximize theirs. Which is how I found myself pinging between writing jobs before picking up and moving to Kenya: after ending my career as a lawyer, I freelanced for a bit, then took a job as a political writer for Cosmopolitan.com, and a year later left that job, too, jumping back in the financially precarious life of a freelancer, this time halfway around the world. I was moving mostly in pursuit of happiness, a career change, and love, but also because it sounded like an adventure, the kind of life I had long wanted but had been too scared to grab hold of. Still, I found myself struggling to explain why a writer who primarily covered American politics was heading to Nairobi. At a party in New York celebrating a friend's new book, I found myself in a conversation with Glynnis MacNicol, a writer I knew only passingly, and she asked me the question I couldn't quite answer: "Why Kenya?" As I stumbled out an explanation about liking East Africa and wanting a change and hoping to do more international reporting and also my boyfriend was moving there—a part of the story that felt particularly unfeminist—she gently interrupted and said, "So you're moving to Kenya because you can."

"Because I can." It was true, but I was still taken aback, and long after that conversation I found myself unable to say those words out loud. In writing this book, I wavered on writing about my own life at all—especially this part of it. I hesitated because a series of unearned racial and social-class privileges makes my experience of American womanhood an overrepresented outlier, but also because I worried any woman who says she does things just because it feels good sounds entitled and not appropriately—and femininely—deferential and self-effacing. Still, Glynnis's words stuck in my mind as a thoroughly modern justification for women's choices, largely unimaginable even a few generations ago. What a reflection of the huge gains women have made, victories for which movements for women's rights get most of the credit.

And yet, for all of the good work feminism has done, equality means very little when you're making yourself equal to men who are struggling too, or when you're seeking equality in a system that simply wasn't designed for you. In this context of such unequal feminist gains, writing about pleasure seems almost flippant; in the context of a culture hostile to female pleasure, a woman who actively pursues pleasure is spoiled, suspect, threatening. "Because I can" is spectacularly freeing. But that kind of freedom, that expanded ability to dictate the course of one's life, is not on offer for most women. For all of the gains women have made, most American women live in a world of "I can't," their opportunities and choices restricted.

That doesn't mean that happiness and pleasure are only available to a privileged few, or that women in challenging circumstances don't have ideas about how happiness and pleasure (or lack thereof) could and should function in their lives. On the contrary, I found that women for whom "I can't" is a daily reality had some of the most incisive ideas for what a society designed by and for women might look like—even if they often reacted with skepticism to my initial premise.

That was certainly true of Janet Rowland, who knit her eyebrows together at the suggestion that there is perhaps a collective social obligation to help women not only survive but thrive. I showed up at Janet's Raleigh, North Carolina, home on a hot August Wednesday, and as we talked, Janet was tired—she was still hurting from a car accident a few months back, and she spent the previous day at the hospital with her daughter, who was having kidney tests and an MRI done (she had just been diagnosed with scoliosis on top of a rare skin disorder doctors found three years prior). All three of Janet's kids were home, along with her niece, who often stays at Janet's place.

"I just don't want to get to the point that I get hospitalized," Janet told me, as the kids chattered in the kitchen, the bigger ones helping the little ones with their ABCs. "My body has broken down from stress, depression. I didn't know that that area was a big impact in my health, and I was hospitalized for a week with health issues. And that is when I learned that stress could kill you."

Janet, it is an understatement to say, is not happy. And as we talked, she explained how much of her life has been ordered around survival, on chasing after a mirage of what she's supposed to have—a job, a house, a partner, children—but which the complexities of poverty, racism, and sexism keep yanking away, just out of her reach. There hasn't been time to sit with herself and ask, "What do I want?" What she wants today is enough gas to drive to the grocery store.

In the course of writing this book, I spoke with dozens of women— some, like Janet, whose challenges stemmed in part from their socio-economic background, and others whose privilege should have opened up a world of opportunity but were somehow still confined. I spoke with women who were already reordering their own lives in ways that better suited their needs and desires and others who believed that if they just followed the rules and tamed their unconventional or simply human impulses, they would be happy, only to wind up disappointed and resentful at all the promises that went unfulfilled. I stayed with one mother raising her children in an "intentional community" of coliving adults in Seattle and another in Maryland whose husband leaned in at home. I interviewed an OB/GYN in Mormon-heavy Utah and a young woman who regretted "saving herself" for marriage, an urban farmer in the Bronx and a sixtysomething adoptive mother. These are not women whose paths are likely to cross or who on paper seem to share many of the same experiences. And yet many of their challenges stem from the same root: impossible expectations countered by constrained opportunities.

I also immersed myself in a trove of happiness research, pop-science treatises on how to be happy, literature on women and work, studies on female sexuality, and surveys that attempt to paint a picture of contemporary American life. These, too, don't offer simple solutions, but together they begin to form a portrait of female satisfaction, experience, and desire that can inform both the individual choices women make to improve their lives and the broader political conversation about how a pleasure-centered policy landscape could more substantially address the stubborn issues and inequalities women continue to face.

Is pleasure-centered policy the magic bullet for American women's happiness and success? Of course not. But at a political moment when even the most basic rights of women are under threat—when Americans have elected a president who brags about sexual violence and who pledges to appoint Supreme Court justices who will dismantle abortion rights—it is crucial to stay on offense and advocate for what we really want instead of cowering in a defense crouch, accepting crumbs. That means countering regressive political forces with our own moral vision of a great society—one that is structured around women and what brings us satisfaction. For several centuries, women have carried disproportionate burdens to underwrite men's pleasure, success, and happiness. Now, it's time we decided that female pleasure isn't an indulgence or a privilege but a social good—and that women deserve more than just equality.

1

Outrageous Acts and Everyday Rebellions: The History of Women's Unhappiness

> Our histories cling to us. We are shaped by where we come from.
>
> —*Chimamanda Ngozi Adichie*

NOTHING CHANGED MY understanding of happiness more than moving to New York City. As a child growing up in the Seattle suburbs, I assumed my path would look a lot like my parents', or even like the white-collar professionals I saw on TV sitcoms: I would earn a degree, get a good job, marry a nice guy, live in a cute house, and have kids. That was happiness.

New York City, where I moved for college and remained for more than a decade and a half, challenged that definition. The city was a particular kind of wonderland, all energy and novelty, a town that fed my own frenetic drive and creative metabolism. It was teeming with striving, ambitious women like me and with endlessly fascinating women who were like no one I had ever met. It was also bursting with little pleasures: the first day of summer when all the pretty girls wear flimsy new dresses, food sojourns to Chinatown or out to Flushing, the magic (and treachery) of new snow on brownstone steps. And, of course, it was full of particular New York trials: the profound loneliness of being left by a lover, magnified by looking out the window at a city so full of people; the one-upmanship in a place of such ambition, where there's always someone smarter, better, thinner, more successful, or more interesting than you.

New York was the first place I felt completely lost and alone, but also the first place where I felt like I made sense. When I initially moved there, I figured I would eventually head back to Seattle, my hometown, where things were easier, and I would settle into an adult life. The longer I was in New York, though, the less I felt the pull of the life my very young self assumed I would want: a house, a husband, babies, the kind of suburb I grew up in. A happy life, I knew, wouldn't look like that for me; "happy" and "easy" were no longer synonymous. Less clear was what other shape my life could possibly take.

For centuries, scholars and philosophers have debated what makes for a happy life, what "happiness" even means, and where pleasure fits in. For such pervasive concepts, both happiness and pleasure remain ill defined, less easily explained ideas than pornography-style "I know it when I see it" feelings.

Out of centuries-long debates and discussions on happiness, two major philosophical traditions have emerged. One is the hedonic tradition, which in oversimplified terms is about feelings and one's mental state and the balance of positive feelings with negative ones. The other is the eudaimonic tradition, which focuses more on one's capacity to flourish, skills and accomplishments, and personal development.

Pleasure can be understood as a component of happiness in either tradition, but it is the hedonic one that assigns it more weight. Pleasure, quite simply, involves stimulating the senses in a way that feels good: indulging, enjoying. This can be tactile and sensory, as well as social and intellectual. Sensual pleasures involve the good aspects of the five senses: taste, touch, smell, hearing, and sight. Nonsensory pleasures are the things that bring good feelings and often involve physiological arousal: achievement, taking enjoyment in the beauty of a person or an object, gratification that comes from socializing, finding pleasure in a process and not just the end result.

When researchers study happiness today, what they typically look at is "subjective well-being." That is, how happy a person says they feel, either at a given time or about their life generally. Subjective well-being encompasses elements of happiness as spelled out in both the hedonic and eudaimonic traditions, but it is skewed in favor of the hedonic one, because it's about how one rates one's own state of mind, not one's aspirations or achievements. Even so, researchers have mostly treated pleasure as a secondary component of happiness, in part because it's hard to determine, exactly, how pleasure measurably impacts well-being and whether that impact is fleeting or carries on after the positive sensual experience ends.

Happiness researchers have reached a number of important conclusions. The first is that governments influence happiness. Happiness differs across borders, and the countries where people are happiest also tend to be more developed, are politically and economically stable, offer a decent social safety net, comply with human rights principles, and have low levels of corruption and high levels of public trust. People need to feel safe to feel happy.

The second is that human relationships impact happiness. Married people are more likely to be happy than those who are divorced or single (and those who never married are more likely to be happy than those who are divorced). People who are engaged in their communities, whether through socializing or attending religious ceremonies or membership in civic organizations, also tend to be happier, and more sociable people are happier than more reclusive ones.

Finally, the old cliché is true: money doesn't make you happy. But this is true only above a certain baseline. Living poverty, or on the edge of it, drives down happiness, and financial security increases it.

This book looks at both happiness and pleasure. It takes as a starting point the notion of subjective well-being, but it seeks to examine those elements of the eudaimonic tradition—aspirations, achievements, purpose, personal development—that many researchers have excised from their definition. It also takes a more expansive view of pleasure—in both its sensory and nonsensory forms—as not just a critical component of happiness but as a right. Happiness in this view is both a state of being, something that involves contentment and pleasure, and also an aspiration, a way of living that considers fulfillment and purpose.

This kind of happiness, of pleasure fulfillment and fulfillment of purpose, is missing for a great number of American women. That's not because women don't pleasure-seek or fail to find meaning in their lives; it's because even though the concept of happiness is written into the founding document of the United States, it wasn't meant for us. Which brings us to one of the central questions explored in this book: How did we start out as a country that made the pursuit of happiness an explicitly political promise and transform into one where pleasure is politically vilified and financially exploited?

The Declaration of Independence promised Americans something unusual. For almost ninety years, ever since John Locke published his two treatises of government, the prevailing Enlightenment view was that government existed to facilitate citizens' rights to "life, liberty and property." Yet the authors of the declaration replaced property in that formulation with another Lockean idea, "the pursuit of happiness," which the English philosopher once called the "the necessary foundation of our liberty."

For them, as for Locke, the "pursuit of happiness" wasn't as sentimental as it sounds now; it was squarely in the eudaimonic tradition, about purpose and personal growth, including the pursuit of knowledge and individual betterment. Government, the founders seemed to think, had a role in encouraging happiness, an idea that was reflected in downstream documents. The Massachusetts Declaration of Rights, which Declaration of Independence signatory John Adams primarily drafted and which was a model for the US Constitution, made explicit that "government is instituted for the common good, for the protection, safety, prosperity, and happiness of the people, and not for the profit, honor, or private interest of any one man, family, or class of men: therefore the people alone have an incontestable, unalienable, and indefeasible right to institute government, and to reform, alter, or totally change the same when their protection, safety, prosperity, and happiness require it."[1]

But just as the line "All men are created equal" didn't apply to all men, let alone any women, the political promise of happiness was one limited by identity. Although they left "property" out of the "inalienable rights" line in the Declaration of Independence, the authors of the declaration certainly valued theirs—including their human property, the slaves many of them kept—over the rights of people who were neither white nor male to pursue their own happiness. Thomas Jefferson impregnated one of those slaves, Sally Hemings, in a sustained series of rapes some historians have rewritten as a love affair. It is perhaps fitting that "property" was removed from the declaration, because a majority of people living in the United States at the time—the women, slaves, and free blacks who collectively outnumbered white men—couldn't legally own any; some were owned as property themselves.

Land-owning white men dominated the public discourse and decision making on politics, happiness, religion, and the very nature of the new American project. The foundation they laid for the country undergirds it today; many of the modern divisions and disputes over what America should be were born in the eighteenth century, including those about the roles of women and pleasure, in public and in the family.

This is not a history book, and given that there are many excellent volumes written on the subject of women in the early republic, this should be taken for what it is: a summary based on the leading scholarship.[2] There are details and nuances left out, especially when it comes to marginalized communities, whose experiences were rarely recorded: enslaved women, free black women, working-class women, Native American women. Trust that life in America post-1776 was richer and more complex than it is presented as here—indeed, than it is presented in most of the scholarship and writing on the era.

Our history, and how we record it, informs our present, and, as much as movements for gender and racial equality have radically changed life in America, they are pitted against centuries of norms, policies, and cultural ideals that continue to shape political and personal life today. For generations, American women have seen their experiences molded not just by their gender but by their race, class, sexual orientation, religion, and immigration status—all of which in turn continue to influence which women can pursue which objectives, including satisfaction, pleasure, happiness, power, money, and family. In the political realm, many women's experiences have been filtered through white, upper-class male norms, with women cast as deviant, dependent, or deserving depending on how our lives and identities are perceived by men in the more powerful castes.

The challenges women face today are not new. At around the same time that America declared its independence from Great Britain, gender norms were beginning to shift rapidly, in some ways that improved conditions for women and in others that continue to confine us even today. In the colonial United States, strict Puritan sexual ethics were set in opposition to the "savage" practices of Native Americans, who imposed far fewer punitive social rules on sexual activity and sexual pleasure seeking; gender roles certainly existed, but many tribes offered much more gender flexibility than did the European settlers, who had rigid views of men and women. Before the eighteenth century, women in the colonies, England, and much of Europe were seen as more lustful than men, easily giving in to sexual temptation and tempting men in the process. Men, as the spiritually awakened gender, were in charge of protecting the moral welfare of their households, either as husbands or as fathers. That all changed with the rise of Evangelical Protestantism, which quickly became the dominant theology in white America, reshaping the family, politics, law—and a woman's place (or lack thereof) in all of these spheres.

"On both sides of the Atlantic, this image of women gets flipped on its head," Christine Heyrman, a professor of American history at the University of Delaware, told me. "Women are increasingly portrayed as holier than men, better than men morally, more able to control their sexual passions. It is at this point where people in the United States come to think of women as the folks who are in charge when a couple starts engaging in sexual congress of any kind—it's the responsibility of the woman now to say no. And in the phrase of the time, women are often characterized as being passionless, as not having a sex drive."

In some ways, this was a step forward, giving women a certain kind of power—morally superior and in charge of controlling the immorality of others was certainly a step above inherently amoral, childlike, and in need of male control. But the image of the holy woman promulgated by Evangelical Protestantism also circumscribed women to the domestic sphere as "angels in the household," because they were seen as so fragile and pure that they could be easily damaged by an outside world that was messy, chaotic, and corrupt.

A changing American economy also reinforced this shift, as home-based farms gave way to commerce and industrialization. The home was suddenly separated from the workplace, and as the division between the public and the domestic spheres grew sharper, women were more clearly confined to the domestic side. As middle-class men began to leave the house for work at the factory or the store, women who once spent their days dairying or spinning wool or raising chickens refocused their energies on the home front—tending to children and housework. Poorer women occupied the domestic sphere as well, in their own homes and in the homes of the wealthy: black and immigrant women often worked as slaves or servants, either inside a richer family's house or on the property it sat on.

A new media landscape also materialized around this time that was focused primarily on women and feeding a reverence for middle-class female domesticity: a woman as her family's moral and spiritual guardian at home was cast as an aspiration for women and men the country over. The first American women's magazine, the *Ladies Magazine and Repository of Entertaining Knowledge,* was published in 1792 and was quickly imitated by other periodicals seeking to reach literate middle-class white women. A few of these magazines discussed politics, but many were focused primarily on domestic life, occasionally touching on moral and social issues. According to one issue of the Boston magazine the *Ladies Visitor,* "The pages of the Visitor, is open to everything which is entertaining or instructing—but closed against *Politics* and *Obscenity*."[3]

Not all women were on board with occupying apolitical domestic roles, and not all women bought the idea that their new moral pedestal was a privilege and not a trap. Around the turn of the century, the English writer and philosopher Mary Wollstonecraft became a leading "free thinker" and feminist voice, latching onto Enlightenment challenges to authority and ideas about the rights of men, and asking, What about the rights of women? Wollstonecraft's philosophies traveled across the Atlantic—especially the idea, radical at the time, that women should be entitled to an education not just to support their husbands' intellectual interests but to develop their own.

Feminist revolution did not immediately follow. Although Wollstonecraft and other free thinkers had something of a following in the United States, it was small, far outnumbered by Evangelical Protestants, and it engendered a robust backlash. "These *Rights of Woman*," warned one Massachusetts newspaper, "would become the *wrongs* of man."[4] Feminist contributions—and Wollstonecraft's in particular—to political thought and Enlightenment ideals became notable in decades and centuries to come, but they didn't move the needle on American culture nearly as significantly as the religious and economic shifts that took place during this era. When it came to feminism, Evangelicals were "attempting to squelch that kind of free thinking because of the strong notion of the importance of marriage to social stability and a gender hierarchy held together by a kind of affection that was loving and passionate, ideally, but also very hierarchical," Amanda Porterfield, a historian of American religion at Florida State University, told me.

And Wollstonecraft, in a bitter irony, given her skepticism of traditional gender roles, died giving birth to her daughter—Mary Shelley, who would go on to write *Frankenstein*.

Enlightenment ideals, religion, and early feminist thought all converged in a new family economy that came into being right around the same time as an independent United States: love marriage. Marriage continued to serve an important economic function, but that was no longer its primary purpose. Reciprocity and mutual happiness, at least in theory, became the new basis for marital unions, subtly undermining the traditional family hierarchy in which wives and children were supposed to be unilaterally submissive and obedient. The husband, of course, still *was* at the top of the family hierarchy, with legal control over his wife and children and a considerable amount of leeway to mistreat them, but the cultural ideal at least implored him not to. Women weren't equal partners, but they were increasingly valued partners, and an emotional connection to your wife was at least as important as her cooking abilities.

As marriage became more romantic, so too did both parenthood and childhood. Parents have always loved their children, but in the days of early immigration to the United States, families needed a bunch of kids to develop their land; because children often died, families routinely had double-digit numbers of them. And children weren't thought of as innocents; they were small humans who had not yet learned how to be moral citizens, and their parents typically treated them accordingly.

"When the Puritans thought about little kids they thought about little devils running around the household, these little depraved beings who had not learned how to submit their will to the will of God and the will of their parents," Heyrman said. "If you've spent any time with three-year-olds, as I have, you know they were not far off. This whole image of kids as little devils whose wills need to be broken is something that goes the way of the lustful daughters of Eve."

As love marriages dominated, as Enlightenment ideas proliferated, and as the family economy changed, children became expressions of their parents' love, not homemade farm workers. And to give each of those children the love and resources parents had newly concluded they deserved, women began having fewer of them.

Between 1800 and 1900, the average white American woman went from having 7 children to 3.5 (broad and reliable data on black American women doesn't exist until about 1850; between 1850 and 1900, the average black American woman went from having almost 8 children to 5.6).[5] This was well before the invention of the modern birth control pill; women still managed to prevent pregnancies and often ended them,[6] although birth control methods weren't particularly effective and abortions not always particularly safe. When familial happiness became a goal, though—when women concluded that they should derive pleasure from their children—birth control and abortion came with it, and by 1850 as many as one in five pregnancies ended in abortion.[7] And with those things also came, eventually, a conservative religious backlash, led largely by men, demonizing contraception and abortion, often with the argument that it's natural for a woman to find joy in being a mother— and wholly unnatural, then, to limit the number of times in which she becomes one. It was men, and male ideas about women's roles, that defined what female happiness looked like.

Although maternal pleasure was certainly the expectation for women in early America, sexual pleasure was not—nor was it a topic of discussion. Men sought out sex before marriage, partaking in a thriving sex industry, and women from lower-class backgrounds who had few other options worked in the sex trade. But the booming commerce in brothels and bars was understood as fulfilling a youthful male sexual desire; women of good social standing of course didn't participate but also weren't seen as having any analogous desires of their own. For them, pleasure came with marriage and children; sex was merely a means to an end. Many women no doubt enjoyed sex, but there was little popular expectation that sex was something women would do for recreation. For men, the recreational aspect of sex was built into the term for patronizing sex workers: "sporting culture."

Still, in the early nineteenth century, as many as 20 percent of births were conceived out of wedlock. The general understanding was that sex should occur only within marriage, but it was more or less acceptable to engage in intercourse if a marital promise had been made—and if marriage didn't follow sex, that would be an unbleachable stain on a young woman's reputation. The reputational damage done by premarital sexual activity was so extreme that a category of lawsuits for "breach of promise" emerged, wherein women sued men who promised matrimony, slept with them, and didn't follow through on their pledge.[8]

These debates around women and sex, motherhood, and marriage— and what they mean for women's pleasure and happiness—are as old as the United States itself. For men, the pursuit of happiness was a central endeavor, and the new American project provided an answer for how to find it: work. As the aristocracy fell away, work became noble: no longer just for peasants and slaves and women and children, working hard demonstrated that you were of good character, and any successes you enjoyed from work were surely merited. There were religious overtones, too, in the idea that the discipline required for hard work was evidence of salvation.

But work was narrowly defined, and a male-only venture. What women did in the home wasn't considered work—and indeed, upper-class women who were able to stay home didn't do much domestic labor. Instead, their new stature as "angels in the home" depended on the work of slaves, black women, immigrant women, and poor women, many of them not even teenagers. By 1850, about one in nine white households had servants.[9]

With white middle-class women in the Victorian era focused on child-rearing and no longer making their own clothing and household goods, and men seeking their fortunes in an emerging capitalist economy, the factory became a new place of production for things like textiles that women had previously crafted at home. Those same factories also became centers of abuse and exploitation, often of less fortunate women and children. According to the historian Stephanie Coontz, by 1820, half of all factory workers were children under the age of eleven. The romantic view of white middle-class women as delicate moral beacons and the stark divisions of labor between white men and women, Coontz argued, "depended on the existence of African-American, immigrant, and working-class families with very different age and gender roles. Sentimentalization of middle-class family life justified terrible exploitation of those other families."[10]

That labor became divided along gender lines did not mean middle- and upper-class white women all stayed home. They may not have worked for wages, but they were often active social campaigners, volunteering in poverty relief efforts, promoting the temperance movement, advocating for the end of slavery, and even fighting child labor and factory exploitation.

For women who were shut out of this white, middle-class Protestant ideal—immigrant women, many of them Catholic; black women; Native American women; poor and working-class women—life was very different, although a limited historical record means scholars come up short on details. The division between public and private was less pronounced in many of these communities, owing to the fact that women as well as men had to work outside of their own homes to make ends meet. Slaves were typically barred from marrying, their children often sold away and their families ripped apart.

The lives of these "others"—the women and men who were not part of the dominant social, cultural, economic, racial, and political classes— may not be well documented, but that doesn't mean they're entirely lost to history. The norms, economies, and cultures of these "outsiders" trickled into the dominant white culture as much as the dominant culture trickled out, especially given that many immigrants and libertines flocked to cities, where public space was more gender integrated and sexual norms a little looser. They also survived and even flourished to some degree outside of the white middle-class ideal—influenced and often rebuked by, but not always bound to, the dominant norms— including norms about happiness and pleasure.

Still, the white Protestant middle-class model dominated in the popular press, setting up the standard from which others were perceived to deviate. "For women, the summum bonum of all happiness is to get married and have children," Heyrman said about the early nineteenth-century middle-class model. "Nothing could be better than to marry a nice guy and have a whole bunch of kids. For men increasingly, the value of individualism, the value of labor, the value of ambition and achievement, of making the most of yourself, making the most of your talents, is—this is for white guys obviously—that's what it's all about."

For anyone with even a passing interest in contemporary feminism or American politics, all of this should sound awfully familiar: a traditionalist push to emphasize marriage as a catchall benefit for women, a view of female satisfaction that is prescriptive and confined to the domestic sphere, and a vision of work and individual achievement that is exclusively male (all of this, of course, premised on white Christian middle-class experiences and ideals). Conflicts that today seem entirely modern—whether they're about insurance coverage for contraception or the value of marriage in combating child poverty or the anger of the working-class white male voter—very much stem from the foundational standards and beliefs that emerged along with an independent United States. In the final days of her run for president of the United States, Hillary Clinton spoke at a traditionally black church in Philadelphia— the city where the Declaration of Independence was debated and ad- opted, and where it now sits on display. "Our Founders said all men are created equal," Clinton, the first woman nominated as a major party candidate for the presidency, said. But, she added, "they left out African-Americans. They left out women. They left out a lot of us."[11]

So it is that more than two hundred years after "the pursuit of hap- piness" was written into the Declaration of Independence, I'm in a living room in North Carolina, asking Janet Rowland to recall the last time she felt happy. She went silent. "Well . . . ," she said and then looked away, blinking rapidly to stop tears from welling in her eyes. She's been working minimum-wage jobs since she was fifteen. She spent her childhood in and out of foster homes. Two of her exes are in jail, one for beating her badly and repeatedly. She isn't pursuing happiness so much as she is dodging the disasters that always seem to befall her just as things are almost in order: the benefits that get cut off because she worked some extra shifts, the poor housing conditions that force her to move and wipe out her meager savings, the car accident that puts her out of work.

There are moments of pleasure, of course—the smell of her chil- dren's skin, the touch of her boyfriend, the precious minutes she sometimes steals in her car, with the doors locked and her eyes closed, listening to music.

And there are dreams, of course—Janet's is to open a shelter for survivors of domestic violence. She's experienced it, she's seen the gaps in the system, and she likes helping people, so it makes sense. She's looked at a few spaces, done a little searching for how she could get grant money, talked to her public defender who has a lot of clients who have, like Janet, been beaten up by men they loved. She knows she could be good at this. "I am positive on this," Janet said. "It's like I can see my vision unblocking. I can see it."

These are the small things she grasps for when the big ones form storm clouds.

There is not now, nor has there ever been, an American happiness ideal for women like Janet. Even marriage and motherhood are not fetishized or prescribed for her. She is poor and she is black, and the long-standing white middle-class ideal that she would stay home with her kids has never been an option, not for her or her mother or the women before her. The places from which she derives pleasure—her children, her family, her partner, her music, her work, her ambitions—are derided, maligned, denigrated, and taken, sometimes by the state itself. She has to build those pleasures with her own hands, and she has to hold tight to them so they don't fall away.

Between the day the Declaration of Independence was signed and the day I sat in Janet's living room, a lot changed. Slavery ended. Women, people of color, and the poor gained the right to vote. Women entered college en masse. It is no longer legal, in most contexts, to discriminate on the basis of race or sex. We've had an African American president; the great-great-great-grandmother of the former First Lady was a slave.[12]

But a lot has stayed stubbornly stuck in the past. We have made dramatic gains toward racial and gender equality, but, particularly in the political realm, much of what we are told we should aspire to remains troublingly similar to what we heard two centuries ago. The ideal of women as self-sacrificing buoys for important male work survives to the present.

With the growth of industry and the shift toward valuing work in the late nineteenth and early twentieth centuries came what the historian Stephanie Coontz called "the cult of the Self-Made Man"—the myth of the man who builds something from nothing without handouts, the Horatio Alger "bootstraps" story. But of course the self-made man wasn't actually self-made; not only did he benefit from a system that was built on the backs of, and systematically disadvantaged, people of color—because the self-made man was invariably white—he could always count on the free labor of his wife, who was expected to sacrifice her own self-actualization and independence to enable his.

"Self-reliance and independence worked for *men* because *women* took care of dependence and obligation," Coontz wrote in her book *The Way We Never Were: American Families and the Nostalgia Trap*. "In other words, the liberal theory of human nature and political citizenship did not merely leave women out: It worked precisely because it was applied exclusively to half the population." Into the first half of the twentieth century, popular culture and literature extolled the virtues of marriage for women and self-sufficiency for men—and the freakishness of any single-by-choice woman. When World War II pulled men out of the workforce, creating a vacuum that had to be filled, 95 percent of women who entered the workforce during the war reported, at the start of their jobs, that they expected to quit and return to their domestic roles when the war was over and the men came back. By 1945, though, women were singing a different tune: nearly as many said they didn't want to quit working, relishing their newfound independence and their own money. Most of them didn't quit, but they did see their jobs downgraded to less challenging and more "feminine" work. As the 1940s slid into the '50s, even women in the workforce were pushed to see themselves as wives and mothers first, and independent breadwinners second (if at all).[13]

The 1950s brought more profound cultural shifts in the United States, and despite the uniqueness of the decade, it remains emblazoned in the American memory as a definitional time. No era seems to be as divisive in the collective American consciousness as that one, on the one hand a rosy-hued *Leave It to Beaver* picture of white suburban prosperity, and on the other a prefeminist cartoon of domestic bondage. Modern conservatives point to the '50s as a time when America was strong and traditional family values dominated; modern liberals and feminists point to the same decade as one in which women were confined to the home and pushed into a narrow feminine ideal, responding with depression and often self-medicating with alcohol or prescription drugs, when African Americans faced legalized discrimination and active segregation, and when gay men and lesbians feared for their lives and livelihoods.

There's truth to both visions of the decade. The 1950s were an economically prosperous time, and white families flourished financially. Various government programs subsidized their new lifestyles, with funding dedicated to helping them buy houses in which to raise their children and build generational wealth, drive affordable cars on newly constructed highways connecting big cities to increasingly prosperous suburbs, and join unions and make collective bargaining agreements that brought reliable pay, medical care, and job security for blue-collar workers. People of color were legally excluded from many of these benefits, further consolidating this new wealth among whites.[14]

Lifted up by this government-sponsored economic security, those same white families also started marrying younger, having more children, and moving away from their extended families into suburban sprawls, forging a kind of nuclear-family independence that required a husband working outside the home, a wife supporting him by working in it, and the federal government footing the invisible part of the bill. Teen pregnancy increased, but these teens typically got married—if they didn't, the teenage girl often went away to a pregnancy home, where she had her baby in secret and saw it placed for adoption. Young families, and sexy young women, became ubiquitous in advertising, sending the message that marriage was a social norm and sexual attraction and fulfillment within marriage a necessity—with women as the object of that attraction and men the ones attracted, primarily to a woman's looks.

The shift among whites to the independent nuclear suburban family also relied on a promise that this new model would make both women and men happy—and that, for women especially, the work they put into the home would pay emotional dividends. Women certainly tried, increasing the amount of time they spent on housework and more than doubling the time they spent on child care. But they also increased their prescription drug use, and many reported a deep unhappiness. Still others broadcast their misery less obviously: *McCall's Magazine* published a piece called "The Mother Who Ran Away" and was inundated with subscriptions, setting a new readership record. Noted one editor, "We suddenly realized that all these women at home with three and a half children were miserably unhappy." *Redbook,* apparently suspicious that its readers weren't quite as content with homemaking as the glossy magazine's ads implied, asked readers to explain "why young mothers feel trapped." Responses flooded in—24,000 of them.[15]

This kind of suburban ennui, and the economic privileges that brought it on, were not the norm for all families. Even in the homemaker-dominated 1950s, 40 percent of black mothers with small children worked outside the home, and a quarter were the heads of their own households. Black, Latino, and other racial minority families were consistently excluded from the government programs that helped white families make their mass exodus to single-family homes in the suburbs, and therefore also excluded from laying the groundwork for future generations to build wealth and do better than their parents. Because what Coontz called "the cult of the True Woman" had whiteness ingrained as a requirement for respectable femininity, women of color and many immigrant women experienced regular abuse and marginalization at the hands of white men who simply didn't see them as delicate, vulnerable, and in need of protection. But neither were these women given the kind of leeway for individuality and professional pursuits to which white men were entitled.[16]

The antiwar movement, feminism, and the civil rights movement exploded 1950s assumptions and norms—at least partly. With challenges to racial hierarchies and traditional family structures came at least a few government interventions aimed at improving conditions for women, children, people of color, and the poor. The Civil Rights Act of 1964 sought to curtail overt racial discrimination, Medicaid provided some health care for the poor, Medicare expanded health care for the old, food stamps helped to feed the indigent, and a variety of other social welfare programs, some part of the earlier New Deal and some more recent, created a more robust social safety net in America than ever before.[17]

But with that safety net came a gendered and racial backlash. Conservatives saw welfare and poverty alleviation programs as undermining the nuclear family, allowing women—and black women in particular—to be government-dependent heads of households instead of husband-dependent domestic helpmeets. The Reagan '80s brought the rollback of many of these programs, often in the name of fighting waste and promoting family values, and with an undercurrent of racial animus and antifeminism. As a result, while children's health had been getting better, that trend reversed itself with the slashing of benefits and the renewed push toward traditional obligations.[18]

Outside of the policy space, feminism and a resurgent conservatism were also going head to head. By the 1980s and '90s, the cultural, political, and media backlash to the feminist '60s and '70s was in full force, with women hearing on repeat that single motherhood set your children up for a lifetime of poverty, that day care was dangerous, that "career" women were destroying the family, and that women were increasingly choosing to opt out of the workforce and find happiness in the domestic sphere. That struggle between those who say the best society is a gender-equal one and those who say the best society is one anchored in the nuclear family, with its clearly delineated roles and obligations, survives to the present. And today, both sides still make the same argument: my vision of an ideal society will make people happier.

At twenty-eight years old, Janet has interacted with many programs and institutions designed to alleviate suffering, keep people alive, and reduce inequality. She's been on welfare and food stamps. She has made the minimum wage or just over it. She's been in foster care, assigned a public defender, and, after she was a victim of a serious crime, saw her assailant prosecuted by the state. Many of these experiences have been traumatic and humiliating, life sustaining only in the most basic of ways—she didn't starve or die exposed to the elements—but certainly not life affirming. No one has ever suggested it is her right to be happy. Instead, she hears she should be appreciative, and maybe a little bit sorry for availing herself of help.

Still, Janet is grateful and quick to list all the ways in which she is, in her words, blessed: she has a roof over her head, there's a little food in the cabinets, her children are bright and kind.

This kind of optimism is very much a female thing. One of the paradoxes of happiness, researchers have found, is that women tend to be happier than men, even when the conditions under which they live—their education levels, income, political and economic rights—are much worse. One possible explanation for this is optimism: women simply don't expect as much, and so they're happier with what they've got, even if what they've got is just a little. If women had what men have—the education, the income, the rights—they would be even happier than they are. But if men had what women have, the same researchers predict, they would be significantly less happy.

Women also live longer, and the psychological stress men experience from their lack of life satisfaction contributes, some researchers theorize, to their earlier mortality. Which is partly why it makes sense to focus pleasure policy on women: figuring out why women are happier despite poorer circumstances offers valuable insight into what "happiness" means and how it's achieved. A political emphasis on women's happiness also has greater potential to lift all proverbial boats. Inter-personal relationships influence happiness, and women are more likely than men to be the only parent in a household, impacting their chil-dren's happiness and development. Women are more engaged in their communities and are often the main point of contact in their husbands' social lives. Women have also traditionally been left out of the project of building political systems and distributing resources. In the United States, many of the systems we operate in—work, school, even the home—were conceived with a particular setup in mind: breadwinning middle- and upper-middle-class men, stay-at-home middle- and upper-middle-class wives, and low-skilled poor men and women making up a low-wage service workforce inside the home and out of it. That is no longer the way most Americans live or how most of us want to live.

Unsurprisingly, American women have gotten less happy over the past four decades. One oft-cited 2009 study found that the subjective well-being of American women has been decreasing since the 1970s.[19] The authors theorized that having to compete and perform in the work-place like men was making women depressed, and so the media head-lines were variations on "feminism makes women miserable." In fact, what seems to be making women miserable is being pulled in too many different directions and dedicating too many hours of the day—more than men—to unpleasant activities rather than pleasant ones. The source of our misery was trying to embody too many roles, to compete in a system built for someone else, with a government and often a work-place indifferent to our lives and needs.

Americans have tried, piecemeal, to adapt to a postfeminist econ-omy with prefeminist government resources, but it's been slow, and the goals often opaque. Progressive parties and activists focus on laudable objectives—gender equality, income equality, public health—but often shy away from the basic premise that making peoples' lives not just healthier but happier and better is the point of politics. If we focus on what makes women's lives happier, healthier, better, more fulfilling, and more pleasurable, many other progressive goals will naturally follow, and we will have a new language with which to frame and advocate for issues of fundamental fairness and egalitarianism.

Part of being a woman in America has always involved giving your-self over to others and defining yourself in relation to them. Women are mothers, wives, sisters, and it is through these relationships that we are supposed to find happiness. Women who think they're entitled to pleasure and happiness for themselves alone are cast as selfish or immoral, even though they're also the primary marketing targets of corporate happiness peddlers. Women who seek out sexual pleasure are sluts or, in the more condescending characterization, "They don't respect themselves." Women who pursue the pleasure of achievement are overly ambitious careerists, and if they're also mothers, then they're probably paying someone else to raise their children. Women who put their own desires even temporarily ahead of someone else's—especially, God forbid, their children's—are unfit parents and bad people.

This cult of female sacrifice, often masquerading as love, has real consequences. There are the obvious ones—if romantic love for women is supposed to mean near-total martyrdom, and finding a male partner is a crucial life goal, then of course women face pressure, internal and external, to stay with men who are abusive or even simply not right for them. But there are more subtle consequences, too. The idea that women should get all the satisfaction they need from their children sets up an impossible expectation, often pushing women to marginalize other valuable parts of their lives—their work, their friendships, their relationships—so that they give their all to their offspring. That also has financial costs. If a mother stops working for a few years when she has children, reentry into the workforce becomes all the more difficult, and she will almost surely find her salary potential handicapped for the rest of her life. When she's out of work, she will be financially dependent on her partner, usually a husband, constraining her options and potentially depleting her power in the relationship. There could be better support to help women who raise children full time not end up bereft if their marriages fall apart, or face less discrimination in returning to the workforce, or less pressure to leave it in the first place. But, instead, women get the head-patting platitude that "Motherhood is the most important job in the world." It should come as little surprise that, contrary to the clichés and the promises, having children tanks women's happiness.[20]

The requirement of female sacrifice also vests in the body. Nearly all American women—as many as 84 percent—report feeling dissatisfied with their bodies at some point in their lives, and most say that dissatisfaction stems from wanting to be thinner.[21] For most women, being thinner means sacrificing food, and with it the pleasure that comes with eating. Or it means more hours at the gym, not because it feels good but because working out promises to make you skinnier. Maybe it means restrictive, tight undergarments to smooth out the wrinkles of human flesh or high heels that lengthen the legs and make one look slightly slimmer, even if they're uncomfortable. It means part of being a woman is striving, wanting, and sometimes hurting.

And it means spending. That desire to shrink oneself fattens the American diet industry to the tune of $61 billion.[22]

Almost none of the weight loss from these diets lasts for the long term, but the emotional weight women carry does. Negative body attitudes are, unsurprisingly, correlated with low self-esteem and eating disorders.[23] Women who are kinder to themselves, who appreciate their bodies and accept or even embrace their appearance, have higher levels of self-esteem, optimism, and even sexual gratification. And they're probably less inclined to spend money on false promises of betterment.

Today, women in America are not particularly happy, but we spend a lot of time, money, and emotional energy trying to be (not to mention the amount of time, money, and emotional energy we spend trying to make other people happy). We also seem to be on the verge of either a breakthrough or a breakdown. We are caught between traditional expectations and more modern desires, hemmed in by institutions and laws and norms built for the men of our grandfathers' generation but energized by a feminist revival that has many of us demanding more and demanding it right now. But we are also wading into the depths of what some of us can see will be a deep, dark, and sustained backlash, the United States now led by a man who ran the most blatantly sexist campaign in modern history, brought to power by followers who espouse a virulent misogyny shocking even to those of us who thought we knew the scope of American sexism.

The confluence of these factors is a source of great frustration and cold fear. It is also a source of enormous potential. America has always been a work in progress, and just as feminists thought we were climbing steadily upward—an ascendance symbolized by a woman who seemed poised to finally break the presidential glass ceiling—we found ourselves collectively knocked down. It's a stinging reminder that, for all of the feminist movement's renewed pop culture relevance, for all of the ways in which women's lives are better than ever, there still has been no full vindication of the rights of women. Advocating for those rights—not just equality in law, but in opportunity, ambition, purpose, and pleasure—remains an act of rebellion. There has perhaps never been a more crucial time to work in the service of hope, social justice, greater equality, and more responsive and representative institutions. There has never been a more crucial time to demand a better way of life for the many of us who have been shut out of the popular political conversation and the promise of the pursuit of happiness.

2

Summer Sisters:
Women and the Power of Friendship

Where does it all lead? What will become of us?
These were our young questions, and young answers
were revealed.
It leads to each other. We become ourselves.

—*Patti Smith, in her memoir* Just Kids

T HE FIRST GREAT love of my life was a girl named Adriene. We met in second grade, both of us short brunettes who liked writing, soccer, and purple leggings. Her mother was young and glamorous, so beautiful I thought she could have been a supermodel—dark hair always done in big loose waves, French-tip acrylic nails she would tap on the grey leather steering wheel of their maroon Volvo station wagon. Adriene and I had sleepovers every weekend, staying up to watch R-rated movies that had been edited for TV but that, for elementary schoolers with only the faintest idea of what sex was, were still wonderfully titillating. When I ran for student government in the fourth grade, she was my campaign manager; when I lost, she was also my companion at our favorite Mexican restaurant, where I wore a too-fancy dress and cried over my bean burrito. We snooped through her parents' bedside table hunting for condoms, and we would put on her mother's red lipstick and use a mascara wand to dot a fake mole above our mouths, like Cindy Crawford, and go holler at construction workers in a neighboring backyard—a kind of wildly inappropriate reverse catcalling. Neither of us wanted to get our periods, and we were happy to make it nearly all the way through middle school without having to figure out how to use a tampon.

We hit high school still inseparable, going to her house during lunch hour to eat chips and salsa and watch *The Golden Girls* (she was Blanche, I was Sophia, her twin brother was Dorothy, and our friend Ann was Rose). We were the two worst swimmers on the swim team. We both tried out for the cheerleading squad and got rejected.

Then she got boobs, and swiftly after, a boyfriend.

Our relationship fell apart. I didn't like the guy she was dating, and at sixteen, I didn't yet have the sense to understand that she probably knew what she wanted better than I did. I was judgmental and critical, and she retreated. The postpuberty years were kind to her, and she became very, very beautiful very, very quickly, growing out of a skinny feather-banged awkwardness into a slender, delicate-boned young woman. I had long venerated her, thinking sincerely that she was the coolest and prettiest girl I knew, and it seemed like suddenly the rest of the world (or at least the rest of the school) caught on. I was both jealous and, being significantly less striking and significantly more bookish, left behind. I made some new friends, who she thought were snobby. Eventually, I went off to college in New York, and she got a job and stayed in our hometown. We haven't spoken since.

It was a long, slow, and painful severing of what was up until that point a lifelong tie—"break" isn't even the right word, because there was no snap, no fight, no moment where we said, "Let's not do this anymore." We just kept our distance until it became too far to cross. That was more than fifteen years ago, and I still think about her with great affection and great regret. I'm "friends" with her still-beautiful mother on Facebook and so get snapshots of Adriene's life—getting married, having a baby—but it's mostly a big question mark. I don't know where she lives or what she does for work. I don't even know when or how she and the bad high school boyfriend broke up. She was my first big heartbreak, the first time I felt a person-sized hole in my chest and wondered, pointlessly, what could have been different.

Since Adriene, I have had more female friendships than I can count. Some have been big and exquisite, profoundly shaping years of my life; others have been small and temporary, filling a hole that eventually found what it needed elsewhere. It has been my friends, much

more often than boyfriends, who have come with me to medical procedures, taken care of me when I was sick, petted my head as I cried,
popped champagne when there was something to celebrate, bought
me dinner when I was broke, snored next to me in a hotel bed. The
biggest decisions of my adult life—and many of the smallest—have
been run past my friends. Plots have been made, pathways to dreams
laid out. Not that these relationships have been perfect: there have
been falling-outs and growing-aparts and long-harbored resentments
and hurtful gossip and needs unmet. But these relationships were how
so many of the building blocks of my life were formed. The particular
kind of intimacy that can grow when you love someone deeply but
don't have a sexual or romantic relationship with them has opened
up a set of experiences and affections that don't rival my romantic
partnerships, but intersect in a kind of emotional Venn diagram—
overlapping in part, but each retaining its own uniqueness, a separate
kind of closeness and impact.

Friends make you happy, and platonic relationships between women
have long been forces for creativity, adventure, love, and sometimes
jealousy. When women were largely relegated to the domestic sphere,
it was other women who formed the contours of their day-to-day lives,
who were their confidantes, their entire worlds, and sometimes their
lovers. Women today have more varied, dynamic, and outward-looking
lives than ever before, and as marriage and even serious romantic partnerships are also delayed, female friendships take on a new role: they
tell the truth that no one person can be everything for another, that our
lives are richer when we get what we crave from a variety of sources.
They help each of us answer the question posed by the title of Sheila
Heti's novel on female friendship: *How Should a Person Be?*

My favorite television shows have always been about gal pals: *Rhoda*
when I was a kid going through a throwback Nick at Nite phase, *My
So-Called Life* in middle school, *The Golden Girls* when I was in high
school, *Sex and the City* when I was in college, *Broad City* in my early
thirties. I gravitated toward them unconsciously, but in hindsight, the
draw was that most of what was on television then and now couldn't
pass the three-part Bechdel Test, which was developed by cartoonist
Alison Bechdel for films but applies to television, video games, theater,

and literature too: (1) the movie has to have at least two women in it, (2) who talk to each other, (3) about something other than a man.

In the shows I watched, the women did talk about stuff other than men (although they talked about men, too). Female friendship looked fun, and it looked cool. In a culture where very little else about being a girl is considered laudable, even a handful of examples of female friendships that aren't competitive or catty can feel revolutionary. The women on these shows offered a model for the kinds of relationships between women that are pervasive in real life but often obscured in popular culture. That does seem to be changing—as feminism has made its way back into the mainstream, female friendship is also having a pop culture moment. But despite the primacy of friendships in women's lives and the fact that our friendships ebb and flow and evolve and sometimes end, their complications and influences are significantly less visible in the mass media landscape than they are in real life. Without rich, persistent, and varied representation in literature and film and television— the kind of representation afforded to romantic relationships—many of us lack the language and the cultural touch points to even adequately describe our friendships, let alone categorize them or accurately assess their influence on our lives.

In her groundbreaking book *All the Single Ladies*, which is also partly a love letter to friendship between women, journalist (and, lucky for me, friend and mentor) Rebecca Traister managed to do just that: put words to the experience of friendship among single women. "Friendships provided the core of what I wanted from adulthood—connection, shared sensibilities, enjoyment," she wrote. "Unlike my few romances, which had mostly depleted me, my female friendships were replenishing, and their salubrious effect expanded into other layers of my life: They made other things I yearned for, like better work, fairer remuneration, increased self-assurance, and even just *fun* seem more attainable."[1]

Friendships can also be sources of shelter, especially for women who find themselves caught up in storms not of their own making. That's one reason many women gravitate toward women like themselves—who share a similar minority background or who have experienced similar difficulties. A friend of mine from high school connected me with her friend Jade, a thirty-four-year-old woman in Seattle; friends, Jade told me, "are my placeholder family and the family that I chose, instead of the family that I was saddled with." When Jade was twenty-one, her mom died; a few years later Jade, who was assigned male at birth, transitioned to living as a woman and fell out with her father and siblings. In those vulnerable years "when I was in those middling stages and finding community," she said, friendships with other trans and queer people were necessary to her survival. Now, she has trans friends and gay friends and queer friends—as well as many straight cisgendered nonqueer friends.[2] What matters is that she feels safe, supported, and loved, that she finds people with whom she has stuff in common, trans or not. "When I need a shoulder to cry on I can have that, when I need someone to give some mothering, I have a friend who does that," she said. "It takes the place of all the things I don't have in place. My friends take on those roles."

Concentric circles of friendships—your closest crew, your good friends, the women you catch up with once a year—are defining aspects of modern female life. Among my closest friends, a few are married but most are not, and none of us married before thirty. We've all been in serious romantic relationships and gone through devastating breakups, but we've all had more single or casually dating years in our adult lives than firmly committed ones. Through these years, it has been our relationships with other women that have largely buoyed us into adulthood and that have shaped our experiences, our preferences, and our ideas about who we are.

In the '70s, as the women's liberation movement was reaching a fever pitch, Gloria Steinem quipped that, for some women, "we are becoming the men we wanted to marry." By delaying marriage, pursuing education and careers, and asking, "Who do I want to be?" instead of, "Who do I want to marry?" some women were finding expressions of self and status well beyond "a doctor's wife" or "a pastor's wife." But the development of self is rarely a solo endeavor. For many women, for a very long time, the act of looking outward to develop one's identity was a gaze toward men, and the imagination of what one could be limited to being an appendage of someone else. That still exists, of course—there is still a status to marrying a doctor or a lawyer, still a kind of self-definition that hinges on one's husband or romantic partner. For most women, though, even those who perhaps relish being a doctor's wife or center their universe on their husband and family, the world of possibility is wider than it has ever been. Very few Americans are getting married or permanently partnered at twenty-two, and many women marry other women.[3] Most women do still marry, and most still marry men, but by the time women wed, most of us have had a solid decade of adult self-definition outside of marriage. Many of us do become the men we want to marry, even if we also marry the men—or women—we want to marry.

But before we marry (if we marry), and as we're in the process of figuring out what our adult selves look like, it is likelier that we are surrounded by the kind of women we aspire to be than that our identities are shaped by men (whether we date men or not). It's through platonic relationships with women, usually more than through romance, that we figure ourselves out. Looking inward is crucial to developing one's self, and years spent adjacent to a diverse group of other women can make that internal exploration deeper and more powerful. Assessing yourself means seeing parts of you reflected in others, observing what you dislike and want to avoid, and noting what you aspire to and want to emulate. A heterogeneous social circle and many more independent years spent in it means more opportunities for self-discovery and more ways to be challenged, loved, and enriched. Young women often talk about having "girl-crushes" on a casual acquaintance—being slightly infatuated with another woman, admiring her intelligence or her style or her humor, wanting not just to be her friend but to be like her, to embody a little bit of what she is. And because friendships are not usually as dyadic as monogamous romantic relationships—there is space for many of them, even if some are more intense that others—the kind of relational development women derive from their friendships is richer than it would be based on romance alone.

"The fact that I was able to develop these sisterhoods with my friends is something that will be of value to me for the rest of my life," my friend Diane, who is thirty-five and considering marriage and children with her partner, told me. "I think it makes me better for my future children. Assuming I'm able to have kids, I'm getting the best of both worlds. I was able to live a full happy life—I sound like I'm talking about death—but I got to live a free life and also got to experience parenthood, and motherhood specifically, and get the benefits of that, too."

In researching happiness, one point that comes up again and again is that women tend to have deeper and more varied social ties than men. We have more friends and we're more involved in our communities. We simply engage with more people—and we tend to engage on a deeper emotional level. This is one reason, researchers speculate, that married men do so much better, physically and psychologically, than their unmarried counterparts: their wives serve as conduits to a fuller social universe. Being married, for men, means you have more friends, simply because women tend to have more friends. These friendships make for a happier life.[4]

One of the strongest predictors of personal fulfillment is having deep-tie relationships. Friendships not only improve one's health; they can aid in recovery from serious illness. One study found that women with breast cancer were more likely to survive if they had a diversity of supportive friendships; others have determined that loneliness is deadly, a consistent predictor of premature mortality. Still another study out of Harvard Medical School determined that as women aged, more friendships tracked with fewer physical impairments, and the more friendships a woman had, the more joyful her life was.[5]

In communities challenged by poverty, high rates of incarceration, and the instability that comes with moving often because of eviction or unsafe housing conditions, these kinds of beneficial long-term bonds can be harder to forge. They can also be harder to sustain, because stress puts cracks in most intimate relationships, including friendships and community ties. But it is precisely these kinds of relationships that also fill the gaps of a punctured social safety net, often with women serving as the pillars that hold up their communities. Janet, in North Carolina, for example, is part of a female-oriented car and truck club called Empowering Sisters; before Janet and I met, she and her girlfriends in the club held a fundraiser for the family of a young man who was murdered in the neighborhood. They raised about $700 for his three surviving children. For Janet, it was important not just to band together with her friends to serve a family in need but for her kids to see the example they were setting: "It is something positive I am doing," she said. "And when I do go out there, I put my kids out here so they have seen the positive that the community can do."

While stress can undermine friendships and community ties, under certain circumstances, researchers have found that it can also bring women together. In one 2002 study at UCLA, one of the first to analyze women's responses to stress, researchers found that women's bodies deal with stress hormones differently than men's do. Both men's and women's brains release the feel-good hormone oxytocin when they're stressed to calm the body and brain. Testosterone, though, tempers its effects, whereas estrogen magnifies them. Men have a fight-or-flight reaction; women are more likely to react to stress by attempting to bond with others, something the UCLA researchers call "tend and befriend." That healthier response to stress helps women to cultivate deeper friendships and enables to them to avoid some of the worst stress-related health detriments and, ultimately, live longer. "There's no doubt," said Dr. Laura Cousino Klein, one of the UCLA researchers, "that friends are helping us live."[6]

But even though friendships between women are pervasive, definitional, and life sustaining, there's often little recognition of them. There are no anniversaries or milestones to celebrate, not even an assumption or understanding that friendships often outshine romantic relationships. There's an expectation—often born out—that women's friendships will recede once they're replaced by the more valid, real, and recognized romantic relationship. There's also no road map for them, especially as women age out of their twenties. They contribute more in terms of health and happiness than just about anything else in a woman's life, and they can cause pain as deep as any heartbreak. They are socially, and sometimes personally, taken for granted.

One of my closest friends is a woman I lived with on and off for a decade, Shannon. I have signed as many leases with her as I have on my own; every time I have moved, I've found one of her sweaters or T-shirts among my things. I know her bra size and her shoe size and that despite being half Italian she has an irrational hatred of raw tomatoes. I can look at a restaurant menu and guess what she'll order. I've eaten more than one first meal in a new apartment with her, sitting on the floor of an empty kitchen, dining out of Styrofoam containers with plastic utensils. We know each other's passwords and PIN codes; we've shared food and money and pets and prescription drugs. When my tiny gray cat Percy became incurably sick a few years back, it was Shannon and my sister who walked me to the vet to put him to sleep, who kept their hands on my back as I held his limp little cat body. Shannon was the one who threw out the litter box and the cat bowls so I wouldn't have to. She was the one who came into my room early the next morning and stroked my hair, knowing it would be the first day I would wake up and he wouldn't be snoozing on my chest. Her phone number is the only one other than my mother's that I have memorized. I trust her absolutely and without question, even to make medical decisions on my behalf, and so she remains my emergency contact on all my medical forms.

Shannon has been my most consistent partner of the past decade. Nevertheless, her name and number scribbled on a few forms is the closest thing to formal social acknowledgment our relationship has ever received.

Friendships make us happy, and they can also make us more radical. The history of movements for women's rights has hinged on women befriending each other, challenging each other, and working together. Although the postindustrial United States was a land of separate spheres—women in the home, men in the workplace and the public— that separation also brought with it an intensity of female connection. Marriage was increasingly a romantic endeavor, but with such enforced gender differences, many marriages weren't as happy as promised. With days spent apart and so few of their experiences overlapping, many wives saw a large gap between them and their husbands; relationships with other women often filled it. Many of these women found each other through philanthropy and activism, areas in which women who didn't work for pay were able to channel their intellect and ambition.

This is how Susan B. Anthony and Elizabeth Cady Stanton met. The two were famously dear friends, and Stanton described being immediately drawn to Anthony upon their first meeting on a street corner in Seneca Falls, New York: "There she stood with her good, earnest face and genial smile, dressed in gray delaine, hat and all the same color, relieved with pale blue ribbons, the perfection of neatness and sobriety. I liked her thoroughly, and why I did not at once invite her home with me to dinner, I do not know."[7] The two remained close friends and collaborators for decades after, working for women's rights and against slavery. "So closely interwoven have been our lives, our purposes, and experiences that [when] separated, we have a feeling of incompleteness," Stanton wrote about her friend. She also credited Anthony with helping to shape her into the woman she was: "I do believe that I have developed into much more of a woman under her jurisdiction," Stanton said. As for Anthony, she chose to remain unmarried, instead molding her life around both her political pursuits and her friendships—and sometimes, it seems, romantic relationships—with other women. "I'm sure no man could have made me any happier than I have been," she told a *San Francisco Chronicle* reporter in 1896. "I never found the man who was necessary to my happiness. I was very well as I was."[8]

The friendship between Anthony and Cady Stanton gave both women the support they needed to work in a radical movement. But while their mutual encouragement in the face of intense resistance was no doubt a necessary life raft to keep them and their ideals afloat, it also may have contributed to the racial myopia that has marred their legacies: when it became clear voting rights for black men were going to come before voting rights for women, Anthony and Cady Stanton together accepted the help of a proslavery politician to promote women's suffrage ahead of black men's, and played on white Southerners' fears about enfranchising African Americans. That decision cost the women a third friendship: the one they shared with Frederick Douglass.

For women living outside the strictures of middle-class white society, the public/private distinction wasn't quite as stark, and proscriptions on opposite-gender platonic friendships not as strict. As a result, radical and life-altering friendships weren't always so intensely female focused. Ida B. Wells, a journalist who risked her life to cover lynching in the South, was driven to do so in part because a close friend of hers, Thomas Moss, along with two of his coworkers, was lynched in Memphis in 1892. Moss and his wife Betty were among Wells's most intimate friends, and less than a year after he was killed, Wells penned one of several columns about his murder. You can feel her heart pulling for her friend and his family, and her own pain radiating off the page: "The baby daughter of Tom Moss, too young to express how she misses her father, toddles to her wardrobe, seizes the legs of the trousers of his letter-carrier uniform, hugs and kisses them with evident delight and stretches up her little hands to be taken up into the arms which will nevermore clasp his daughter's form," she wrote. "His wife holds Thomas Moss, Jr., in her arms, upon whose unconscious baby face the tears fall thick and fast when she is thinking of the sad fate of the father he will never see, and of the two helpless children who cling to her for the support she cannot give."[9]

For other women at the margins, and even many who occupied public roles in mainstream white society, not all of these transformative female friendships were strictly platonic. As the historian Lillian Faderman has extensively documented, many intense female connections were also romantic and sexual; others adopted the language of romance, and there remain outstanding questions about whether the women who wrote so loquaciously to each other were sexually involved. As Faderman notes in her book *To Believe in Women: What Lesbians Have Done for America—a History,* Susan B. Anthony wrote adoring, effusive letters to Anna Dickinson, often inviting her into bed. Dickinson, too, once wrote to Anthony, "I want to see you very much indeed, to hold your hand in mine, to hear your voice, in a word, I want *you*—I can't have you?" Whether the two women were actually sexually involved is less clear, but the depth of affection, and the intense flirtation, is obvious.

And they weren't the only ones. Women's rights and antislavery crusaders Mary Grew and Margaret Burleigh lived together and shared a bed. When Burleigh died, Grew wrote to a younger suffragist, "To me it seems to have been a closer union than that of most marriages. We know that there have been other such between two men, & also between two women. And why should there not be. Love is spiritual, only passion is sexual."[10] Love between women—romantic, sexual, and platonic—has been a cornerstone of the women's rights movement from the beginning.

Female friendship also shaped the second-wave feminist movement. For many middle-class white women, the retreat to suburbia was profoundly isolating; for those who stayed home with children, it was a next-door neighbor or nearby sister or the members of bridge club who provided a crucial social outlet. And it was those same female relationships that eventually radicalized so many women. Feminists formed consciousness-raising groups as a way of connecting their individual lives to broader social dynamics, a remarkably simple and stunningly effective grassroots strategy. Across the country, women would gather and talk about the many things they thought of as individual, personal problems. Some of those issues were as seemingly small as a husband who always left his socks on the floor to be picked up by his wife or the shame of never having had a vaginal orgasm, which women in the 1950s were told was the only "mature" way a woman could experience sexual pleasure. Others were much weightier, like a husband who hit when he was angry, or a pregnancy that just couldn't be, or a rape that was kept a secret, or a baby born to a teenager that was sent away never to be spoken of again. The process wasn't just psychologically cathartic; it was radicalizing. Suddenly, these problems weren't so individual at all—they were systemic, endemic to being a woman. This is what feminists mean when they talk about the theory that "the personal is political." It is from these conversations between women that the mainstream (and often white-dominated) feminist movement set its goals: more expansive laws against domestic violence and rape and better enforcement and treatment from the police and the courts; the right to birth control and abortion; research and education on reproduction and female sexual pleasure; expanded rights for women who placed their children for adoption; more aid and less stigma for single mothers.

It is also from consciousness-raising sessions that black feminists pushed back on the assumptions about womanhood that proliferated when white middle-class women were given the most airtime. While women of color had been organizing for women's rights from the beginning, imbalances in racial power meant that issues most relevant to white women were cast as general "women's issues," and it was white women who took leadership roles and got the lion's share of the media coverage for their feminist work. As a result, some black feminists found that their work was isolated—both from white-dominated feminism and from the work of other black feminists. In her essay "Anger in Isolation: A Black Feminist's Search for Sisterhood," originally published in the *Village Voice* in 1975 and later in the anthology *All the Women Are White, All the Blacks Are Men, but Some of Us Are Brave: Black Women's Studies*, writer and academic Michele Wallace critiqued both white domination of the feminist movement and the patriarchal impulses of the Black Power movement. She wrote, "But for now, Black feminists, of necessity it seems, exist as individuals—some well known, like Eleanor Holmes Norton, Florynce Kennedy, Faith Ringgold, Shirley Chisholm, Alice Walker, and some unknown, like me. We exist as women who are Black who are feminists, each stranded for the moment, working independently because there is not yet an environment in this society remotely congenial to our struggle—because, being on the bottom, we would have to do what no one else has done: we would have to fight the world."[11]

Despite these challenges (or, arguably, because of them), black feminists, feminists of color, lesbian feminists, and other women often pushed to the side of the mainstream movement did just that—and while some did it individually, many worked collectively. The Combahee River Collective, a group of black feminists and lesbians formed in

Boston in 1974, released a statement of its feminist aims, developed over many meetings, conversations, consciousness-raising sessions, and a half-dozen group retreats—women-centered spaces where participants discussed, debated, found strength in shared experiences, and further expanded the feminist project by pushing back on restrictive narratives of universal womanhood. "A political contribution which we feel we have already made is the expansion of the feminist principle that the personal is political," the statement reads. "In our consciousness-raising sessions, for example, we have in many ways gone beyond white women's revelations because we are dealing with the implications of race and class as well as sex."[12]

Female friendships, or at least intense intellectual relationships, have played no smaller role in the resurgence of feminism today. In the early to mid-2000s, feminist blogs provided a kind of modern consciousness-raising effort, bringing women together online to talk about the roles, status, and challenges of women. For almost a decade I wrote for one of those blogs, called *Feministe,* where I shared the masthead with a rotating cast of other women (and a few men) and discussed and debated a wide range of feminist questions. A few of those online relationships grew into more robust friendships, some just over g-chat or, earlier, AOL instant messenger; others transitioned into real life. As feminist blogging gave way to a mainstreaming of feminist thought in newspapers, magazines, and other publications both online and off, feminist writers—many of whom lived in places like New York and Washington, DC—connected, chatted, and often met up in person. For a half-dozen of my good friends and several dozen of my less-close ones, the answer to "How did you meet?" is, "The Internet." Specifically, the feminist Internet. What's powerful about these connections, too, is that they can transcend physical space, distance, social class, and race. Feminist blogs and websites brought together women who would likely have never met in real life and if they did, probably would have passed each other by, not discussed feminist theory and the female experience.

This is part, I suspect, of what has made even mainstream modern feminism so much more attentive to race and class than its predecessor movements: voice and leadership aren't as contingent on access to a mainstream platform as they were before. Today's feminism still suffers from blind spots, and it is still educated, upper-middle-class white women who are often selected to embody the movement in magazines or newspapers, while women of color or trans women or poor women are pushed aside, representing "black feminism" or "intersectional feminism" or something other than feminism full stop; women who are not white and relatively economically stable are still not seen as the everywoman. But slowly, as more versions of womanhood become visible and as feminists are able to forge relationships across what were once wide gulfs, the feminist movement itself is becoming a bigger tent—and a more accurate representation of how a diversity of women experience womanhood. This brings with it a fair share of conflict, frustration, anger, and sometimes intramovement splits; it is nonetheless a remarkable strength.

Modern feminism's grandes dames of female friendship are Ann Friedman and Aminatou Sow. The two women met at a *Gossip Girl* watching party in Washington, DC, in 2009 and quickly became inseparable. A few years into their friendship, after Ann moved to Los Angeles, they started "a podcast for long-distance besties everywhere" called *Call Your Girlfriend,* where they riff on feminism, pop culture, politics, and relationships—including their own. One staple of their discourse is Shine Theory, coined by Amina and loosely based on lyrics from the Killers: "If I don't shine, you don't shine." The theory is a simple one: surrounding yourself with intelligent, successful women you admire makes you all the better and pushes back on the idea that there are only so many seats at the table for women. "When you meet a woman who is intimidatingly witty, stylish, beautiful, and professionally accomplished, *befriend her,*" Friedman wrote in *New York* magazine. "Surrounding yourself with the best people doesn't make you look worse by comparison. It makes you better." It's more than a feel-good ode to platonic ladylove; it's a political act, countering the belief, Friedman wrote, "that there are a limited number of spaces for [women] at the top."

The kind of friendship that Ann and Amina have—that so many women find in each other—is radicalizing in a smaller, simpler way, too: it's a reminder that the stuff we do and the things we like matter. Culturally, "girly stuff" is denigrated while men's stuff is elevated: fashion is shallow and women's magazines are trashy, but sports are a valuable national pastime and men read *Playboy* and *Esquire* for award-winning journalism alongside photos of barely clothed women. If parents give their daughter a traditionally male name, it's cute, even cool and edgy, and if enough parents start giving girls what was once a boy's name, the name first crosses over to being "gender neutral" and eventually becomes simply female: Lesley, Ashley, Sydney, Taylor, and Reese. But the opposite doesn't happen; girls' names almost never become boys' names, and it's not cute to name your boy after a woman. The same goes for clothing: "unisex clothes" are traditionally men's clothes that women can also wear. Women have taken up wearing pants en masse, but most men do not wear skirts or dresses. Women can embrace guy stuff and it's a sign of clout and authority; men who embrace girl stuff are weak, less powerful, gay. And women, too, have to walk a tightrope between femininity and power: act too masculine and you're an unlikeable bitch, but act too feminine—wear too much makeup or too much pink, talk "like a girl" using upspeak or a high-pitched voice—and you won't be taken seriously.

There's a status that comes with being the only girl in the room or the only woman at the table, and a status that comes with liking "guy stuff" to the exclusion of girly stuff—being the kind of girl who drinks whiskey, eats burgers, and watches football. There are fewer culturally accepted, let alone erotically venerated, ways to be a girly straight man. Feeling unique and special by being "one of the guys" is a pretty common twentysomething female experience, so pervasive it's a cliché. But you can't blame the guys' girl for embracing what everything else in American culture makes clear: girl stuff sucks. And by extension, girls suck too.

Female friendships offer a tiny refuge from that misogynist drumbeat. Throughout law school, I would get together with two girlfriends for weekly manicures. It was a little luxury I allowed myself even though I was a broke student, a time we could all sit down and just talk. It was a feminine ritual, it kept us connected, and it felt good. Carving out those women-centered spaces, even if they hinged on "girly" stuff like manicures and yoga and joint bathroom excursions, has been a consistent if tiny reminder that frivolity can be fun— and that a lot of girl stuff is pretty great.

Even for women who aren't in to "girly stuff," girlfriends can be lifesavers. Being the only woman in the room can be gratifying, but it only goes so far—it's rare that the one woman at the table is the big boss. For women whose hobbies are coded as male—video games,

NASCAR—being the only girl can become isolating, and being "one of the guys" can segue into becoming either invisible or a sex object. To use an outdated reference, lots of women got sick of always having to play the princess—the one female character—in Super Mario Bros. Another woman in the room broadens the roles women can take on. In describing her college extracurricular activities in theater and comedy, comedian Alexandra Petri, the youngest person to have a column in the *Washington Post,* told Cosmopolitan.com, "Back then, I was super excited to be in a roomful of guys. The one thing I wish I could go back and tell younger me is that if you're in a room of all guys, it doesn't mean there's something special about you. It means there's something wrong with the room."[13]

When my childhood friendship with Adriene fell apart, I took away the lesson that, if you're not careful, men can cleave apart even the strongest female bonds. So I promised myself I would never be the type of girl who let a boyfriend suck up all of her oxygen, whose primary source of affection and the whole of her social life was a guy. Through college and beyond, I knew those women: the ones who had back-to-back serious relationships, who were never single, who seemed to disappear wholly into the men they were dating, the codependent types who married soon out of college or high school. That would not be me. I spent a lot of years casually dating, meeting men I liked well enough, but none who I wanted to change any aspect of my life to be with. And then I started dating Ty.

We didn't live in the same city, so there were a lot of weekend trips overseas, not blending of social groups. When he was in my city, our time together was so brief I didn't want to share it with anyone else. I had simply never liked someone as much as him; I had never been so immediately drawn to someone or felt myself so eager to talk to someone. Because I saw him so seldom I jealously wanted every minute to myself. We started talking about what we wanted our lives to look like, and, for the first time, I had found someone with whom I was on the exact same page: we both wanted to write, to work, to travel, to adventure. He was moving to Kenya for work; would I come?

To even be in that position—falling in love, knowing what I wanted in a long-term relationship—was very much a direct consequence of

having spent more than a decade dating men and befriending women. I
had had hundreds of intense conversations with my friends about what
we wanted: Was it enough that a guy was kind and intelligent and good
to us, or was there some other, intangible thing that it was okay to crave?
How much does that X-factor feeling matter if the guy otherwise doesn't
check a lot of your boxes—if he's not ambitious or if he can be unkind?
Did we want kids, and how do you even know if you want kids? How do
you know when to take a big risk? By the time I met Ty, I had a pretty
good idea of what I wanted out of a relationship, what my checkboxes
were, how much I valued passion, and the general direction I wanted
the rest of my life to take me. I had figured some of it out through failed
previous relationships; I had figured almost all of it out by talking it
through, again and again, with my friends.

To a great extent, the friendships themselves informed what I was
looking for in a romantic relationship. I knew the characteristics I liked
in my friends, the ways in which they challenged me, and when to let
go when the relationship was no longer serving me well. I knew what it
felt like, in the company of women, to be listened to and really heard, to
have my feelings and my opinions respected, to not be condescended to
or insulted for being too feminine or too emotional. I had shared homes
with women and knew what egalitarianism felt like, both in the intimate
realm of putting in the emotional work to sustain the relationship and
the practical one of who was going to clean up after dinner. I knew what
it looked like to show up for someone else, to act with kindness and out
of love, not just sexual desire or obligation. I knew I expected that same
consideration from a partner. With a life that was already full of love, I
didn't need to settle romantically. Nothing felt like it was missing.

"The worrywarts of the early twentieth century may have been right
about the competitive draw of female friendship, about the possibility
it might inhibit or restrain a desire for marriage, especially bad marriages," Traister wrote in her book. "But the real problem with having
friendships that are so fulfilling that you prefer them to subpar sexual
affiliations is that when you actually meet someone you like enough to
clear the high bar your friendships have set, the chances are good that
you're going to *really* like him or her." That's what happened to Traister,
and to me, too.

Ironically, all of that preparation, and the relationship it allowed me
to develop, put me in a curious position: In a new country with my

boyfriend as my primary social outlet, he is sometimes the only person I talk to in the course of a day. For the first time in my life, I live in a place where I do not have many friends.

I'm not the first person who has found it challenging to adequately tend to both my romantic relationship and my platonic ones, to let them flourish equally. Through my twenties, the women I spent the most time with were the four corners of a quad of college friends: Anne, P, Jules, and me. For years, the Friday night question wasn't, "Are you free?" but, "What are we doing?" The four of us spent every New Year's holiday together, often going away for a long weekend, and every New Year's Eve, with a few glasses of champagne in us, we would turn to the others and talk about how lucky we were, how much this little unit mattered to the four of us, how the intimacy and connection we had forged felt so special and so rare. It was our Thanksgiving.

Just before Ty and I started dating, P was the first member of our foursome to get engaged, and a year and a half later she was married. We were all happy for her, but it put a strain on the friendship. In theory, nothing had to change—she was already living with her now-husband, and the engagement was just a ring, the wedding just a big party. But something shifted. Her fiancé worked late hours, so they didn't see each other as much as either of them wanted; when he would text that he was getting off of work on the weekends, she would leave whatever we were doing to go meet him. We were used to spending so much time together that scaling back to even once a week, or once every two or three weeks, felt like a big loss. Intellectually I understood that P was being pulled in different directions, and that, with only so many hours in the day, it was reasonable that she wanted to spend more of them with her partner. But emotionally it was hard. Planning a wedding meant P had even less time to hang out, less money to spend on going out, and less emotional energy to put into her friendships. I vacillated between missing her terribly and resenting her absence. The gaps grew. A year after P's engagement, we stayed in New York for New Year's so that she could spend it with her partner, too, and we threw a house party. P left before midnight so she could celebrate with her fiancé. The three of us left behind understood; we also knew it would be our last New Year's all together.

This is all a normal part of growing up, falling in love, and growing apart—the intensity of your friendships can take a hit if a romantic relationship takes the place of primary importance in your life. There are few models for how friendships balance out with romantic partnership, especially if you aren't friends with a couple but friends primarily with one individual. Marriage, especially, is a kind of crossing-over for many women, a point at which they increase their focus on their home, on their partner, and often on having children and building out their families. There's less space for Thursday night drinks, Saturday manicures, and Sunday walks to the farmer's market. "Couple friends," where all the partners get along, replace old girlfriends. When kids enter, "mom friends" seem to take over—women with kids around the same age, who can be a part of the same playgroup, and who can relate to what you're going through on an intimate level. It's a natural thing, friendships ebbing and flowing and adjusting, and new ones emerging as you enter a new stage of life. But, when you don't get married at twenty-five and when you do spend more than a decade cultivating a life in which rich female relationships are at the foundation, it can be especially jarring to have those building blocks disintegrate. It can be jarring to realize you've shifted your own foundation, and it now rests largely on a man.

Sometimes, though, this all comes back around: breakups, divorces, and deaths have a way of bringing friendship back to the fore of women's experiences and helping women persevere. Researchers have confirmed what many have individually observed: women who have close friends do better after the death of a spouse than those who don't, and the ones with good friends are less likely to develop new ailments than those who don't have other social outlets. I've seen something like this in generations of my own family. When my grandmother and grandfather divorced, my grandmother was reliant on her friends and her sister, something my own mother observed and internalized. "I remember my Aunt Eva coming over, girlfriends coming over, sitting in the living room for hours and smoking and drinking instant coffee after instant coffee," my mom recalled. "As a little girl I used to think, what in the world do they talk about? This is ridiculous, those old ladies, all they do is sit and drink coffee. Of course that's what I do now, except I do it in a coffee shop." In hindsight, my mother said, she realized it was the ladies down the block "who she called on when she had to run one of us to the hospital, when the hot water tank broke. The women would try to fix it first."

That model of forging and maintaining female friendships served my mother in her own life, especially when she and my father divorced shortly after I left for college. "My life got turned on its axis," my mom said. "But I just bucked up and took each day at a time. I never missed a day of work. And my girlfriends, they weeded themselves out real fast. I watched Grandma during her hard times, she had her girlfriends and Aunt Eva, and I had my sister Rose and my girlfriends." Those girlfriends carried my mother through some of the toughest years of her life. And when they went through their own losses—divorces, husbands who became very ill or who passed away—the favor was repaid. In her early sixties, my mom now has her own group of single lady friends (and some married ones, too). They go on long walks. They travel together. They hold book club meetings and watch each other's dogs. They have their own sisterhood. It keeps them physically active and mentally engaged. Most of all, it seems to make them really happy.

3

Playing in the Dark:
Sex, Pleasure, and Pain

> In touch with the erotic, I become less willing to accept powerlessness.
>
> —*Audre Lorde*

A S A KID, one of the most explicit messages I got about sex came from an unusual place: Christian horse camp. Like lots of preteen girls, I had a thing for horses, and the closest, cheapest, and easiest way for my parents to let me get my fix was to send me off for the weekend to a camp run by a local religious group. I was, in Christian horse camp parlance, "unchurched," and the evening sermons, led by a Cool Guy youth pastor, were a new experience—especially the one focused on the evils of the Nike slogan, "Just Do It." We should not, we were told in no uncertain terms, "just do it," and it was the special job of girls to make sure that when we were with boys, no one "just did it." I came home asking my parents for a promise ring, a silver band you wear on your wedding ring finger to symbolize a promise not to have sex that you trade out for a wedding ring from your husband.

"Jill, you are twelve," my mother said. "I think you're a little young to be making this decision." She told me, though, that it was my body and I could and should do what I wanted with it. So I got myself a little band and put it on the third finger of my left hand. By the time I started high school, my short-lived religiosity had waned, and I took the ring off. My understanding of what it meant to be a desirable and good young woman had shifted too, in part because of peer expectations and in part based on what I heard from the adults around me. When I tried out for (and did not make) the cheerleading squad, the coaches emphasized that cheerleaders were role models for the other girls at school and for little girls in our community, who would see us cheering on the sidelines. We could be kicked off the team if we were caught partying or drinking, and we were expected to behave appropriately with boys. Part of the uniform was "spankies," underwear that was visible when the cheerleaders bent over and their skirts flipped up, with the school's initials, SW, printed on each butt cheek. We were sixteen years old, and this was the sweet spot: sexy, with plausible deniability that any of it was actually sexual.

A decade and a half later, I write a lot about sex, and very little of it is sexy. Time and again I find myself covering the moments in women's lives that are often some of the most difficult, as well as some of the most common. In ten years of writing about women and sex (usually nonconsensual sex or political efforts to curtail nonprocreative sex or the aftermath of sex), it has been rare for me to report on sex as purely a recreational activity, let alone on what makes for pleasurable sex.

But even in moments of their lives when they had been hurt sexually or when cultural hostility to sex was a source of trauma or frustration or inconvenience—just after they had been screamed at for walking into a Planned Parenthood to get birth control, for example—most women I met still either had or craved fulfilling, pleasurable sex lives. That kind of complexity and resilience—the ability to experience profound sexual pleasure even after sex has been a source of pain, the fact that pleasure is central to so many women's sex lives even as we're told we are sexual objects but not sexual beings—is perhaps definitional to the American female sexual experience.

In my own life, a burgeoning feminism brought with it better relationships. As I became more engrossed in movements for gender equality while in college and later as my work focused on women's rights, I found myself becoming both more assertive with my own needs and more careful to ask about my partner's. Just as I pushed for better and fairer compensation in my professional life, I pushed myself to talk to the people I dated more honestly not just about sex but about the contours of the relationship: whether one of us was doing more emotional

labor, what we expected from each other and whether those expectations were shaped by biases and stereotypes we wanted to challenge. It
didn't mean I always got exactly what I wanted, but it did force me to
identify what that was and exposed whether I was in a relationship that
would offer it. Without a doubt, feminism made my professional life
better, my love life better, and my sex life better.

It turns out this is not an anomaly. Feminist gains and feminist-
minded relationships mean better sex across the board. Research has
found that women who embrace nontraditional gender roles report
higher levels of sexual satisfaction,[1] and women who are able to assert
their desires and have those desires met in their relationships are happier in bed.[2]

By contrast, women who play by the feminine social script of partner pleasing end up having worse sex. Women who have sex to please
a partner are both more inhibited and less satisfied, while women who
have sex to foster intimacy tend to be both more satisfied and more
autonomous individuals.[3] And women who conform to traditional gender norms tend to be more sexually passive, which correlates with lower
rates of sexual arousal and sexual function—and, predictably, less sexual satisfaction.[4]

Americans have a disordered relationship with sex and pleasure, and
female pleasure in particular. Narratives about female sexuality tend to
put us in a few boxes: we're objects of male sexual desire, we're sluts im-
properly wielding our sexual power, we're alternately prudish or proper
for withholding sex, or we're victims of sexual exploitation or abuse. We
talk more about sex and watch more sexually suggestive and explicit
material, it seems, than ever before—ubiquitous online porn, racy television shows and ads, shock-value "It happened to me" stories of sexual
endeavors and humiliations on popular websites and in magazines, the
Fifty Shades of Grey series where a virgin who has never even masturbated enters into a BDSM relationship with a sociopathic billionaire
and finds true love.

Although American pop culture is soaked in sex, our politics remain
at best uncomfortable with and at worst actively hostile to female sexual
pleasure. Nearly a century after its invention and after decades of wide
usage by American women, the birth control pill remains a source of
debate in Congress and even the Supreme Court. Abortion is a peren-
nial election issue, opposition to it always listed in the Republican Party

platform. The idea of poor women or the wrong kind of women having too much sex, or the wrong kind of sex, has been used to justify cutting the social safety net, decreasing women's access to reproductive health care, taking children away from their mothers, and sterilizing women without their consent.

The United States, and the world, remain vastly unequal places, marked by profound political, economic, and social disparities between men and women. Much of it boils down to sex, and in particular how heterosexual men's desires and experiences exist as standard, while women's desires, experiences, and sexualities remain a kind of deviant from the norm, understood primarily in relation to men. That informs not only our sex lives but our politics, our ideas of how men and women should be, our family structures, and, ultimately, our happiness.

To learn how we got to this thoroughly sexually dysfunctional place, and to figure out to go forward, I started looking back. The quest for female pleasure has long been a feminist endeavor, and the importance of an independent female sexuality, apart from women's relationships with men, long a part of feminist thought. In the nineteenth century, feminist and "free love" proponent Victoria Woodhull wrote, "I have an *inalienable, constitutional* and *natural* right to love whom I may, to love as *long* or as *short* a period as I can; to *change* that love *every day* if I please, and with *that* right neither *you* nor any *law* you can frame have *any* right to interfere."[5]

Woodhull's views shifted the popular dialogue but didn't catch on widely in practice. Perhaps the most striking thing about women's sex lives in the early United States and through the post–Civil War period is the silence: sexual pleasure for women just wasn't discussed, although it was widely understood that marriage was the proper confine for sexual activity. While young men frequented prostitutes—almost always women of lower social and economic status than the women those same men would marry—young women were largely expected to be chaste until marriage, or at least offer that appearance. Which doesn't mean women were all virgins until marriage. In 1690s New Haven, Connecticut, 19 percent of young women were pregnant on their wedding night.[6] But the key was, once pregnancy happened, they got married.

Given that for centuries women were cast as sexually insatiable, we can safely assume that many women throughout history have enjoyed pleasurable, heady sex lives. But the legal authority men long had over women, and the social condemnation of sexually active unmarried women, often impeded women's sexual pleasure, or made it entirely dependent on the whims of her husband. Men had sexual desire, while women—the good ones, at least—were chaste but sexually attractive.

This view of women's sexuality was laid out in *Satan in Society: A Plea for Social Purity*,[7] a runaway hit when it was published in 1890, after the death of its author, the Rhode Island physician and professor Nicholas Francis Cooke. Despite chapters on the topic of "female self-abuse" (opening line: "Alas, that such a term is possible!"), Cooke summed up what most people thought of women when he wrote, "Many of the best mothers, wives, and managers of households, know little of or are careless about sexual indulgences. Love of home, of children, and of domestic duties are the only passions they feel."[8] Even the vast majority of women who had given birth, Cooke noted, "are innocent of the faintest ray of sexual pleasure."

The publication of Cooke's book, regressive as it was in its full-throated hostility toward masturbation, birth control, abortion, a woman's right to vote, and women's rights generally, still marked a subtle shift in American views of female sexual pleasure—that is, that women had a right to it at all. In describing the thoroughly miserable sexual conditions of many marriages, Cooke was critical, not applauding. He implored men to treat their wives with care and kindness, even telling them to bring their wives to orgasm during sex, partly based on dubious science but partly out of concern for "the pleasure to which the woman was justly entitled."

Women, too, didn't universally expect sex to be pleasurable. Between 1892 and 1920, Dr. Clelia Duel Mosher interviewed forty-five married women, most of whom were born before 1870, about their sex lives. Although the women said they wanted sex to be had only when both parties desired it, they also understood that mutuality was up to their husbands. One woman described her husband as "an unusually considerate man" because they only had sex when she also wanted to. Her experience, though, was an outlier. A similar study conducted in 1929, this one by Katharine Bement Davis of more than one thousand women, found that most of their husbands controlled when and how marital sex happened. Although they were displeased with that arrangement, many were resigned to it. "My mother taught me what to expect," one subject said. "The necessity of yielding to her husband's demands had been a great cross in her own life."[9]

By the turn of the twentieth century, female sexual pleasure had fully crept into ideas about Christian marriage (including theories about pregnancy being easier, and certain female ailments avoided, if women had orgasms during sex). But that pleasure was wholly contingent on men. If a woman was lucky enough to marry someone who took her physical enjoyment of sex seriously, then she probably had enjoyable sex. But if her husband saw sex with his wife as his right—and he would be correct, given that a husband's right of sexual access to his wife's body was enshrined into law—he might exercise that right at any time, without regard to his partner's opinion on the matter.

Gains in women's social power in the first half of the twentieth century went hand in hand with gains in sexual power. Sex was still very much a male-controlled thing, but as women increasingly entered the workforce and sought higher education, even in very small numbers, their sexual negotiating powers increased, and by the 1950s, female sexual pleasure in marriage was a standard expectation—even if the ideal marriage wherein the husband treated his wife well, including sexually, was far from the universal norm. What really changed the slow-moving tide toward marriage-centric female sexual pleasure into a cultural tsunami was the birth control pill and, later, legal abortion.

For most of human history, women had attempted to separate sex from maternity. Herbal abortions, sheep-intestine condoms, half-lemon cervical caps, rudimentary barrier methods, syringing chemical mixtures into the uterus,[10] even infanticide were all common ways women tried to determine for themselves the number and spacing of their children. And they got pretty good at it: in the 150 years before the birth control pill was invented, the average number of children born to American women dropped precipitously, from an average of 7 children per family in 1800 to just over 2 in the 1930s (it picked up in the 1950s, when the average number of children peaked at 3.7, and then went back down).[11] But the Pill offered, for the first time, a reasonably safe and very effective way to not get pregnant.

Much has been written about the Pill's impact on gender equality and how the ability of women to postpone childbearing allowed them to go to college in record numbers, work outside the home, forge independent lives, and die from childbirth a lot less often. For women's sex lives, the Pill did something equally radical: it allowed women to have sex for fun, without anxiety and without signing up for ten months of pregnancy, a painful and potentially life-threatening birth, and then at least eighteen years of caregiving.

Modern conservatives often point to the Pill, and the sexual revolution that followed, as the point at which the traditional family began to fall apart. They are partly correct: sex for fun did totally undermine a family model in which women were dependent on male partners for both economic support and, if they were lucky, sexual pleasure. In pre-Pill America, conservatives and feminists alike presciently understood the potential impact of reliable birth control: feminists advocated for it as a means of improving women's health and safety, and conservatives fought against it—most notably with the Comstock Laws of 1873, which criminalized as "obscene" imparting even information on birth control—because they feared it would upend traditional gender roles and obligations.

It is important to emphasize that the Pill did not simply pop up. It was a purposeful, feminist invention, dreamed up by public heath crusader Margaret Sanger as a "magic pill" that would allow women to control pregnancy. Sanger, who worked in poor communities in New York City and was also a target of the Comstock Laws, went to jail more than once for her work educating women about their reproductive capacities, and for running an organization that was the predecessor to what is now Planned Parenthood. Sanger wanted her magic pill, and so did Katharine McCormick, one of the first women to graduate from the Massachusetts Institute of Technology, who forwent a career in the sciences and married a rich man. At Sanger's request, McCormick wrote a $40,000 check to fund research for contraception—a significant sum in 1953—and within a year, they had a pill.[12]

By 1964, the Pill was the most popular method of contraception in the country. By 1965, the Supreme Court held that there is a fundamental right of sexual privacy, giving married women the right to use birth control. Seven years later, the same court held that the right to birth control extends to unmarried women as well. And a year after that, the court used that theory of sexual privacy to legalize elective abortion.[13]

Like the invention of the Pill, these legal victories were not happenstance. They were the result of an increasingly vocal movement for women's rights forged in the 1960s and '70s, as much an outgrowth of the newfound freedoms offered by the Pill as a backlash to the often suffocating, hyperdomestic 1950s. Feminist arguments for abortion rights, for example, were more radical than even today's mainstream prochoice arguments: the line was "abortion on demand, without apology," not a tepid request for rights because without safe abortion women might die in back alleys (although certainly women did die in back alleys, and their plights were also folded into the movement for legal abortion).

While some early second-wave feminists, including *The Feminine Mystique* author Betty Friedan, thought of feminism as a way for women to have marriage, children, and meaningful work outside the home, others, including Gloria Steinem, began to advocate not just for something other than marriage but for a politics of sexual pleasure. Steinem came under fire from fellow feminists for always having a male partner, and she herself noted that her good looks, sex appeal, and whiteness were part of what made her such a tolerable icon for what was often viewed as an intolerable set of beliefs. But as much as her unapologetic and active sex life sent the soothing message that not all feminists were man-hating hags, it also forged new ground: that liberation and sex for pleasure, outside of marriage, went hand in hand.

Also forging that path, although not always from a feminist perspective, was Helen Gurley Brown. Her book *Sex and the Single Girl* was published in 1962, and sold some 2 million copies; within three years, Gurley Brown was the editor of *Cosmopolitan* magazine, which she swiftly remade from a family publication to one targeting a new market of single, career-oriented, often sexually active young women. "Theoretically a 'nice' single woman has no sex life," Gurley Brown wrote in her 1962 book. "What nonsense! She has a better sex life than most of her married friends. Her choice of partners is endless." Gurley Brown was regressive in a whole series of ways, particularly in her obsession with pleasing men and remaining physically attractive and as thin as possible, but her position on female sexual pleasure was more progressive than that of even many feminists of her time. "A woman who even occasionally enjoys an orgasm from the roots of her hair to the tips of her toes is sexy," she wrote, an ethos she brought to *Cosmopolitan*, and into the living rooms of women around the world.[14]

A decade after *Sex and the Single Girl*, Gloria Steinem and Dorothy Pitman Hughes, along with editors Letty Cottin Pogrebin, Mary Thom, Patricia Carbine, Joanne Edgar, Nina Finkelstein, and Mary Peacock, founded the seminal publication *Ms.* magazine. Pre-*Roe*, the magazine published a petition titled "We Have Had Abortions," signed by several dozen women, including Gloria Steinem, Billy Jean King, Nora Ephron, and Anaïs Nin. It published an unflinching and disturbing photo of a woman's bruised face, taken after her husband beat her, opening up a national conversation about domestic violence and later about rape. Certainly the magazine, and its feminist contemporaries, were interested in sexual pleasure, too—but they focused first on sexual and other physical abuses, trying to change laws and social norms to protect women.

The same year *Ms.* printed its first issue, a feminist collective in Boston published the women's health manual *Our Bodies, Ourselves*. It talked openly about female sexuality and abortion and women's frustrations with male-dominated medical care, sought to demystify menstruation and childbirth, and illustrated the problem of unwanted pregnancies and lack of reproductive control. "Picture a woman trying to do work and to enter into equal and satisfying relationships with other people when she feels physically weak because she has never tried to be strong," reads the introduction to the 1973 edition of the book. "When she drains her energy trying to change her face, her figure, her hair, her smells, to match some ideal norm set by magazines, movies and TV, when she feels confused and ashamed of the menstrual blood that every month appears from some dark place in her body; when her internal body processes are a mystery to her and surface only to cause her trouble (an unplanned pregnancy, cervical cancer); when she does not understand or enjoy sex and concentrates her sexual drives into aimless romantic fantasies, perverting and misusing a potential energy because she has been brought up to deny it. Learning to understand, accept, and be responsible for our physical selves, we are freed of some of these preoccupations and can start to use our untapped energies."[15]

They may not have known it at the time, but these two movements—one explicitly political, advocating for women's rights, health, and safety, and the other focused on women's enjoyment and desires—enabled and perpetuated each other. Better access to reproductive health care, including contraception and abortion, made it easier for women to have sex on their terms. Increased legal protections and freedoms made it easier for women to both avoid and leave abusive relationships; a culture increasingly accepting of a woman's right to independence and sexual pleasure gave women an increased ability to find fulfilling and pleasurable relationships, marriages, and sexual encounters.

Pleasure, then, has always been a feminist project—and sometimes a not-quite-feminist one, ushered in partly because of feminist gains. But as the rapidly changing politics, policies, and social mores of the 1960s and '70s segued into the 1980s, a backlash was brewing. Sex, and female sexuality, was still everywhere. Popular late '70s and early '80s films like *Fast Times at Ridgemont High* and even *Grease* were saturated with teenage sex. But political forces were increasingly hostile to this newfound norm of female sexual freedom. A neotraditionalist moment took root, with "family values" advocates—usually religious conservatives opposed to birth control, abortion, and gay rights, many of them coming from failed movements to uphold racial segregation—firmly entrenching themselves within the Republican Party. President Ronald Reagan, once a prochoice governor of California, quickly evolved into an icon of this new Right: an antiabortion, pro-Christian, traditionally masculine man leading the country back to order after the gender and racial upheavals of the '60s and '70s.

Efforts to turn back the clock on sex, though, didn't work. Although many right-wing policies made birth control and abortion harder to get while simultaneously cutting welfare benefits, hamstringing affordable child care, and making working motherhood (and especially single motherhood) particularly difficult, Americans still didn't stop having sex for fun. Nor did American women stop using birth control or having abortions. Instead, 1980s right-wing policies, and the continuation and sometimes expansion of those policies today, functionally restricted pleasure, making it a privilege instead of a right. Pleasure for women was never public policy, but conservative backlash politics relegated it even more to the realm of private enterprise and corporate exploitation—a treat and an advantage if you could afford it, a moral failing if you could not. Through the 1990s and early 2000s, female sexual pleasure became increasingly monetized, packaged, advertised, and sold. *Cosmopolitan,* by the '90s a decades-old bible for the single career woman, careened straight into please-your-man sex tips, each more ludicrous than the last;

sex-toy parties became the '90s woman's Tupperware parties; and *Sex and the City*, with its eroticization of designer shoes as much as sex, replaced *Sex and the Single Girl* as a generation's clarion call to independence.

Where sexual pleasure did tip into the political realm, it was met with scandal. In 1993, President Bill Clinton appointed pediatrician and public health expert Joycelyn Elders as surgeon general of the United States. Early in her tenure, Elders caused controversy by supporting contraception access and sexual health education in schools—a fairly standard public health strategy but a controversial political position. "Joycelyn Elders is at it again," wrote columnist Suzanne Fields in the *Washington Times* in 1993. "The surgeon general is pushing sex educa- tion for children from the kindergarten through 12th grade. She wants 'the plumbing lessons' to start for tots as young as 2." Instead of sex ed and contraception as a strategy to reduce unintended pregnancy, Fields suggested, "the solutions that might actually work include restoring stigma to illegitimacy" and "restoring strict codes of conduct and dress." For teens, she added, we could send the message that "maybe it's hip to be a virgin."[16]

That vision did not ultimately win out, but neither did Elders's. A year later, at a United Nations conference on AIDS, Elders was asked about masturbation as a way to prevent the spread of HIV and remarked that "I think that it is part of human sexuality, and perhaps it should be taught." That comment and the political backlash that followed forced Elders to resign.[17]

Bill Clinton's affair with Monica Lewinsky, and the subsequent in- vestigation and publication of the *Starr Report* for any younger reader with an Internet connection to peruse—including yours truly—further entrenched sex in the public eye, simultaneously normalized and scan- dalized. And the increasingly powerful gay rights movement, itself active alongside movements for women's rights and coalescing partic- ularly in the Reagan '80s as HIV/AIDS ravaged gay communities and the president stood by and did nothing, saw at least marginal gains through the '90s. Those turned into significant victories in the 2000s— including nondiscrimination ordinances, adoption rights, and, finally, the right to marry.

The Internet, and the easy access it provided to porn, sexualized chatrooms, and increasingly frank discussion of all things sex related, also, finally, moved recreational sex into the category of wholly normal and expected, to the point where now online subcultures of men and women who don't feel sexual desire, or don't feel much sexual desire, thrive. These folks, many but not all of them young and many connecting on social media and blogs, have a host of self-identifiers: asexual, demisexual, demiromantic. They often position themselves as sexual minorities, mistreated in a culture that now sees sexual activity, and the quest for sexual pleasure, as the only normal and natural way to be.

Two hundred years after Victoria Woodhull's free love movement, her vision is increasingly a reality, and the push for gender equality, including sexual equality, has been good for the collective sex lives of American women, especially the more feminist ones. Sex, too, is now a thing we study, and so researchers are better able to pinpoint what makes for happy, pleasurable sex lives.

Politicians have been remarkably slower to adjust to the new sexual normal. And so perhaps the next step in the American feminist trajectory of sexual pleasure is to insist that politicians and lawmakers use the conclusions of researchers to craft policy—and that its goal be enabling and promoting the pleasurable experiences of women.

In 1995, the year I bought myself a promise ring, I became one of 2.2 million adolescents across the United States to take a virginity pledge.[18] According to a study conducted a decade later, nine in ten of those pledgers didn't adhere to their promise. Studies also found that virginity pledges actually increased risky sexual behavior, such as not using birth control or condoms, and pledgers are as a result as many as eight times more likely than the general population to contract a sexually transmitted infection (STI).[19] Virginity pledgers are also more likely than their nonpledging peers to engage in sex acts that they believe preserve their technical virginity but are often less pleasurable for women, such as fellatio and anal sex.[20]

Even with the stunning failure of efforts like virginity pledges to return Americans to a more culturally conservative age, and even as feminism is having a pop culture comeback, it has not gotten any easier, or any less confusing, to be a girl in America. As I write this, abercrombie kids sells a fragrance to its prepubescent audience called Sparks Fly.[21] Walmart sells girls' tights that look like thigh-high stockings; according to the sales page,

"These adorable faux thigh highs are sure to spice up any ordinary outfit."[22] The store also sells leopard-print girls' panties branded Sweet n Sassy, an underwear set printed with the words "I ☒ My #Selfie,"[23] a child-sized coconut bra,[24] and a training bra that reads "Sweets for you and me."[25]

According to a 2012 study, when offered a choice between a sexy doll wearing a black miniskirt and bra top and a doll in jeans and a sweater, 68 percent of girls between the ages of six and nine said they wanted to look like the sexier doll.[26] Another study of girls' clothing sold at fifteen national retailers found that 31 percent included sexualizing features, such as emphasizing girls' chests or backsides, or displaying sexualized writing.[27] In ads and in pop culture, adult women are routinely made to look younger or invoke sexiness and childishness at the same time (Katy Perry performing in a schoolgirl uniform), while girls are adultified, dressed and made up to look older than they are (children's beauty pageants have little girls in heavy makeup, large wigs, and fake teeth).

It's not news that women and girls are objectified in media, advertising, and American culture. Women who mostly fit a very narrow beauty ideal appear in women's and men's magazines—often posing in ways that suggest sexual readiness. The many seemingly interchangeable sexy women surrounding male stars in music videos is common enough to be a misogynist cliché: the "video ho." Women on film are routinely sexually desirable but also keep their mouths shut—just 30 percent of speaking roles in the seven hundred biggest movies went to women between 2007 and 2014, and not a single woman over the age of forty-five held a lead part.[28] One 2008 Wesleyan study looked at 1,988 ads from fifty American magazines and found that women were presented as sex objects in half of them.[29]

The bombardment of hypersexualized images of women has serious cultural, social, and psychological impacts on women, girls, men, and boys. According to the American Psychological Association, self-objectification occurs when people "internalize an observer's perspective on their physical selves and learn to treat themselves as objects to be looked at and evaluated for their appearance."[30] That's now endemic among adolescent girls, who see images of women and girls in media and couple them with the judgment and negativity leveled at actually sexually active women. Of course girls and young women internalize the message that their job is to be aesthetically pleasing and sexually enticing without being sluts who have too much sex (what counts as "too much" is never defined).

It's the Paris Hilton ideal. Hilton was famous in part for her sex tape, in which she often looked bored during the actual sex but more animated and sexy-acting when she knew the camera was turned on her. At the height of her fame, she tellingly revealed in *New York* magazine, "My boyfriends always say I'm not sexual. Sexy, but not sexual."[31]

While the "be sexy" message is a broader one coming largely from mass media, popular culture, and advertising, the "don't be sexual" message is often more formalized, coming from parents, schools, religious institutions, and peer policing. At the same time girls in kindergarten are learning that their bodies exist at least in part for the aesthetic gratification of others, they're also hearing that normal sexual curiosities are no-nos, inappropriate, or dirty. As girls hit puberty, this combination of sexualization and sexual shame gets worse. In late elementary school sex education classes, where those classes even exist,[32] information about the penis and ejaculation is front and center. For girls, though, the education is about the inside parts that make and carry babies— ovaries, fallopian tubes, the uterus. In many diagrams of the female reproductive system, there's no clitoris, and certainly in sex ed programs there's almost never discussion of the female orgasm or the reason most people have sex, which is for pleasure. There's usually no discussion about same-sex relationships or intercourse, let alone the existence of transgender people. And thanks to $1.7 billion spent since the 1980s on sex ed that tells students the only appropriate sexual choice is remaining abstinent until marriage, if you stepped into an American classroom any time in the past three decades, you might have heard a teacher read a script like this:

"Girls need to be aware they may be able to tell when a kiss is leading to something else. The girl may need to put the brakes on first in order to help the boy."

"A guy who wants to respect girls is distracted by sexy clothes and remembers her for one thing. Is it fair that guys are turned on by their senses and women by their hearts?"

Fewer than half of all states mandate the teaching of sexual education in public schools; thirty-three states require HIV/AIDS education.[33] Yet thirty-seven states require that when sex ed is taught, abstinence until marriage be covered—and twenty-five of them say that abstinence must be stressed.[34] As a result, more than 75 percent of high schools teach abstinence as the most effective method of preventing STIs and pregnancy, while just over a third teach how to correctly use a condom.[35]

This is the flip side of the hypersexualization coin. In both the demands that girls look sexy for male approval and that they refuse sex to control male desire, it's male desire at the center, and girls' feelings, desires, and priorities orbiting around it.

It should not be surprising that this doesn't work out particularly well. The United States has the highest teen pregnancy rate of any developed country. We have the highest STI rates, too, and the highest rates of unintended pregnancies generally.[36] Students who receive abstinence-only sex education aren't any more likely to wait until marriage than their peers who receive more comprehensive sex ed, but like virginity pledgers, they are less likely to use contraception or condoms when they do have sex.[37] They are also more likely to become pregnant unintentionally. And, despite the fact that fewer than half of American youth now define their sexual orientation as heterosexual, the overwhelming majority of abstinence curricula teach only about sex between men and women and don't even touch on safer practices for people who sleep with members of the same sex, let alone discuss pleasure for people who identify as gay, lesbian, bisexual, or transgender, or who aren't sure how they identify.[38]

This combination of sexualization and sexual shame is something many American women know well. It's also a uniquely American phenomenon—while other countries and cultures certainly have their own issues with women, girls, and sex, the American sexual schizophrenia is at once hypercapitalist (using sexualized images of women and girls to sell more stuff) and hypermoralist (using sex as a metric of a woman or girl's virtue, value, and character). Sex is the thing that many women report brings them the most pleasure, and also one that has brought many of us the most pain. Even feeling agnostic about sex, or not having it at all, is a point of anxiety, relief, or identity for many women. Sex is, at least for now, necessary to continue the human race, something that can be transformatively good, and also the act onto

which we have piled our anxieties and bigotries and neuroses the highest. Sex is, in many ways, a gateway to understanding what it means to
be a woman in the United States today.

In my early thirties, I worked as a political reporter at the publication
that is perhaps the epitome of the American sexual paradox: *Cosmopolitan*. I wrote mostly for the website, covering contraception access,
abortion stigma, and women's rights abroad. It was a job I loved, in large
part because I was hired at a time when the publication once known for
man-pleasing sex tips had pivoted to publishing sex positions for lesbians and guides on how to have a safe abortion. The first week of 2015,
my editors sent me down to Louisiana to write about how antiabortion
groups were blocking the construction of a new Planned Parenthood
clinic. I combined the assignment with a New Year's trip with girlfriends
to New Orleans, a city that, for me, exudes pleasure, indulgence, and
hedonism. In between fire-flamed oysters and swizzle-sticked cocktails,
I forced myself, for the sake of journalism, to head to the place where
sex, capitalism, and overindulgence collide, on the French Quarter's
famously touristy (and, depending on who you ask, either gloriously de-
bauched or aggressively trashy) Bourbon Street.

   If you have ever been on Bourbon Street, you know the feeling of
having either wandered into a hedonistic paradise or descended into a
feminist purgatory. When I was there, it wasn't Mardi Gras, so the tits-
for-beads economy was temporarily suspended, but sex was everywhere:
on the signs for the Scores and Barely Legal clubs, in the plentiful shots
poured at all hours (sex on the beach, slippery nipples), and on the
to-do list of the many people chugging from go-cups and not-so-subtly
eyeing the hundreds of young, lightly clothed bodies congregating in the
crowded street. Although a lot of it seemed like fun, there was very little
about it that struck me as sexy.

   A few days later and back on assignment, I left the French Quarter
for a coffee shop off Magazine Street that shares a parking lot with a strip
mall to meet Dr. Julie Finger, an adolescent medicine physician in an
underserved area of New Orleans far from Bourbon Street. We sat at a
table in the back so we wouldn't disturb the line of workday coffee-to-go
drinkers, and Julie, the mother of a young child, listened attentively and
spoke intentionally, choosing her words with care and clearly reluctant

to play political activist. She was willing to speak with the media about Planned Parenthood, though, because she works with kids in New Orleans. As she talked about her patients, and all the resources they don't get, her language grew more forceful, and her fists clenched.

Julie doesn't work at Planned Parenthood, but she works with a similar demographic as the one that organization serves. The young people who come to Julie's clinic often face a series of challenges: poverty, communities with high rates of HIV and other STIs, burgeoning sexual identities without much support. Routinely, Julie said (and as I first reported on Cosmopolitan.com), she finds herself asking her teenage girl patients why they're having sex "and having the answer be because their partner wanted to, and them not having a voice in that decision." One of the most important parts of her job, she said, is "asking them, 'What do you want?' And having them realize, 'Oh I actually have a part in this process.'" Another part of her job: giving young people very bad news.

"We had a horrible winter," Julie said, visibly flinching. "We had three new [HIV] infections in a three-week span: seventeen, nineteen, twenty-one. One of whom was a heterosexual male, and when we told him he was infected he was stunned. He couldn't fathom that he possibly could be infected because he's only had sex with women, and in his mind, that's not how you get HIV."

The problems Julie tries to combat one patient at a time—girls who see sex as something they're obligated to give to boys and men, teenagers who are naturally sexually curious but lacking the knowledge and tools to make fully informed sexual decisions—are not natural disasters, but very much man-made. In Louisiana, sexual health education is not mandatory. If schools do teach sex ed, they are legally required to promote abstinence until marriage. Attempts to introduce comprehensive sexual health education were repeatedly blocked by conservative former governor Bobby Jindal, who also barred representatives from Planned Parenthood from teaching sex ed in schools.[39]

"One frustration with all of this is a lot of the sex ed that needs to happen is not specifically sex ed; it's, 'How do you have a healthy relationship, how do you avoid dating violence, how do you become a healthy adult?' It's a shame that we can't impart that to our youth," Julie said.

Jindal also tried to cut funding for Planned Parenthood entirely, attempted to exclude the group from the state's Medicaid contracts, and signed into law a series of abortion restrictions, making the procedure exceptionally difficult to get in the state. And he refused the Medicaid expansion under the Affordable Care Act, which made it more difficult for low-income folks—and Louisiana has some of the highest poverty rates in the nation—to get affordable health care, including contraception and reproductive care.

Recognizing those challenges, Planned Parenthood, one of the largest providers of women's health care in the country, decided to invest millions of dollars in building a state-of-the-art clinic in New Orleans, which was supposed to open in 2015. But because Planned Parenthood provides abortions elsewhere in the country—the group doesn't perform abortions in Louisiana, although it makes no bones about the fact that it would like to offer that service as part of its full slate of reproductive health care—local religious organizations launched a coordinated effort to keep the new facility from opening despite the state's desperate need for expanded sexual health services. Antiabortion activists interrupted church services of congregations that support Planned Parenthood; contractors working on the clinic saw their children's schools picketed by protesters; construction workers were threatened and intimidated; the state refused licenses and permits for no discernable reason.

The clinic opened anyway, albeit more than a year behind schedule. It plans to see some 13,000 patients a year, offering annual exams, STI testing and treatment, sexual health education, cancer screenings, and contraception.

Louisiana needs it. The proabstinence, prolife push under Jindal may have been politically satisfying for his conservative base, but the state now ranks first in the nation for its rates of gonorrhea, second in chlamydia, and third in both syphilis and HIV.[40] Sixty percent of the pregnancies in Louisiana are unintended, and nearly 80 percent of unplanned births are publicly funded, costing the state and federal governments $651 million in 2010, the last year for which data is available.[41] Louisiana is also one of just two US states that saw its abortion rate increase between 2010 and 2014 (Jindal was first elected in 2008).[42] In 2015, as Jindal pushed to yank funding from Planned Parenthood, the state was in the midst of a massive syphilis outbreak.[43] Louisiana, Jindal has bragged, is "the most pro-life state" in America.[44]

Luckily, when it comes to sexual health, not every state looks like Louisiana. With increased access to long-acting contraceptive methods, a health-care plan that made contraception free for most American women, and eight years of more liberal sex education policies under the Obama administration, unintended pregnancies have dropped off precipitously nationwide, and teen pregnancies have fallen to an all-time low.

That more liberal social policies have led to better results is not surprising, as there is little debate in the public health community about what improves health outcomes: education, affordability, and access, including access to reproductive health care, such as birth control and abortion. After thirty years and more than a billion dollars of federal funding for abstinence promotion, the data is in, and it's clear that policymakers couldn't have thought of a more effective way to waste government resources. Teaching teenagers to just say no to sex has been a massive failure by all measures. Still, these programs are how many kids in the United States learn about sex, and as a more conservative administration moves into the White House, many public health experts are concerned.

"There's a wonderful quote from a sexual health educator who said, 'What if we approached teaching our kids swimming the way we approached sex education in this country?'" Julie told me. "So you would have this pool but you'd put walls around it and keep the kids locked out, and they'd hear all this splashing going on and people laughing but you would never tell them what swimming was or what was happening in there. And then one day you decide that they turn eighteen or whatever and you open up the doors and you say, 'Now you can go swim.' Some of the kids would jump in and do just fine. And some of them would drown."

Samantha Pugsley played by the rules for girls and sex, and it almost ruined her marriage. She grew up attending a Baptist church and took a purity pledge, promising to abstain from all sexual activity until she was married. At twenty-two, she married her high school sweetheart, walking down the aisle a virgin.

I talked with Samantha by phone, after finding an essay she wrote on the website xojane.com called "IT HAPPENED TO ME: I Waited Until My Wedding Night to Lose My Virginity and I Wish I Hadn't." I had been hunting online for real stories of wedding-night virgins that weren't on abstinence-promoting websites, and Samantha's was one of the top hits. I wanted to know more than just the headline—not only that she wished she had made different choices, but why virginity had mattered so much to her, how she navigated a sex life that went from zero to sixty in one day, and what her marriage was like now. She agreed to talk, and I called her at her home in Charlotte, North Carolina, where she lives with her husband and works as a photographer.

"I had this feeling that I was above everybody else, that I wasn't doing the bad thing, that I was being the good person," Samantha, who speaks in a bright voice with a southern accent, said of her purity years. "God is really happy with me, look at how strong I'm being."

After the wedding ceremony, everything changed.

"I actually had a panic attack on my wedding night," Samantha told me. "When we got married nothing felt different. So we went on our honeymoon and I'm looking at this man who now all of a sudden I'm allowed to be intimate with, and I couldn't flip a switch and say now it's totally fine for you to be a sexual person, it's allowed biblically. I couldn't understand what that meant and why it was suddenly okay. It was very scary."

Terrified and too embarrassed to let her new husband know what was going on, Samantha emerged from what should have been a romantic vacation feeling isolated and traumatized.

"Everything I had ever learned came crashing down," she said.

According to a study out of the University of Washington that focused on male virginity pledgers, keeping the pledge to stay abstinent until marriage comes with its own set of consequences. Primary among them: poor sexual communication with their wives and, it's not hard to imagine, the less-than-great sex that comes with it. As one of the men put it, "For me to come home from work and say, 'Hey, did you like it last time?' I mean that would be—that would be such a weird question for me to ask."[45]

Once married, some female virginity pledgers also report struggling with intimacy and communication and, sometimes, sexual abuse and violence. Christine Webb, a young woman who describes herself as "incredibly conservative" and runs a blog called *The Vintage Housewife,* wrote that although she was glad she and her husband didn't have sex until their wedding night, "there is a huge mental/emotional block that comes with suddenly becoming sexually active. There is nothing else on earth that is completely forbidden one second, and then with a few

'I do's,' it's suddenly not only permissible, but essential to the health of your relationship. That is super strange. I was supposed to be 'pure pure pure' one night and then a veritable porn star the next."[46] Eden Strong, a writer for the site YourTango and another wedding night virgin, was sick on her wedding day and scared on that night, so she told her husband she wanted to wait. "He told me he had waited long enough," Eden wrote. "I don't even remember much of what happened after the initial struggle, all I know was that one minute I was a virgin and the next . . . I wasn't. I remember sobbing." Eden's husband spent the rest of their marriage raping her, physically overpowering her when she resisted and berating her when she cried.[47]

Samantha's husband was warm and generous. But the narrative that sex was bad was impossible to shake just because she was married. "Any time I was faced with the possibility that sex would happen, I would have this visceral panic reaction, almost like a fight or flight thing," she said. "I would go in the bathroom and shut the door to change my clothes because I was terrified of being naked in front of my husband. It escalated more and more, where I would avoid triggers. And the triggers were doing anything that would be natural for a husband and wife to do—hold hands, cuddle on the couch, kiss for any length of time, change clothes in front of each other."

Eventually, Samantha was so tense that sex became physically painful. But the messages she received as a girl about male and female sexuality—that husbands needed sex and wives needed to give it to maintain a happy marriage—kept her quiet; she was afraid that if she took sex off the table, her husband might leave her. After more than a year, she cracked.

"I knew it wasn't sustainable and I couldn't see our marriage working if I continued to hide it," she said. "I tried to hold it together for a while but eventually it gets so bad that you can't anymore. That was a bad day."

Her feminist-minded husband was horrified and backed off immediately, giving Samantha room to heal physically and psychologically. She started going to therapy to treat PTSD related to the sexual trauma she experienced. Slowly and with much patience, they are rebuilding their sex life, but significant challenges remain.

"Now we even have problems where he feels scared to initiate something because he's worried, 'Are you just doing this to make me happy or because this is what you're supposed to do?' So even though I'm getting better, we still have those obstacles," Samantha said. "It's a never-ending thing. It's not something that fixes itself with some therapy overnight."

Despite its value in American purity culture and in cultures around the world, there is no medically agreed-upon definition of virginity. Nor is there a socially agreed-upon one: If it's the breaking of a hymen, what about girls who broke theirs riding horses or bikes? If it's vaginal penetration with a penis, is a fifty-year-old lesbian who has slept with dozens of women a virgin? Does oral sex count? What about anal sex?

Talking to Samantha and reading online narratives of women who waited, even the ideal waiting-till-marriage stories seemed like recipes for unhappiness. According to most proponents of premarital chastity, young people should abstain from all sexual activity until their wedding nights. That term "all sexual activity" is itself a little vague—is kissing a sexual activity?—but the hard line seems to be drawn at genital touching for sexual pleasure, whether those genitals are someone else's or your own. In the best-case scenario for purity proponents, a young man marries a young woman, and neither of them has ever been sexually touched by anyone, including themselves. They are supposed to go from experiencing no sexual activity to having penetrative vaginal sex in a single night, and this is supposed to be both wholesome and satisfying.

But maybe I was missing something, and there was some great benefit to cramming what is for many people a years-long sexual trajectory in one night and doing what conservative blogger Christine Webb called the "instantaneous mind-switch" of sex being dirty one day and righteous the next. On Twitter, I found Dr. Leah Torres, feminist OB/GYN who works in Utah and sees many religious patients. I wanted her take on American sexual culture from her vantage point in Salt Lake City, where no sex before marriage is the standard plan for many young people.

"No sex before marriage is the worst plan ever," Leah told me when I called her. "It's the zero to full throttle thing, but it's also exploring and getting to know your partner. Why do we not have room in our culture for that? We should have room for exploring our partner, who we may or may not spend the rest of our lives with, including the physical, including the sexual."

Before you marry someone, Leah notes, you would want to know if you're compatible on a variety of levels—whether your life goals mesh, whether you have the same financial priorities, whether you want kids, whether you feel emotionally and mentally satisfied together, whether you have similar desires for intellectual stimulation and cultural engagement. Leaving sex off that list, she says, "doesn't make any sense, and it speaks to the whole view of female sexuality being something that is not important or somebody else's property."

Utah, with its large Mormon population and cheery social conservatism, is in many ways a model for the kinds of traditional sexual relationships the "wait until marriage" crowd values. Utahans marry younger than residents of any other state in the nation (perhaps because of the Mormon Church's strong prohibition against premarital sex), with men typically marrying at 25.6 and women 23.5, three and a half years younger than the national average.[48]

Even with its conservative social mores, Utah also has a higher-than-average divorce rate, something researchers have linked to its high rates of early marriage.[49] And despite the state's religiosity, a 2009 study found Utah to have the highest rate of pornography consumption in the nation (although several Mormon groups have questioned the study's reliability). A few years later, Utah became the first state to declare porn a "public health hazard," with a bill condemning pornography and asserting it is "linked to lessening desire in young men to marry."[50]

That view of sex as a vice until a wedding ring turns it into a virtue comes up when Leah is asked to conduct "premarital exams" on female patients before their wedding day. "You can look in every medical textbook under the sun and you will not find such an exam, but it exists here, because culturally, before they were married, girls would go to the OB/GYN and have their hymen inspected," Leah said, adding that such exams are not as standard as they used to be, but she still fields requests for them.

"When these young ladies come in, they have not had any sort of sexual activity, they say they have not masturbated because that's what the church tells them to do, and they say, 'I'm about to get married, what do I do?'" she said. "I don't care what their hymen is doing, I talk to them about what the looming wedding night is going to entail. For them, that's consummating the marriage, and that's the first time, supposedly, that they're having sexual activity with another person. I talk about consent, I talk about active consent, I talk about comfort, I talk about communication, about exploration of each other's bodies. I tell them, 'You don't have to have penis in vagina sex the first time,' and they look at me like I've just shattered the earth."

Most Americans are not religious Mormons or virginity pledgers, and more than 95 percent of Americans have sex before marriage.[51] For all their problems, surely virginity pledges and promise rings are not the sole or even primary cause of America's collective sexual dysfunction. Looking at rates of sexual activity, there is no question that women like sex and have it for fun. There is, though, an outstanding question of whether sex could be better for many women. The answer is yes.

I don't remember the day, the year, or the reason I eventually took off my promise ring, but I do remember sitting in my college dorm room, listening to a friend describe how a few days earlier, her boyfriend had quickly removed his penis from her vagina and forced it into her anus. She told the story not to describe a rape or even a violation of trust, but to worry he thought it was gross. I remember that conversation in particular, but it was not the only time a friend described a nearly identical chain of events—the consensual vaginal sex, the "surprise" anal. There were others, too: women whose heads were forced down by men who felt entitled to oral sex, women who were black-out drunk and woke up naked in the bed of a man they thought was a friend. And there were the less extreme and less violent stories that still hurt to hear: the friend who had painful sex she didn't enjoy because her boyfriend wanted it and she wanted him; the friend who didn't have sex when she wanted to because she thought the guy she was dating wouldn't respect her afterward; the friend who said she just didn't like receiving oral sex not because she was self-conscious or anything, but you had to admit vaginas were kind of gross.

It's not just religious women or women in conservative pockets of the country for whom sex is often done to please men, or withheld to gain some other benefit, or performed out of sacrifice or while in physical pain.

On one extreme is sexual violence, including rape and other forms of sexual assault. Depressingly, sexual force and coercion are common aspects of women's sex lives. According to a 2015 fact sheet from the National Sexual Violence Resource Center, one in five American women will be raped in her life, and nearly half of women report experiencing sexual violence other than rape.[52] In what is perhaps the most obvious result of all time from a scientific study, women who reported having sex that was unwilling or entered into coercively were significantly less happy than those who did not report experiencing forced or coerced sex.[53]

In the course of writing this book, I spoke with dozens of women about their sex lives. I also drew up a survey and asked friends and friends of friends to forward it on to people I may not have come across in my everyday life. I asked for details of various aspects of peoples' sexual beliefs and histories. Of the hundreds of people the survey reached through this unscientific distribution scheme, I got thirty-five responses, mostly but not all from women, ranging in age from their early twenties to midsixties. I was surprised, first, by how candid and descriptive the respondents were, writing in detail about some of the most intimate aspects of their lives. And I was struck by how almost none of their stories fit neat narratives about pleasure, violence, sex, and desire.

For the women who responded, sexual violence and coercion were the rule, not the exception—reading through survey after survey, it was a relief (and a rarity) to find one in the pile where a woman reported no abusive experiences with sex. All of the women who were abused were abused by men they knew.

"On two occasions [my ex-boyfriend] was so rough that he ruptured my bladder and I peed blood for days," wrote one twenty-four-year-old woman. "I loved him, so I never did anything about it." Another was molested as a child by a seventy-eight-year-old neighbor and later raped by a boyfriend. A forty-eight-year-old woman had an elderly male piano teacher grab her crotch twice when she was eight; in her twenties, "a boyfriend/friend tried to coerce me into sex by forcefully grabbing me and trying to pin me down on the floor, when I was alone with him at home," she wrote. "That was frightening but he did back off when I resisted." One sixty-one-year-old wrote that she was raped more than once, after a childhood of physical and emotional abuse. "One of my assailants was a gynecologist, and he used digital penetration in a very forceful way, repeatedly," she said. "I still do not enjoy having fingers in my vagina, especially deep or forceful repeated thrusting."

Not all of the women who experienced what could be called a sexual violation defined it that way. "I've never experienced sexual violence or coercion, really, but I did have a male partner who didn't bother with a

condom and was sort of just inside me before I realized what was happening," wrote one thirty-year-old woman. "We were naked and making
out (which was fine) and then BAM! unexpected penetration. It really
didn't feel consensual, but at the time I was so uncomfortable and surprised that I didn't know what to do so I just let him finish. I felt really
grossed out by that experience and remember taking a really long hot
shower and just scrubbing myself all over."

In much of pop culture, experiencing sexual violence means women
either end up in a body bag or with lifelong emotional scars. The reality, women reported, was more complicated—for many, the trauma of
sexual coercion or abuse eventually recedes, or at least coexists along
with a happy, dynamic sex life. "I was coerced into a lot of situations by
my husband because of his addictive-like craving for experiences of all
sorts," wrote another woman, now sixty-four. "Hard on me but in retrospect I learned a lot about myself and how to hold boundaries and when
to let them go." There were also six or seven years, she said, where she
and her husband "made love three times a day," and she described their
sex life as featuring "hours, hours, transformational, kundalini experiences, visions, out-of-body, and just long, luxurious encounters."

There's no smooth trajectory from "victim of sexual assault" to "sur-
vivor," and no point at which sex becomes universally "good." For most
women, it seems pleasurable sex is a kind of ebb and flow, a lifetime of
experiences that are usually positive and sometimes negative and often
somewhere in between.

A fundamental problem in traversing this in-between lies in defining
"pleasurable sex" for women. It turns out there isn't much of a definition:
some sex researchers determine pleasure by number of orgasms, something many feminists have criticized as patriarchal, while others use
self-reported measures of satisfaction. Those measures, though, often
don't distinguish between physical satisfaction and emotional satisfaction—and women routinely factor in emotional satisfaction when eval-
uating their sexual satisfaction, while men are more prone to evaluate
the frequency of intercourse.[54] That women fold emotional feelings into
physical ones is not a bad thing—factoring in your partner's pleasure
to your own can make for much better sex and more intimate relationships—but it gets complicated in a culture where women are expected
to be servile, decorative, and self-denying and where men are expected
(or allowed) to be sexually voracious, aggressive, and self-focused.

It gets complicated, too, when so much of how women (especially but not exclusively heterosexual ones) see, understand, and even desire sex is filtered through male experiences and norms. None of us is a blank slate, starting from scratch; what we eroticize and fetishize are very much products of the world in which we live, which is one where violence against women is commonplace, female sexiness is commercialized while female sexual desire is politicized, and men dominate in nearly every realm. "In a world ordered by sexual imbalance, pleasure in looking has been split between active/male and passive/female," wrote the feminist film critic Laura Mulvey. "In their traditional exhibitionist role women are simultaneously looked at and displayed, with their appearance coded for strong visual and erotic impact so that they can be said to connote to-be-looked-at-ness."[55] Women, to paraphrase both Mulvey and film critic John Berger, watch themselves being watched, hyperaware of how they appear to men and adjusting their behavior accordingly, while men can take pleasure in simply sitting back and watching. In the sexual realm, this means women are often as concerned with looking sexy as they are actually enjoying sexual touch and experience. Worrying about whether your partner thinks you're sexy can be a real impediment to being wholly present during sex and being able to wholly enjoy it. It can also make pleasure contingent not just on pleasing another but on being a conventionally sexy, aesthetically pleasing object.

There is probably no such thing as "authentic" female sexual pleasure absent cultural dictates, being as it is that all of our desires and feelings are filtered through multilayered cultural assumptions and individual experiences. But when a central part of womanhood is the demand that we be self-sacrificing as well as objects to be wanted, the ability of women to just want falls further away. A wealth of psychological literature details how girls are raised to be conflict avoiding and give without taking, and how women are expected to be supportive helpmeets and objects of male longing. There isn't much of a road map for basic female demands, let alone female desire—even though desire is foundational to how women live.

The women I surveyed and interviewed for this book used words like "sweet," "ecstatic," "joyous," "passionate," "intense," "exciting," "affirming," "blissful," and "tantric" to describe their sex lives. Getting older and having more sexual experience seemed to make sex better. Many described first feeing sexual excitement as children, followed by a somewhat rocky initiation into sexual activity with other people, and finally lessons learned that improved their sex lives—how to be more accepting of their bodies and perceived physical flaws, how to establish clear boundaries with partners, and how to accept and eventually celebrate their sexual orientations and desires.

That enjoyment tracks with the research on women and sexual pleasure. In one study of one thousand employed women, sex was what they identified as making them the happiest. And the more often both men and women have sex, the happier they are.[56]

Still, sex is often less pleasing for women than it is for men. According to one study, straight women who have sex with a regular partner only orgasm about 63 percent of the time, while men orgasm 85 percent of the time. Other studies have found even lower numbers, indicating that women orgasm less than 30 percent of the time.[57]

Orgasms are not the only indicator of sexual pleasure, of course, and sex can be fun without them. But far more women seem to be having orgasm-less sex than men, and it's tough to imagine many men saying that they never orgasm with a partner but they're still fully satisfied with their sex lives. Indeed, in one survey of more than 3,200 people between the ages of eighteen and twenty-six in heterosexual relationships, the young men reported both more frequent orgasms (87 percent of the men surveyed said they came all or most of the time they had sex, while just 47 percent of the women did) and higher levels of sexual satisfaction.[58] Other studies have found that young women routinely engage in sex they don't find particularly pleasurable because they want to make their partners happy.[59] Women are also much more likely than men to experience painful sex and to tolerate that pain in order to continue having sex. And many women, especially younger ones, who report never orgasming with a partner do not feel especially upset, cheated, or frustrated by that fact.

This is not because women's bodies are inherently more mysterious or difficult to navigate than men's. Lesbians orgasm 75 percent of the time,[60] which is almost as often as men who have sex with women orgasm, suggesting the problem is less the female body than either male sexual aptitude or male sexual effort. There's also the question of attraction and whether some women might be more sexually satisfied with women but either don't realize it because of social norms that emphasize heterosexual relationships or because they actively push away

attraction to women. One thirty-five-year-old woman I spoke with identified as heterosexual before meeting the woman she married. "When I
finally met [my wife], it was like, oh, this is what everybody talks about
when they talk about sex," she said. "This is why it's a big deal. I got it.
Whereas before, I would say I had had good sex, but I had never had a
connection with somebody like I did when I was finally with a woman."
The universalizing of heterosexual women's experiences—a universalizing that is reflected in much of the research and as a result I recognize
is happening in this book, too—constrains our ideas of what could be
and what we might enjoy.

Some straight men, especially younger ones, will also readily admit
they don't put effort into making the women they sleep with come—
especially if the woman isn't a girlfriend and is therefore considered disposable, or a slut. In one study of college hookups, researchers found,
unsurprisingly, that orgasms were closely related to sexual satisfaction,
with women reporting five to six times more satisfaction when they
orgasmed versus when they didn't. College women also had the most
pleasurable sex—and the most orgasms—in the context of committed
relationships.[61] College-age men reported simply not caring as much
about women they were hooking up with and so not trying nearly as
hard to make the experience pleasurable for them. And many heterosexual women often lack both sexual knowledge and a sense of orgasm
entitlement: in one study of college students, nearly a third of young
women couldn't locate the clitoris on a diagram of the vulva. A greater
proportion of young men were able to find it, despite not having one of
their own.[62]

In her book *Girls & Sex,* journalist Peggy Orenstein interviewed dozens of young women and in a section about fellatio wrote, "Whether they
hoped to attract a boy's interest, sustain it, or placate him, it seemed
their partner's happiness was their main concern. Boys, incidentally, far
and away, said that the number one reason they engaged in oral sex was
for physical pleasure." According to one study, the primary reason high
school girls give oral sex is to improve their relationships. Nearly a quarter of high school girls report giving oral sex to make their relationships
better; only about 5 percent of high school boys give it for the same
reason.[63]

It should come as little surprise, then, that women report higher
levels of sexual satisfaction when they're in monogamous relationships,

where their sexual needs are better attended to. Such relationships are not always easy to forge—nor, for some women, are even satisfying casual dates. "The well has kind of gone dry," Jade, who dates both men and women, told me about her love life posttransition in Seattle. "I date pretty regularly, I have, but especially with men it's changed dramatically. The men tend to be kind of slimy, and don't really know how to treat a trans partner—they sort of act like rocks. I've gone on entire first dates with men and had them stare at me silently like I'm some sort of mythological creature, like they can't believe they managed to actually find one, and they don't know what to do."

Not all women crave monogamy, of course, even if most do express a desire for sexual pleasure and generous partners. The many women I surveyed and spoke with described wanting, and usually experiencing, a variety of sexual (and nonsexual) relationships, from unenthusiastic abstinence to intentional celibacy to random hookups to nonmonogamous sex to polyamory to traditional monogamy. A few don't have sex at all. "I can't say I am satisfied or not satisfied with not having sex," wrote one thirty-three-year-old woman. "It is just the situation of my life."

Some expressed a hint of regret that their current happy monogamous relationship may mean they don't have any more sexual partners. "Assuming I remain faithful to my fiancé—which I plan on—I will probably wish I'd had more partners, especially women," wrote one woman. "But honestly I'll think it was 'good' based on how loving it's been." The thirty-three-year-old woman who doesn't have sex at all said she identifies as asexual but that she at least wants to give sex a try. "I would hope that I experience sex at least once in my life and that it is a good experience," she said. She isn't willing, though, to compromise her comfort. Women who did say they wanted a monogamous partner also said they hoped to have a variety of sexual experiences before finding the right person. "Ideally, after spending time exploring what I like sexually with different people, I eventually would like to be with someone long term who I have great adventurous sex with throughout our years," wrote one young woman. That expectation to have a long, rewarding sex life was summed up most clearly by a woman in her early sixties, who wrote, "I hope to still be enjoying sex at eighty."

To the extent that feminism encourages higher self-esteem and auton-omy in women—and those are certainly two of its goals—it also con-tributes to better sex. Young women who feel better about themselves, who are more autonomous, and who have greater empathy also expe-rience greater sexual satisfaction.[64] Feminist movements have long en-couraged women to get to know their own bodies, and while the 1970s instructive to break out the hand mirror and get a good look at your vulva may sound silly now, it's valuable nonetheless: young women who are uncomfortable with their genitals engage in riskier sexual behavior, have fewer orgasms, and are less sexually satisfied than women who are comfortable with their vulvas. In another study, college-age women who gave oral sex to men often reported feeling bad about themselves, but those who received it were more self-aware, open, and assertive.[65] In citing these studies and another showing that girls who masturbate during hookups or relationships are twice as likely to orgasm as girls who don't, *Girls & Sex* author Peggy Orenstein wrote, "So how young girls feel about 'down there' matters. It matters a lot." How they feel about themselves as whole people—how much the promises of femi-nism have reached them—matters too.

That seems like an obvious calculus. But for many women (and men), American cultural discomfort with sex for pleasure, coupled with a lack of realistic sexual education and airbrushed, hyperscripted pop culture representations of sex, means we're too sexually confused, inhibited, self-conscious, and ignorant to enjoy ourselves as much as we could.

Leah Torres, the OB/GYN who works with many religious women in Utah, said patients routinely come to her asking for a checkup be-cause they don't feel like having sex as much as they think they *should* be. When she asks whether they're having sex as much as they *want* to be, the answer is often yes. Other patients ask for tests because they are having difficulty reaching orgasm; when Leah asks whether they've tried exploring their own bodies, they say they don't masturbate because of their religion yet assume something is "wrong" because they don't orgasm with a partner.

"It's such a confounding issue, but it's also an issue where society tells us one thing and then shames us for that one thing it tell us," Leah said. "What I hear from patients is, 'There's something wrong with me, check my hormone levels.'"

What's wrong, she said, isn't usually hormone levels. It's a culture that symbolizes sex with the female body but expects that the person inhabiting that body will be satisfied by the display alone. Sexiness—being perceived as sexually attractive to men—is the point; female sexual desire and pleasure is not, at least not beyond the desire to be admired and the pleasure that comes from being desired.

"We have cultural messaging thrown at us 24/7 that's sex sex sex, if you don't have sex there's something wrong with you," Leah said. "The flip side of that coin is that if you want sex you're bad. So it gets very confusing for women out there."

And yet both having sex and not having a lot of sex are completely normal. The average American adult has sex two to three times per month.[66] Younger folks have more sex, with American adults under the age of forty having sex about once a week on average. Only 10 percent of Americans under forty are having sex four or more times a week, and the same percentage are celibate, having no sex at all. When you look at all adults, the numbers grow starker: just 6 percent are having sex four or more times a week, and 22 percent have no sex at all. There are also a lot of benefits to having just as much sex as you want, whether that's four times a day or four times a year: according to one study in China, the frequency of sex being "just right" was associated with a big jump in happiness and satisfaction.[67]

If there is one feminist solution to hang-ups and issues with sex, it's giving every woman the tools to find that "just right" spot for herself. That's harder, though, than it sounds—especially given the fact that feminist movements rarely represent all women equally.

Feminist gains, significant as they are, have disproportionately benefited women at the top: upper- and middle-class women, white women, able-bodied women, heterosexual women. Gains in sexual pleasure and autonomy have similarly been unequally distributed.[68] Women of color, working-class women, and less educated women report lower levels of sexual satisfaction but higher levels of sexual activity—that is, they're having slightly more sex than their white, upper-class, educated counterparts, but they're liking it less.[69] That in turn implies that some of that sex may be forced or coerced—and indeed, 40 percent of black girls report experiencing coercive sexual contact before they reach adulthood, Native American women are raped at a rate three and a half times higher than that of the general female population, and women of color are both more likely to be incarcerated (where they are frequently sexually assaulted) and less likely to report sexual assault to the police than are white women.[70] Among transgender women, half have been sexually assaulted or abused,[71] and men who rape or even kill trans women are routinely let off the hook by using the "trans panic defense": the claim that when they discovered their date was transgender, they experienced something akin to temporary insanity.[72] The ever-present threat of rape and murder complicates and sometimes poisons the romantic and sexual landscape for many trans women, and makes an easy and pleasurable sex life all the more difficult. Lesbians, too, are sexually assaulted in astounding numbers, and although men are statistically many times more likely to commit assault than are women, women who are assaulted by other women—including by their romantic partners—can have a hard time finding resources for both healing and legal action.

It's not just sexual violence that leads to less pleasurable sex. It's also health and time, both of which are in shorter supply in poor communities, marginalized communities, and communities of color. Homelessness, which is endemic among young trans women and gay and lesbian youth, ups the probability of a whole slew of health challenges in addition to increasing the risk of violent victimization. Working-class women, who are disproportionately of color and have lower educational levels, often work long, hard hours, which means coming home exhausted. Stress also decreases sexual satisfaction, and women who are worried about feeding their kids or paying the electric bill or who combat regular racism certainly have that in spades.

Health issues like diabetes and hypertension, which can impact sexual function and desire, are also disproportionately seen in African American and working-class communities. Access to health care is lower in those same communities, and so if women do have an issue with their sex lives, they have fewer medical resources. And women lacking resources are also more likely to be stuck in unhappy, dysfunctional, and abusive relationships because they're more financially dependent on their partner.

Feminist gains in access to abortion and contraception have made it easier for women to have sex without worrying about the act leading to a baby. But both contraception and abortion are less accessible and in turn used less often (and for contraception, less effectively) by poor women.

Today, feminism is en vogue, and intersectionality—the idea that people exist at the intersections of various oppressive forces based on race, class, gender, religion, and other characteristics, and that movements for social justice should reflect those realities—is increasingly mainstreamed not just into the feminist movement but into American society generally. Sheryl Sandberg's *Lean In* faced criticism for focusing on white-collar, and by extension mostly white, female workers. African American feminists pushed back on mainstream media narratives of the Black Lives Matter movement that talked only about black men killed by cops, insisting that those within the movement and outside of it mention the names of black women shot or assaulted by police. There's an increased push to talk about sexual assault not just at elite, traditionally white, universities, but also at historically black colleges and in communities where most people don't go to college at all.

When it comes to sexual pleasure, though, there's little discussion of how overlapping identities of gender, race, class, sexuality, and religion shape women's experiences, and how the downstream impacts of racism, classism, and sexism on women's time, our health, our choices, and our options offer unequal access to satisfying sex. The more I talked to women about their sex lives, and the more research on sexual pleasure I pored over, the more clear it became that this—disparities in access to the things that allow for pleasurable sex, and the resulting disparities in pleasure—is both a pressing feminist concern and a problem solvable with better public policy. But to decide that inequality in sexual pleasure matters, we would first have to conclude that sexual pleasure matters. And for all the progress American women have made, we are not there yet.

I started writing this book at thirty-two, living in New York City with no children, no husband, my own apartment, and what felt like several full-time jobs. I have a college degree, a law degree, and a nearly full passport. Early on in the process of thinking about women and pleasure, I noted to myself that none of this—the things that make me extraordinarily happy, the things that let me be free, the things that contribute to a healthy sex life—would have been possible without access to birth control and abortion.

Looking around at the women I know, there is no question that all of our lives have been shaped, and so many doors opened, by the ability to not get pregnant, or not stay pregnant, when we didn't want to. Our sexual and romantic lives have also been improved by being able to have sex for fun, because we want to, without risking our educational futures, our jobs, our health, or what we wanted in our partners, relationships, and lives. For so many American women, contraception and abortion are nearly unparalleled social goods. They make sex better. They make life better.

Unfortunately, the American political class either understands little about what makes for good sex and a pleasurable sex life, doesn't care, or is actively hostile to it. Thanks to feminist efforts, many of our laws have changed, and some of the things that explicitly made sex bad or painful for women are no longer generally permissible—rape, adolescent marriage, criminalization of same-sex relationships, the prohibition on contraception and abortion. But rarely have the ways in which liberal politicians pushed through these gains been pleasure-centric. Rather, the modern Democratic Party, behind which today's feminists largely put their electoral energies, has situated itself as a health-focused, social justice–seeking, reality-based alternative in opposition to the morality-obsessed, science-questioning Republican one. Feminist organizations, too, set out their goals along vectors of health and rights: the right to equal pay, the health benefits of safe and legal contraception and abortion, the right to not go to jail because of who you have consensual sex with, the right to marry the person you love, the necessity of maternity care for healthy women and children.

These are not bad arguments, but they are framed differently from those of the Right, which positions itself as a moral authority. "The most offensive instance of this war on religion has been the current Administration's attempt to compel faith-related institutions, as well as believing individuals, to contravene their deeply held religious, moral, or ethical beliefs regarding health services, traditional marriage, or abortion," the 2012 GOP platform read.[73] In 2015 debates over federal funding of Planned Parenthood, one antiabortion advocate, Citizens for a Pro-Life Society's Dr. Monica Miller, decried Planned Parenthood's sexual immorality, telling a religious radio show that the underlying problem with the organization isn't just that it performs abortions; the problem is that "the kind of sexual ethic that Planned Parenthood promotes is sex for recreation, sex for mere pleasure."[74]

Today, opposition to abortion is a plank of the GOP platform. Contraception is also met with hostility. No national "prolife" organization supports birth control access, and many point to the "contraception mentality"—that women should be able to avoid pregnancies they don't want—as a cause of abortion. "This mentality views human life as something that is not always welcome and, when unwelcome, can be disposed of," wrote Reverend Walter J. Schu, LC, in a publication for the United States Conference of Catholic Bishops. "Sexual intercourse tends to be reduced from an act of personal self-giving to one of mutual sensual gratification freed from any tie to responsibility to new life."[75]

Under the guise of "religious liberty," conservative legal organizations convinced the Supreme Court that public companies should be able to refuse to provide employees health insurance that covers birth control. State-level restrictions on abortion have made the procedure nearly impossible to access for a great number of women, and many are again turning to illegal and often unsafe methods to end pregnancies.

The discourse around abortion tells us less about American reverence for fetal life than it does about our shaky relationship with female sexuality and pleasure. Browse the arguments against abortion rights, and even American opinions on the legality of abortion, and the hostility to women having sex becomes quickly apparent. According to Gallup, 29 percent of Americans support legal abortion under any circumstances, and another 12 percent support it under most circumstances—not exactly overwhelming numbers in the prochoice camp.[76] When you break abortion rights down into the reasons a woman might need an abortion, a telling trend emerges: three-quarters of respondents support abortion when the woman was impregnated by rape, and 82 percent if the pregnant woman's physical health was at risk. But far fewer—just over a third—agree that abortion should be permissible when a woman can't afford to raise a child. In other words, support or opposition to abortion rights is less about fetal life than a woman's reasons for having an abortion—whether that reason stems from having consensual sex in the first place, in which case she deserves to be punished for her indulgence, or whether the pregnancy isn't technically her "fault" because of rape.

The argument that abortion is a "rejection of personal responsibility,"[77] which is how many prolife groups frame it, only works if you think sex for pleasure and pleasure alone is by definition irresponsible. The argument *does* work because the idea that sex is wrong if it's for pleasure and pleasure alone is baked into our politics.

We see this in how little we support pleasurable sex and how negatively Americans react to supporting the right of women to have sex without babies—even as most of the sex Americans have isn't intended to make babies. Women who can afford the luxury of sex for pleasure— who can pay for their own birth control pills and to terminate their pregnancies, who can bring a pregnancy to term and parent their child while still having the time and space, and often the domestic labor enabling it, to focus on their romantic relationship—are largely seen as entitled to it.

Women who cannot afford the luxury of paying for all of the things that allow unfettered sexual activity and the pleasure that goes with it— low-income women—see their options restricted from all sides and face intense and negative social scrutiny for pleasure seeking. Under US law, federal funds can never pay for abortion, and so women who rely on federal programs like Medicaid for their health care don't typically see the procedure covered. In 2015, congressional Republicans tried to pull the plug on Title X, the federal program that funds contraceptive services for low-income women across the United States. Yes, that's right: the antiabortion party tried to pull all funding to the very program that provides birth control to poor women and reduces the abortion rate.

What's missing in American politics today is a left-of-center moral argument for sexual pleasure. Sex for pleasure and pleasure alone may be the way most Americans actually have sex, and it may be enabled by the policies embraced by progressives and feminists, but it is not yet reflected even in mainstream liberal discourse. Instead, the Right dominates the conversation on sexual morality, their values sounding more or less like Tea Party activist Jerome Corsi's, who at a political event in 2013 told audiences in Oregon, "Sex is not about fun. If you want to have fun, read a book, go to a movie."[78]

The vast majority of Americans will have sex in their lifetimes, most of them outside of marriage, most of them with more than one partner, many of them with people of the same sex. Most of them will report that sex makes them happy. Among the heterosexual people having sex, the vast majority will use some form of birth control to prevent having a child, placing sex firmly in the realm of recreation and only a relatively small number of times in the territory of purposeful reproduction. Sex might be the most popular recreational activity in the United States.

Politically, though, we treat sex like it's a vice instead of a normal part of human behavior—a sinful defect but also a consumer product. The bulk of that dysfunction falls on women, who are tasked with being the safeguards of appropriate and moral sexual activity but whose nearly naked bodies also serve as stand-ins for sex itself, to the point where we all understand the clichéd observation "sex sells" really means "women's bodies sell things." It's women whose decisions about sex and reproduction face state interference and moral hand-wringing. It's women who are legally punished for sexual and reproductive choices that deviate from some often-shifting and unreasonably high bar for what a "good" woman does. It's women against whom sex is used as a weapon, and whose pleasure is left almost entirely out of the way we understand, teach, and talk about sex.

It's easy to write sex off as a vice or an act of selfish hedonism or a loss of control. It can be all of those things. It can also, at its best, be transformative and life affirming and crucial to one's health and happiness.

In feminist writer Jessica Valenti's memoir *Sex Object,* she asked the provocative question, "Who would I be if I didn't live in a world that hated women?" There's a reason the word "sex" is in the book's title: sex is the locus at which women are so often made to feel bad, the thing we are both shamed for and made to embody.

And so it's worth asking too, *What would the world be if sex was just good?* The answer: The world would be a sweeter place. We would expect our political leaders to help create the conditions for more fulfilling sex lives and voluntary reproduction. And the entire experience of womanhood—the definition of womanhood—would be unrecognizable.

4

Life Among the Savages:
Finding Pleasure in Parenting

Female possibility has been literally massacred on the
site of motherhood.

—Adrienne Rich

O N A LATE July weekend in Bedford-Stuyvesant, Brooklyn, two
dozen thirtysomethings eat jerk chicken in the backyard and sip
on cold white wine inside a roomy brownstone, the women in high-
waisted cutoffs and crop tops, the men in thin white T-shirts and dark
sunglasses. And then there's Aiden: an animated four-year-old, zooming
between people's legs, knocking himself over, and popping back up to
race around some more before anyone can ask whether he's okay.

Amy Lucas, Aiden's mom, is in the kitchen, one eye on her conversation with girlfriends, the other steadily tracking her son. These summer
weekends, when Aiden isn't in school or at one of his many activities
and she's not at work, are her favorite days. "My life is very structured,
outside of weekends," Amy tells me later in a phone conversation. "By
Sunday it's a free-for-all. So that's good."

These unstructured days also offer a chance for her to reflect on her
relationship with her son. "I look back at old pictures and old videos
and see how far he's come," Amy said. "Wanting to read, the curiosity,
the questions, I love it. That has to be the most rewarding part of this
whole deal. You're raising a human being. This person is going to go off

and live his own life, and everything he's experiencing now is going to be the framework that shapes who he becomes as an adult. Just to be a part of that is amazing."

No experience, relationship, or condition has been as definitional to womanhood as motherhood. This has been true for all of human history; across cultures and borders, the locus of women's oppression, and of our status, comes from our capacity to reproduce. And throughout history, few social changes have been met with as much backlash as efforts to give women full control over reproduction.

In art, literature, religion, and politics, motherhood has been long filtered, imagined, and understood through the eyes of men—all of whom have mothers and many of whom credit themselves with turning their female partners into mothers. The idealized mother is unendingly generous, quietly sacrificial, asexual; she exists in opposition to the mere woman, who retains the ability to be selfish, independent, sexual (or at least sexually tempting). Pain in birthing children was the first biblical punishment, physical agony the price women must forever pay for curiosity and knowledge seeking. The path to motherhood is punitive. But motherhood itself is redemptive.

As an American woman in my early thirties with a professional degree, the possibility of motherhood has only recently tiptoed into my consciousness. Like most women in my cohort, I never even considered the possibility of having children before I was out of school, gainfully employed, and probably married. Now, the question of whether or when I'll have kids isn't an abstraction but a time-limited choice. It's also one I would rather avoid, because I don't feel a biological pull toward parenthood, nor is there some hole in my life begging to be filled by a child. My fascination with motherhood—and its relationship to pleasure—began as an outgrowth of my own ambivalence toward it. My own parents tell me having a child brings indescribable, life-changing happiness. But I've also watched as the virtually unending needs of children and our culture's equally onerous demands on mothers have thwarted the potential of so many women, undermining the kind of attention to self that has been historically required to make great art or explore challenging intellectual pursuits.

I am content with my life the way it is—and averse to interrupting it with children. Most parents, I presume, are having kids for the same reason I am not: because they think it will make them happy. But even in a world profoundly shifted by feminist gains, it remains a challenge for a woman to become a mother and remain wholly herself.

It is also clear that there is no singular experience of motherhood. It is only in our very new post-second-wave-feminist America that mothers' own stories of motherhood have found a wider audience and that the intimate experiences of mothers have become part of our mainstream discourse. So much of women's experience was lost to history as mothers were cloistered into the domestic, with middle- and upper-class white women largely in their own homes, and working-class women, immigrant women, and women of color tending to their own domestic spheres as well as laboring in the homes of others.

And although we silenced mothers themselves, we also converted a subclass of them into venerated idols. The white middle- and upper-class women who were "angels in the house" saw that role magnified by the post–World War II economy, the home becoming the place where a mother would find the most fulfillment—raising children, keeping house, meeting her husband's sexual needs. African American women, who were usually considerably poorer, more likely to work outside their own homes, and to face daily racism and discrimination, weren't appreciated for their maternal capabilities—at least not when it came to raising their own children—and less able to enjoy the satisfaction that came from postwar prosperity. "While they have seldom been 'just housewives' they have always done their housework," Angela Davis wrote of African American women. "They have thus carried the double burden of wage labour and housework," often forced to neglect their own homes and children to serve another family.[1] Happiness in the eudemonic, Aristotelian sense—the pursuit of excellence and knowledge, the hunger for an interesting and challenging life, the politicized happiness Jefferson was referring to in the Declaration of Independence—wasn't on the table for women, and certainly wasn't supposed to be an aspiration for mothers, no matter their race or class. Mothers were supposed to find happiness in their nearly limitless sacrifice for others.

Even so, women have spent much of history at least attempting to pursue their own interests and take control of childbearing; once they had the tools to effectively do both, the role of women and mothers in American society radically shifted. Feminist texts on motherhood, gains in reproductive freedoms, and the feminist movement's insistence that isolating mothers and their children in suburban nuclear families

was psychologically devastating for women has shifted both the experience of motherhood and the social understanding of it. Female writers,
artists, filmmakers, and other culture shapers increasingly give voice
to what motherhood feels like for actual mothers. Most mothers now
work, bridging the man-made divide between the public and the private. Motherhood is more optional than it has ever been, and more and
more women are defining themselves outside of, or in addition to, their
parental status, or forgoing children entirely.

Most women do still have children. Many women still care for children full time and without pay. And still, a narrow motherhood ideal
persists, centered in sacrifice and rewarded with head-patting condescension in lieu of real support. According to one stay-at-home mom
website, being a stay-at-home mom isn't just a job; it's the hardest job
there ever was. "Granted it's not your cushy 40 hour a work week job,"
the site said. "Nope, ours is the 24/7/365 kind."[2] Another survey suggested that a stay-at-home mother is also a "Day Care Center Teacher,
CEO, Psychologist, Cook, Housekeeper, Laundry Machine Operator,
Computer Operator, Facilities Manager, Janitor and Van Driver."

These decrees aren't all that different from one 1950s Bell Telephone
ad, featuring one woman in five different outfits. "This Is Your Wife,"
the ad said. "She's the family chef. And the nurse. And the chauffeur
and maid. And when she's all dolled up for an evening out—doesn't she
look just wonderful! How does she do it?"[3]

It's easy to brush off this sort of bluster as a sanctimonious effort
to bring some minor affirmation to women who, in raising children,
are doing something that the overwhelming majority of women have
managed to do through all of human history without laying claim to
employment in fifteen different sectors. By this same calculation, as a
freelance writer who lives with her cat and boyfriend, I am also a veter-
inarian, travel agent, maid, psychologist, CEO, cook, laundry machine
operator, computer operator, nurse, and accountant. Except I am none
of those things, only a woman who cleans her own house, tends to her
relationship, and manages her finances.

And yet as much as I roll my eyes at the "It's the hardest job in the
world" pronouncements, they speak to a very real lack of respect for
mothers, and a very real sense of dissatisfaction that brings. Mothers,
whether they work outside the home or not, know motherhood matters, and they want that recognized. And yet there is next to no real

investment in mothers, no political groundswell of support for this allegedly crucial occupation. In a country where the overwhelming majority of the most highly paid, prestigious, important jobs are occupied by men, only a tiny number of fathers are full-time caregivers for their children. If being a full-time parent is more valuable than being a CEO or a neurosurgeon, it seems odd that more men don't do it.

The American economy, in both its capitalism and its focus on men's lives and experiences, keeps mothers' labor largely invisible and mothers' experiences marginal. At the same time, the expectations for modern mothers are so high that it can be difficult to adequately meet them and still retain an identity outside of, or in addition to, one's status as a mother. Which is perhaps why women who are the most privileged—who are likely to have other socially respected sources of identity outside of maternity and for whom the bar for perfection is extraordinarily high—are more likely than their middle-class peers to commit fully to one path or the other: either dedicate themselves to full-time motherhood or forgo it entirely.

Although nearly every mother I have talked to said children bring extraordinary pleasure and unimaginable pain, in America, the pain is more acute: the happiness gap between parents and people who don't have kids is wider in the United States than just about anywhere else.[4] Motherhood today is still definitional to female identity, still paid in lip service, still unrecognized for its power. And although women are still told motherhood will bring happiness, the conditions under which women mother remain set up to bring the opposite.

Amy is a single mom, living in her Bed-Stuy brownstone with Aiden and working full time as a consultant. She has a good relationship with Aiden's dad, although their romantic one didn't work out; he typically takes Aiden every other weekend. Much of the time, though, Amy is on her own.

"It can be hard," she said. "Sometimes it's like, I don't want to read you a story today, I don't want to play with the Legos today. But if there's no one else to do it, you have to do it. I'm sure when two parents are there it's like, 'Okay, Mommy doesn't want to do it, go ask Daddy,' and it gets done." Aiden has a great example of both a mother and a father, but it would be nice, she said, to show him a more traditional family unit, with a mom and dad under one roof. And so Amy is trying to make time to date, which means shelling out for a babysitter if one of her relatives or Aiden's dad can't help out, in between working full time, managing her two properties, preparing to take the real estate exam, and planning a move out of the city. But when it comes to a partner, she said, "I'm not going to bring in just anybody."

Sometimes Amy's mother, Lauretta, a petite immigrant from Sierra Leone who raised Amy and her two sisters in New York City, comes over and helps out; so does Amy's dad, and an uncle to whom Amy rents the downstairs apartment. Aiden's aunties Diane and Adrienne also see him often, along with a cadre of their friends. Add that to piano lessons, school, and soccer practice, and Aiden, apple cheeked and bright eyed like his mother, is rarely alone.

Which doesn't mean it's been easy. When Amy became pregnant at thirty-four, the timing was imperfect: she was in the middle of the long process of buying a house, plus juggling work and a relationship. "But at the same time, it was like, eh, I'm thirty-four years old, when is going to be the perfect time?" Amy said. "There wasn't really a doubt in my mind; I never thought oh should I or shouldn't I. It was definitely a happy surprise."

"White people don't force black people to have babies out of wedlock," Fox News Channel personality Bill O'Reilly sputtered on his show in 2013, in a segment about the murder of African American teenager Trayvon Martin. "That's a personal decision. A decision that has devastated millions of children and led to disaster, both socially and economically."[5]

Single motherhood in the United States is the new norm, with 27 percent of US children living in a single-parent family[6] and some researchers predicting that half of all children will live with a single mother at some point before their eighteenth birthdays.[7] But contrary to the narrative pushed by conservatives like O'Reilly, the American single mother is more likely to be an adult white woman than the stereotypical African American teenager, and about half of single mothers live with their child's father when they give birth.[8] Women across demographic groups are having children later than ever and having them alone more often than ever, though African American women are about twice as likely as white women to have a child without being married.[9]

This demographic shift toward single parenthood has been met with a lot of hand-wringing from conservatives and liberals alike. To an extent, there's a good reason for that: it's true that, everywhere in the world, single mothers fare worse financially than married mothers. This is in large part simple math: two adults in a home means more time, and two incomes means more financial resources. But it's especially true in the United States, where the difference in poverty rates between single mothers and their married counterparts is wider than in most economically comparable nations.[10] Single mothers like Amy, who own their homes and make enough money to send their children to private school, are a minority of single moms. Sixty-three percent of American families headed by a single mother live in poverty.[11]

That 63 percent is actually similar to the poverty rates of single mothers in other wealthy nations when calculating by household income only. There are some demographic differences underlying these statistics: even though American single mothers are more likely to be employed than single mothers in other countries, they are also much more likely to work in low-wage jobs. And American single mothers are less likely to live with a romantic partner (for example, 38 percent of "single" mothers in Sweden share a home with their boyfriend or girlfriend). But what fundamentally differentiates the United States from other countries when it comes to the experience of single motherhood is that American women don't have access to the robust social safety net most other advanced nations provide. Even when you take into account the impact of social welfare programs like food stamps and financial aid to needy families, just over half of American single mothers remain in poverty. This isn't the case in our economic peer countries, where more generous cash assistance, better unemployment insurance, and government child allowances mean single motherhood isn't a direct ticket to the poorhouse: in those nations, only a quarter of single mothers are poor.

In other words, we have made a choice in the United States to allow single mothers and their children to languish in poverty. Politically, we have decided not only that married motherhood is better, but that we will create economically disastrous conditions for women who have children outside of marriage—or, given that many single mothers were at one time married, we have chosen to craft disastrous conditions for mothers who have the bad luck to be widowed, separated, or divorced.[12]

Many of the ills commentators attribute to single motherhood—instability, lack of time to spend reading to a child or helping with homework, exposure to violence and crime—are less about a mother's marital status than her economic circumstances. But American conservatives—and a number of liberals—pin the blame on a woman's marital status, and the message they send is clear: single mothers are by definition lacking. And by extension: mothers are not enough.

This is especially telling when you consider that the loudest critics of single motherhood are often proponents specifically of *traditional* marriage, wherein a wife and mother is the primary caretaker for the children and is financially dependent on a working husband, who spends considerably less time with the kids. In that formulation, the father is a source of financial security and authority but not necessarily an integral part of his children's lives emotionally or developmentally. The key question, it seems, is whether it's better for children to rely on the financial contributions of their father and the emotional ones of their mothers, or whether the state should endeavor to provide a baseline level of support for all children, regardless of their parental configuration, and support families whether the financial and emotional sustenance comes from one parent or two. The US government could decide, as the governments of many countries have, that whether a child is born to married parents shouldn't dictate whether that child lives in poverty.

The US government could also decide that single mothers—and the majority of single parents are indeed single mothers—deserve not only sustenance but happiness, that parenting shouldn't be an exercise in getting by but an experience made easier and a relationship allowed to be primarily joyful. We have a pretty good idea of what fosters maternal happiness: time to spend with children and recover from childbirth, financial stability, good health. For most single mothers, and many married ones, none of that is automatically on offer.

"Joyful" is not the way we think about single motherhood—or motherhood at all, but single mothers come in for a special kind of dourness. Multiple studies show that single mothers are less happy than married mothers, even accounting for factors like income and education. Single American women, many of them mothers, are nearly twice as poor as single American men. Our country allows this because we judge single mothers harshly: compared to people in our economic peer countries, Americans are the most disapproving of nontraditional families.[13] According to a 2014 Pew survey, some 60 percent of Americans, including 58 percent of millennials, agreed that the trend toward single parenting is "a bad thing for America"—more millennials disapprove of single mothers than have shared a selfie.[14]

But that doesn't mean motherhood itself is bad for single women. According to a 2007 survey by Pew, married and never-married parents alike say their children are crucial to their life satisfaction, and almost every parent who was asked to rate the importance of their children to their personal happiness and fulfillment gave them a 10 on a 0–10 scale. "The difference is that the overwhelming majority of married parents also give the same rating of '10' to their relationship with their spouse," the Pew survey said, "whereas never-married parents rate no other aspect of their lives as being nearly as important as their children."[15]

Culturally, we carve out a little more space for maternal joy among single mothers we collectively decide are deserving: the high-earning professional women with lots of resources, usually in their late thirties or early forties. We seem to increasingly agree that single motherhood is more acceptable if a woman has paid her dues and just couldn't find the right man but can afford the feminist dream. Stigma remains, to be sure, and there's plenty of judgment to go around. But the white-collar single mom is at least a little more acceptable than she's ever been.

"I am a single mom, but I don't think I'm your stereotypical single mom," Amy said. "My child doesn't want for anything. People can judge if they want, but I've never had anyone come directly at me or give me a weird look, or if they did I didn't notice it. If anything, because of the stigma, people do go out of their way to commend me. I do notice people are like, 'Oh you're doing a great job,' and I'm absolutely positive that's because of the single mother stigma."

Although financially stable black single mothers like Amy may experience a kind of "you're doing great!" condescension, the broke, black single mom is more often the target of widespread derision. She's the martyr or the welfare queen, either sacrificing it all and working herself to the bone or living large off the government dime. In public policy discourse, her children are mistakes to be avoided, not sources of delight and nourishment for her soul. She is not cast in the soft focus of newly married couples cradling their infants. There is no cliché that for her, motherhood is the most important job in the world, and certainly no expectation that she will fulfill her maternal duty by staying home full time. For black mothers today, single or not and especially if they're poor, the social expectation is the same as it's been since the days of slavery: work.

The first time I talked to Janet was for a story on minimum-wage workers that I was writing for *Cosmopolitan*. I talk to a lot of women from all over the country in the course of my work, but my conversation with her stood out, and when I began work on this book, she was the first person I reached out to. It was largely because of what Janet had told me about Christmas.

Christmas is hard, she said in that initial conversation. There usually isn't enough money for toys, so Janet borrows from friends to buy the basics—clothes, shoes. She gets a few gifts from her local Toys for Tots charity. She wants her kids to have something from Santa to unwrap, but that's not the most important part of the holiday in her house. "Every year at Christmas, we go through their clothes and toys, and we drop some things off at the Salvation Army," Janet told me. "I tell my kids each and every night, 'Be thankful for what we have, because there is someone else out there in a worse situation.'"

Janet may have been the type of single mother Bill O'Reilly was thinking of when he made his hateful comments. But scratch the surface and the stereotypical single mother isn't such a stereotype.

When I met with Janet at her home in North Carolina more than a year after we first spoke, she told me that she had planned on waiting until her thirties to have children, but two different forms of birth control, the implant and the shot, failed, resulting in three pregnancies. This is not unusual. Women with college degrees tend to be better able to afford not only birth control but the annual doctor's visits required to get it, they're more able to take time off during the day every month to get their pills refilled, and their lives tend to be stable enough that their addresses, local pharmacies, and health-care benefits don't change very often. For poorer women, none of that is an assumption, and even finding bus fare and getting time off work during pharmacy hours can be a challenge. Poorer women are also more likely to have a higher body-mass index, and researchers increasingly suspect that traditional hormonal birth control methods don't work as well for heavier women.[16]

As a result of all these factors, low-income women are far less likely to use birth control at all and less likely to use it effectively and consistently when they are able to access it.[17] More affluent and educated women are also more likely to use abortion as a backup when their birth control fails. That's not because of some class-based moral difference over abortion; it's largely because US government policies intentionally make abortion unaffordable and inaccessible to low-income women. Under US law, federal Medicaid dollars—the way most poor women get their health care—cannot pay for abortion services, leaving the most vulnerable to pay out of pocket for procedures that start at $500 and can run into the thousands. Wealthier women may have private insurance to cover the cost or have an easier time coming up with the money they need; choosing abortion lets them delay childbearing until they're emotionally and financially ready, putting them on steadier footing for the rest of their lives.

Although poor women and wealthier women have about the same amount of sex, poor women are five times as likely to have an unplanned birth. Still, all the contraception and abortion access feminists could want would be unlikely to make poor women's reproductive patterns look exactly like rich women's—and, indeed, even more well-heeled women are having children outside of marriage far more often than they used to. As much as being a single mother is difficult and overwhelming, it's the circumstances, Janet said, and not the kids, that are the problem. Researchers have shown time and again that for young women growing up in poverty, the incentives for delaying pregnancy are different than they are for middle-class women, for whom an early pregnancy can mean derailment from college and a stable, middle-class life. For a woman without a college education working a low-wage job without much promise of breaking into the middle class, having a child in her twenties—and most low-income mothers are having children in their twenties, not as teenagers—is in many ways a rational choice: she's at the prime of her health, she's not earning enough to take a big financial hit, and her own mother is still young enough to help with child care.[18]

Perhaps more importantly, children often give women of all income levels a sense of purpose. They also serve as markers of adulthood. If there's no college graduation, no down payment on a house, and maybe no wedding to serve as a ritual induction into a grown-up life, the status of mother works just as well. Working-class women value marriage just as much as their wealthier counterparts but are more inclined to have children while they're looking for the right person to marry, while richer women tend to wait longer and marry before they reproduce.[19] This makes a lot of sense. Unlike wealthier women, who also regularly interact with and date educated and financially stable men, lower-income women are more likely to become romantically involved with men they don't view as ideal husbands—men who are less likely to be financially stable and more likely to have been incarcerated, something that further (and often unfairly) limits their job prospects. Women may calculate, rightly, that marriage will mean another mouth to feed without a counterweighing benefit. And there is the simple matter of finding the person with whom you want to end up—for women rich and poor, that person may not come along until you're in your thirties or beyond, but there are still plenty of people you may like, love, and want to have sex with. The push for poor women to marry, and the suggestion that childbearing should always come after marriage, assumes who you marry doesn't matter much and turns the whole concept of a lifelong love into a luxury item.

Motherhood also gives many women a new sense of resolve, a feeling that is especially valuable for those who felt aimless before their kids or who may have been teetering on the edge of a destructive lifestyle. That, Janet said, is her story. "Before I had my kids, I was hanging in the streets smoking marijuana, having parties, always drinking and stuff," Janet said. "And when I had my babies, my life really changed. I really made a 180 in my life. This is no longer the hangout house. No more parties. My kids, they really changed me."

They also gave her more of a connection to her community. For many women, the experience of having children makes them more inwardly focused. There are simply fewer hours of the day to spend with friends or to volunteer; and, indeed, those without children spend more time volunteering their services to benefit their communities as a whole,[20] while parents are more likely to put their efforts toward their own child's success by spending their free time at the kid's school. Friendships shift toward other parents with similarly aged children. But, for Janet, kids meant more connection and the chance to demonstrate what being a good neighbor means. There's an elderly man nearby who gets only twelve dollars a month in food stamps, and so "when I go grocery

shopping, I tell him come ride with me and I'm going to get you a couple things," Janet said. Some other people in the community have also
given her referrals to a local food pantry so she could put food on the
table when things were tight, and she tries to pay that forward. "I'm old
school," Janet said. "I believe it takes a community to raise kids, so if I'm
able to help regardless of what I'm going through, we're going to tough it
out together. If I'm riding on empty, if I'm going to the food pantry and
you need to come, you can ride with me. We run out of gas, we are going
to walk together to make sure the kids are good."

Talking to Janet as her kids sit in the kitchen and do their homework, it's obvious she loves them; what's less obvious is that she has the
time to fully enjoy being with them without stress or worry. The stakes
for her, and for them, are high, and there's no room for error. So Janet
is strict: no playing outside during the week, no television, schoolwork
always comes before play. Although more mouths to feed means less to
go around, it's Janet's kids who have kept her alive through depression
and given her a greater sense of purpose and determination. "They are
my motivators, so I can't stop," she said. "There are days I really want
to give up but then I think about, if I end my life or if I just quit, who's
going to take care of them? Because nobody's going to raise them like
I do."

When Corinne Moss-Racusin and her husband Ranjit decided to have a
baby, they approached it the same way they had approached the rest of
their lives: "We calculated it to the moment," Corinne said. The couple
lives in upstate New York, both of them pursuing demanding careers,
Corinne in academia and Ranjit as a licensed clinical psychologist; they
determined that having a baby in December of Corinne's second year
on tenure track would be ideal, giving them the longest maternity leave
(winter break, then spring semester, then summer) while not interrupting her career trajectory. They mapped out the fertility timeline and
started on the first day. "We first started trying assuming it'll happen,
because the idea is it's just natural," Corinne said. But months went
by without a pregnancy. She read Internet forums and downloaded
pregnancy apps. Still nothing. "It was tough to do the two-week wait—
overinterpreting every little twinge or not-twinge, only to get my period.
It was every month, this reminder of something that felt like we had

failed. And neither of us were used to that feeling. I felt like effort is supposed to equal outcome, there is supposed to be a linear relationship between my trying and succeeding, and it just wasn't happening. It brought up all these feelings of what is wrong with me? This is supposed to be my natural path and gift to the world. It really hurt. And on Facebook every time I logged in I saw friends posting, *here's my ultrasound picture!* It was dark, and we were sad."

For all the fetishizing of the perfect mother, there's a remarkable quiet when it comes to the complexity of actually having a baby. The average American woman wants two children, and the average American woman has 2.4—which means women are often having more children than they plan for.[21] It also means three-quarters of an average woman's reproductive life is spent trying not to get pregnant, while she spends a mere three years trying to become pregnant, pregnant, or postpartum.[22]

The "average woman," of course, looks different across social subgroups. For women with lower levels of educational attainment, family size is larger. Among mothers who didn't graduate from high school, a quarter have four or more children; fewer than one in ten women with graduate degrees do. The differences are less significant by race, although still notable: about a quarter of black, white, and Asian women have just one child, but one in five Hispanic mothers, and nearly the same number of black mothers, has four or more children. Only about one in ten white and Asian women is the mother of four or more kids. White women and women with graduate degrees are also the most likely to not have children at all.[23]

What these statistics obscure is that although the birds and the bees seem straightforward enough—have sex, get pregnant, have a baby, be happy—that's not how it works.

Although most women are fertile into their forties—contrary to much of the fear-mongering about our eggs wasting away—the vast majority of individual events of sexual intercourse don't result in a sperm fertilizing an egg. Even when fertilization does happen, most fertilized eggs never implant in a woman's uterus. Among the minority of embryos that do implant, many come loose before a woman even takes a positive pregnancy test; many others are lost in miscarriage, sometimes very late. Other pregnancies go tragically wrong because of fetal defects, and there's no healthy, happy baby at the end. Still others are terminated, usually for the simple reason that a woman cannot have a baby at that moment—she doesn't have enough money, she's in school, she's with the wrong partner, her whole life is ahead of her, this just isn't what she wants.

Reproduction is a messy, imperfect, naturally sloppy process; reproductive choice adds a whole new layer of complication. All in all, the chances of a fertilized egg developing into a baby are remarkably slim, and any given pregnancy's chance of ending in birth is far from a guarantee. Even when a baby is the end result, happiness eludes many women—and many suffer the deep shame of not feeling as happy as they think they should. This is a reality many women know intimately. But because it's not something many of us talk about, the reality of reproduction remains a source of suffering and isolation for a great many women.

After six months of trying to get pregnant, Corinne and Ranjit got a positive pregnancy test. "We were over the moon and terrified, and it just felt like finally everything is happening the way it should," Corinne said. "And then at eight weeks, I had a miscarriage."

"I would say in retrospect, one of the toughest things was the expectation of silence," Corinne said. "It's messy, it doesn't fit the cultural narrative about how joyful and effortless motherhood and parenthood is going to be." In the middle of miscarrying, she had to teach a class about gender and motherhood; back in her office after teaching, she was staring blankly at the wall when a colleague came in to discuss some administrative minutiae. "I remember thinking, if it was any other kind of loss, I could say to my colleague, 'I'm grieving, I'm suffering, I can't come to work for a few days.' And my colleagues are great people, they would have put together a card and sent e-mails of support. But this just felt like, to tell anyone what was happening would be an imposition on them, it would be inappropriate, it would be forcing the messy reality of my body and this process on someone who wouldn't want to hear it or wouldn't be comfortable hearing it." And so she felt very, very alone.

She was also in a lot of physical pain. When the miscarriage began, Corinne and her husband went to their obstetrician, and Corinne was offered three choices: she could have a procedure to remove the fetus, she could take medication to speed its passing, or she could let it pass naturally. These are not necessarily the choices on offer to every woman. Reproduction, fraught as it is with moral, religious, and ethical judgment, is treated differently at some religious hospitals than it is at secular ones. In Corinne's case, her fetus's heartbeat had stopped, and so the options would likely have been the same at any medical facility.

But a woman miscarrying a clearly doomed pregnancy where the fetal heart is still beating may see her options immediately curtailed if she goes to a Catholic hospital, where doctors routinely refuse to help a woman manage the miscarriage by conducting a procedure to help remove the fetus. Instead, they basically make her go through birth—even if it puts the pregnant woman at greater risk of infection. So too are Catholic hospitals notoriously backward in handling ectopic pregnancies, where a fertilized egg implants outside of the uterus, usually in the fallopian tube. Some Catholic facilities stick to the standard medical protocol, which is an injection into the egg that essentially dissolves it, preserving the woman's life and her fertility; others refuse to do that, and instead remove the whole tube, compromising a woman's ability to have future pregnancies and putting her at greater risk.

Having been given a set of medically sound options, Corinne decided to let the miscarriage pass naturally. "The bleeding intensified over the next couple days," she said. "Saturday morning I woke up to a pain I had never experienced. It was a version of labor; I was passing someone. And that lasted for a day or so, and it was horrible. Labor you get through because it's pain in the service of something. This was pain that I did not want, because it's such a loss."

Afterward, she wasn't sure who to talk to or how to address such a significant but culturally hidden tragedy. "It was so hard to be hurting that way in my heart and my body and not have space to have a conversation about it," Corinne said. "I stub my toe, I post about it on Facebook. But here my Facebook was silent. I had nothing to say."

She threw herself into exercise and her work, eventually injuring her shoulder so badly she had to get surgery. Corinne spent long nights sleeping in a recliner because she couldn't lie flat, knowing intellectually she would make it out the other side but not seeing how. "I just wanted to hold my baby in my arms," she said. "I don't know any more intellectualized way to put it. It was just this yearning. I'm sure it was biological in part, I'm sure it was my hormones, but it was like my body was crying out for this in a way I didn't think was possible. I thought it was a trope. But I experienced it."

After the miscarriage, they stopped trying for a while, giving Corinne's body and both of their spirits time to heal. Two and a half weeks after they went on what only academics would term a "vacation"—Corinne went to a conference and Ranjit came to meet her—Corinne woke up at 4 a.m. and, feeling funny, decided to take one of the many pregnancy tests she had stocked in her bathroom. "I was staring at this blank spot in the test," Corinne said. "One line comes really quick, the test line, and I had seen that happen a million times. And suddenly there's this other beautiful line. The shock of everything, I started laughing hysterically. It was the greatest feeling. I ran into the other room and woke Ranjit up and said, 'I'm pregnant!' And he said, 'I knew it!' And that was our daughter."

There was another miscarriage scare, but the pregnancy lasted. "She was the most beautiful thing I have ever seen, from the first time I saw her tiny beautiful wavy line to when I saw her on the ultrasound until this morning, when I sent her off to day care," Corinne said. Her pregnancy was, all things considered, relatively easy. She had some common issues—acid reflux, sciatic pain, nausea—but her earlier pregnancy loss shifted Corinne's perspective, and she felt grateful every time she put her hand on her belly. When it was time to start planning for the birth, Corinne and Ranjit decided they wouldn't have a rigid plan—their trouble getting pregnant and the previous miscarriage solidified for them the futility of planning such a complex event. Referencing the documentary by natural birth advocate Ricki Lake, Corinne said, "In this post–*Business of Being Born* world, birth plans are a big . . . industry is the wrong word, but there's a lot of emphasis on it. I never understood that—it's like, 'What's the theme of your wedding?' Wedding. 'What's your birth plan?' Having a baby. And I don't care how she gets here, as long as she gets here. I just want to hold my baby at the end of this and I'm completely open to how that happens."

The birth was ultimately "empowering," Corinne said—something she hadn't expected. She had told her husband earlier that she didn't want pampering; she wanted coaching, athletic encouragement, and that's what she got. "Everyone talked to me that way, and it was just fucking awesome," Corinne said. "The nurse was like, 'You are born to do this, you are a natural, I can't believe these pushes!' They got the doctor back in, and he said, 'One more push and she's going to be here.' I was exhausted. It was the hardest thing my body has ever done. They had me on oxygen, I barfed at one point. But he said, 'One more push.'" And so Corinne pushed. "I just dug deep into a place of strength that I didn't know existed and I brought her here. I remember the nurse yelling, 'Corinne look down look down!' And her shoulders were out, and she was present."

When they put the pink-grey baby on Corinne's chest, she said, time stopped. "I just kept saying, 'Hi! Hi!' I think what I was trying to say in that moment was you're real. I can touch you in a way I haven't before. In one way you're further away than you've ever been, but in a much more profound way, you're closer than you've ever been. She was crying and I wrapped my arms around her and she stopped and just stared at us. It felt like the most profound meeting."

Although the birth made Corinne feel strong and capable, her life postpartum was less satisfying—in large part because of less-than-adequate parental leave policies. Corinne got time off; Ranjit didn't. For a couple that had always been dedicated to doing things 50-50, and for Corinne as a new mother suddenly left alone with an infant, that abrupt change was overwhelming and devastating. "I've always worked and I am not a homebody, and here's where some of the institutional stuff really messed with our initial experience," Corinne said. "Ranj was working an hour away, crazy hours, so he would leave the house at 6:00 and get home at 10:00. And Alia had colic. That means twelve to sixteen hours alone, clueless about how to take care of an infant who is inconsolable, just screaming. I remember saying to my mother on the phone, 'I am her mother, she is supposed to come into my arms and be soothed,' and she was soothed by nothing. That was really hard and lonely. It was the biggest moment in my life where I could see that a change in policy and how institutions work would affect me for the better so profoundly and so personally. The fact that my husband cannot be here is incredibly detrimental to the health and well-being of our entire family right now."

Breast-feeding was also hard, but Corinne took seriously the maxim that "breast is best." In breast-feeding class, "we learned that there are four hold positions and breast-feeding is an endless joy and they will do the breast crawl from your womb, with the umbilical cord still attached, to your nipple and gloriously and magically suckle until they are two years old—that is the message you get," Corinne said. It's a good counter, she added, to the shameful practices of companies pushing formula, especially to women who can't afford it or who don't have clean water to prepare it. "But the pushback against that, the breast is best, really isolates women for whom it's not that natural. The secret no one wants to talk about is that's most of us. I have one or two stories of people who have that beautiful angel wings surrounding you as your child drinks away, but most people don't have that moment. And then what? Because all you've heard is this is supposed to be lovely."

They tried supplemental nursing, where a tube is attached to your nipple on one end and a medicine dropper on the other, encouraging the baby to eat—doing it every ninety minutes, even through the night. There was no sleeping, just constant rounds of pumping, feeding, cleaning up, and starting all over again. A lactation consultant helped, and Corinne nursed her daughter exclusively for two months, but it was never easy and it never felt good. Oversupply made her breasts ache excruciatingly; thrush, a yeast infection, passed back and forth between the nipple and the baby's mouth, bringing with it stinging nipple pain and stabbing breast pain. Then she got mastitis, an infection of the milk duct that makes you horribly ill. "I had a fever of 103, I couldn't keep ice chips down, I couldn't lift my head off my pillow," Corinne said. "And the kicker is you have to keep nursing, because otherwise it makes it worse. I was vomiting over my child's head while I was nursing. That was the moment Ranj turned to me and said, 'We need to think about our quality of life now. Half the time you are with each other you are both in tears.'"

Corinne's mother and therapist had been telling her it was time to stop, but her husband's statement sealed the deal. "Once I got over feeling like it was my failure, life got so much better. I had my body back, and I don't think I realized how much that mattered to me." Her daily schedule was no longer contingent on nursing. She could hold her baby and not feel the pressure of counting down until the next breast-feeding session.

Eight weeks after birth, when the breast-feeding was at the height of its difficulty, Corinne had also gone back to work. She was still bleeding, her body still healing. She wasn't sleeping, and she was in a lot of pain a lot of days. She worked hard to make sure she performed well as a professor, and her evaluations were good, but "it was bad for our family," she said. "I really accepted that I had some postpartum depression and anxiety at the end of semester. It was almost like if you imagine that you have a wound and somebody is applying pressure to it. When the pressure comes off you might say, 'Oh it feels so good to have the pressure off.' But then you realize how deep the wound is, because it starts gushing."

Corinne went to therapy and began taking medication for postpartum depression and anxiety. She found it helped. She wasn't dejected or unable to bond; she went too far in the other direction, feeling like "I have so much love in my heart for this helpless creature it is going to crush me," Corinne said. "No amount of data in the world would convince me she was okay. I could not stop worrying about her." Part of her postpartum challenges were just her: an analytical overachiever, prone to anxiety. But part of it, Corinne said, were the conditions under which she was expected to parent in those early days, alone and isolated. "I wish I had more time. I deeply wish Ranj had been able to be home with me. We have said from the beginning, if we do this again, we are going to make it work that we are both home for longer. We need twelve weeks, and we need twelve weeks for both of us. It shouldn't be crazy to ask for that."

The experience left Corinne feeling like she'd missed out on something that should have been a source of great happiness. "I think I felt a little bit robbed of the joy of her early days," she said. "I was so scared for her safety, and for my own well-being. They were long days of crying and trying to nurse and it was hard. I don't think I was able to delight in her in the ways that I deserved to."

Today, Alia is nine months old, a smiling, happy baby. As Corinne and I talk, it's summer, so her teaching schedule is less demanding, and she's relishing the time with her husband and child. They're also working out the new division of labor in their relationship. Before Alia, "we defined equality in our relationship in a very literal sense: you took out the trash yesterday, I'll take it out today; you cooked, I will clean up," Corinne said. "We split everything. And that's what we thought of as an egalitarian partnership. With parenting, in the context of a heterosexual relationship where one person is giving birth, the biological reality is you cannot have that be your definition of equal. Equal can't mean the same. If you're relying on sameness, you're fucked." It was Corinne's body going through miscarriage and pregnancy; it was her who was vomiting with morning sickness and in pain breast-feeding. Her husband felt sad and stressed and worried about her, but the fundamental imbalance in what they were contributing to the family came into sharp relief. "That we really had to grapple with: What does it mean to have a true partnership when the easy ways to be equal are not available to us? We really had to hash that out," Corinne said. "I think for him he's had a lot of moments of, 'I thought I knew what it means to be a feminist partner for my wife, and how do I give to her when she's doing so much for us?' Our daughter is here yes because of him, but she's physically here because of me. And he wrestled with that. For us, what it has meant has been to be very talky and explicit about 'What can I do to make you feel supported as you're doing something I can never really repay?'"

That kind of careful dedication to fairness, if not perfect equality, has brought benefits for both of them. Ranjit gets up every morning to feed Alia so Corinne can sleep; those early mornings have become, Corinne said, "some pretty magical times for them." That one-on-one affection also means that Alia reaches for both her parents, not just her mommy, and that Ranjit is just as capable of soothing her and attending to her needs as his wife. "The way we think about having a feminist home or an egalitarian partnership is we aren't going to be doing the same things, but what is the sum of these parts?" Corinne said. "What is the whole we are trying to achieve, and what are the different contributions we can make to that whole? That is not how I thought about it at nineteen—if my partner wasn't doing the same things as me, if he wasn't doing the laundry, I was being taken advantage of. Because there is so much history to the laundry. The cards are stacked against us. But biology is real. And if one person is going to carry the baby, you have to be more nuanced than 'you do X, I do X; you do Y, I do Y.'"

When class starts up again in the fall, Corinne will return to work full time, something to which she looks forward. But she's also enjoying this stage of Alia's life and getting to be with her more often now that she's out of the fragile infant stage and is a little more robust and communicative. She feels a deeper bond with her husband, too. "Looking at my husband now, he's so much more than the dude I met at the bar, more than my boyfriend or fiancé or my husband or my partner or my best friend or my lover," she said. "He is my daughter's dad. It's not that he's that thing before all those other things, but it is knowing she looks at him the same way she looks at me that binds me to him in a way I didn't know was possible to feel with another person."

With a child under one, Corinne's and Ranjit's lives haven't returned totally to normal—they would both choose sleep over sex most days, and both hope that at some point that changes. But while they look forward to that kind of intimacy returning, they're enjoying the new intimacy of doing this project of creating and raising a tiny human together.

"We try to make time for intimacy in all its different forms, but it is not the center of what we are doing," Corinne said. "We are deeply, cumulatively exhausted. If the engine of our relationship was sex and physical intimacy, that engine would be sputtering out. The engine is something different. It's a different kind of connectedness."

And little in her life up to this point, she said, has been so transformative. Falling in love with her husband opened up a line of romantic affection and a deep well of connection that has only grown fuller, her passion for her work has brought a sense of purpose and intellectual satisfaction, and now her daughter has ushered in a new kind of love and sheer delight. These different and sometimes overlapping loves and devotions, Corinne said, have been the greatest gifts of her existence. She just wishes there had been more light shone on the dark parts and some more help getting through them, so she could have known she'd make it out and into the sun.

"For all that darkness, for all the moments that could have been better or clearer, there is a profound joy that I experience every day in knowing that this little person is here," she said. "I think it's presumptuous to say you can't understand it unless you're a parent—there are a ton of things that could bring you that same understanding—but in my life, this is a joy that is unique to her. I share it with my partner, our ability to take such joy in someone else and her experience and her inquisitiveness and her smile and her little sleeping body. It's an intensity of experience that I hadn't gotten to. It's a way of seeing yourself through someone else's eyes, or just experiencing emotion because of another person. It's really humbling and it's really exciting, and at the end of the day, there's a satisfaction that comes along with it that I couldn't have predicted. There are all sorts of challenges I couldn't have predicted either, but there's just this joy that I had also not experienced before, and for which I am so profoundly grateful."

Part of what has made Corinne so grateful for her experience as a parent are the challenges she and her husband overcame—and the fact that having a child was a hard-earned choice. Corinne and I are the same age and went to undergrad at New York University together. Through college and graduate school, we both made the same choice as the overwhelming majority of our female classmates: we took proactive steps not to get pregnant. For most of us, this meant birth control of some kind—pills, patches, rings, injections, IUDs, condoms, sometimes less reliable methods like a partner who pulled out or fertility tracking. And for many of us, this also meant ending pregnancies so that we could have babies when we were ready, if we decided to have babies at all.

If pregnancy is a gift, it can also be a burden, and the choice to bring a child into the world or decide not to is a fundamental right vested in the same bodies that carry that weight. Carrying, bearing, and caring for a child is a great responsibility, and the ability to choose to, or to choose not to, a significant source of power. Feminist writer Lindy West wrote about having an abortion in her book *Shrill,* saying that although it wasn't a huge life-changing experience, "it was my first big grown-up decision—the first time I asserted, unequivocally, 'I know the life that I want and this isn't it': the moment I stopped being a passenger in my own body and grabbed the rudder."

By most estimates, one in three American women will have an abortion in her lifetime. Most of these women are already mothers at the time they end their pregnancies; many of those same women, and most of the rest, will go on to have children afterward. The decision to end a pregnancy is, for some women, a difficult one, made in the absence of better choices; for other women, it's an easier calculus, a throbbing "NO" from the moment they read their positive pregnancy test. Despite claims to the contrary by antiabortion activists, depression after abortion is less common than depression after childbirth. Although many women may look back and wish circumstances could have been different, most never regret their decision.

With the legalization of abortion in 1973 with *Roe v. Wade* also came watershed liberation for American women. Women have been attempting to prevent and end pregnancies for as long as women have been able to get pregnant, but the legal right of women to decide for themselves whether to bring life into the world or not—this was new. And it spawned a deep social, cultural, and political rift that has yet to be mended. Few things, it seems, are as overwhelmingly powerful—and as overwhelmingly terrifying—as letting women choose motherhood for themselves or avoid it at their wish.

Few women in the United States today know this as intimately as Merle Hoffman, a seventy-year-old feminist activist, journalist, psychologist, and abortion clinic owner. Merle spent the early 1970s working

three jobs to put herself through college; one of them was for Dr. Martin
Gold, who ran a health clinic in Queens. After abortion was legalized
in New York two years before the *Roe* decision, Dr. Gold and a medical
partner told Merle they were opening a small clinic for women who
wanted to terminate their pregnancies and asked whether she wanted
to be involved. "I had no idea what they were talking about—I wasn't
following feminism or any of the politics," Merle told me. "When they
explained it to me, it seemed extremely pioneering and romantic, because no one had done it before. So I said sure, I'll get involved. And
after I counseled my first patient, I became wedded to the movement."

She helped open the Flushing Women's Medical Center, which
would become Choices Women's Medical Center, and eventually
opened a second clinic as well. She had an affair with Dr. Gold, and
after nearly a decade, they married. She had never wanted children, and
in the midst of her work as an advocate and health provider, she became
pregnant at thirty-two. "I had all the props that should have allowed me
to have the child without major issues," she said. "But I knew almost
immediately that I would have that abortion."

She did. "I didn't see myself as a mother," Merle said. "This child
had come at a time when I was in the full flush of my being a warrior,
building Choices, helping to lead the movement, debating all the anti-
choice people. I was in my reality, and I was not going to stop or change
or alter anything I was going to do." It's a decision she said she has never
regretted and one that allowed her a life of exploration and passion. But
it's also one she sees as part of the normal continuum of the female
experience—and of motherhood. "I've never been of the thinking or the
political feeling that it's just blood and tissue, it's no big deal—it is a big
deal," she said. "You're making a decision not to let this potential life
come into being."

For herself, and for the thousands of women she met over the course
of her work as an abortion provider, she saw that the choice to end a
pregnancy was a morally complex one, tied up in power and potential,
age-old obligations and the persistent human desire to shape the course
of one's own life. "The things that these women spoke about, that I
spoke about with them," Merle said, included "what their meaning of
life was, how they felt they were defined as being a parent or being a
mother, what it meant to live their lives, the way their lives were saved,
their lives as they projected them, their future as they saw it. Having the

abortion allowed them to, if not fulfill them, at least try to become what they foresaw for themselves. For all of these things, the fulcrum was the decision whether or not to bear this child. I saw it as an extremely powerful decision."

She advocated for her patients, instituting the kind of woman-centered counseling now standard at abortion clinics. She also advocated for the cause, even as her clinic faced protests and physical and financial attacks. She kept it open, sometimes, it felt, by sheer force of will. Her message was a clear one—she once papered St. Patrick's Cathedral in New York City with pamphlets reading, "Women are full moral agents with the right and ability to choose when and whether or not they will be mothers." The opposition was just as clear: women are not only inherently intended to become mothers but, should they become pregnant, obligated to. The ability to decide unilaterally when and whether to use their bodies to bring new life into the world was simply too momentous a right to allow mere women.

The choice to become a mother was not one Merle thought she would ever make. Then, her husband, Dr. Gold, who she had been with for more than thirty years, died. Her mother died. Her stepfather and two dear friends died. "I had lived a long time, and I had many great triumphs, and I had tremendous challenges," Merle said. "And all this loss was with me." She woke up one morning and decided to act on an idea with which she had often flirted and ruled out: she would adopt a child. Half Russian and long enchanted by great Russian writers and composers—Dostoevsky, Tolstoy, Tchaikovsky—Merle zeroed in on Russia as the place from which to seek a child. She would be an older mother, already almost sixty, but she was curious about experiencing a new kind of love in her life and knew that older children and those who had been in orphanages for extended periods of time were often not adopted. So when the adoption agency called her to say they had a three-and-a-half-year-old girl from the Siberian city of Omsk, Merle got on an airplane to meet her daughter, Sasha.

Still, the prospect of being a mother scared her, especially what it meant for life as she knew it. What she's found, she said, is that some of her fears have indeed come to fruition—but it's been okay. "I remember the night before I adopted her, I was in Omsk with my friend who had come with me, and I was having an anxiety attack, a horrible anxiety attack, and I said, 'Oh my god what happens, what if I don't love her, what if she doesn't love me?'" Merle said. "I had this vision of myself locked in a bathroom with a book because I wouldn't be able to read." She looks back on this anecdote and laughs, because in the years she's been Sasha's mother, "that's happened to me," Merle said. "I do go in and lock myself in the bathroom sometimes."

It's also difficult to drop Sasha off at school among twenty- and thirtysomething moms, who assume Merle is a grandmother. Her age also "puts into strong relief my mortality," she said. "If somebody says, 'Well, in five years she'll be going to college,' what goes through my mind is, 'Will I be around in five years?' I'm very aware that I won't be around for the majority of her growing life, even if I live fifteen or twenty years more." But older parenthood also brings with it patience, wisdom, and a fullness of experience. What she likes best is sharing, and adjusting her own assumptions and patterns for her little girl. "I think in teaching you grow yourself, and I've seen this with my daughter," Merle said. "She'll ask, 'Why?' about things, and I start to give this formulaic response I might have given to fifteen other people, but because it's her, I'll stop and I'll rethink it. It allows me to break the kind of static you get into with your answers—the sun rises here, it sets here, is there a God? I deal with all these ethical and philosophical issues on a macro level, but with a child they come up every day on a micro level, and it challenges me so much to be my personal best."

There is an ease, too, in being an adoptive parent as opposed to a biological one: Merle has no genetic expectations for her daughter and doesn't see her as an extension of herself but as a fully separate human being who she gets to nurture into an adult. Merle's own parents placed high expectations on her, and it sometimes felt as if their love was at least partly conditional on her success. With Sasha, "I accept and love her as who she is." She has no expectations that Sasha go to Harvard or play piano or enjoy opera; when Sasha wanted a basketball hoop in the backyard, Merle, not a sports fan, put one up. "I want her to be happy," Merle said. And her definition of happiness asks, "Are you doing the most you can do? Have you had intense experiences? Have you loved passionately?" These are the things she hopes for her daughter.

Merle's own experience of motherhood is indelibly shaped by her ability to choose it—and the ability, decades earlier, to choose not to do it. Our lives are not straight lines, and each choice we make shifts our course; for women who end pregnancies and go on to have other

children, it is not as if, without the abortion, they would have their existing families plus one more. So too is it with Merle. Had she had a baby
at thirty-two, would she have adopted Sasha at nearly sixty? Maybe.
Probably not. Which is partly why being a mother "deepens my commitment to choice," she said. "I made a choice of when I could have a child,
and even though it was at fifty-eight years old, I am the best mother I
could be now. It deepens my understanding of why it is so important
that women maintain the ability to make that choice, that they must be
the chooser, not the state, not the doctors, not the political class."

I asked Merle whether there's anything she would do differently. No,
she said. "I am the result of the choices that I made. And that question
really asks me, how do you feel about the result of who you are? And
the way I feel is very good. Does that mean I'm happy all the time? Not
at all. Am I adding to the good in society? Absolutely. And that's a very
strong criterion. Is the world a bit better because I was in it? I hope so."

Her experience as a mother has brought profound pleasure. But so
too did her decades-earlier choice not to become one—it let her pursue
her political passions, her business, the love of her life. The things that
have made for a happy life—the intellectual pursuits, the excitement,
the intense experiences, the passionate loves for her work, her partner,
and now her daughter—all of these things were the result of choosing,
and of getting to choose, what her family and her work looked like.

"I saw how being a mother was important first and foremost, and the
decision to allow this life to come into being, how powerful that was,"
Merle said about her abortion care work. "And how powerful the decision was to decide not to."

For middle- and upper-class women who decide to have children—
which is most of them, eventually—motherhood isn't just one choice
among many.[24] It's a choice that seems to lock in hundreds of subsequent choices, from how to meticulously plan your birth to whether
to exclusively breast-feed for a year or more, all of them aimed with
hyperfocus on doing everything right and in the service of your child.
The expectations for kids are higher than ever before, but so too are
the requirements for motherhood—and they seem to only magnify as
babies grow into children. Mothers bear more of these burdens than fathers do, and they're expected to make it all look effortless. Consider, as

Adrienne Rich pointed out in her book *Of Woman Born: Motherhood as Experience and Institution,* that "mothering" is a verb, understood as encompassing birthing, nursing, nurturing, loving, caring, and protecting—an ongoing relationship, synonymous with unending care. "Fathering," on the other hand, is momentary—when you father a child, you've done little more than impregnate someone.[25]

As more and more of my friends became pregnant and had children, I watched how the most down-to-earth women and the most tightly wound alike faced the pressures of maternal perfection, of doing "mothering" right. More than one woman I know has been driven to tears in a Brooklyn park by other mothers implying she's failed in some way by not yet signing her child up for the best local preschool—many of these women were still pregnant. Another described the stress of reading other parents' Facebook updates about their children's early accomplishments, and feeling like she was failing because her five-year-old wasn't fluent in French. Others resent being shamed by a child's teacher for not volunteering in the classroom—something fathers, who are assumed to be working, don't face. Many shudder at the mention of Pinterest, a relic of too many hours spent going down a rabbit hole of "easy kids birthday ideas" that are actually hours-long crafts and projects requiring the skill of an artisan or professional baker.

One of the more common examples of this shift toward intensity is attachment parenting, a theory that encompasses everything from childbirth to breast-feeding to sleeping to potty training, and that does offer some real benefits. Some mothers find baby wearing, where your child is attached to your chest by a sling, lets them be more mobile. Others say cosleeping makes it easier to breast-feed through the night. But the requirements for "attaching" are almost entirely centered on theories (many of them weakly supported) of what babies desire, with little regard given to the mother's needs, wants, or life requirements. One celebrity proponent of attachment parenting is the actress Mayim Bialik, of the CBS show *The Big Bang Theory.* Bialik practices "elimination communication," which involves largely forgoing diapers and watching for nonverbal cues that your infant or child has to go to the bathroom.[26] "Since I was the 24/7 at-home caregiver for the formative years, it worked for us," Bialik wrote in a 2011 op-ed (she and her husband divorced a year later). "EC is not impossible if you are not an at-home parent; however, the 'best' results generally speaking come from being in close consistent physical contact and communication with your child." Never mind that most parents, even those who stay home full time, are not staring at their children's faces watching for poop cues at all waking (and, one imagines, sleeping) hours of the day. The lesson, even for women who would never consider EC, is that women should sacrifice their ability to do literally anything else if they so much as vaguely suspect it could have even the tiniest benefit for their child.

Of course mothers and fathers should do whatever they believe is best in raising their children. But it's hard not to see practices like EC and other attachment parenting recommendations—cosleeping, extended breast-feeding—as increasingly onerous demands on mothers that are fundamentally at odds with the idea that women should do anything other than cater to their children 24/7, or that mothers are separate human beings and not physical appendages of their babies.

It seems nearly every woman finds herself pressured, in one way or another, to be the mother who sacrifices the most, who tries the hardest, or who at least keeps up with ever-more-demanding parenting requirements. "Motherhood has been elevated—or perhaps demoted—to the realm of lifestyle, an all-encompassing identity with demands and expectations that eclipse everything else in a woman's life," writer Heather Havrilesky argued in the *New York Times*. "Somehow, as we've learned to treat children as people with desires and rights of their own, we've stopped treating ourselves and one another as such." For middle- and upper-middle-class women in particular, "the current culture demands that every mother be *all in,* all the time."[27]

In response to Havrilesky, one college-educated stay-at-home mom wrote a letter to the editor in defense of the "true beauty" of mothers who "work tirelessly" at motherhood and take it as their identity. "It is *my choice* to stay at home, so why wouldn't I go 'all in,' just as I assume that women who work outside the home go 'all in' at their day job," she wrote. "Why is it viewed as somehow compromising my own identity? Personally, my sense of self is only enhanced as I navigate through the crazy day-to-day mayhem of motherhood. After all, I'm a mom. First and foremost, that's who I am. It is my identity, and I wear the label proudly."[28]

Parenthood has undergone a radical shift since my mother's generation, and families today are more varied than ever before. Record numbers of same-sex couples are married with children; kids are routinely raised and sometimes adopted by grandparents, aunties, or other kin; single mothers are the new normal; first-time mothers in their forties are no longer a rarity. But for many affluent, educated, married couples with children, things look as traditional as ever, with a working husband and stay-at-home wife. Although most stay-at-home mothers are low income, there is a subgroup of the hyper-elite where the breadwinner father / at-home mother persists. Among graduates of Tier I American educational institutions—Ivy League colleges and other prestigious schools, like Stanford and Duke—women with children are much more likely to stay home than mothers who graduated from less elite schools.[29] Compared to their peers at lower-ranked institutions, women with MBAs from these top schools are 16 points less likely to be employed.

To get into and graduate from these top schools requires hard work, diligence, and intelligence, and it's easy to see how the characteristics of elite graduates might translate into the characteristics of intensive mothers. And why not, if your husband is also a graduate of an elite institution and brings in a hefty income and you believe you're doing what's best for your child?

One reason not to stay home with your child is that it doesn't matter: researchers have found that it's quality of time, not quantity, that makes a difference for children.[30] The number of hours parents spend with kids has virtually no impact on how they turn out. What does matter is spending quality time with them—having one-on-one conversations, eating dinner together, reading to them. The demands of intensive motherhood can actually have a negative impact on children if their mothers are anxious, stressed out, exhausted, or guilt ridden. And full-time caregiving doesn't lead to kids who are better off: children of working mothers do better in school and have lower rates of depression and anxiety, adult sons of working moms spend more time on housework and child care, and adult daughters are more successful academically and professionally.[31] There is also the simple fact that working outside the home can add a richness of experience that can be passed onto one's children: more varied dinner table conversations about topics other than what happened inside the house today, and the messages that pursuing one's own interests matters and women don't exist solely to serve the needs of others.

Staying home full time is also not a recipe for parental happiness. Both mothers and fathers spend more time today with their children than they did in decades past, but given that there are only twenty-four hours in a day, that often cuts into time couples spend together—and less time together often means decreased marital happiness. Among reproductive-age Americans, current parents are the least happy; those with kids who have flown the nest or who haven't had kids at all are considerably more pleased with their lives. This is particularly pronounced among women who grew up in a more feminist world and who sought out equal partnerships with men they expected to be involved, active dads. The usual absence of paid paternity leave coupled with the biological reality that women are usually the ones birthing and feeding new babies means that many previously egalitarian heterosexual couples find themselves sliding into more traditional roles with the birth of a new infant: new moms do both more child care and more housework while new fathers, anxious about fulfilling their own role as the family's provider, spend a greater number of hours at the office. This unexpected traditionalization of the relationship is a primary cause of women's declining happiness when they have children.[32] Research on the impact of children on same-sex couples remains insufficient; it will be telling to see whether couples who don't have this built-in gender difference will experience the same destabilization when and if they have kids.

For women who see marriage as a vehicle to the nuclear family they desire—a more traditional view—children, and the traditional roles they often spur, may actually be less disruptive. But for women who marry because they believe they have found a soul mate with whom to share in romantic love and blend their lives while maintaining and nurturing each other's individuality, children can knock everything badly off kilter—and no one tells you it's coming.

Intensive parenting is also intensely inward looking, seeking to improve life for *my* kid. And the work that parents—mostly mothers—do for free in service of that improvement takes the onus off of the government and the general public to provide good services for all children, no matter who their parents are.

Take schools, for example. The offspring of well-to-do parents are already at an educational advantage, with access to better public schools and the money to afford private ones if the public options aren't up to their standards. Public and private schools alike are increasingly reliant on parent volunteers—and "parent" almost always means mother. In wealthy areas with concentrations of highly educated stay-at-home moms, the local schools benefit from thousands of hours of high-quality free labor. That means more hands-on attention for each child. It means fundraising help from women who don't just organize two-dollar-a-cookie bake sales, but used to work in finance or as professional event planners, and come with iPhones full of the numbers of well-heeled friends and neighbors. It means the person helping a fifth-grader with their fractions might have a degree in economics; the parent volunteering to supervise the school newspaper might be a former professional journalist.

Over in Bed-Stuy, Amy feels the residual expectations for her own son. He's only four, but already he's enrolled in piano lessons, swim lessons, and soccer, and the list of activities gets longer as he grows. "I want to make sure he is on the mark or above it," Amy said. "It's so hard—you want to make sure he's prepared for what's to come in the future. Those are the types of things I worry about more than anything else."

Amy isn't your stereotypical "helicopter mom," and Aiden isn't a micromanaged child. But in some ways their family is typical of households with an educated parent. Mothers who finished college spend four and a half more hours per week with their children than mothers who didn't go to college at all—even when these highly educated mothers work outside the home.[33] The intensive motherhood practiced by the upper classes and broadcast out—whether it's Gwyneth Paltrow's *GOOP* newsletter suggestion for a kid's lunch box of nori-wrapped vegetable sushi[34] or Bialik's advice that you not give a puking kid Gatorade because it has high-fructose corn syrup[35]—gets slowly integrated as the new parenting normal, even for those without the resources, time, desire, or ability to meet these ratcheted-up demands. This has costs both to the middle-class mothers who dedicate significant time and resources to keeping up (often at the expense of their own happiness, their marital satisfaction, and their professional success) and to the lower-income and working-class mothers who can't keep up. The raising of the "good mom" bar also means that mothers who don't or can't meet it are "bad," and sometimes deemed criminally neglectful. In 2014, South Carolina mom Debra Harrell let her nine-year-old play at the park alone while she went to work at McDonalds; the daughter had a cellphone, and the park was filled with some forty other children and several adults. Harrell was arrested for "abandoning" her daughter, and the girl was put in foster care.[36] That same year, Ashley Richardson was arrested in Florida and charged with negligent child abuse because she let her four children play in a park while she went to a local food bank.[37] Arizona mother Shanesha Taylor was homeless and seeking work when she landed a much-needed job interview in 2014; unable to afford child care during the forty-five-minute appointment, she left her two children in the car with the windows cracked. She was arrested and charged with two felony counts of child abuse, and Child Protective Services took her children.[38]

It is not a coincidence that most of the mothers deemed neglectful for trying to survive are poor women of color. The good mother is wealthy and she is white, and it is through the lens of what she is able to do that so many other moms are judged—and found lacking, sometimes by the law and sometimes by themselves.

Most parents try to do what they think is best for their children, so of course the ones with the greatest resources dedicate more to their own kids. It is too easy, and too simplistic, to blame the lack of resources offered to poorer kids on the abundance of time and energy that richer mothers can afford to give to their offspring. This remains a systematic problem: the way female labor in all its forms, but especially caregiving, is rendered invisible and left uncompensated; and the way the norms of the upper classes shape policy and standards for everyone, even while the disparity in resources between the richest and the poorest grows.

If you're as ambivalent about babies as I am, this is a pretty good time to be alive, especially if you're in a liberal urban center—look around and you'll find a lot of women just like you. With the ability to reliably postpone pregnancy came the ability to pursue many other opportunities, and today American women are having children later than ever. This is true across educational and income levels, although most of the media attention is dedicated to the highly educated, often high earning women who push childbearing into their thirties and forties. Much of this attention is negative, concerned that women are forgoing their biological duties in favor of selfish enjoyment of life. "The retreat from child rearing is, at some level, a symptom of late-modern exhaustion—a decadence that first arose in the West but now haunts rich societies around the globe," wrote Ross Douthat in the *New York Times.* "It's a spirit that privileges the present over the future, chooses stagnation over innovation, prefers what already exists over what might be. It embraces the comforts and pleasures of modernity, while shrugging off the basic sacrifices that built our civilization in the first place."[39]

Not all concern about older parents comes from such a place of moral judgment (not to mention ignorance about what creativity, innovation, and experience may look like for many women); some of it is a legitimate inquiry into what this entirely new cultural dynamic might bring. Journalist Judith Shulevitz has reported on early research suggesting that children born of older parents—including older fathers—may be more likely to have certain developmental disorders, like autism, or chromosomal abnormalities, such as Down syndrome or Edwards syndrome, of which half of afflicted babies die within a week of birth.[40] In an interview with the *Washington Post,* Shulevitz pointed out that women are not going to start having children earlier unless the United States commits itself to "putting in place much more child-friendly policies and making it possible for women and men to a) put their careers or education on hold to spend time with their babies without being forced out of the work force or suffering a lifelong reduction in earnings and b) put their kids in affordable, reliable child care."[41]

I'm less convinced. For some women, better policies would surely make it easier to have babies earlier. But Shulevitz herself is an example of where that gets knotty: she didn't meet her husband until she was well into her thirties. For women who don't want to go at child-rearing alone, who don't want to get married just to have a baby, and who also have a deep understanding of what they want in a romantic partnership, all the child care and social welfare in the world won't make them have a kid at twenty-six.

It's also not the case that thirty- and fortysomething women's reproductive prospects are as dire as many seem to believe. Good research is surprisingly rare, but the more reliable studies point to the conclusion that even through their fortieth birthday, about 80 percent of women remain fertile.[42]

And there are significant benefits to having children on the later side. For younger mothers, having a child often results in a quick happiness spike that rapidly tanks. For women who have a child after thirty-five, though, that happiness spike is higher, and it doesn't decline nearly as much. With a more established career, the financial stressors are fewer. The hit to workplace earnings may be lower. And although some are concerned that later childbearing means moms who become infirm or die while their children are still young, women who have children later in life tend to live longer than those who have them young—women who have their first child after forty are four times more likely than younger mothers to live to their one hundredth birthday.[43]

In other words, there's no perfect time, and I suspect most women would agree that more options are better than none. Still, not every reproductive option is created equal, and "choice" is only one of many competing values. What do women owe their children? Is there an obligation to have a child earlier if it means there's a small chance the child could be healthier, even if doing so would complicate women's well-being? How much should parents weigh the probability they will be alive for most of their child's life? When is it permissible to have a child by relying on the labor of another woman, who is likely poorer and has fewer resources and options in her own life? How much does one's own desire for a child, and the happiness one believes a child will bring, count in weighing the moral and ethical dilemmas of the new ways we build our families?

"None of us thought we'd be in our late thirties and single," said Tamara (not her real name), a thirty-nine-year-old technology company employee who, along with several of her friends, froze her eggs. "Shit didn't go the way we thought it would go. You're trying to maximize your options, your option to have a baby the old-fashioned way with your husband in a healthy way and the way you imagined you would, and you're trying to squeeze a few more years out of that option. We all would have had babies earlier had we met the guy. And we just haven't."

Tamara had looked into egg freezing years before she actually had the procedure but wasn't able to afford it; she finally went through with the procedure when she moved to a company that paid for part of it. The wave of technology companies that now pay for egg freezing has even some feminist-minded women nervous that women are either thoughtlessly delaying pregnancy, confident in the promise that they'll be fertile forever, or are being pushed to delay by unscrupulous employers. "It's hard not to perceive the inclusion of egg freezing coverage as an attempt to squeeze more value out of women before they abandon the industry altogether," wrote journalist Samantha Allen in the *Daily Beast*.[44]

That narrative, Tamara said, couldn't be further from the truth. "You would never look at a thirty-eight year old man and say he doesn't have kids yet, he must be really ambitious," she said. "You look at women and the automatic assumption is that they're going through egg freezing because they're trying to get ahead in their careers. Not one woman I know, including myself, has done it because they wanted to advance their careers." Three-quarters of women who freeze their eggs say they're waiting for the right partner, according to a study out of New York University, while needing to finish school or establishing themselves in their careers comes in a distant second.[45] Even though egg freezing is more effective the younger a woman is, most workplaces do not offer it, and the procedure remains rare: in 2013, just under 4,000 women froze their eggs in the United States.[46]

American prolife groups are either hostile to egg freezing or silent on it; the Catholic Church opposes it. Judy Brown of the American Life League said freezing one's eggs is "self-absorbed" and a "violation of nature itself," and lamented that "today, due to radical feminist influence, many women execute decisions once made only within the context of a loving marriage between a man and a woman."[47] In other words, egg freezing gives women too much control—and men too little.

The same antiabortion and religious groups often oppose IVF as well; advocating for the rights of frozen embryos to survive is a new, marginal prolife cause (although tellingly, the same people who protest abortion clinics because they claim every fertilized egg is a human being don't do the same at fertility clinics, where a great many fertilized eggs perish). Even secular critics of reproductive technology often point to mental health issues, suggesting that undergoing IVF or freezing one's eggs makes women depressed—a careful reading of the medical literature, though, paints a more complicated picture, and medical studies have not determined that IVF itself leads to depression or PTSD.

Which of course doesn't mean women shouldn't be informed of all of the risks. In 2012, the IVF market alone was a $9.3 billion industry[48]; today it is surely higher, and when you add on egg freezing and other innovations, fertility treatments are a huge cash cow. The incentives may be less about serving women and their families and more about cashing in, and there are numerous stories about clinics selling IVF to women using tactics like those of used car dealers. That's what happened to Sally Kohn and her partner Sarah, who both live in New York. Sarah had trouble getting pregnant, despite using sperm that was procured from a local sperm bank and presumably relatively potent ("As someone who's never slept with a man in my life, I've always been under the impression, and my male friends have told me, that sperm is not all that hard to come by," Sally told me. "But you put it in a bank and suddenly it's very expensive"). So they visited a fertility specialist, who scared the pants off both of them with a fear-based rapid-fire sales pitch—that Sarah probably only had a few eggs left, that they had to start IVF right away—before slipping in a $20,000 price tag, virtually none of which would be covered by insurance. Luckily, intrauterine fertilization, where the fast sperm are separated from the slower ones and the quick swimmers placed directly in the uterus, worked for Sally and Sarah. Nine months later, they had Willa.

"She was the greatest thing in the world, then and now," Sally said about Willa, now eight. "It's the coolest thing. It's also the hardest thing. Someone wrote once that having a child is like having your heart walking around outside of your body. There's no better description for it. It's a level of vulnerability and awareness that you're suddenly not just yourself."

And yet for all the joy they bring to women who want children, fertility treatments are often met with disdain. "People who spend thousands of dollars on fertility treatment are selfish and should instead adopt a child already in this world," reads one Reddit message boards[49]; similar assertions pepper nearly every comment section in an online article about fertility treatments. Adoption and fertility treatments aren't necessarily opposite choices: Sally adopted her daughter after her partner birthed her. But adopting a child whose birth mother isn't your partner or even someone you know is not nearly as straightforward. Adoption has become something of a trend among evangelical Christians in the United States; they host adoption drives and encourage their followers to pluck orphans from the developing world to give them a better (and Christ-centered) life. According to evangelicals, there are hundreds of millions of orphans in need, and it's the calling of Christians to bring these children "home." Even more secular people more or less agree adoption is an act of great selflessness, a gift to a child in need.

Just one problem: as journalist Kathryn Joyce reported in her book *The Child Catchers,* most of the hundreds of millions of alleged orphans actually have one living parent or live with extended family—in other words, they aren't orphans at all.[50] Joyce also zeroed in on the women who are so easily erased: birth mothers. Adoption, she asserted, is almost always a tragedy, involving a mother who gestated and birthed a child who for whatever reason she wasn't able to keep (or, in some circumstances, was taken away without her consent). The paucity of efforts to help mothers keep the babies they birth, Joyce said, are obscured by the idea that adoption is a selfless act.

It is true that there are children in need of adoption—most of them, though, are not healthy infants. As contraception and abortion became legal in the United States and as protections for birth mothers grew more robust, the pool of adoptable babies went down: today just 1 percent of babies are placed for adoption, down from 9 percent of babies born before abortion became broadly legal, which is why so many potential adoptive parents now look overseas. Most women don't want to gestate and birth a child only to relinquish her, and in the United States, only 15 percent of non-stepparent adoptions are of babies whose American mothers placed them for adoption voluntarily; the majority of babies adopted in America come through the foster care system, and were removed from mothers who were deemed unfit or unable to provide basic care.[51] And both domestically and internationally, many children who are up for adoption have serious health or psychological issues, or are older, like Sasha, who was three and a half and had spent most of her young life in a Russian orphanage before Merle Hoffman adopted her. There are simply not millions of adorable healthy babies awaiting their "forever home," and many potential adoptive parents decide they are not equipped to parent a child with special needs or a history of trauma. Adoption, even in the best-case scenario—with loving adoptive parents and a child placed in better circumstances—is often a tragedy for someone. That doesn't make it a bad choice—it's often a great one for adoptive parents and children alike—but it does make it thornier than the "win-win" many adoption proponents say it is.

For families who want biological children but can't have them on their own, either because of fertility issues or because both partners are men, surrogacy is an increasingly popular option—and, for feminists, a complicated and often troubling one. In surrogacy agreements, the woman who gestates the pregnancy is not (at least in theory) the woman who will raise the child. Sometimes the surrogate has a biological connection to the baby—she's the egg donor. Other times, an embryo is implanted in her uterus, and she has no genetic connection to the fetus she carries. In an ideal surrogacy arrangement, the surrogate is happy to carry another couple's child, is compensated fairly, and feels she has done a service for a couple in need. And that happens.

But sometimes it doesn't. Most wealthy women do not sign up to carry pregnancies to term when they aren't going to keep the resulting child, and so surrogates, especially when they aren't family members of the couple seeking a surrogacy arrangement, are almost always significantly poorer than the couple or individual who wants a child. Pregnancy may be safer than ever before, but it still comes with a significant chance of death or serious injury; even the healthiest pregnancies mean time off work, significant changes to your body and mobility, and the physical pain of childbirth. There are no workplace protections, and the laws governing surrogacy vary widely from state to state. Even when the parties have what seems to be an ironclad contract, much of what individuals may want isn't enforceable.

For example, a couple may make clear to their surrogate that they want only one child and expect the surrogate to abort any multiples, or that they do not want to continue a pregnancy if the fetus has a condition incompatible with life or one that will make life painful and short. A surrogate, though, cannot be legally forced to have an abortion— although she may have to pay the couple damages if she continues the pregnancy against their will, and the couple may be able to refuse guardianship of the resulting baby. The law is also inconsistent across state lines on the question of who is the legal parent. In most states, women who place their children for adoption have the right to walk that decision back within a certain time frame (a few days or even a few weeks). For surrogates, it's much more dependent on which state law regulates the surrogacy contract and whether the surrogate contributed her own genetic material. In some states, the labor of pregnancy and childbirth gives the surrogate certain claims to parenthood; in others, she is treated as a vessel for a child who legally belongs to someone else. Feminists, ethicists, and legal scholars remain divided on how to best regulate this industry, and the law is dreadfully behind the technology, leading to a lot of heartache.

Many couples also seek surrogates abroad, precisely because gestational surrogate mothers in places like India have virtually no legal protections or claims to the children they carry, they come at a cheaper

price than American women, and their behavior can be easily moni-
tored and controlled—many surrogates are housed in dorm-like (or
prison-like) units with dozens of other women carrying children for for-
eigners, where they are guaranteed to eat healthily, not smoke or engage
in activity that could threaten the pregnancy, and remain under the care
and monitoring of medical staff.

For feminists, this is a tough ethical calculus. On the one hand,
shouldn't women have the right to make their own reproductive choices,
including getting paid to carry another woman's baby? It seems condescending and antithetical to the philosophy of supporting female autonomy to tell women that they can't make money if there's a demand
for reproductive labor and they're willing to meet it. But, on the other,
can we really call this a freely made choice when there are significant
economic incentives targeting and coercing the poor—is the feminist
dream one in which rich women can have babies using poorer women's
bodies?

The idea that it should be up to women to determine for themselves
when, whether, and how to become mothers is a good one. But it becomes less neat when theory butts up against rapidly shifting reproductive realities. Motherhood, for many women, does bring incalculable
happiness. Many women crave it. What we haven't figured out is how
to weigh the individual happiness of having children with the potential
moral costs of some of the new ways we have them.

As I inch closer to the point where having my own children will become difficult and eventually impossible, I understand more viscerally
the appeal of interventions like egg freezing, IVF, and surrogacy, as well
as the promise of adoption. They don't stop the clock from ticking, but
they slow it down. What many women want is the same thing men have
always had: more time. More time to find a suitable (or even ideal)
partner, more time to get to a stable point in your career, more time to
decide whether parenthood is even for you.

At every stage of my young adulthood I knew, definitively and without
question, that the answer to the kids question was "not now." But the "yes
now" never seemed to come. By my late twenties, I decided I would have
them under two conditions: if I had a real desire for them, the kind of
craving women in my cohort described as feeling their ovaries twitch at

the sight of an adorable baby; and if I had a partner who wanted children more than I did, and was committed to doing more than half the work of raising them (given that men tend to overestimate the time they spend with their children and women to underestimate it, I figured a man who planned on doing 70 percent would end up meeting me halfway).

Neither of these conditions has been met, and as my eggs and I age, I look around at my life and not only fail to see how a child would fit but actively do not want to invite a child into it. This does not feel like a loss or something I am forgoing; it feels like the avoidance of a disruption that would end the life I have worked so hard to build.

Still, the question of regret nags at me. I lack the confidence in my future self's desires to be sure she will be happy having never had children. There is of course no cultural space to say you regret having children, but there are women who say they wish they had. What if, I think in the moments of self-doubt, I end up one of them?

This pervasive ambivalence seems to be the norm among my peers. Even the women I know who are sure they want children remain plagued by the question of when—and no time, it seems, is the ideal one. No one is looking for children to fill some empty hole in their lives; instead, the women I know worry about how they can be the best mothers possible while also retaining their own identities and their own work and their own interests.

The profound social changes that have brought about this ambivalence have also caused more women than ever before to skip having kids entirely. Today, one in five American women hits the end of her childbearing years without becoming a mother.[52] Overall, there are nearly 2 million American women in that age range who have never reproduced, and just six nations have childlessness rates higher than the modern United States.[53] As fewer women and men have children, social stigma around being child-free also adjusts. In 1988, only about a third of Americans disagreed that the childless "lead empty lives"; by 2002, 59 percent of Americans objected to that statement.[54]

But Americans aren't totally accepting of women who decide to forgo motherhood: according to a 2009 Pew survey, 38 percent said that the move toward childlessness was bad for society.[55] And it doesn't take much hunting to find people who claim the childless are "selfish, shallow, self-absorbed," as the title of an anthology of child-free writers cheekily put it.[56]

Increasingly common though she may be, the childless woman is still a source of both pity and scorn—a crazy cat lady or a selfish hedonist. In either case, she's alone. But the choice not to have children is often a pretty good one, if you ask women themselves. According to an analysis of a study comparing married women with children to married women without that was conducted in 1979, when being childless was far more stigmatized, the women who voluntarily did not have children "more frequently engage in outside interests with their spouses, more frequently exchange stimulating ideas with their spouses, express a greater desire and determination to continue their marriage, report a higher degree of marital happiness, report more agreement between themselves and their husbands on matters of household tasks, career decisions, leisure time and interest, and activities."[57] Additional research shows that, even in older couples, children are not a significant predictor of marital happiness for women—although they are for men.[58] And women without children are consistently happier than women raising them.

Not all childlessness is by choice—some women don't have children because of infertility or circumstance. Researchers estimate that only about 5 percent of married couples between the ages of eighteen and thirty-five expect not to have children; because more than 5 percent end up without children, it seems many change their minds somewhere along the way, and many others find they can't have the children they want. Unsurprisingly, those who chose not to have children were happier than those who didn't have them because of circumstances outside their control.[59]

Among the voluntarily childless, many cite the same reason for not having children as I do: enjoying one's freedom and enjoying one's life. In one study of people without children, 72 percent of women cited positive feelings of freedom and independence. Very few decided to forgo children because they didn't like them.[60] And the overwhelming majority had close relationships with children in their lives—nieces and nephews, godchildren, and children of friends.

Perhaps the most interesting aspect of research on childlessness, though, is the finding that the voluntarily childless think deeply about their decision—and many parents do not. Parenthood remains the social default, something a lot of people just do because it's culturally expected or because it's just how you think of family. That's certainly how I thought about it—and had I not had good reasons to wait, I might have ended up with children myself. One study of the child-free that surveyed previous research on the topic bears this out, concluding that while people without kids spend years considering their decision and have a fairly accurate view of what either having children or forgoing them will mean, "many parents often do not realize the full meaning of having children. If parents would consider the consequences of having children, as much as the childless couples have, it would result in improved quality of parenting and maybe a little less quantity of children." [61]

There are of course many parents who deeply consider the choice to bring a child into the world—particularly those to whom pregnancy doesn't come easily or who are partnered with people of the same sex and have to take even more proactive steps to have a baby. But as with any social norm, many people who follow it don't consider it as deeply as those who make a conscious decision to break it. And it's probably not a coincidence that the women with the most resources—the highly educated and the more affluent—are the ones more likely to make the choice not to reproduce. Although some may write that off to career women forgetting to have babies, I suspect a more common reason is purpose: if you have a demanding, interesting job that stimulates you intellectually and brings with it a sense of importance, a need many people fill with children is met. Everyone wants purpose in their life. Children offer a sense of meaning, an everyday project of molding someone small into a capable adult. If you have that sense of function and fulfillment elsewhere, and if your job also gives you a kind of autonomy and financial freedom that would be curtailed by children, it's easier to see why you might decide not to have them.

For women with all-consuming creative lives, children pose a particular challenge. "I had three abortions because I was convinced that it would be a disaster for my work, that you only have so much energy in your body and I would have to share it," the artist Marina Abramovic told the German newspaper *Tagesspiegel*.[62] "That is my view on the reason that women in the art world are not as successful as men. There are plenty of talented women. Why do men take all the important positions? It's simple: love, family, children—a woman does not want to sacrifice all of that."

"There are good artists that have children," the artist Tracey Emin said in 2014. "They are called men."[63]

In *New York* magazine, the writer Kim Brooks penned a long medi-
tation on the inherent conflict between motherhood and writing, after
watching so many of her artist friends either cut back on their creative
work or stop entirely. She recounts a conversation with a writer-mother
friend[64]:

> I pressed her again on the question I'd been turning over in my
> mind: Why is it that writing (or really any creative pursuit) seems to
> be in such conflict with parenting?
>
> She answered calmly, hardly raising her voice. "Because the point
> of art is to unsettle, to question, to disturb what is comfortable and
> safe. And that shouldn't be anyone's goal as a parent."
>
> I don't know why it took me by surprise when she said this. I
> knew it to be true. I recalled an interview I read with one of my first
> writing teachers, Deborah Eisenberg, in which she said, "Art, it-
> self is inherently subversive. It's destabilizing. It undermines, rather
> than reinforces, what you already know and what you already think."
> Oscar Wilde said it is the most intense mode of individualism the
> world has ever known. Hippocrates tells us "Art is a revolt."
>
> People make art, in other words, for exactly the opposite reason
> they make families.

What Brooks wrote feels true, and anecdotally, I've observed the
same—and yet of course there are a great many exceptions. In a piece
for *New York* magazine on fiction writer Shirley Jackson, biographer
Ruth Franklin wrote that Jackson's children opened up a new way for
her to see the world, both giving her a look through their inquisitive eyes
and letting her observe the kind of raw, untamed humanness children
embody. The daily demands of caring for four kids also set a predictable
cadence to Jackson's life, one that helped her organize her thoughts as
she did housework, and pushed her to be efficient with her words when
she had time to sit and type out her stories. "She needed the children
as much as they needed her," Franklin wrote. "Their imaginations energized her; their routines stabilized her. More important, their heedless
savagery was crucial to her worldview."[65]

Motherhood perhaps doesn't handicap art so much as cast a pall
on writers who are mothers. Mothers are conservative, boring, and domestic—stereotypes that are in direct opposition to our ideal of the

risk-taking, brooding, uncontained artist. What does ring true in the question of whether art and motherhood can coexist, though, is how the all-encompassing demands of motherhood don't leave much room for the kind of work that many creative-minded people can't segment off into working hours or when the nanny can come or when the husband is home. This is a man-made problem, not one of biology or some natural female state of being, but it is a real problem nonetheless. Nor is it just the problem of the artist or the writer. Although women with children are often more productive at work than their counterparts without them—trying to jam as much into their workday as possible so they can get home—women with small children are less productive. Kids, especially very small ones, suck up time and energy.

I consider this when thinking of my own job as a writer: I write when I can write, and that's not always between the hours 9 a.m. and 5 p.m. When I am working on an important piece, it is all consuming, and the quality of my work depends on being able to stay up late into the night, get up very early in the morning, work weekends, and travel on a whim. There is no question in my mind that I would not be nearly as productive if I had a child to think about and raise. For men, it is different: fatherhood has never been as wholly demanding as motherhood, the role of "dad" never requiring the same kind of sacrifice as "mom."

And that, it seems, is the whole of the problem.

5

Wife: The Feminist Transformation of Marital Happiness

> "And now," I said, approaching a very delicate subject on tip-toes, "tell me one thing more. Were you ever in love?"
>
> "In love?" she laughed merrily. "Bless you, Nellie, I've been in love a thousand times!"
>
> "Really?" I gasped, taken aback by this startling confession.
>
> "Yes, really!" nodding her snowy head. "But I never loved any one so much that I thought it would last. In fact I never felt I could give up my life of freedom to become a man's housekeeper."
>
> —*Nellie Bly interviewing Susan B. Anthony*

LUCY'S MARRIAGE TO her husband was a kind of American love story we've heard before: He was a military cadet, she nineteen and living in New York City, taking a gap year between high school and college before going on to work as an elementary school teacher. They fell in love quickly and got married when she was twenty-five. "It was very much the ideal that I had as a little girl: I'm gonna grow up, I'm going to meet a man, I'm going to get married, and I'm going to have a family," said Lucy, who lives in upstate New York. "I was enamored with Disney princesses, and that's what my life was supposed to look like." Their setup was fairly conventional: she made more money, but he believed that as the man he should make more of the financial decisions, and so he did; there were things he thought she, as the woman, should be doing—more tidying of the house, making fewer demands on him—and so she tried to shape herself into what he wanted in a wife.

The princess fantasy, it turned out, didn't work so well with this particular prince. "It was very much me trying to force a square peg in a round hole," Lucy said. Her husband had anger issues and alcohol abuse problems. They separated and got back together. He became vi-olent. Their marriage flagging, they decided to try an open relationship, and when Lucy mentioned an attraction to a female coworker a year later, her husband, not considering a woman a real threat (and perhaps imagining his participation in a potential sexual encounter) encouraged her to pursue it. The first night Lucy went out with Nadine, "it was im-mediate. It was like, yes, I want this person in my life," she said. "It was the quintessential, what's a lesbians' second date? Renting a U-Haul. We went out with friends and the next night we went out just the two of us and spent three consecutive days together, and after that did not spend much time apart for several years." Within a week of meeting Nadine, Lucy left her husband (both Lucy and Nadine are pseud-onyms). Now they're the married parents of a baby boy, sharing work and child care, enjoying both a love Lucy didn't know existed and an egalitarianism she hadn't imagined. "It's very hard to describe. I didn't believe in soul mates until I met [Nadine]. And then I did. I didn't understand my life before her and I can't imagine my life without her," Lucy said. "It's different because it really truly is a partnership."

This is "traditional marriage" in the twenty-first century.

For all the change marriage has undergone in the past hundred years, aspects of it remain stuck in the past. In my late twenties and early thirties, I watched as my peers dated and married their educational and intellectual equals, many living with men who were perfectly proficient at tidying up the apartment or changing the cat's litter box. But when I looked at my colleagues and coworkers a decade older than me, I saw something very different: a more traditional arrangement, with women who scaled back professionally to take on the bulk of child care and men who scaled up at work, excelling in their careers and enjoying the approving nods of strangers who admired their weekend dad duties.

As my friends and I discussed how we thought our own marriages and families would look, the women who dated women (or both women and men) often questioned whether to marry at all—marriage may have been a newly minted legal right, but would entering the institution mean folding themselves into a kind of staid, conservative heterosexual norm? Sally Kohn, who has a long-term partner and a child but doesn't want to marry, told me she is "not a big fan of the state putting relationships into boxes and saying that they will only grant benefits and recognition to families that fit in certain narrow forms." If religious or cultural institutions want to recognize marriage, have at it—the government intervention is what she dislikes. "It's the state seal of approval—these relationships are valid and these aren't equally valid, and okay now we're going to include gay families in this, but what about grandparents raising their kids or long-term friends in a nonromantic but very mutually reliant relationship?" she said. "Why can I only give my social security inheritance to my spouse and not to my aunt if that's my most meaningful relationship? Why do we define worth or benefits in these hierarchal ways?" That said, "from a practical perspective, it's kind of stupid that I won't get married. But there you have it."

Sally is only a few years older than I am, and in my peer group, those of us who dated men tended to be less concerned about the marriage question, not chomping at the marital bit but quietly assuming it would probably happen at some point. The big question was what would happen next, especially if we had kids. None of the bright, ambitious women in my social circle saw themselves as future stay-at-home moms. But neither did any of us have an interest in marrying men who would be stay-at-home dads (or women who would be stay-at-home moms). We found ourselves attracted to the people we dated in large part because of their intellectual curiosity and their ambition. None of us wanted to come home at the end of a long workday to a person whose primary social interaction had been with a toddler and whose universe was dominated by diapers and playdates; neither did we want to be the person whose universe revolved around a child. And none of us wanted the burden of being our family's sole financial provider or relying fully on someone else's provision.

A truly 50-50 marital model wasn't something I had seen often among
the heterosexual couples long permitted to legally marry, even if on the
surface it looked like both partners worked and cared for their children.
In my own family, my mother scaled back to part-time work when I
was born. I knew lots of women who intentionally worked less when
they had their children, but not a single man. I knew lots of women
who continued to work just as hard after having a child; their husbands
did the same, but it still seemed like it was mom who was in charge of
wrangling the nanny and keeping track of the kid's vaccine schedule. I
knew virtually no couples who both scaled back, especially if it meant a
cut in pay and prestige for the father.

Whey Lucy and Nadine had their son, Lucy, who carried the pregnancy, took five and a half months off; when her time was up, Nadine
then took five and a half months, which meant their boy was home
with one of his parents for almost the entire first year of his life. "When
he was born, he slept on [Nadine] for the first week of his life, so at
night they were skin to skin," Lucy said. And the fact that Nadine was a
woman with breasts meant that even though she didn't carry the pregnancy and wasn't lactating, she could also allow her son to suckle and
experience the particular, and for many women profound, physical connection of nursing a child. "Starting around six weeks she was able to
comfort nurse him, which was such a relief for me," Lucy said. "There
are some things that she's able to do that if I were married to a man,
he wouldn't be able to do. It also allows us to do what we're both really good at. So if I'm really good at putting him down to sleep, or if
[Nadine] is really good at that, we are able to draw on those strengths,
rather than 'this is what I'm supposed to be doing.'"

Lucy and Nadine's marriage looked a lot like the kind I wanted. But,
even without kids, men complicate things.

American marriages today are fundamentally different than they
have been for nearly all of human history, not least because they are increasingly optional. There are more unwed adults in the United States
today than at any point in our country's past, and people are marrying later than ever. Nothing has redefined marriage more than feminist
gains, and for the most part, they've made married people happier and
more satisfied (especially wives).

Far from being an attack on traditional marriage, this modern marriage economy has largely been a boon for the women who embrace

it. Women who marry after thirty make more money than their single counterparts—an $18,000-a-year average bump for women with a college degree, and a $4,000 bonus for women with a high school degree and some college.[1] And women who marry later divorce less often than their counterparts who marry in their teens and twenties; college-educated women are also less likely to divorce than women who didn't finish college or never went at all. According to some studies, marriage makes people happier (others suggest that the happiness boost is fleeting or that the people who get married were happier in the first place).

The feminist marriage revolution, though, is a stalled one. While most women today exist in a marital landscape that is far preferable to the options of a century ago, they're still in a strange limbo where men's actions haven't totally caught up to women's expectations, where institutions and laws lag further still, and where the scourges of racial and economic inequality mean some women benefit from social shifts in marriage and others are left painfully behind.

This new standard, of marrying an autonomous individual only once you're an autonomous individual yourself, is what marriage researchers call the "capstone" model: marriage as the final marker of a solid, stable life, as opposed to a cornerstone of one. Educated young people today see marriage as something they do after most of their other ducks are in a row: they have a college degree, they're working at a stable job, they can afford a wedding. And most crucially, they want to marry someone who is a great match and from whom they derive emotional and sexual fulfillment, not simply someone who plays a complimentary role—that is, an employed man looking for a woman who would be a good mother and homemaker, and vice versa. Americans say a happy sexual relationship is one of the primary things that makes a marriage work, second only to faithfulness; more than 60 percent also agree that sharing household chores is crucial to a successful union.[2] Of unmarried young people today, about a third say they haven't tied the knot because they're looking for the right person. About the same number say they don't feel financially ready.

That capstone model means that women and men are marrying later than ever before, if they marry at all—and many don't. The most well educated and financially prosperous, though, continue to wed, building their families like the children's rhyme: first comes love, then comes marriage, then comes a baby in a baby carriage.

The kind of marriage I and many of my peers assume we will have, whether we marry at all and whether we marry a man or a woman—a union of equals, entered into out of love, with things like kids and housework negotiated and discussed—is worlds apart from the average marriage even a generation ago. This kind of modern marriage is possible only because of feminist activism and women's social gains, many of them in the form of legal changes well before marriage was expanded to include same-sex couples. One of the more profound shifts saw the status of married women transformed from men's chattel into individuals in their own right. But we've seen social and cultural shifts, too. In the 1950s, intelligence didn't even crack the top 10 qualities American men said they wanted in a wife (it was ranked 11, tied with education).[3] More important than intelligence were a woman's cooking abilities, her housekeeping skills, and her pleasing disposition. By 1996, intelligence crept up to number 5. And by 2015, it topped the list of what men look for in women they marry.[4]

Even this new kind of egalitarian marriage, wholly unprecedented in most of human history, remains vastly imperfect. Those who believe marriage is best when it's "traditional," with a breadwinning husband and a domestically focused wife, point to feminist gains—contraception, women working outside the home—as forces undermining the family, womanhood, and children's welfare. Those same people are fighting an uphill battle—marriage has changed, and it's going to take some work to convince women to walk these gains back—but they have the benefit of a clearly defined social vision and the soft glow of nostalgia for what they present as an easier, more moral, bygone era of suburban conventionalism and the traditional family.

"Marriage is based on the anthropological truth that men and women are complementary, the biological fact that reproduction depends on a man and a woman, and the social reality that children need a mother and a father," wrote Ryan T. Anderson in a paper published on the website of the conservative Heritage Foundation.[5] "Just as the complementarity of a man and a woman is important for the type of union they can form, so too is it important for how they raise children. There is no such thing as 'parenting.' There is mothering, and there is fathering, and children do best with both."

For feminists, the question of what marriage should be is more difficult to answer. This new marriage model is in its adolescence, and the growing pains are tough. Some advocates for women's rights, including me, wonder whether opposite-sex marriage can ever be fully egalitarian, let alone feminist. Like many women, I grew up assuming I would get married, and by high school had it all planned out: I would go to college, work for a few years, get married at twenty-seven, and have my first of two children at thirty. It didn't quite work out that way: twenty-seven is when I quit my job as a lawyer to become a full-time writer, and back then I was far more focused on running full-speed into a new job than picking out a white dress. At thirty, my then-boyfriend wanted to move in together, a step I interpreted as one foot closer to the altar—I panicked and said no. Not only did I not feel ready to get married, and not only would he have been the wrong person for me to marry; I realized I may just not want to get married at all—and that forgoing marriage could be a very good option.

This view was shaped in part by the stable, happy, but lukewarm marriages I saw around me. People hit a certain age—late twenties or early thirties for my law school cohort, a few years younger among people I attended high school with—and it seemed that, as long as they were in a secure relationship with a similarly sensible person they loved, they got married, and had children a few years later. These are thoroughly reasonable, risk-averse unions, with women I knew marrying the same kind of men I often dated: dependable, kind, career oriented. But the decision to marry them often seemed like a vehicle for something else both people ultimately wanted: an end to dating, a consistent partner, a nuclear family, an upper-middle-class life, kids, and a steady environment in which to raise them.

Had any of those things appealed to me, perhaps marriage would have as well—the responsible-partner marriage model is a rational, intelligent choice if you see marriage as one part of a family package, the foundation upon which you build the rest of your life. That was not the foundation, nor the life, I envisioned. Instead, in my midtwenties and increasingly confident I didn't want children, I made a conscious decision: I would not marry Mr. Good Enough. I would rather have a string of loves and heartbreaks than marry someone fundamentally decent but about whom I felt the least bit tepid. It wasn't that I never wanted to get married; it was more that the conditions under which I would be willing to get married were so extreme that I never expected to meet them. Finally making that decision felt like a huge relief—and taking off the "is this it?" pressure made dating a lot more fun.

And then, in an extraordinary turn of luck, in my early thirties I met someone better than anything I could have envisioned or expected. To my great relief, he also had little interest in a traditional nuclear-family life. But it turned out there was one exception: about a year into our relationship, he told me he wanted to get married.

No longer an abstraction, I forced myself, for the first time in my life, to really consider marriage and interrogate my immediate recoil from the mere suggestion of it. I was in the middle of a love affair unlike anything I had ever experienced, at once exhilarating and steady, with both of us fascinated by each other but also carefully and intentionally laying down the building blocks of what we wanted a long life together to look like. There was no question in my mind that this was the person for me; the idea of lifelong commitment didn't feel scary or daunting but appropriate, a desirable and feasible challenge. But when I thought about being someone's wife, my stomach turned.

Because I write about gender and feminism and because I'm a woman in a culture that still holds up marriage as a woman's ultimate achievement, I spent a lot of time thinking about marriage as an idea, well before it became immediately relevant to my own life. And although I had written thousands of words on all the ways in which feminism had improved marriage and even saved the institution from irrelevance, I still questioned whether marriage, the paradigm of a patriarchal institution, was even a thing feminists should care about, let alone fight for or encourage. On the one hand, the brutally misogynist history of marriage should have rendered it obsolete long ago. But on the other, marriage has evolved so much, especially with the expansion of marriage rights to same-sex couples, it's hard to argue that the institution itself is irreparably broken. Feminists get married, I reasoned, and that had to count for something. But I remained unconvinced that more egalitarian shifts in the institution meant that marriage itself was desirable.

Even if marriages are more equal than ever—and like many women, I work under the assumption that should I get married, my relationship will remain more or less equal—marriage still, in many ways, remains definitional for women and tangential for men. I saw over and over again how marriage still clips women's wings. I had settled comfortably into my identity as a single woman and all the freedom and room for folly it brings with it. Would getting married obscure this person, an individual who defines herself in large part by her autonomy and self-sovereignty?

It's with that frame that I entered this project, wondering whether marriage actually makes women happy or if by its nature it subsumes women into their male partners—and whether any of that changed when we expanded marriage to include same-sex couples. Can marriage ever be *good* for women—and can marriage be feminist?

Most importantly, what kind of family, community, and bonding arrangements would make women, men, and families happiest? What does a pleasurable marriage, or alternative to marriage, look like—and did I ever want one?

A century and a half ago, early feminists pointed to marriage, and the attendant forcible sex and compulsory motherhood, as a root of women's displeasure. More equal marriages—or none at all—were the solution.

"Did it ever enter into the mind of man that woman too had an inalienable right to life, to liberty, and the pursuit of her individual happiness?" Elizabeth Cady Stanton wrote in a letter to her friend Gerrit Smith in 1855. "Our present laws, our religious teachings, our social customs on the whole question of marriage and divorce, are most degrading to woman; and so long as man continues to think and write, to speak and act, as if maternity was the one and sole object of a woman's existence—so long as children are conceived in weariness and disgust—you must not look for high-toned men and women capable of accomplishing any great and noble achievement." Marriage, she wrote, "is the starting-point; here is the battleground where our independence must be fought and won."[6]

For centuries, "traditional marriage" meant near-total male authority over women. Old English law and its American offshoot relied on the doctrine of coverture, wherein a wife became subsumed into her husband: "The husband and wife are one person in law: that is, the very being or legal existence of the woman is suspended during the marriage, or at least is incorporated and consolidated into that of the husband: under whose wing, protection, and cover, she performs every thing," according to William Blackstone's eighteenth-century treatise on English common law. The wife's job was to love, honor, and obey. The husband's was to love, cherish, and protect.[7]

Under coverture, women could not own property, work for pay, file a lawsuit, accrue debt, or make a contract.[8] Coverture was an exchange of legal obligations, tied up in other restrictions of women's political, economic, and social rights: men were obligated to financially support their wives and families, and in turn they were the heads of those family units, existing as the liaison between the family and society as a whole. It was a man's privilege to vote, and woman couldn't—her vote was thought to simply replicate her husband's, and he was the family's political representative. If women wanted political influence, one senator said, their best bet was to "attach themselves to some man who will represent them in public affairs."[9]

Unsurprisingly, early feminists viewed marriage with deep skepticism. "The signing of this contract," Elizabeth Cady Stanton said in 1854, "is instant civil death to one of the parties."[10]

Women's roles in marriage and society were front and center in the contentious debates on dismantling coverture and, later, women's suffrage. Giving women voting rights, one American religious leader and academic wrote scornfully, would redefine the marital unit into "simply a copartnership, with 'all rights reserved.'"[11]

Today, women not only have the right to vote, but they remain their own distinct legal entities, even when they marry. Marriage today is very much a copartnership, if an often imperfect and unequal one, but at least one with all rights reserved.

Which doesn't mean marriage is now a panacea. One "traditional" requirement of marriage that hasn't completely disappeared is a woman's loss of her bodily and sexual autonomy. In marriage, women once became the property of their husbands, and that near-total ownership extended to their genitals, too. Nineteenth-century rape laws were careful to say that "a husband does not become guilty of rape by forcing his wife to his own embraces" and that a rapist might be "any male of the age of fourteen or over, not the husband of the female." For centuries, there was little debate about marital rape. The idea that it's impossible to rape your wife because she is by definition her husband's sexual property was so deeply integrated into American law that some courts determined it was "a material and necessary part of the definition of the offense" that the alleged rapist not be married to the victim. Sir Matthew Hale, a chief justice of the Court of King's Bench in England, wrote in an influential legal treatise that "the husband cannot be guilty of a rape committed by himself upon his lawful wife, for by their mutual matrimonial consent and contract the wife hath given up herself in this kind unto her husband, which she cannot retract."[12] That sentence was published in 1736, but it guided American law well into the 1970s, when the marital rape exception finally started to crumble.

It wasn't until 1993 that marital rape was outlawed in all fifty states, and even today some states have laws on the books treating marital rape differently from "rape-rape"—for example, if you drug your wife in Ohio and then have sex with her without her consent, it's not rape.[13] And the view that marriage creates a sexually proprietary relationship wherein the husband deserves sexual access to his wife whether she wants it or not remains alive and well. Conservative commentator and Eagle Forum founder Phyllis Schlafly argued as recently as 2007 that marital rape doesn't exist, because marriage itself is open consent to sexual activity. "I think that when you get married you have consented to sex," she said. "That's what marriage is all about, I don't know if maybe these girls missed sex ed."[14] American president Donald Trump was also accused of raping his first wife, Ivana, while they were married. His lawyer's defense when the accusations became public during the early stages of Trump's campaign: "You cannot rape your spouse."[15]

Historically, men and not women were the ones with the right to sex: they could traditionally sue for "loss of consortium" if death or injury to their wife meant she was no longer sexually available. But it was a claim only the husband could make—wives were their husband's chattel and had no similar expectation of sexual or other services.[16] The first time a wife won on a claim of loss of consortium wasn't until 1950. Adultery, too, was a privilege men were entitled to engage in, and an injury from which they were permitted to recover if their wives strayed. Men could sue their wives' affair partners for claims including alienation of affection, enticement, and criminal conversion because an affair defiled the marriage (and the husband's property—his wife)[17] and because it threatened to give his inheritance to offspring that were not his.[18] Women could not.

That early view of sexual pleasure as a thing men get and women provide exists still, both socially and, in a few instances, legally. So does the view that a woman is folded into her husband, if mostly socially and linguistically. The vast majority of American women still take their husbands' last names upon marriage. And we still tear up when a bride's father walks her down the aisle and "gives her away," like property, to her new male authority. The legal groundwork is different today, but the traditions remain. For as far as we've come, suppression of women's very selves in marriage persists.

And yet we have come far, and fast. In the grand scheme of human history, the skyrocketing status of women is virtually unprecedented. It's not fast enough for those of us who believe women are fully human and deserve to be treated as such, but it is worth taking a moment to recognize the incredible speed at which these changes have occurred—and to extend gratitude to the generations of feminist activists who ushered them in. Nineteenth-century feminists earned women the right to vote but were just as concerned with women's rights to their own bodies within the marital relationship. Twentieth-century feminists carried that forward, reshaping marriage at light speed in the second half of the century.

"The women's movement itself was enabled and encouraged by several structural changes, not all of which were necessarily profeminist," historian and marriage scholar Stephanie Coontz told me. "One was the invention of the Pill, which made it more possible for people not to have to rush into shotgun marriages, and to delay for education. Another was the development of a new kind of service economy that recruited women as second-class workers, but once you gave them access to the salary and the experience, you set in motion a chain of events that led some of them to challenge the relegation to second-class status. All of those things paved the way. But I think you need to give credit to the woman's movement itself, which insisted that the laws be changed."

Today's women live in a world where marriage is more feminist than ever, but where marriages themselves are rarely truly fair. That promise of egalitarianism leads to deep dissatisfaction when it butts up against the realities of entrenched sexism, a political climate hostile to women, and widespread inequality across gender, racial, and economic lines. We have a pretty good idea of what makes marriages stable and what makes married people happy. Now, we just have to make those things a reality, and that requires a frank reckoning with some of our most deeply ingrained and closely held ideas about marriage, men, and women.

When same-sex marriage became legal in New York in 2011, Lucy and Nadine decided to tie the knot. "We wanted to make a commitment to each other, and we wanted that commitment to be taken seriously, so for us that meant doing it legally," Lucy said. For her, legal status mattered quite a bit—being recognized was important to both her and Nadine—but wasn't the heart of what marriage meant. "Standing up in front of our friends and family and dearest closest people and having them hold us up and support us and love us as we made this commitment to each other, that for me was the more meaningful piece," she said.

That same-sex couples can now marry across the United States is a triumph of the overlapping movements for gay rights and women's rights, and a natural outgrowth of the incredible changes gender equality has made to marriage. In the opinion in *Obergefell v. Hodges,* the Supreme Court case that legalized same-sex marriage across the United States, Justice Anthony Kennedy wrote:

> As the role and status of women changed, the institution further evolved. Under the centuries-old doctrine of coverture, a married man and woman were treated by the State as a single, male-dominated legal entity. As women gained legal, political, and property rights, and as society began to understand that women have their own equal dignity, the law of coverture was abandoned. These and other developments in the institution of marriage over the past centuries were not mere superficial changes. Rather, they worked deep transformations in its structure, affecting aspects of marriage long viewed by many as essential.
>
> These new insights have strengthened, not weakened, the institution of marriage.[19]

And that, along with other legal precedent, justified expanding marriage rights to same-sex couples in all fifty states.

Conservative opposition to same-sex marriage relies on a "complimentary" marital model—the idea that marriage is inherently about the distinctive and dissimilar roles of husbands and wives. In amicus brief after amicus brief filed by conservative groups in the Supreme Court marriage equality case, the position that marriage is by definition about joining two people with separate, gender-determined roles was offered as a justification for denying same-sex couples the right to marry. According to one amicus brief by seventy-six conservative marriage scholars, "Most obviously, by requiring a man and a woman, that definition conveys that this structure can be expected to have both a 'masculine' and a 'feminine' aspect, one in which men and women complement each other."[20] Challenging that structure harms society, the scholars argued, because "such legal changes are especially likely to undermine those norms among heterosexual men, who generally need more encouragement to marry than women."[21] According to another brief, "Marriage is an inherently sexual institution where hair color distinctions would be arbitrary, but distinctions in gender composition—the 'vital core' of the institution—are neither trivial nor superficial."[22]

It's no longer particularly couth—or particularly realistic—to come right out and say that husbands should work and wives should stay home or that men should be in control of women, so the language of "traditional marriage" is increasingly coded. According to a paper by Rob Schwarzwalder of the Family Research Council, who served in the George W. Bush administration, "Men and women are different"—for example, "guys still take such pride in their machines, while women often care more about maintaining a clean home."[23] The same organization issued a paper opposing the UN Convention on the Elimination of All Forms of Discrimination Against Women because it would "de-emphasize the role of mothers and increase incentives for them to work rather than stay home to care for children."[24] According to Focus on the Family, an influential conservative organization, "The woman brings life; the father brings strength . . . the abiding pattern, the divine design, gives power to the father."[25] And marriage isn't about happiness between the married people but about pleasing God.[26]

These conservative ideas have trickled out into social policy. More than forty years ago, Congress passed a universal child-care bill that would have created and funded high-quality day-care centers across the United States. It was almost a reality—until religious fundamentalists opposed it down for being "antifamily" and President Richard Nixon vetoed it.[27] Attempts to establish high-quality child-care centers in the late 1980s also met conservative opposition from those who thought even a child-care tax credit disadvantaged "traditional families" with a stay-at-home mom. At the core of the GOP's positions on family is the idea that the role of government is not to assist existing families in being healthy and happy but rather to promote a particular, increasingly rare familial structure: a working father, a stay-at-home mother, and children.

That may have been a key to social stability and marital satisfaction in the 1950s (although the popularity of both prescription drugs and

Betty Friedan's *The Feminine Mystique* suggest otherwise). But it's not the world we live in today. One of the most significant marital shifts over the past century has to do with what makes married people happy. According to Coontz, predictors of marital happiness have essentially flipped since the 1970s, and today the copartner model brings the greatest benefits. "What we're seeing really is that a lot of the rules of engagement are changing," Coontz said. "The things that used to make for a happy marriage no longer necessarily do, and the things that used to be disruptive to marriage—a wife having more education than her husband, egalitarian division of house care—are now predictors of marital and sexual satisfaction."[28]

The "success penalty" that educated women used to face in finding both partners to marry and later marital happiness is now gone[29]; marriages where the husband and wife are both educated are some of the happiest and longest lasting.[30] (Given the recent advent of marriage equality, there is scant research on married same-sex couples.) Feminist marriages are particularly happy ones. According to one study out of Rutgers University, women with feminist partners have healthier heterosexual relationships, while men married to feminist women see more stable relationships in which they report higher levels of sexual satisfaction.[31]

And yet although marriages are more equal than ever, truly equal marriage is far from the norm.

"Though marriage is more egalitarian now than it used to be, it's still the case that it's gendered," W. Bradford Wilcox, an associate professor of sociology and the director of the National Marriage Project at the University of Virginia told me. "So, yes, contemporary husbands do more housework and more child care, a lot more than their fathers and grandfathers did, but women still do about twice as much child care as men in contemporary families. And about 69 percent of married family income on average comes from the husband. So we're in kind of a neo-traditional moment."

Indeed, college-educated men married to college-educated women bring in about the same proportion of household income—around 70 percent—as men in couples where neither partner has a college education. In 2012, the mean annual income for married college-educated men was around $90,000; for their wives, it was under $40,000. Married men without a college degree made slightly *more* than $40,000 a year, while their wives made closer to $15,000.[32] In other words, even across classes and education levels, the man is still usually the primary bread-winner in any married couple—and there's not much of a difference in the supposedly more egalitarian marriages of the educated. Marriage has changed, but perhaps not nearly as much as we like to think.

And for all the gains women have made in the past century, men have been a bit slower to catch up. The feminist movement has, rightly, focused on women and girls, fighting discriminatory laws, telling us we can be anything we want to be, and expanding opportunities and op-tions for the female half of the population. Some of that has trickled down to men, too, as they're expected to be more present at home and participate more in child care. But still, only a tiny number of men are full-time caregivers for their children. Men mostly say they want equal partnerships. But when push comes to shove, they don't actually make many sacrifices or adjustments to do it.[33]

Although millennial men are more progressive than their fathers, they aren't quite a feminist vision of twenty-first-century males yet: more than a third of employed millennial men without kids say that men should be the breadwinners and women should stay home with the children. And the numbers get worse among those who are already fathers: more than half of millennial fathers think heterosexual couples should fall into traditional roles.[34]

Moreover, what heterosexual men say they want, and then what they actually do, are very different things. There's also a stark divide between what women expect from their male partners and what those male part-ners expect to do (and end up doing), even among those with the great-est resources and abilities to provide for themselves. Women assume they will have egalitarian marriages where both partners' careers are of equal importance and both share in child care and household duties; men are more likely to expect their careers to take precedence. The men end up being right.[35]

Men are often raised to believe their biggest contribution to a family is financial; they also know that money and career advancement mean power and freedom, something women who are financially dependent on their husbands lack. The idea that masculinity and being a good husband is linked to being a financial provider is an idea that men have been slow to shake. Getting rid of it entirely will require a big cultural shift in how we define maleness and how much we reward and expect men to participate on the home front—just as women have entered the workforce en masse. More conservative marriage scholars agree. "I think if marriage is going to be stronger in this century, we need to think about a newer model of masculinity that both the average woman and the average man can buy into and that doesn't depend upon them being the primary or the sole breadwinner," Wilcox said.

Where the feminist model and the more conservative one differ, though, is in what that "new masculinity" looks like. For scholars like Wilcox, it means retaining distinct gender roles, whereas for many feminists, the ideal is roles based on individual interest and talent, with each partner having the space and ability to exist outside of prescribed roles attached to their sex. As it stands, there are such strong and divergent expectations for women and men that of course women seem to be "better" at child care and housekeeping, and men seem to be "better" at contributing financially and working the long hours necessary to make it in today's economy. That's shifting, but women's roles are significantly more flexible than men's—women are still the vast majority of full-time caregivers, and most women also work outside of the home. Although strangers may coo at a daddy wheeling a stroller, there's less social space and fewer cultural rewards for men to be the primary caregivers for their children or other family members, and caregiving carries with it an emasculating stigma.

What marriage scholars across the political spectrum can agree on is that depressed wages among working-class men make them less marriageable—women don't want to marry men who can barely support themselves, and the men themselves don't feel marriage ready because their idea of male adulthood is so tied up in economic stability and provider status. In a vastly unequal country where many men will simply never make the kind of money their fathers were able to earn through low-skilled labor, the old marriage model may never be a feasible option for those who see the ability to provide for a family as a prerequisite. Still, most people want to get married. So if the conditions for a traditional marriage are increasingly daunting, the question now is, What replaces it?

Some six hundred miles south of Lucy and Nadine's New York home, in Raleigh, North Carolina, Janet lives with her three kids in a square two-bedroom brick house, one of two dozen identical units lining a long thruway. On the day I visited, there was a fourth kid running around—her niece Makaiya, a skinny, hopping little girl with tight cornrows, in hot pink shorts and a teal shirt that matches Janet's. Janet eventually puts the kids—Takarah, eight; Shaniya, seven; Jayvion, five; and Makaiya, three—down for a nap, but as we I talked, we could still hear their slow tiptoeing as they snuck around the house, too amped up by each other's company to sleep. What Janet and I talked most about was money—or, rather, how she doesn't have it and how a lifetime of just hanging on has left her depressed and physically ill.

Looking at Janet's situation, it would have been easy to conclude that marrying Rome, her then-boyfriend, and moving into the same house might be an easy fix. They'd save money on expenses, because they would be sharing the rent and utilities, and he would be a source of emotional support for her and her kids. Indeed, that's the solution that many conservative scholars have been pushing for decades. In many ways, Janet and Lucy are both emblematic of what Wilcox called the "growing marriage divide" in the United States, which he asserted is "leaving millions of men, women, and children in poor and working-class communities without ready access to the stability, emotional security, and financial resources afforded by marriage."[36]

There is a wealth of research to suggest that the children of single parents fare worse than the children of married couples and that declining marriage rates are associated with poverty and low education levels. For Wilcox and many others, a clear solution is to encourage marriage in communities where it has flagged, and recenter the nuclear family as the norm in American life. And it's not just social conservatives promoting marriage as a cure; the US government is too. Clinton-era welfare reform allowed states to spend welfare funds on marriage promotion, and under the George W. Bush administration, marriage promotion programs—efforts to counsel welfare recipients to wed—received more than $1 billion.[37] This money came from a pot previously set aside to help those in need: "Displaced funds included $14 million from child welfare, $6.1 million from a child support enforcement program, $9 million worth of support for refugees, and $40 million from a development strategies program focusing on Native Americans," journalist Madeleine Schwartz reported in the *LA Review of Books*.[38] The policy of encouraging poor people to marry continued under President Barack Obama.

The goal of the often-religious, lightly tested marriage programs of this era wasn't just getting people to tie the knot; it was to end women's financial dependence on welfare and shift that dependence from the government to a husband. In justifying the program's cost, Robert Rector and Melissa G. Pardue from the conservative Heritage Foundation asserted, "This sum represents one penny to promote healthy marriage for every five dollars government currently spends to subsidize single parenthood. Moreover, this small investment today could result in potentially great savings in the future by reducing dependence on welfare and other social services." Welfare, they wrote, "serves as a substitute for a husband."[39]

The marriage programs, it turned out, didn't work. In most of the places where they were implemented, they had no impact; sometimes, they actually made things worse[40]: a program called Building Strong Families cost $11,000 per couple and offered relationship skill–building for 5,000 unmarried partners with children, and yet compared to a control group that didn't participate in the program, participant couples were no more likely to be married three years later and were in fact less likely to have stayed together at all. Fathers who participated in the program were less involved in their children's lives and less likely to support them than fathers who hadn't. Some states, like Oklahoma, nevertheless channeled 10 percent of their welfare spending into marriage promotion programs, many of which are sexist and homophobic to boot. Sociologist Melanie Heath chronicles this in her book *One Marriage Under God: The Campaign to Promote Marriage in America,* observing one marriage program leader read from the Bible: "Wives submit to your husband as to the Lord. For the husband is the head of the wife as Christ is the head of the Church, his body, of which he is the Savior."

The reason these marriage promotion programs have failed so spectacularly is that they tried to solve the wrong problem: marriage itself, and not the underlying stressors, many of them financial and some of them gendered, that force couples to delay marriage and cause relationships to dissolve. It's not that low-income Americans don't take marriage as seriously or have worse marital skills than their higher-income peers; on the contrary, low-income Americans have more traditional views of marriage than do higher-income Americans, and they have comparable romantic expectations and problems with relationship skills.[41] It may in fact be these more traditional views, stoked by the political Right and funded by marriage promotion programs, that keep marriage rates depressed among the American poor and working class. A key element of traditional marriage is a breadwinner husband, and while educated, affluent American men are typically able to provide for a family, lower-income men often can't. The flood of women into the workforce—to the point that, now, never-married women are more likely than their never-married male counterparts to be employed—has also contributed to the marriage gap because of traditional views of gender and marriage.[42]

"People say over and over again that they want to meet a certain financial bar" before they marry, Coontz said. "And it's not an over-the-top material one, it's like, 'I don't want to have to take out payday loans or to rely on the government.' When people meet that bar they tend to marry. I think that it's pretty clear that the way to solve these problems is to get living-wage jobs, to rebuild the social safety net, and then you have a win-win situation. All the evidence suggests that people will marry if they feel that economic security is in their future."

When men aren't able to find steady work, they don't get married. That's both because they don't believe themselves to be marriage material, and because women don't, either—nearly 80 percent of unmarried women say it's important for a spouse to have a job. The view that economic independence is a prerequisite for marriage is nearly universal among young people of both sexes: 91 percent say they will be ready to marry once they are fully financially independent. And one in five young people reports postponing marriage because of the current economy.

For the very poor, the incentives for avoiding marriage are even more material. Getting married can mean losing benefits like food stamps and Medicaid if total household income creeps up, even if the amount of money coming in isn't realistically enough to support a family. And in a country where a third of young people believe they should be able to pay for their own wedding before getting married—and where weddings routinely cost tens of thousands of dollars—it's no wonder marriage seems like it is at best a frivolity and at worst a financial death wish to women like Janet. For lower-income, less-educated women, the modern view of marriage as a final achievement—once the rest of your life is straightened out—means it often doesn't happen at all. Even if women abandoned the capstone model and started marrying before they had a steady job or a child, that wouldn't necessarily bode well for marital stability: early marriages, entered into in one's twenties, are significantly less stable than marriages between two people in their late twenties or early thirties. The same groups that are the most likely to get married— the educated, the wealthy—are also the least likely to divorce, especially when they marry after thirty. Those who take a more traditional path by marrying young are more likely to split up, as are those without a college degree.

Marriage proponents emphasize that getting married offers financial benefits, and that's true. With a slew of rights and benefits offered to married couples, partners who are committed and cohabiting but unwed face penalties: they pay more in taxes, they have fewer legal protections if the relationship ends, and because they often cannot share health insurance they are less likely to be insured.[43] But while less-educated women do see a financial boost when they get married, it's not nearly as large as that of their higher-educated counterparts, and the risks posed by divorce are significantly more dire: low-income women are not only more likely to get divorced, but they suffer more financial disruption when they do. That makes sense: financial stress puts a lot of strain on a marriage, and, when there are few resources to go around in the first place, trying to divvy them up and losing some of them after severing a relationship can push a precarious economic situation over the financial cliff. Although some marriage advocates, including Wilcox, believe marriage is one solution to endemic poverty, others, like Coontz, say it's an inadequate answer to a much more complex problem, and that selling marriage as an antidote to poverty and diverting money away from welfare benefits and toward marriage promotion may be exacerbating the issue rather than curing it. "A lot of these correlations between marriage and success and successful child-rearing are just correlations," she said. "The people who can commit to each other, who have the stability to raise their kids, are the ones who get married. The ones who don't, don't tend to get married, or if they do get married tend to get divorced."

The American divorce rate has fallen significantly since the 1970s and '80s, and experts estimate that two-thirds of marriages entered into in the 2000s will last.[44] But divorce remains commonplace—in large part because of much of America's fetishization of "traditional marriage." The parts of the country where it's most prevalent aren't the highly educated blue-state bastions of feminism but politically conservative and evangelical areas. That's partly explained by poverty and partly explained by the fact that religious couples tend to marry early instead of living together or dating into their late twenties. But there's something else at play as well. According to the Council on Contemporary Families, religious, politically conservative pockets of the United States breed certain norms around marriage that mean even nonreligious folks in those areas tend to divorce more often than people living in more liberal, secular areas: sexual activity before marriage and cohabitation are frowned upon, and so there's a push to marry young; limited information about sexual health and contraception, coupled with stigma and limited access to abortion services, mean marriage is often the solution to unintended pregnancy; lack of educational opportunities and lack of support for secular education means young people have few reasons to delay marriage and childbearing, and they get married and have kids before they're fully mature; and lack of education translates into financial stress. All of that is a perfect storm for failed marriages. It's also solid evidence that a nineteenth-century view of marriage doesn't work in the twenty-first—and that feminism makes for happier marriages.

It's no mystery why women whose lives are plagued by instability and pocked with violence may hesitate before legally binding themselves to a man. One in ten American men will go to jail at some point in his life, and the men who go to jail are disproportionately poor and of color. That's a lot of men who, by virtue of being behind bars, are off the market. And, even when they do get out, people with arrest records and convictions have a harder time finding steady employment, making them less appealing partners—even though most Americans who go to jail are there for relatively petty, nonviolent offenses.

Janet lives that challenge. Her children's fathers have been in jail, and she, too, has an arrest record, keeping her trapped in low-wage labor. For Janet, marriage sounds nice but isn't on the table right now. And when she ticks off her list of past boyfriends, it's hard to argue, as many conservative advocates do, that she would have been better off marrying any of them. Two of her children's fathers beat her. Shaniya's father never laid a hand on her, but he's locked up for robbery; Janet said he's by far the best man of the three. Before he was incarcerated, he embraced both of her daughters, even if he wasn't always able to be a financial provider. "He was a good father to the girls, talking to them and spending time, but actually spending on them, that was the issue,"

Janet said. "When he came to pick up his daughter, our daughter, he made sure to pick up my other daughter as well. Even when he's been locked up he told his mother, 'That's my daughter, too.'"

Janet does her best to explain to her children why their little family remains fractured. "I explain to them what's going on; I keep it open," Janet said. "I don't sugar-coat anything. When their father got locked up, instead of telling my girls, 'He's on vacation,' I'm not going to do that. I did it with my brother when he was locked up, and my girls they started asking questions like, 'Ma, why are we going to this building to see my uncle? Why can't he come with us?' I say, 'You know what, I'll tell you the truth.' I always tell them people have choices in life. Some people make good choices, and I said some, they make bad choices. I always tell my babies, even myself, you make bad choices there's consequences behind that."

Janet's life was made harder by many of the men she encountered, and in that she is far from alone. Men remain the biggest threat women face, and women are usually beaten, injured, raped, and abused by men they know, and often men with whom they are in intimate relationships. Of the spousal murders in the United States, husbands commit 83 percent.[45]

That isn't to say that most men are abusive—they aren't. But it's impossible to separate women's increasing reticence to marry men from the systematic violence men impose on us. For most of marriage's history, that violence was seen as a private matter, and police officers and courts were loath to get involved—unless "permanent injury has been inflicted," the courts were unlikely to intervene.[46] It wasn't until feminists in the 1960s and '70s catapulted intimate partner violence to the forefront of the social and legal conversation that law enforcement began to consistently treat wife beating as a real crime.

Feminists also advocated for no-fault divorce, in part so that abused women could exit their marriages more quickly and easily. Religious and "profamily" organizations opposed the liberalization of divorce laws, suggesting that no-fault divorce would cause the divorce rate to skyrocket. In the short term, they were right: divorces did go up substantially. A generation later, though, the divorce rate has significantly decreased and leveled off, suggesting that there was a surge of people exiting toxic marriages, and now that marriage is somewhat less compulsory and entered into later in life, people are marrying partners they want to stay with. Opponents of no-fault divorce also suggested that making marriages easier to end would erode marriage as a near-obligatory social status, the foundation of American society and a key marker of adulthood. They were right about that, too. But they were wrong that this erosion was a bad thing.

Today, too many women are still in abusive marriages. But many others simply don't marry their abusers and are often better able to leave their relationships because they aren't legally bound to them. "Marriage has changed enough so that it is no longer the major source of violence against women, and women can leave it," Coontz said. "We've seen domestic violence rates really go down, women can leave a marriage, and of course the more they have access to the gains of the feminist movement, the easier it is for them to forgo or to leave a marriage that will be a source of violence and oppression."

With no-fault divorce, the shift toward seeing marriage as a choice rather than an obligation, and the related decrease in the number of women trapped in abusive relationships, came a series of benefits, not the least of which is fewer men murdered by their wives—in a society where marriage was more compulsory, women who were badly abused sometimes killed their husbands as an escape route. As the broader culture accepted the idea that beating your wife was not a "private" matter but a serious crime, important pieces of legislation, most visibly the Violence Against Women Act of 1994, were put into place, standardizing law enforcement strategies for handling domestic violence and bolstering a national network of shelters for women fleeing abusive partners. The cultural and legal shifts giving women basic rights to be protected from violence have in turn influenced male behavior. Twenty years after the Violence Against Women Act passed, nonfatal incidents of domestic violence are down 63 percent.[47] The number of women killed by their partners declined 26 percent.[48]

If the long history of marriage has been one of partnership, it has also been one of violence. This, like much else about marriage, is changing—although not fast enough.

In large part because of her history, Janet took her relationship with Rome slow and didn't rush into marriage. But she was committed to him, and he to their family. A few days before I met with her, Janet and

Rome had taken their children to the park. ("He has two biological kids but then he also claims his other daughter from his baby mama as well," Janet told me. "I claim her too. So altogether we have seven kids.") While they were walking, Janet noticed her son Jayvion starting to act out, clearly jealous of Rome's other children. "So me and Rome, we were talking about it and Jayvion was like, 'I'm gonna start calling Rome Daddy,'" Janet said. "And I told him, 'That's fine.' Rome, he's been in my life for three years and he made it clear to all three of my babies that he is not going nowhere."

What stressed Janet and Rome out the most wasn't their unusual family makeup; it was money. When they faced relationship strain, Janet said, it was largely because there just wasn't enough to go around, and both adults were under enormous pressure. When I met with Janet in her home, she was optimistic about her future with Rome. A year and a half later, though, they had split up.

The strain finances and instability put on romantic relationships is a fixable problem, and improving the financial realities of those who are struggling would be much more helpful than getting them hitched. Most welfare benefits in the United States, though, are punitive, requiring recipients to work and penalizing recipients both for finding employment and for failing to, while also neglecting to provide child care or to fully treat education like work. Recipients are often required to demonstrate they are either working or looking for work, and have to meet with job counselors and case managers or risk losing their benefits; school or vocational program hours often don't fully count as working hours, limiting the ability of women to move into more steady and remunerative jobs. Many socially conservative welfare reform advocates recognize that these sanction-based welfare systems create disincentives to marry and breed marital instability, but their aversion to welfare dwarfs their promotion of marriage. "The only way to eliminate the anti-marriage bias from welfare entirely would be to make all mothers eligible for these programs regardless of whether they are married and regardless of their husbands' earnings," wrote Rector and Purdue of the Heritage Foundation. "Structured in this way, the welfare system would be marriage-neutral: It would neither reward nor penalize marriage." Still, they didn't get on board, saying it would be too expensive. Instead, they wrote, "a more feasible strategy would be to experiment by selectively reducing welfare's anti-marriage incentives to determine which penalties have the biggest behavioral impact."[49] In other words, play around with cutting benefits and keep the punitive structure in place; just see which cuts lead to more marriages and fewer divorces.

One social welfare program that did succeed in bolstering marriage among the poor wasn't a marriage promotion program at all—it was a liberal welfare reform initiative. Beginning in 1994, the Minnesota Family Investment Program took a commonsense but, sadly, rare view on welfare benefits: make them relatively easy to apply for, and don't put them in conflict with paid work. Low-income Minnesotans were able to retain some of their benefits even if they landed paid jobs. So although their paychecks would make up the majority of their earnings, they still got some help from the government in the form of cash payments, food stamps, and child-care benefits so that parents didn't have to shoulder a massive additional expense just to make sure their kids were safe while they worked. The plan boosted family income and helped lift some households out of poverty, but it had another unexpected benefit: women who utilized the plan were both more likely to get married and more likely to stay married than women on more traditional welfare plans, where benefits are routinely cut off as a result of employment or marriage that marginally increases household income.[50] Even more striking, women utilizing Minnesota's welfare program were significantly less likely to be in abusive relationships. More money, it seems, means both more freedom from violent men and more stability to make relationships work with the good ones.

For all its successes, though, the Minnesota program lasted only a few years, victim to antiwelfare conservative ideology. And so low-income women today, most of whom say they want to marry someday, are in a particularly tough spot—and even though there are proven fixes, the American aversion to social welfare and direct financial aid to the poor outweighs any conservative desire to see marriages work.

In a strange twist after more than a century of skepticism, many feminists have morphed into marriage proponents themselves. Increased gender equality, feminists say, is the key to happier, healthier, and longer-lasting marriages—another argument in favor of feminism. Even some more traditional marriage advocates are coming around—to an extent. "What's good about the net impact of feminism is that it has basically encouraged men to embrace life in the home in a much more serious and interesting way, and I think that is a good thing," Wilcox of the National Marriage Project said. But the feminist emphasis on equality has also contributed to the marriage gap, at least in the short term. "I think where feminism or egalitarianism in particular have had a downside is in the ways in which for a lot of spouses, there isn't a road map for how to do things when it comes to a working family," Wilcox sad. "That can be confusing and a source of conflict. And there's a huge class divide in American life when it comes to marriage."

The new expectations for egalitarian marriages swept in by feminist gains mean that "when you look at the interviews with working-class women, they're more likely to fall back on self-reliance if they can't have equality in a relationship," Coontz said. "To the extent that working-class women are demanding more equality and more consideration in a marriage, and working-class men are less likely to compensate for any failures in those regards by being able to support the women, well yes, that has destabilized marriage."

But that isn't necessarily a bad thing. "People are absolutely rational to be frightened of entering a marriage now that both couples have earning potential," Coontz said. "It's not like a man needs a woman to take care of the home anymore or iron his shirts. He can do that himself or buy the drip-dry shirt. A woman doesn't need the man to earn the money. Increasingly, people want someone who can pull their own weight economically, and if that person can't pull their own weight economically or is emotionally immature and misuses the resources, then you will be better off alone."

Feminism, in making marriages more equal, has made them better—but the benefits of those better marriages are not equally distributed. For women who are educated and financially stable, marriage is both relatively easy to enter into and a winning economic deal, which perhaps explains why college-educated—and disproportionately white—women are more likely to get married than those who don't have a degree.[51] Once those women marry, they tend to stay married, and their relative economic power means their husbands pitch in more around the house (and how much housework he does contributes to overall marital happiness).[52] These couples also have more sex than their unmarried counterparts and report higher levels of sexual satisfaction.[53]

In many ways, I see these statistics, and how they're shaped by the educational, racial, and economic privilege of my cohort, reflected in my own not-yet-marital relationship. My partner and I both have graduate degrees, we make about the same amount of money, we split the rent 50-50, we go grocery shopping as a pair and cook dinner together most nights, and we both do whatever needs to get done around the house without one of us taking on the bulk of the labor or giving the other a chore list. There is a long list of reasons I would marry him, but his ability to provide for me isn't one. That I can set aside his earning potential is a privilege, and a feminist victory in more ways than one—the fact that I can earn my own money and that I don't tie breadwinner status to masculinity or male desirability.

This, many liberal scholars say, is the solution to today's marriage gap. Giving women more opportunities for financial stability in their own right may widen the gap in the short term, especially if men are slow to catch up. But expanding the ways in which families can thrive and continuing to challenge traditional gender roles could close the gap in the long term. "I don't think you're seeing that feminism has gone too far," Coontz said. "It's that it hasn't gone far enough."

If current patterns hold, a quarter of millennials will never get married, and young women and men will routinely stay happily single into their thirties, forties, and beyond. The ties and status marriage once offered are increasingly tenuous, as young people find community, affection, and purpose outside of a single monogamous relationship. More single women and men in college, in the workforce, and in their communities mean it's more common to find love and companionship in life-altering friendships than it is in sexual relationships. A full and varied life may mean women and men, but especially women, are less likely to settle than they once were, seeking out a mate who truly adds value to their already rich lives instead of marrying young because marriage and motherhood offered purpose they wouldn't find elsewhere. According to a 2011 Pew report, two-thirds of young adults between the ages of eighteen and twenty-nine say that "society is just as well off if people have priorities other than marriage and children."[54]

A full and varied life also means that, for many women, it's not just traditional marriage that doesn't cut it but traditional ideas about family and community. We're still ironing out what that looks like, though. As much as I approached marriage with some skepticism, I also wasn't sure what in my life would take its place if I decided to forgo it. Would I be isolated? Lonely and ultimately alone? Before I met my partner, I sometimes fantasized about being a Golden Girl: moving in with a few good friends, maintaining our own outside love lives but sharing a female-only space like family (muumuus optional but recommended). With most of my friends—and eventually myself—on the marriage track, this has become less feasible, but I'm far from the only person who has dreamed of an alternative to the nuclear family model: a small but growing number of adults in the United States do decide to live in shared, family-like spaces without the traditional bonds of marriage or blood. And while some of them are overgrown frat boys concentrated around Palo Alto, many are real grown-ups, seeking the benefits of connectedness and kin without the burdens and expectations institutions like marriage bring.

Back in my hometown of Seattle, I met one of those people, a wavy-haired mother of two named Jennifer Becker. She's college educated, middle class, works full time as an administrator at a hospital, and lives in a comfortable house in a trendy neighborhood. On the way to get vegetarian Thai food and, later, around her big wooden dining table, she told me about her life before this—a life that, on paper, looked like the kind that many Americans aspire to. "I did the very traditional nuclear family," Jennifer said. "Got married right out of college, had two children, bought a house." She and her husband worked and focused on raising their children, zeroing in, as many parents do, on their tight family unit.

This was the dream. "But I felt," Jennifer said, "deeply isolated, lonely, and very unhappy." Eventually she and her husband divorced, and she found herself seeking the kind of connection marriage traditionally brought, without the marriage itself.

As Jennifer and I chatted, two other people joined us at the table: her roommates, Anna-Brown and John, both, like Jennifer, in their forties. A third roommate, Dan, was upstairs and a fourth was out of town. They call their home an "intentional community." Jennifer's kids live there half-time, as does the child of the housemate who was gone the day I visited. The whole thing is very, well, *Seattle:* the community makes its own kombucha, there's a hierarchy of yogurt purchasing (making their own failed, so now the first choice is the organic Bulgarian variety from the co-op, followed by Greek), and they dedicated several minutes of the house meeting I attended to discussing sprout cultivation. On one wall there are a half-dozen sheets of butcher paper on which they'd written their ideals, their goals, and their activities in colorful pen—words like social justice, restorative justice, spirituality, dance, yoga. Anna-Brown and John do gender and racial reconciliation work, helping to heal the wounds of racism and sexism; Dan runs a men's group and is also active in environmental causes. There are weekly meetings and regular house retreats where all five housemates bond and discuss the doings of the community, and decisions get made through a system of "whole-ocracy," a hierarchy-free governance strategy. Conflicts are resolved first through an honest sharing of needs and desires, and if that doesn't work, with restorative justice, a community-based system of accountability. Discussions involve a lot of "I" statements and evaluations of what "resonates" and a radical emotional honesty—there's no beating around the bush of what you want or passive-aggressive commentary.

Yes, it's kind of crunchy. It is no surprise that two of the housemates have backgrounds in psychotherapy. And the guiding principles of this house are not for everyone (although the accountability they required of men and the careful egalitarian distribution of power warmed this feminist author's cynical heart). But in creating an alternative community based in deep social connections, this little house may be onto something.

Jennifer learned about living in an intentional community through a man she was dating, Karl. He invited her into the early stages of community-based living. "I was terrified, like, could I do this? This was so very different from what I was used to," Jennifer said. "It was an experiment, I wasn't sure how it was going to go, but it felt huge because it impacts my children and I wanted to take a lot of care before making a change." Now, Jennifer said, living in a space where adults consciously choose to live out their collective values, "there's a deep nourishment and there's a fire."

Two of the greatest predictors of a happy and long life are connectivity and conscientiousness—living healthily, carefully, and investing time in the people one holds dear. In a remarkable eighty-year study of the lives of 1,500 men and women born in California around 1910, modern researchers looked at length of life, health, and happiness and concluded that "a society with more conscientious and goal-oriented citizens, well integrated into their communities, is likely to be a society of health and long life."[55] For men, that connectivity usually came through marriage. But for women, it took many forms, and the most connected women—although not necessarily the most sociable—lived the longest, healthiest lives. The study found that steadily married women lived the longest out of all groups of women, but they lived only marginally longer than their single counterparts. And the single ladies outlived the women who divorced and then stayed single as well as the women who divorced and remarried.

Many of the women who truly thrived were those who bucked the social conventions of their time: who didn't marry, who traveled the world, who worked exciting and satisfying jobs—women, in other words, who were not tied to the nuclear family domesticity so definitional of their generation. These women didn't lack connectedness; they made connections, a huge number of them, in their own out-of-the-box way, and it served them well. For many women then and now, forgoing marriage for a life driven by other purposes and desires isn't a kind of failure or a recipe for loneliness in middle age but rather an emboldening choice that can lead to a long, pleasurable, and happy life. For others, more traditional social connections serve a similar purpose. In the longevity study, religious women were among the happiest; that happiness wasn't from prayer or dogma but simply from being a part of a purpose-driven community. People with large social networks live longer, as do people for whom compassion and helping others is integral to their lives— church provides both, but so do many other things. A survey of nine hundred Texas women showed that, when accounting for all the hours in their day, the women were happiest when their tasks were completed in the company of others.[56] Another study that analyzed data from eighty countries over more than twenty years found that the amount of time a person spends in relational activities such as volunteering or spending time with friends and family correlated quite strongly to their self-reported happiness, and that the correlation stayed strong even when controlling for variables like education, culture, geographic region, and age.[57] There's little question that of all the factors that lead to well-being and happiness, connectivity and kinship are among the most important.

For a long time, those factors came through the nuclear family, and that family's formal civic and personal connections, usually organized and spurred on by mom: holidays with the extended family, Sundays at church, PTA meetings, children's play groups, adult book clubs. Our connections now look different, in part because of the decline of these formal institutions and in part because of technology. They are broader—thanks to Facebook I know what more people I went to high school with are up to than my mom did at my age—but also shallower, insofar as I know virtually nothing about those same peoples' struggles or daily lives, or even what their voices sound like. Without those more traditional institutions facilitating connectivity, and with marriage happening later and later if it happens at all, there are a lot of us seeking connections elsewhere. Coliving is one of them—and could, for the 5 million Americans who live with roommates,[58] be a satisfactory substitute for my parents' generation's ideal of the single-family suburban house with two kids and a fenced-in yard. To be sure, most of these home-sharing adults don't see themselves living this way forever. Many are living with roommates because it's too expensive to live alone (I and everyone else I know lived with roommates in New York at some point and often left our roommates to cohabitate with a romantic partner). But for others, coliving, whether as roommates attracted by a shared interest in affordable rent or as members of a carefully cultivated community built around shared values, may be a way to foster connectedness and happiness in the shadow of a nuclear-family model that no longer works for many.

Which doesn't mean everyone has to share one house and learn to make kombucha in a communal kitchen. Jennifer's dream, she said, is a multihome community built around collective ideals—she would love to buy a whole city block and build several small houses around a community center, with group dining and socializing areas. Families, whatever they look like, could have their own spaces and benefit from that privacy, while still reaping the benefits of living in community.

One challenge, though, is diversity. In much of the country suburbs have traditionally been segregated by race, and certainly those with higher incomes clustered together. Communities based on shared values also face the critique that they are segregating themselves by ideology—do we really want housing enclaves where everyone is an antiracist liberal feminist, and in the next city over where everyone is a Libertarian, and in the next over where everyone is a religious conservative? There are many benefits in sharing a living space with those who share your values and nurture your best impulses, but there are some downsides, too, including the broader social cost of increasingly fragmented social clusters. When everyone who lives near you believes more or less the same things you do, it can be easy to assume not only that your views are universal but that they are always correct and righteous. Connectedness is crucial for personal happiness, but connecting outside of one's own comfort zone may be even more necessary for a cohesive society.

The night I stayed over in Jennifer Becker's community house, Dan was hosting a men's group meeting upstairs. Together in weekly sessions, men gather to discuss positive masculinity, question social norms, foster connectivity among men, and combat violence, depression, and shame. It's not a church, but its function in the community is just as important—nurturing connections, offering resources and information, promoting shared values and responsibilities, encouraging attendees to evolve into better versions of themselves. As church attendance in the United States is as low as it's ever been, union membership is declining, and young people are increasingly both secular and single, there's something of a vacuum for traditional civic engagement. Groups like Dan's are trying to fill that void.

Unlike a religious group, though, Dan's men's group doesn't enjoy tax breaks; the house reaps no financial benefits from offering its space. Economists and sociologists have long noted that individuals in societies with high levels of trust, connectedness, and civic engagement are more willing to act for the greater good, even if they incur a cost themselves—for example, people in Nordic countries are more likely than people elsewhere to return a wallet full of money.[59] These are the values Dan's group helps to foster, and even though they have tangible social benefits, they see no formalized social support.

The American tax code also isn't particularly nimble when it comes to our modern living situations and new institutions cropping up to facilitate them. It's no longer the norm to become a two-parent married couple with children as soon as people are out of their teenage years; married couples tend to be older and more prosperous. But still, they benefit disproportionately from our tax structure. Individuals living with roommates, single parents, and other sorts of "nontraditional" relationships that are increasingly common go generally unsupported. Jennifer Becker's community has eight people sharing three bathrooms and one kitchen. They save a lot of resources compared to five different families living in five individual homes, but the realities of their household are not reflected in how they file taxes; nor is it clear what their rights would be if the relationships in the house severed.

Janet's efforts to foster connectivity are similarly unsupported by the government. Whether it's taking care of her neighbors and coworkers, watching the kids in the community, or sharing child-rearing responsibilities with friends and relatives, none of it is rewarded with a tax break—or even just recognized and commended. Still, Janet prioritizes fostering feelings of kin and family for her children. She asks male relatives to come over and act as surrogate father figures; her oldest daughter's father isn't in the picture much, but his brother is, and Janet does her best to keep those two connected. "Me and his brother were like peanut butter and jelly," Janet said. "Whenever he has free time he would come over here and talk to my daughter. He claims all my kids; because we all say we were like brother and sister. He tried to keep the communication open with my daughter."

All of this requires some amount of stability, leisure time, and a sense of trust and safety. But Janet's community is unstable and shapeshifting for reasons outside of her control. People often disappear because of incarceration, mental or physical illness, poverty, or violence. She doesn't always feel safe—while we sat in her living room on a bright summer day, she had the shades drawn and the door locked.

The old models for cultivating community—church, marriage, even labor unions—are increasingly obsolete. Across the country, though, new institutions, formal and not, are taking shape, where people can come together, talk about their values and their hopes, and advocate for each other's needs. They're in Seattle houses. They're in New York City yoga studios. They're in Little Rock backyards. They're in housing project parking lots. They're still largely unrecognized by government, the way the old institutions were subsidized. But the more we breed positive community connectedness, the less it may matter whether individuals marry or not.

With so many other options on the table, why promote marriage above the others? Wilcox of the National Marriage Project said that marriage is fundamentally an institution of social organization, a way to order our lives and society and "to govern our fundamental urges and desires to be in communion with another person."

"Marriage exists to lend meaning, purpose, direction, stability to intimate human relationships and any kids that come along," Wilcox said. "I'm not one who says marriage is perfect or everyone experiences a high-quality marriage, but I would argue that marriage is the best way that societies organize this. And of course marriage through time has and will continue to evolve and must do so if it's to survive in this century into the next."

How it evolves, though, is central to the tension between traditionalists and progressives. "I think marriage is an expectation of lifelong commitment," Wilcox said. "It's about enjoying the trust and security that come with the horizon of commitment, and enjoying commitment to mutual investments, practical, financial, and emotional, both in one and other and also in your relationship and, if you have kids, in your family as a whole. Of course that sounds kind of loveless. But that would be one way of framing marriage."

In the months I spent discussing and considering whether marriage was for me, Wilcox's frame only partially resonated. I did crave that trust and security, and the idea of investing in a lifelong partnership was appealing. It also felt like, having met the person I wanted to be with forever, calling him my "boyfriend" indefinitely—putting him in the same category as the guy I dated at sixteen—felt deficient, disrespectful, and inaccurate. But I did wish there were other options for recognized, respected ways of organizing a family. Marriage could be one institution for people who have found a partner with whom they want to form a lifelong romantic commitment and enter into a set of legal benefits and obligations. But there could be additional statuses with diverse sets of benefits and obligations, meeting the needs of people entering into various relationships with different levels of commitment and obligation—kids, shared property, joint finances. Making marriage one recognized and supported relationship choice among many—not the pinnacle of a relationship, not a cap to an adult life, not the point of dating—seems like it would make marriage all the more special and valuable, while offering institutions that could meet peoples' needs and address many of the social ills that come with holding marriage to such a high bar.

"We have to come to terms with the fact emotionally and policy-wise that marriage is not the only game in town, and it's not the only game people will play over the entire course of their lives," Coontz said. Organizing societies and systems around marriage makes little sense when people are single for longer periods than ever, more unmarried women and men are having babies than ever before, and many never marry at all. But even as its role in American society has changed, marriage remains the norm. And, depending on where you live and your socioeconomic class, there comes an age when people start to worry if you remain unmarried. In more conservative enclaves, that might be twenty-five. In liberal corners of Manhattan, it's more like thirty-five. But the age does come, and most women end up married close to their community's arbitrary deadline. The later that deadline, the better their marriages do, but there are a great many couples who marry because they're a certain age, they've been together a certain amount of time, and getting married is simply the next logical step.

In going through the arguments for and against marriage, there was a lot that turned me off about the "marriage as the next logical step" model. Women's lives, their accomplishments, and their happiness, much more than men's, are shaped by the person they marry. Among women in the longevity study who did marry, who the women married mattered a lot more for their happiness than who the men married. A husband's well-being matters a lot more to both partners' quality of life than a wife's; that is, a difficult, unhappy husband is more likely to pass that misery onto his wife, to the point where it shortens her life expectancy. A difficult, unhappy wife doesn't have the same impact on her husband. Neurological studies also indicate that prolonged exposure to marital stress results in shorter responses to positive stimuli, something that is associated with lower levels of well-being. It's obvious that stressful marriages can make you unhappy, but they actually train your brain to be less happy about most everything else.[60]

Divorce, too, is a major source of instability, depression, and early death. The ripples of that unhappiness trickle down to children, who are in turn less healthy and have shorter lives if their parents divorce. Divorce, of course, gets a bad rap, and not all of it is deserved—ending an unstable, miserable relationship is better than continuing it. Making divorces difficult to get keeps women physically, psychologically, and economically vulnerable, which is why feminists fought so hard for no-fault divorce laws. But although divorce should be easy to get, it's still better to avoid it, if possible. One way to do that is to marry later—the human brain isn't even fully developed until the midtwenties, and it seems ridiculous to encourage people that young to enter into what is in theory a lifelong contract with another individual. Later marriage also means more time to build stable financial footing, to date, to test out different kinds of relationships and develop the attendant communication skills and emotional competencies that it takes to support a stable marriage. And testing out different relationships means an individual has a better idea of what they want in a partner, and what jibes with their personality and what clashes.

One obvious way to decrease the divorce rate is to encourage life paths that push back marital age—accessible and affordable higher education, for instance—and to curtail the kind of pervasive inequality and economic hardship that leads to marital stress and discord. People divorce for a lot of reasons, but money is chief among them. An economically stressed couple is at an immediate relationship disadvantage compared to a financially stable one. Offering even a small cushion in the form of a living wage, social welfare programs, and affordable child care could go a long way, especially in the lower economic classes where divorce is endemic, to helping marriages last longer.

Another way is to just not get married. That brings its own set of disruptions, especially if there are children involved. But it would be nice if lifelong single status wasn't considered some kind of failure or lack or even a bold choice, but rather was simply unremarkable—and if there were other options for organizing one's life and the society in which one lives. Surveys of divorced people tell us a lot about the degree to which marriage itself continues to benefit men more than women: very few divorced women—just 15 percent—say they want to remarry, while twice as many men do. More than half of divorced women say they never want to get married again.[61]

Still, I may eventually be one of the people who keeps marriage from going extinct. Ultimately, I adjusted to the marriage idea, not because I was interested in redeeming a knotty social institution, but because, imperfect or not, these institutions continue to matter. Marriage feels appropriately validating of my relationship. It also seems like a monumental challenge, and one I am increasingly ready to take on. After dozens of conversations with family and friends, I whittled down my view of marriage to this: in getting married, not only are you making someone else a part of your family, but you get the rare opportunity to both choose that family member and to commit yourself to staying family even if you temporarily fall out of sync; and you get to see what a commitment that deep, enduring, and intentional looks like on the other side of the inevitable challenges. I thought about my sister, who I adore, but with whom my relationship was difficult through our bratty teenage years. We were family, and we continued to love each other, but there were periods where we didn't like each other very much. And there were others in which we were best friends, each other's biggest fans and favorite people. Many of my happiest moments have been with my sister, and the depth of our relationship is borne of its complexity. Had she been just a friend, maybe we wouldn't know each other anymore. But she's my family, and so she is here, mine always. I wanted that kind of familial tie with my partner: starting in these amazing years when we are mad for each other, making a choice to carry through the inevitable ebbs, and seeing how and in which directions the relationship blooms when it breaks through the hard parts.

This is perhaps not the most romantic view. But the more research on marriage I read, the more I felt secure in the knowledge that I'm at least approaching it with every advantage and every possible tool at my disposal. I've also become convinced that although marriage doesn't create happiness out of thin air, it can create the conditions for everyday pleasure and lifelong contentment to thrive. There should be a greater diversity of romantic and connection-based institutions and statuses; that much is obvious, and we would all be the better for it. But there isn't, and in the absence of a plethora of options, I concluded that not putting this particular relationship on the culturally agreed-upon pedestal of marriage would do the relationship, and the two of us in it, a disservice—and potentially breed discontent.

It's still not clear whether marriage is something we will do. But if it is, I imagine the day we finally do it will be a turning point in our relationship, even if we go home to our shared apartment and co-cat and nothing looks any different. It won't be the most important day of either of our lives, nor the most monumental, nor either of our greatest accomplishments. But I do hope, as far as individual days go, it'll be one of the happiest.

6

Bossypants:
Making Work Work for Women

Independence is a heady draught, and if you drink it
in your youth, it can have the same effect on the brain
as young wine does. It does not matter that its taste
is not always appealing. It is addictive and with each
drink you want more.

—*Maya Angelou*

IF YOU HAD asked me as a child whether there were girl jobs or boy
jobs, I would have told you no, that I could be anything I wanted. And
what I wanted to be was Nellie Bly or Linda Ellerbee: an enterprising
journalist who cared about the world and reported stories that changed
it. I don't remember admiring, let alone really knowing the names of,
many male journalists, despite their dominance in the field. Would I
have seen journalism as a viable career path at such a young age (I was
under ten when I first read a Nellie Bly biography) if the occupation's
only public faces were male? Maybe. As a small child I begged my parents to write down my stories before I knew how to write a sentence,
and in my preteen years I read so much my father once disciplined me
by not taking me to the library; maybe that love of words was enough
that I would have become a person who wrote for a living whether or not
I had ever seen another woman do it.

Maybe.

More probably, seeing Linda talk about the five Ws of journalism—
who, what when, where, why—on Nickelodeon and reading and re-
reading books about Nellie allowed me to see my future reflected back
at me in a way that wouldn't have happened if I had only watched Tom
Brokaw or read about Upton Sinclair. In this, I was not alone: girls of
my generation grew up seeing women in nearly all sectors of employment—rarely in equal numbers to men but enough that they were visible. In 1992, when I was nine, a record four women were elected to
the US Senate, bringing the total number of female senators up to six.
This achievement was apparently so monumental that 1992 was deemed
"the year of the woman." One of the newly elected senators was Patty
Murray from my home state of Washington—a woman who years earlier
had been denigrated in a campaign for school board as "just a mom in
tennis shoes," an insult that so roiled my own mother she intentionally
laced up her own tennis shoes to go vote that year and cheered when
Murray held up her practical footwear in victory. Sure, ninety-four out
of a hundred senators were still men and a female president still seemed
laughably far off. But at least there were six.

Part of being a "good girl" when I was growing up in a middle-class
suburb of Seattle was demonstrated by achievements, and so we—the
girls—racked them up. By high school, advanced placement and college
prep classes were dominated by young women. And the girls weren't
just book smart. Among the group of young women who were in my
AP classes, I'm hard-pressed to think of a single one who didn't have
a robust list of other talents: there were varsity swimmers and basketball players, accomplished cellists and violinists, thespians and student
leaders, photographers and painters. Many of us went to colleges where
women also outnumbered men.

The environment in which I grew up was in many ways a perfect
postfeminist storm. Legal discrimination was at least in theory a thing
of the past; no state would tell a female lawyer, as they once did, that
she could not practice law because of her gender; colleges were no longer male-only domains; and girls went to college to get a job, not a
Mrs. degree. Female role models could be found in just about every
occupation—not many of them, but at least one or two. And young
women lacked the sense of entitlement and full liberation enjoyed by
many young men, so many of us played by the old rule of femininity

that demanded women and girls please authority figures. But we did it in a new context where that pleasing—getting top grades, striving for academic and extracurricular achievement—put us at a real advantage.

Today, about 60 percent of college degrees are earned by women, and women also hold about 60 percent of the advanced degrees awarded in the past decade.[1] We earn just under half of law degrees and degrees in medicine.[2] Among law firm associates, women make up 45 percent.[3] For women under thirty, the gender pay gap is the smallest it has ever been, with women making nearly as much as their male colleagues. When Nellie Bly was doing her groundbreaking reporting on abuse of the mentally ill in New York asylums, she was one of only 208 female journalists working in the United States, out of 12,308—just 2 percent of the profession.[4] Today, we still aren't at parity, but nearly four in ten reporters are female.[5] When my mother was my age, just 4 percent of wives outearned their husbands. Now 40 percent do.

Decreases in economic discrimination have come with marked up-ticks in women's health and well-being. And decreases in political discrimination have brought benefits not only for women but for also for men—according to one 2007 study, women's increasing visibility and power in the political realm are tied to increases in men's life satisfaction. Those positive effects of female political participation go double for women.[6]

We have, per Virginia Slims, come a long way, baby. Which is part of the reason I was so shocked when I started working as a first-year associate at a Manhattan law firm and noticed it was always the female partners, of whom there weren't that many to begin with, placed in charge of ordering lunch.

It was a small thing, but it was one in a series of small things I began to notice the longer I was in the workforce: all of the secretaries and most of the paralegals were women. Many of the male partners had stay-at-home wives enabling them to work the long hours they in turn demanded of younger lawyers; as far as I could tell, none of the female partners had a full-time stay-at-home spouse. The firm offered a part-time option; a handful of mothers took it, but no fathers.

As far as we have come, women still lag behind men. Although the gender wage gap has been cut in half in just a half century, pay differentials persist even when women do the same job for the same number of hours, and they are much worse for black and Hispanic women. Although jobs are less segregated by gender than they were in the past, with women pouring into traditionally male-dominated fields, occupations that are majority female are chronically underpaid and low status. And although women have more financial freedom than ever before, too many still say they are stressed and stretched to the limit.

Study after study shows that working brings women better health, more independence, and greater happiness. But social expectations, unconscious biases, constrained choices, and a system built around the outdated model of a male-headed family mean that, for women, the benefits of work are offset by a long list of downsides. Our workplaces have changed dramatically over the past several decades, but our workplace policies have been slow to catch up—most American women work outside the home, but our government and many businesses still operate as if all families have two parents, a working husband, and a stay-at-home wife. More households are headed by single women than ever before, and even in heterosexual two-parent homes, men typically don't do their fair share of child care and housework, leaving women with a "second shift" after their paid workday is done. These challenges could be overcome with political commitment, corporate changes, and individual betterment: policies and regulations that treat workers like people who first and foremost deserve to enjoy their lives, companies that choose humanity over ruthlessness, and men who fully show up at home. Instead, the hodge-podge of policies aimed to improving workplace conditions that have been tried so far often end up pushing women even further out of the workforce rather than making it easier for them to thrive there.

With less pay and greater demands, it's not hard to see why even women who love their jobs would fantasize about calling it quits or conclude they would simply be happier at home full time. In the face of inhospitable workplace policies and a political climate often outright hostile to the interests of working women, problems that are in fact political are reframed as individual: we hear that women with children can simply make choices about whether to work or stay home, that each family's decision is personal, that what matters is "balance"—and yet somehow it's always women charged with doing the balancing, and women who are hurt when they fall off the tightrope.

My first job was that mainstay of preteen girls everywhere: babysitter. I took child-care classes at a local community center, learned basic CPR, charged five dollars an hour, and can still remember getting home from my first official gig and opening my palm to see a twenty dollar bill. It was all mine, and it felt sweet.

In high school and some of college, I worked as a lifeguard and a swim teacher at a few local pools. At the strong suggestion of my mother, I dutifully put a little bit of my earnings away in a retirement account; some of the rest was saved for college, some spent on new clothes and cheap beer. It was freeing, having my own money, but it was more than that: I met new and interesting people; I gained skills and confidence; and when I helped a clingy, whimpering four-year-old named Adrian grow into a back-floating, water-happy five-year-old, I felt a sense of profound satisfaction. At the end of the summer, he shyly presented me with a maple-leaf-print pencil case from a family trip to Canada. I still keep it in my childhood bedroom.

For all of American history, women have found a sense of identity, purpose, and freedom in work—even in jobs we don't think of as careers. But the past century has been particularly radical for women and work. In 1890, 63 million people lived in the United States, but only 4 million women and girls (then, girls aged ten and up could legally get jobs) were either employed outside the home or wanted to be; three out of four of these women were single. Although most married women worked at home or on their farms, less than 5 percent of them were in the work-force outside of their own property.[7]

From the late nineteenth century through 1920, unmarried women filtered into the workforce, but according to economist Claudia Goldin, most were poor; many were the children of immigrants, and the work was dirty and difficult, and the majority left the workforce when they married.[8] Industrialization created a neat divide between at-home work and the paid labor force, and women were routinely excluded from the latter, both formally and informally. Labor unions, seeing single women as competition for jobs, routinely barred them from membership[9]; women started their own, but they were often smaller, less influential, and less powerful. From the turn of the century through 1930, women's labor force participation crept up marginally but remained at about 20 percent.[10]

New jobs for women opened up in the 1920s, '30s, and '40s, and many of them were in offices as secretaries and clerical workers, where the days were shorter and the work less perilous. In 1926 New York City, the Barbizon Hotel for Women opened to house exactly these kinds of young women: upwardly mobile, newly educated, and always single, "ambitious, discriminating young women," as one advertisement put it.[11] ("Modern amazons in the making" was the *New York Times'* take upon seeing women fencing, swimming, and playing squash in the Barbizon's athletic facilities.[12]) The quarters were small and dorm-like, but it wasn't the property that was the sell; it was the propriety: yes, single women were coming to the big city, and, yes, they could date and set themselves on the path to marriage by having men to their social engagements and in public waiting rooms, but strict supervision meant that no men were allowed in their bedrooms. The Barbizon was, according to *Time* magazine, "one of the few places in Gomorrah-on-the-Hudson where a girl could take her virtue to bed and rest assured it would still be there next morning." And although some girls came for a long career—the Barbizon housed a striking number of women who would go on to be famous models, actresses, and writers, from Grace Kelly to Joan Didion—there was a time limit. "If you were living there when you were over 25, it was *over*," Betsy Israel, author of *The Bachelor Girl*, told *Vanity Fair*.[13]

Before it was over, though, it was fun. "My room was about as big as a mailbox, and I shared a bathroom with another girl," wrote actress Susan Kohner. "But I felt wonderful because I was paying my own way. I was on my own." The sliver of independence offered by the Barbizon could be life changing, even for women who jumped from there straight into traditional marriages. "I think most of us can look back at that time and feel like it was a place where we felt safe and happy," former Barbizon resident Sandra Hart told *Bust* magazine. "It was the beginning of us all spreading our wings and leaving home, and developing our own stories."[14]

Most single working women, of course, were not Barbizon girls—Barbizon girls were nearly all white and middle class, with parents who could afford to send them to New York with a little pocket money. But the kind of young woman the Barbizon catered to—educated, working for a paycheck, and dating to pick a mate instead of courted with parental approval—was a new invention, and one starting to thrive outside of the big city, too.

World War II brought with it both an economic boom and a substantial uptick in employment for both single and married women.[15] Some 5 million women entered the labor force between 1940 and 1945,[16] many of them married. During the war, about 60 percent of single women were employed outside the home, as were close to a quarter of married women.[17] That influx of female workers, and the patriotic message behind it, profoundly shifted cultural narratives about women and work: according to historian Stephanie Coontz, a 1943 poll of more than 30,000 high school girls found that 88 percent of them wanted to have a career.[18]

That didn't happen quite as easily as those high school girls might have expected. By 1947, after the war was over, employers had laid off more than 3 million women. A year earlier, a poll by *Fortune* magazine asked Americans whether women should have equal employment opportunities: only 22 percent of men and less than a third of women said yes. Around the same time, Coontz wrote, came the publication of the book *Modern Woman: The Lost Sex,* a runaway hit "in which [the authors] described feminism as a 'deep illness' and accused career women of seeking to symbolically castrate men."[19]

In the postwar years, the average marriage age dropped, and the number of children per family rose for the first time in a century, as what Coontz called the Cult of Domesticity took hold. Single women were fewer and farther between, and their employment rates steadily decreased as well. But, as the 1960s turned to the '70s, the numbers of single working women again skyrocketed and has more or less been on an upward trajectory ever since.[20]

What single women found in work was what men, single and married, always had: money, freedom, a social life outside of the home. Not all women had glamorous jobs or high-flying careers—most didn't and worked in more menial positions—but for legions of women, work has meant an identity that is just theirs and not contingent on their status as a wife, mother, or daughter.

"Sometimes I get concerned about being a career woman," Mary Tyler Moore's character, Mary Richards, said on Moore's eponymous show, which aired from 1970 to 1977. "I get to thinking that my job is too important to me. And I tell myself that the people I work with are just the people I work with. But last night I thought, what is family anyway? It's the people who make you feel less alone and really loved."

For single women today, work is a normal part of life. Unless you have a trust fund and don't want to work, are in school full time, have a disability that means you can't work, or can't find a job, if you're a single woman in America, you almost surely work for pay.

But how we work, and how we think about work, remains gendered. Women are more likely than men to work in care professions—child care, elder care, nursing, social work. And there is still no cultural consensus that women could, or should, derive a sense of identity from work, that delaying marriage and working is an acceptable choice, or that it's a good thing to have an identity outside of a relational one (mother, wife).

"The so-called rise of women has not threatened men," conservative author Suzanne Venker wrote for *Fox News*'s website. "It has pissed them off. It has also undermined their ability to become self-sufficient in the hopes of someday supporting a family. Men want to love women, not compete with them. They want to provide for and protect their families—it's in their DNA. But modern women won't let them."[21]

For young single women, the drumbeat of tradition still plays in the background: although more of us are going to college than ever before and most will work at some point in our lives, many women plan on getting married and taking time off when they have children—even well before they've met a person they plan to marry. Others who don't plan to drop out of the workforce are nevertheless fed a steady diet of articles and panels on "work-life balance," consistent reminders that for women, having a job isn't a given part of life but a challenge to be reckoned with. And women are still, on the aggregate, less likely than men to see their careers as definitional to their lives and identities.

All of that combined means that women are more likely than men to underestimate the amount of time they'll spend working, and accordingly make fewer investments in their careers.[22] It was a point Sheryl Sandberg made, to some controversy, in her book *Lean In,* when she implored women, "Don't leave before you leave." Despite some pushback on the idea that women have one foot out the door even before they have babies, several studies have shown that when women reach their early twenties, both when they are in the formative stages of their careers and when they may be considering marriage, fewer express plans to work than do women who are teenagers or who are over the age of thirty-five. Being married makes women less likely to plan on working; so does having kids. Black women are more likely than white women to plan to work, but a similar pattern of dipping work plans in the early twenties holds across races.[23]

So although 67 percent of white eighteen-year-old women and 73 percent of black eighteen-year-old women say they plan on working, less than half of white twenty-three-year-olds and 61 percent of black twenty-three-year-olds say the same. But the average American woman is twenty-six when she has her first child—black women are, on average, twenty-four, and white women twenty-seven.[24] And the average American woman is twenty-seven when she gets married.[25] That means many women assume they'll stop working before they've even walked down the aisle or taken a positive pregnancy test. And it's hard to blame them, given the mix of toxic messages, from the childhood princess fantasies (that Mr. Right will sweep you off your feet and financially provide) to the feminist-minded admonishments (that no one, or at least no woman, can "have it all") to the family values lectures (that kids need their mom at home, and that being a mother is the most important job in the world). Even for young single women, motherhood is presented as both a goal and a career-derailing threat (or promise). Lots of women adjust their expectations accordingly.

By the age of thirty-two—when, presumably, more of them have dropped out of the workforce—the proportion of women who plan on working in the future ticks back up: 67 percent of white women plan to work by thirty-five, as do 82 percent of black women.[26] Perhaps the women who change their minds and decide they would like to go back to work are reacting to a financial necessity; perhaps they've decided traditional gender roles aren't all they're cracked up to be. But the conflicting messages women hear while they're single, the cultural landscape that remains skeptical of women's full workplace participation, and the conscious and unconscious choices many women make in response, can handicap women's achievement, even long before they have children.

They can also make her pretty unhappy.

In 1953, Dana Mazurek's life looked a lot like other women of her generation. Born Dana Wyatt in rural West Virginia, she met Ed when she was a striking raven-haired twenty-one-year-old. He was a handsome Marine four years her senior who had recently returned from the Pacific theater. They were married within a year and headed for Chicago to live near his Polish American family. Using the GI Bill, they bought a house on the South Side, in a middle-class neighborhood populated mostly by Jews and, as Ed called them (and himself), Polacks. By the time Dana was thirty, she was a homemaker with five kids, each a year and a half apart, all skinny like their mom and blond like their dad, with the kinds of names that sound perfect for a charming family sitcom: Rosie, Mikey, Vicky, Timmy, Mary.

Behind closed doors, though, life didn't look like 1950s TV. "These days we call it domestic abuse," Mary, Dana's youngest, told me. But back then she would just say, "He beat me up." "They didn't have those fancy words back then," Mary said. "You were allowed to hit your wife, you were allowed to hit your kids. Back then, the cops would just say, 'Stop,' or, 'Come on, be a better wife.' So it was just very, very different."

Dana stayed, until she didn't: she and Ed divorced when Mary was two. "When I was an adolescent, probably twelve, I found some pictures of her that had been taken obviously when she had been beat up by Dad," Mary said. "They were pictures of large bruises, on her legs, her arms, she obviously had to have those for court. She never knew I saw them, I never told my siblings, but they haunted me for a very long time. Now my dad swears up and down on the good old Catholic Bible he never did anything, but I don't think my mom was out gallivanting with five kids."

Nor was she gallivanting after the divorce. Dana was thirty-two with five kids under the age of twelve, two of them still in diapers, to support on her own, in an era of staunchly conservative family values— single mothers were rare, and divorced women pariahs. Unable to afford tuition, the older kids had to leave the local Catholic school, and the church was unwilling to help them out. "The Catholic Church turned its back on her because now they were divorced," Mary said. "When my dad wanted to get remarried, his marriage to my mother was annulled— what does that make us five kids? That also irked her and hurt her—*I had five kids and what do you mean I didn't exist?* That's some of the resentment that I think the divorce left me with; resentment toward some establishments that turned their back on divorced women."

That annulment, and Ed's remarriage, came almost twenty-five years after Ed and Dana divorced. When they split up, Ed moved back in with his mother, where he stayed until he remarried, and continued working as a bookbinder at the printing company RR Donnelley, which back then printed the phone book and many of the big magazines, including *Life, Time,* and *Sports Illustrated.*[27] Dana got the house and the children. "She was not June Cleaver," Mary said. "They never showed you the Cleavers when the kids had the measles or diarrhea. They never showed June washing shitty diapers, or June with five kids a year and a half apart, and June is a single parent who couldn't afford a babysitter even if she could find one."

Dana didn't have formal education past high school or much in the way of work history, but she got to work anyway. Someone had to keep the lights on, and the minimal child support that she had to take Ed to court to get wasn't going to cut it. "She had to fight to get fifty-six dollars a month for five kids," Mary said. "I remember the checks coming every month. When I turned eighteen there was a note with the check that said, 'This will be the last money you will ever get from me.' It was like, 'Happy Birthday Mary.'"

To keep the house and put food on the table, Dana had two or three jobs at a time: she would work as a crossing guard from 8 a.m. until 3 p.m., and then as a waitress from 4 p.m. until midnight. She took other odd jobs as well, selling Avon for a while, working at a soap factory for a while—whatever would pay the bills.

"All my life I remember her always saying her legs hurt," Mary said. "'My legs are killing me, my legs are killing me.' She was always on her feet. She had to wear high heels as a crossing guard and panty hose; as a waitress she at least wore waitress shoes. But her legs killed her all the time. She was never off of 'em very much."

This was not the typical 1950s womanhood. In 1955, most adult women were married. Fewer than a third of married women worked, and fewer than a quarter of marriages ended in divorce; even most divorced, widowed, or separated women were not in the paid workforce.[28] This reality was the result of long-standing expectations for women: in 1939, 90 percent of people said married women shouldn't work if their husbands were employed—perhaps a reaction to job losses during the Great Depression and the sense that a woman working was taking the rightful job of a man. And even in 1941, nearly 90 percent of school districts had a policy of not hiring married women.[29]

Nevertheless, in some ways, it was easier for married women to work than it had ever been: regulations barring married women from work had largely been rescinded,[30] and the influx of women into the economy during the war had shifted perspectives, at least somewhat. Although the vast majority of women with children under six stayed home, increasing numbers took jobs once their children were in school or out of the house. By 1950, nearly half of the female workforce was married.

Even so, the 1950s and early '60s saw a peculiar reversal in progressive trends, including those toward women's rights. The *Leave It to Beaver* era was a historical aberration, but one many Americans continue to idolize as authentic, traditional America. Perhaps the defining characteristic of the era was women's turn to the domestic, wherein they got married sooner and had more babies than their mothers—the first time in recorded American history that marital age went down and the average number of children a woman had went up. The prevailing sensibility was that for women, life as a suburban housewife was supposed to bring ultimate happiness. But women were still working and many didn't want to quit, so the rules shifted: white, middle-class women could work, but the job had to be an extra little thing, not a real career or something that defined her identity, and her husband had to be the primary breadwinner.

In her book *A Strange Stirring: "The Feminine Mystique" and American Women at the Dawn of the 1960s*, a history of the social conditions that led to the groundbreaking book *The Feminine Mystique,* Coontz unearthed a 1954 advice column in *Coronet,* a then-popular general interest magazine, where a woman, Jacqueline, was described earning a decent salary while single; when Jacqueline married, the magazine recounted approvingly, she "gave up her job, and took one that paid less, because she knew how important it was for her husband to feel he was unquestionably supporting her." In a 1956 issue of *Life* magazine, the journalist Robert Coughlin interviewed a number of psychologists about marriage and gender. In summing up their expert views, he wrote that women who worked out of desire rather than necessity were "rejecting the role of wife and mother." Any woman who did so, he added, "may find many satisfactions in her job, but the chances are that she, her husband and her children will suffer psychological damage, and that she will be basically an unhappy woman."

Work, women were told over and over again, would make them miserable; sacrificing their own desires for their families was the true path to happiness, and during her childbearing years, a woman's life "should reflect her full emotional acceptance of the role she is living: receptive, bearing, nurturing," as the psychiatrist Edna Rostow put it in a 1962 issue of the *Yale Review.* Doing otherwise "can adversely affect the development of her full identity"—because a woman's full identity was that of a mother and wife.[31] Coontz summed up this new justification for an old requirement thusly: "The assignment of women to a passive, secondary role in social life, which had once been ascribed to duty, social custom, God's will, or innate differences in ability, was now declared to be a woman's only route to personal fulfillment."

But the pursuit of personal fulfillment and pleasure, it turned out, was less about what actually made women happy and more about money—and men being able to make it without competing with women, and men's ability to "have it all." Men's wages rose steadily through the 1950 and '60s, while women's stagnated. Although women had earned more than 63 percent of what men did in the early 1950s, by 1963 they made less than 59 percent. The share of women in high-status jobs also went down.[32]

By the time Betty Friedan's *The Feminine Mystique* was published in 1963, a generation of women had largely been at home most of the time and told they should be the happiest women on earth; if they weren't, it was their own psychological dysfunction. The book that asked mostly white, middle-class women to ask themselves, "Is this all?" sold millions of copies to women who realized the nagging dissatisfaction they felt wasn't because they were crazy but because they wanted more.

At the same time, the picture of what would enable women to actually *have* more was coming into focus. Reliable birth control was increasingly available and more and more women were using it to plan their families. A vibrant civil rights movement had been breaking down racist laws and norms, and many African American women were pointing to the hypocrisy of their own third-class status, their rights hampered by both race and gender even while they were among the bravest and most vocal advocates for equality. More women were going to college, and a few were graduating with plans for a lifelong career as well as, or sometimes instead of, a husband. By the early to mid-1960s, the cultural blip of the hyperdomestic '50s was showing signs of decline.

Mary, Dana Mazurek's youngest daughter, was ten when *The Feminine Mystique* was published. Her older sister Rose had just graduated from Jones Commercial High School, which was set up to train America's future secretaries. Vicky, another sister, went there too; both Vicky and Rose learned shorthand, typing, and a whole set of marketable skills, and got clerical jobs soon after graduation. When Mary entered high school, both Dana and Ed expected her to attend Jones Commercial as well.

"This is the late '60s with the Vietnam War, with women's lib starting, and the rules for this secretary school were you had to wear a hat, white gloves, your skirts had to be midknee, and you had to wear pantyhose and heels," Mary said. "This is when kids were in jeans. I would have to walk down the street in a hat and gloves and pantyhose, going to secretary school when everybody else was having sit-ins. I hated it. After six weeks I begged my mom to let me go back to the regular high school, and she never batted an eye—she said yes."

Mary was shocked. Her sisters, at least, were trained for something, "and I came out of high school and I was trained for nothing," she said. "But I was different from my two sisters. The world was changing, and I was changing." It was, she said, "my own internal stirring." And although she didn't realize it at the time, looking back several decades later, she was part of something bigger. "I think it was happening for a lot of women," she said. "That secretarial high school ended up closing a few years later, due to lack of applicants."

Nor did her sisters continue on as secretaries. Vicky joined the Air Force; Rose, many years later, became a lawyer.

After Mary graduated from high school, she and her mother moved from their house on the South Side of Chicago to an apartment on the North Side, which they hated. Mary's best friend, Marlene, had a mother named Helen who lived in a mobile home in the south suburbs and invited them by, noting there were a lot of single women around. It was a nice place, so Dana bought a mobile home, and she and Mary moved to the park. "As a twentysomething living in a trailer, I did feel a little embarrassed, but it was very nice," Mary said. And she got to live there rent-free while she figured out what to do with her life—her brothers were in college, funded by her father, but he wouldn't pay for the girls to go. Marlene was in community college to be a licensed practical nurse, and encouraged Mary to give it a try. "She said, 'Mary, why don't you do that?' I said I didn't want to," Mary said. "But she dared me.

Back then I was still one to take a dare, so I tried one class, I aced it, I liked it, and it opened up a door."

She also became, she said, something of a militant. "I was just pissed off," she said. "I was from a divorced family, my mom was single, she didn't have a highfalutin job. The boys got to go to college, and they got umpteen chances to blow college, and I never got one chance.

She asked her father why he paid for college for the boys, who got arrested and kicked out, but not for the girls. "My dad said, 'Well, for women it's a waste of money. They go to college, they get married, and they get pregnant.'" And Mary thought he kind of had a point: while she knew she was going to college to get a job, she didn't necessarily expect it to last forever. "I don't think I gave it a whole lot of thought, but I think I thought I would stay at home and have children," she said. "That's how I envisioned life. I didn't envision myself being like my mom. I didn't aspire to be like my mom. I aspired to not ever get divorced, to have a nice house, kids, to live the traditional life with two kids and a white picket fence."

She paid her own way through community college, and at nineteen started dating Mike, a guy from her South Side neighborhood. In 1978, when he was twenty-five and she was twenty-four, they got married—after paying his way through law school by working at the local steel mill, he had taken a legal job in Ottawa, Illinois, eighty miles away. "We were trying to commute back and forth and we decided, well, we'd better just get married," Mary said. "It wasn't an on your knee proposal, there was no asking my father, it was just one of those next steps—very unromantic, but very pragmatic." By 1981, they were off to Seattle, Washington, for Mike's job. She worked as a nurse the whole time, and at twenty-nine she had her first child—me.

"Don't take this personally, but the only reason I got pregnant is my doctor said, 'You're gonna be thirty, you've gotta start having a family, or you'll be a high-risk pregnancy or you won't be able to get pregnant,'" she said. "And I went, holy moly, then I'd better start a family!"

I was born in 1983, and my sister was born a year and a half later. My mom scaled back, working the night shift two days a week so she could be home with us during the day. Leaving her kids was wrenching—having children was "a love affair," she said, and "there are not descriptive emotional words to explain the thought of being away from your babies"—but the family needed her income, and she also liked her job and what it meant for her independence.

"I said to myself, I will never be unable to get a job. I will never be fully dependent on a man. That's a little bit of the cynicism I have toward men. Every month that check came in, and every month it was a reminder to my mom: here's the man that beat me and I have to take his money."

Unlike my grandmother, whose status as a divorced working mother made her an outlier, my mother was a woman of her generation. Between 1950 and 2000, the number of hours married women spent at work more than doubled.[33] In the 1970s, when my mom was working her first few jobs, women across the country were surging into the workforce, and for the first time more than half of American women between the ages of twenty-five and fifty-four worked outside the home. By the time I went to college, more than 75 percent of women in the same age group were in the labor force.[34] I expected to be one them.

For all the emphasis modern adults place on the dreams of the young— asking children what they want to be when they grow up, telling them they can be anything they want—Americans remain ambivalent about whether adult women working, and especially mothers working, is actually a good thing. This starts young: girls not only do an average of two more hours of chores per week than boys, they're less likely to be paid for them.[35] There's a broad understanding that work is valuable for men, that it feeds their sense of importance as providers and meets some existential need related to identity and sense of self. This, indeed, is a very Psych 101 idea, illustrated by Maslow's hierarchy of needs: humans require food and shelter, and then security, as baseline needs. Once those are met, one can address psychological needs of belongingness (love, friendship) and self-esteem (feelings of achievement and accomplishment). And finally, if those psychological needs are satisfied, one can achieve one's full potential in self-actualization by harnessing personal creativity and innovation.[36]

This final stage was not supposed to be on offer for women, a foundational point in Friedan's *The Feminine Mystique*. Historically, women weren't supposed to have their need for individual identity formed in part through their work, because women weren't supposed to have individual identities at all: they melded into their husband's identity when they married ("the husband and wife are one, the one is the husband," according to the laws of coverture), and they were supposed to find satisfaction by caring for their children and husbands. Women's identities have long been relational—daughter, wife, mother—rather than individual. Which is perhaps why women finding individual identities tied to their work makes so many people uncomfortable.

In one 2013 *Fox News* segment, commentator Lou Dobbs introduced a discussion on breadwinning women by saying, "I want to turn to a study from Pew Research, a study showing that women are becoming the breadwinners in this country, and a lot of other concerning and troubling statistics." He went on to note that "we're watching society dissolve around us."[37]

This is not the 1950s, and the vast majority of Americans—nearly 80 percent—do not think women should return to traditional wife-and-homemaker roles. But something shifts when you replace "woman" with "mother": just over half of Americans believe children are better off with a mother who is at home full time and does not hold a job. Only 8 percent said the same thing about fathers.[38] There's a kind of schizophrenia happening in the United States when it comes to women and work. Most women do work, and few think a return to strict gender roles is desirable or even possible. But the idea that a woman's first obligation is to her children and that it's best if she tends to them full time, remains—and it's clearly not the case that this is a gender-neutral desire to simply have one parent home. It's a demand placed specifically on mothers.

Even among feminists, it's difficult to have honest conversations about the value of mothers working, in part because the workplace is so inhospitable to women generally (and mothers especially) that work often doesn't feel particularly pleasurable, in part because so many women are stuck in low-status, low-wage jobs and in part because many of us hesitate to say anything that could be perceived as criticizing other women's choices to not work, lest we set off another battle in the Mommy Wars. Conservatives have a clearer vision, one that flat-out says it's best for women to stay home and rely on a breadwinning husband, at least when their children are young—a vision that relies on having not only a husband but one who can make enough money to support an entire family. That feminists are so often unable or unwilling to say that working outside the home isn't just a necessity but that it's good for women—that it's good for mothers—is perhaps one reason we have not yet seen the political groundswell necessary to pass the workplace policies we so desperately need.

This lack of a coherent and vigorous moral argument in favor of women working is especially unfortunate given that women are better off when we work outside the home: working correlates with better mental and physical health, and working women not only report higher levels of happiness than women who don't work, but the more hours women work, the happier we are (with the exception of women who have very small children and work very long hours; more on that later).[39] Mothers who work are also good for families: daughters of working mothers tend to be higher achieving, make more money, work themselves, and spend more time with their own children than do daughters of women who did not work; men who were raised by working mothers do more work at home and help more with child care than sons of stay-at-home moms.[40] And women in the workplace is good for women in the aggregate: men who have stay-at-home wives are more likely than men with working wives to penalize their female coworkers, denying them promotions and viewing them unfavorably.[41]

Not working also puts women at risk. Without financial independence, they are more likely to get stuck in abusive or simply unhappy relationships. Staying home can be isolating and often means fewer options for making friends and connections outside of an unhealthy relationship. Many marriages end in divorce or death, and others are thrown into turmoil by disability, illness, or separation; women who drop out of the workforce can find themselves in quick financial ruin if their partner leaves them, gets sick or injured, or dies. Although many women who take time off to have children assume they can come back into the workforce easily, that's often not the case, and even a few years off can have a lifelong impact on earnings. And although there's no doubt women are unduly penalized for taking time off, it does seem odd to assume there would be no consequences—I haven't worked as a lawyer for more than three years now, and it would almost certainly be impossible for me to resume working at a law firm at the same position and pay scale as before, even though I've remained in the workforce in a different capacity.

Working confers benefits on the individual working woman and to women more generally—especially when there are women in power. Although the number of women working at a given company doesn't typically influence the adoption of female-friendly policies, having women in core positions does.[42] Women, in other words, have to have a seat at the table in order to make decisions that impact other women. Yet women at the decision-making table makes many, including self-described feminists, skeptical. Collectively, we seem to hold women to a higher standard, something I saw when my female colleagues at the law firm would express frustration at the lack of mentorship from female partners. There were a handful of women in senior positions and a glut of young female lawyers vying for their mentorship; the female partners had as much work to do as anyone else and were also in charge of much of the at-home stuff the male partners didn't worry as much about. While the female partners were mentoring a half-dozen young women, many of the male partners didn't mentor anyone at all, or had just one or two young men to focus on. Yet it was the women many of my own colleagues branded as insufficiently helpful—women, it seemed, were obligated to help other women, while men were not.

The problem with getting women into decision-making roles is a bit of a circular one: because we aren't used to seeing women in power, we often react badly to women either in or seeking power, and that keeps women out of power, which in turn makes it harder to normalize women in power and break this whole cycle. Women who are "firsts" or perceived as figureheads are often held to impossible standards and made to jump through hoops men simply are not. Women are also appraised more harshly than men for the same behaviors, while men get professional boosts just by being men. Take, for example, the Howard/ Heidi study conducted at Harvard Business School: Students were presented with a case study of a venture capitalist, alternately named Heidi Roizen or Howard Roizen, but otherwise identical. According to Frank Flynn, one of the authors of the study, "Students were much harsher on Heidi than on Howard across the board. Although they think she's just as competent and effective as Howard, they don't like her, they wouldn't hire her, and they wouldn't want to work with her. As gender researchers would predict, this seems to be driven by how much they

disliked Heidi's aggressive personality. The more assertive they thought
Heidi was, the more harshly they judged her (but the same was not true
for those who rated Howard)."[43] Being aggressive may be an important
characteristic for a venture capitalist, but women who demonstrate it
are nonetheless penalized. Women who act in more traditionally feminine ways don't fare any better—they may be well liked, but they are
less respected than their male peers. And so women seem to have a
choice: they can be respected but disliked, or liked but not respected,
the bitch or the bimbo. Presumably, this will change when more women
are at every level of power—and indeed, studies have demonstrated
that greater political power for women has brought with it significant
improvements in women's life satisfaction (and men's life satisfaction
as well).[44] Getting there, though, remains difficult.

I thought about my grandmother, who passed away in 2008, when I was
in Janet's Raleigh living room. She was sitting down, body sore, giving
me a modern rundown of many of my grandmother's same woes: domestic violence, unplanned pregnancies, unending financial stress. Janet,
like most of the women in her family, has worked from a young age in
low-wage jobs. She's usually managed to eke out a living, but barely, and
not always—supporting her three kids has been a blur of crises, including bouts of homelessness. But not working at all? Until she was injured
in a car accident, that hadn't occurred to her.

   "I've been working since the age of fourteen," Janet told me. "I have
a passion for doing hair—so my first job, I was fourteen, was working at
this hair salon. I was the washer; washing hair and watching the beau-
ticians doing hair. My talent was, I could watch someone do hair and
in my mind I can do it, and even when I get home I could do the same
thing here as well."

   Janet worked at two different beauty salons and went to school, where
she had a hard time—her home life was turbulent, and she wanted out
of high school and into the real world. At eighteen, she started working
in restaurants and in retail; like at the hair salons, she realized she had a
gift for working with people.

   "I love working with customers," she said. "I don't know why, but I
love the older people. . . . I love putting a smile on their faces, asking
them for their IDs—you know, saying they don't look their age, because

they asked for a senior's discount, and I'll be asking for their IDs. Just putting a smile on their faces makes me feel good."

In the United States, African American women have, at least anecdotally, worked outside the home in greater numbers and for longer hours than their white counterparts. The Bureau of Labor Statistics didn't start looking at race until the 1980s, so reliable figures from the first half of the twentieth century are hard to come by, but historians generally agree that there is a more entrenched tradition of work for pay among black women than white women.

Today, it remains true that a plan to work is more common among African American women than white women. Still, a greater proportion of white women are in the workforce than black women,[45] and the unemployment rate for black women is twice as high[46]—suggesting that many African American women didn't "opt out" but are rather looking for work and can't find it. Studies also find that although having a child and having other family income (usually from a husband) significantly decreases white women's workforce participation, it doesn't impact black women's nearly as much: African American women with children work on average forty-six fewer hours per year than African American women without children—less than an hour per week. (Hispanic women show similar patterns.) But white women work on average two hundred fewer hours per year than their counterparts without children at home.[47] Unsurprisingly, married women who work outside the home tend to have partners who do more of their fair share domestically, and that is certainly true of black women. African American husbands do much more at-home work than white husbands, spending more hours on both housework and child care.[48]

Which doesn't mean anyone is living the feminist dream. The American labor market remains deeply segregated by both gender and race, although gender segregation is more pronounced.[49] Male-dominated jobs are more racially segregated than female-dominated ones—white men, essentially, find themselves often working alongside other white men, while female-dominated jobs tend to be both lower paying and more diverse.[50] Women, then, are both underpaid generally and underrepresented in high-status, well-remunerated fields, with black and Hispanic women paid the worst.

Statistics on the gender wage gap are as ubiquitous as they are hotly debated. Among full-time workers, women make 79 cents for every dollar men make; the gap is worse for African American (63 cents), Native American (59 cents), and Hispanic women (54 cents).[51] Critics of these numbers point out that they aren't comparing apples to apples: white men make more, they say, because white men tend to be better educated and in higher-paying fields. Some critics, like the antifeminist Christina Hoff Sommers, say women choose to make less money than men: "Women, far more than men, appear to be drawn to jobs in the caring professions," she wrote in the *Daily Beast*. "In the pursuit of happiness, men and women appear to take different paths."[52]

But even when you compare apples to apples, women make less. And that's true when you control for a whole slew of factors that could explain differentials in pay—occupation, college major, hours worked, length of employment since college, age, marital status, geography, type of college. The American Association of University Women found that just a year after college, men with the same characteristics as their female colleagues made 7 percent more. Ten years after graduation, the gap had nearly doubled, and they made 12 percent more.[53] And when industries shift from being male dominated to female dominated, wages drop.[54] It's not that women freely choose low-wage work in the pursuit of happiness; it's that jobs we think of as female—and into which women are often funneled—are accorded less respect and lower pay.

Women with kids face particular penalties, and the discrimination has nothing to do with their choices or qualifications. Studies have found that mothers applying for jobs are both less likely to get an offer and if they are offered the job, are extended a lower starting salary than both women without children and men; fathers, on the contrary, are more likely to get the job and are offered more money than men without kids.

Women are also more likely than men to scale back or drop out of the workforce, which obviously impacts their earnings. In the American Association of University Women study, 23 percent of women had quit working ten years out of college, and another 17 percent had gone part time. Among men, just 2 percent were part time, and only 1 percent had dropped out.[55] Maybe that's just a "choice." But when you look at the people who have the most flexibility—high-earning, college-educated men and women—relatively few choose to drop out of the workforce entirely. Contrary to the stereotype of the stay-at-home mother as a toned blonde in Lululemon yoga pants, stay-at-home moms are more likely to be poor and more likely to be immigrants: 34 percent of them are poor, compared to just 12 percent of working mothers.[56] They also tend to be less educated: nearly half have a high school diploma or less.[57] Only 5 percent of stay-at-home mothers with working husbands have a master's degree and a family income exceeding $75,000—few, in other words, fit the stereotype of affluence that allows them to choose to opt out. The overwhelming majority of affluent, highly educated stay-at-home mothers are white or Asian; just 7 percent are Hispanic, and just 3 percent are black.[58]

Janet is now technically a stay-at-home mom, although she doesn't see herself that way. Having grown up partly in foster care, she was declared independent at seventeen, at which point she took over guardianship of her two younger brothers, one in eighth grade and the other in ninth. She worked full time at a grocery store to support her family; when she missed a day of work, she got fired. At twenty, she had her first daughter, while living in a homeless shelter after she fled an abusive relationship. She had been planning on going to cosmetology school in Atlanta, but when she got pregnant decided to stay in Raleigh instead. She ended the relationship with her oldest daughter's father, a man she started dating as a teenager, and starting dating the man who would be the father of her second daughter. He was kind, Janet said, but had other problems and ended up in and out of jail. They split up, and she met the man who would be the father of her son, the baby of the family. It was good, at first, until he became abusive as well.

"Because I didn't have a mother or a father growing up, I needed someone to be there for me, to love me," Janet said. Having never witnessed a functional relationship up close, it was hard for her to identify signs of abuse before the situation escalated. She tried to leave; he wouldn't let her. He went to jail, but as soon as he got out he was back at her house, breaking her windows, stalking her in the bushes, showing up at her job.

"It was a couple of times that we'd come home and he had broken into my house. He was upstairs in the house, that right there's scary," Janet said. "I was trying to save up to move out of here, so I was doing a little bit better, working a full-time job, I got my first vehicle. He busted my tires, trying to bust up my windows in my vehicle—money I don't have. When we were in the house he would bang on my door, from ten o' clock at night all up until the morning."

Janet got a restraining order, and another one. Her ex did so much damage that her landlord tried to evict her—and couldn't only because the restraining order proved she was a domestic violence victim. The manager at the restaurant Janet worked at helped her keep her job, until he was replaced; the new manager fired her. She got a new job at a fast food restaurant, and shortly after her ex beat her up again—and this time she was arrested because, she said, she fought back. "I had two black eyes, a busted lip when I got locked up and I suffered a concussion," Janet said. "When I got out that night, I went to work the next day."

When Janet went to drop some of her ex's clothes off at his father's house, her ex showed up and tried to kidnap her son. Again, there was violence, and Janet ended up jabbing him with her keys several times in an effort to get her son back. He tried to press charges against her and failed; instead, charges were filed against him. Two police officers familiar with Janet's case called her every day to check in and drove her to and from the trial. "Officers Leonard and Marcel, they had picked me up and made sure that I got back and forth to court," Janet told me in her living room. "This is the first time I'm talking about it and not crying. So, I'm proud of myself."

Five witnesses came forward and testified on Janet's behalf. Her ex is now serving a forty-one-year prison sentence.

When Janet did work, it was, like my grandmother, two jobs back to back, usually for just above minimum wage. The hours were often inconsistent, which would throw a wrench in her child-care plans. As her family's sole earner, she was one of many low-income single women to hold the role of breadwinning mom: 40 percent of mothers are their family's sole earners, and more than two-thirds of women whose families rank in the bottom 20 percent in terms of income make the same or more than their husbands. And that's if they have husbands or partners who are employed full time at all—something just 14 percent of low-income women can say.[59] Janet didn't get maternity leave when she had her oldest daughter; when she had her son, she was given three weeks through North Carolina's Work First program, despite the fact that she had a C-section and needed more time to recover. She ended up ripping her incisions out and had to be hospitalized.

About 17 percent of American workers have the kind of unpredictable schedules Janet has long dealt with, according to the Economic Policy Institute.[60] And like Janet, most American private-sector workers do not get paid maternity leave—just 12 percent have the option of taking paid time off when they have a baby.[61] About 60 percent can take unpaid leave, but for the many workers who work because they need the paycheck, unpaid maternity leave isn't particularly helpful.[62]

Janet was with Rome for more than three years, and the additional income he brought in was beginning to stabilize the family. But then a car accident put her out of work and landed her back in a precarious financial situation. "When the doctor first told me I wasn't able to work, I did not tell my job because it was like, if I tell my job I'm not supposed to work, how am I to pay my bills?" Janet said. "I'm a single mom. No one's giving me any money." Work did eventually become too painful, and she's now relying on North Carolina's Work First program again for the first time since she had her oldest daughter. "I'm getting $297 a month," Janet said. "I will receive that check once I see my job counselor. I have to see my job counselor every two weeks. For some reason the government thinks that people can live off of $297." She's on several different pain medications and not supposed to drive, but she has to drive to see the job counselor; the unemployment office tells her to get a sit-down job, but there aren't many of those on offer, and Janet doesn't see how she's supposed to drive back and forth to work while taking medication that makes it dangerous for her to operate a car. And so for now, she's stuck in her house, frustrated and unhappy, spending too much of her meager income on gas.

"I have a therapist come out here every Saturday for me and also for my babies," Janet said. "I got diagnosed with depression, multiple stress disorder, also borderline personality disorder; and not working—that really turned my life upside down. I can't stand being in this house like this. I've been through this stage last year, when I was out for the longest, I got to the point where I was suicidal. I overdosed several times on my medication."

The physical and psychological strains created by Janet's history, coupled with her precarious economic situation, are the new normal for American workers, particularly those who don't make enough money. In a 2011 American Psychological Association survey, 36 percent of workers reported feeling stressed out, with many saying low pay contributed to that tension.[63] Multiple studies have found that workers who feel insecure in their jobs suffer a bevy of physical and mental health problems, and employees who work nonstandard shifts—the night shift or irregular hours—not only have a higher risk of serious health issues (eating disorders, heart problems) but see their marital happiness decline, their sex lives worsen, and their chances of divorce go up. The kinds of insecure and temporary jobs that tank psychological well-being are also the kind of jobs populated largely by poor women and women of color. And although work does generally improve women's health and well-being and working longer hours is actually associated with better health in women, having a preschool-age child reduces those health benefits. For mothers of small children, working longer hours is associated with poorer health, although there seems to be a sweet spot: mothers of six-and-under kids who work between one and thirty hours per week report better health than both women with small children who work more than thirty hours a week and women with small children who don't work at all outside the home.[64] It's the time bind, not the work itself or the child, that seems to make women less healthy. And that time bind is something we could fix with policy—if we wanted to.

The one thing that keeps Janet afloat is her children. The dream, Janet said, is a combination of basic financial stability and that coveted "balance": that she could both enjoy time with her children and work full time at a job that would actually bring in enough income to support her family. Both time and money, though, have proven elusive, no matter how hard she tries and no matter how much she sacrifices one for the other.

"If I was able to work full time and still be able to spend time with my babies, that would be the most important thing to me," she said. "My babies will live better than how I'm living right now. I missed my baby's first two years, and that is my oldest child. And, you know, that's very important. I wasn't even there when she started walking because I was working two jobs. It hurts. I don't even remember when she started talking. I was always working all the time."

She was there when her second daughter walked, but only because she was unemployed. She had found a new job by the time she had her son, and so she missed his first steps, too. "When I work, I get up 4:30 in the morning," Janet said. "I work. And then normally I'd do doubles and get home at about one o'clock in the morning and my babies were asleep. This is the most time I ever spent with my kids. And I've been sitting here thinking about that. I worked all of these years."

A few years after I graduated from law school, I was working at a law firm in Manhattan and casually dating a rotating cast of low-maintenance men who were happy to meet up late if I got off work after 10 p.m. and wouldn't get bent out of shape when I had to cancel dates at the last minute for long nights in the office. That narrowed the dating field to marginally employed Brooklyn creatives for whom a midnight beer at a dive bar on a Wednesday was normal enough courtship and other lawyers, who were inevitably less interesting but always up for a late-night whiskey. One of those nights with one of those lawyers, I started to vent: the only reason the partners at the firm could work the hours they did is because so many of them had stay-at-home wives who took care of every other aspect of their lives, managing their social calendars and raising their children, and making it possible for them to "have it all." I was a single woman—no one was picking up my dry cleaning for me, or stocking my fridge with food, or making small talk with clients' wives so I could focus on business.

A few weeks earlier I had been at a fundraiser where the firm had a table. I attended, largely because it was an important cause but also because it would be a good opportunity to network and get to know some of the partners better; instead, I was seated next to one senior associate's wife, and although she was a very nice woman, she was a full-time caregiver for their children who was very sure that being a mother was every woman's most important calling. I spent the evening answering questions about why at twenty-seven I wasn't married yet and why I hadn't yet put the pieces in place to have children. It was sexist bullshit, I told this lawyer I was dating. He was the same age as I was and at the same point in his career but was regularly invited to play golf on the weekends with his male bosses and felt confident he would make partner.

My observations, my date said, were correct, and he had seen the same dynamic—which was why he would only marry a woman who agreed to stay home with their kids. Children need full-time care, he said, and the period in which he would be marrying and having children was the same time in which he planned to make partner. It's not that women have to stay home, but someone has to, and it wasn't going to be him. A stay-at-home wife was the only way to make it work.

We stopped dating not long after that. This was not a guy I planned on marrying or even dating seriously, but he was also not the last man I met to express a similar view. I was struck at the time not just by how much his comments surprised me—like all of my high-achieving girl-friends, I was attracted to ambitious, driven men and wanted to marry someone with an interesting career, and I had naively assumed that most men felt the same way about ambitious, driven women—but by how blithely the stay-at-home wife plan was offered.

It turns out this kind of division in expectations is endemic, even—perhaps especially—among highly educated Americans who work in white-collar professions. In a 2014 study of Harvard Business School students, men and women were equally ambitious and equally desiring of both professional success and personal happiness.[65] But the similar-ities ended there. Nearly all of the women surveyed expected that in their marriages, their careers would be equally important as their part-ner's. The men, though, mostly said that their careers would be more important than their wives'—and their expectations were exceeded. Among Gen X men, for example, 61 percent expected their jobs to take precedence; in 70 percent of marriages, it did. Ditto child care: about half of women thought they would be their children's primary caregiv-ers, and in reality, more than two-thirds ended up in that role. Eighty-six percent of Gen X and Boomer men also expected their wives would be in charge of caring for the children, and they were usually right.

Among Harvard MBAs already in the workforce, many more men than women reported high levels of professional happiness—and many more men than women also reported that they were given high-level re-sponsibilities and occupied senior management roles. The overwhelm-ing majority of women stayed in the workforce, and those who did drop out rarely preferred to devote themselves to full-time motherhood; in-stead, researchers found, "the vast majority leave reluctantly and as a last resort, because they find themselves in unfulfilling roles with dim pros-pects for advancement." In other words, men wound up with as much at-home support as they expected and were able to build their careers accordingly; women wound up doing more at home than they wanted to or intended, and found themselves frustrated and disappointed.

For women, though, better options don't really exist. In the conversa-tion with my lawyer date, I was simultaneously fascinated and appalled by how easy this man thought it would be to set up a traditional life, and how emulating the powerful men in his office by securing himself a stay-at-home spouse was a rational and readily available life choice. I realized that, even if I wanted to imitate those same men (which I most surely did not), I probably couldn't—for all the jokes men my age would make about wanting to be a househusband, staying home full time and being financially dependent on a woman is not a thing the vast majority of men do willingly. Just 7 percent of American fathers are stay-at-home dads, and only one in five of *those* stay-at-home fathers have chosen not to work in order to care for their children—close to 80 percent either can't find work, are too sick or disabled to work, are in school, or are retired.[66] That means there are only about 420,000 dads who stay home and care for their kids by choice—less than half a percent of the US population.

Even though women and men work at near-equal rates, work in the United States remains a man's world. Our institutions and policies don't serve women much better today than they served my grandmother when she had to navigate them as a single working mother in the 1950s.

Traditionally, both stay-at-home spouses and the US government have helped men to build their careers and expand their wealth. Neither source of support has been available to women. Today, we think of "welfare" as something that helps poor single mothers, and feminist pushes for things like paid parental leave and government-funded child care are met with derision from self-appointed family values advocates. The conservative Heritage Foundation called government-funded preschool "Nanny State Childcare" and stated that "preschool and childcare should remain the domain of families, community preschools, and church-based care."[67] During his successful run for governor of New Jersey, Chris Christie called the state's child-care program "glorified babysitting."[68] Paul Smith, a Republican politician in Maryland, opposed funding the state's Head Start program, explaining his reasoning by quoting a pamphlet from the Mormon Church: "By divine design, fathers are to preside over their families in love and righteousness and are responsible to provide the necessities of life and protection for their families. . . . Mothers are primarily responsible for the nurture of their children."[69]

But as much as they emphasize the importance of that maternal nurturance, conservative lawmakers have declined to support it, especially for women on welfare—there isn't the same value placed on their at-home maternal care. North Carolina's Work First program, for example, "is built upon the belief that all people have a responsibility to their families and community to work and provide for their children"; it's not a way to enable women to care for their kids at home.[70]

The paternal responsibility of providing, by contrast, is one the federal government has been quite keen on enabling—they don't call it welfare, but the federal government has taken significant steps and spent vast amounts of money to improve the welfare of its white male citizens. In the 1930s, the Federal Economy Act required that only one member of a married couple could work for the federal government; although the law was technically gender neutral, more than three-quarters of the spouses who resigned were wives. In her book *Under the Bus: How Working Women Are Being Run Over,* Caroline Fredrickson wrote that "the National Recovery Administration explicitly pegged women's wages below men's, even when they were doing exactly the same work. For example, men in the garment industry coded as 'Jacket, Coat, Reefer and Dress Operators, Male,' earned $1 per hour, while the code 'Jacket, Coat, Reefer and Dress Operators, Female' paid only 90 cents per hour."[71]

The New Deal brought with it reforms that both conceived of workers as white and male and overwhelmingly benefited those same men. Domestic, agricultural, and retail labor were excluded from the Fair Labor Standards Act, which required a minimum wage and other labor protections, hanging women and especially women of color out to dry while improving conditions and pay for labor that was disproportionately male.[72] "Ninety percent of black working women received no benefits from the new laws providing for a minimum wage, maximum hours, and assistance for the unemployed and elderly," wrote Fredrickson. "By leaving out these workers, New Deal Legislation actually ensured that, relative to other workers, African American women particularly, and domestic and agricultural workers generally, would be worse than before." Even today, many domestic workers lack basic legal protections.

The federal government also shoveled money into infrastructure projects like highway systems, which simultaneously employed lots of men and made possible the kind of male-headed single-family household that came to symbolize traditional 1950s suburbia. These unearned benefits for white men in turn made the labor of women and people of color cheaper and more perilous. All of this helped form the building blocks of today's economy, where women still do more low-wage care and domestic work, and male-dominated work still pays more. Even jobs that require similar skill sets, like being a housekeeper versus being a janitor, pay differently depending on which gender they're more closely associated with (housekeeping, a traditionally female job, pays less on average than traditionally male janitorial work and tends to come with fewer benefits).

In the 1950s, federal GI benefits—like the ones that helped my own grandfather buy a house—were available to 40 percent of the twenty- to twenty-four-year-old male population; those benefits extended low-interest mortgages with low down payments to millions of male-headed families, most of them white.[73] Even Social Security explicitly excluded certain classes of workers who were disproportionately female and of color, including domestic laborers and farm workers. Those same categories of workers were excluded from the National Labor Relations Act, which among other things allowed employees to advocate for better treatment through collective bargaining, until the 1970s.[74] Other social welfare programs including Medicaid and worker's compensation mostly helped the white middle class, and white male workers in particular—something I saw in my own family.

"As you fast forward and grandma turns sixty-five, what she gets out of Social Security is zippo, because she was a waitress," my mother told me. "She had squat for Social Security, versus what my dad got for Social Security, because he got to work full time at a good-paying job. She got half of his distribution. So if he gets $1,000 a month, she gets $500, but he still gets the thousand. There is no reward, no credit, no recognition for raising children. So what grandma got in Social Security was penalized again, slapped again, ostracized again. You have no value, again. Because you were poor and uneducated and had to work in low-paying jobs, all you get is low-paying Social Security based on your low-paying jobs."

Twenty-four percent of the federal budget in 2015 went to Social Security spending—$888 billion.[75] And make no mistake, it's crucial that the government supports people as they retire. But Social Security remains attached to earnings, and men—white men in particular—earn more than women and are in the workforce more consistently in part because women support them with unpaid labor, which goes largely unrecognized in Social Security payments. (American women spend almost twice as much time on unpaid work as men but slightly less in paid work, so while women work more total hours than men, they get paid for fewer of them.[76]) Spending on programs intended to help women who work or who have dependent children is tiny compared to Social Security.

At the same time as government programs are failing to meet the needs of modern families, the demands of workplaces have gotten more intense. Only about 7 percent of companies offer child care either on site or near the worksite,[77] even though the irregular hours required in many professions can make it difficult to plan your own child care. Americans simultaneously work too much and too little: white-collar workers are putting in more hours than ever before, while low-wage workers are often unable to get enough hours to make ends meet. Americans take less vacation than workers in our economic peer countries. And this is notoriously one of the only countries in the world without government-mandated paid maternity leave, and certainly the only rich nation on earth that doesn't help new mothers take time to recover and bond with their babies without risking financial ruin.

As a result, families are stressed out and miserable, and women especially are. In 2009, much was made of a study finding that women were less happy than they were in the less feminist 1970s.[78] "Liberated and Unhappy" was one representative headline from *New York Times* columnist Ross Douthat[79]; "Did feminism make women miserable?" asked Barbara Ehrenreich at Salon (her answer was no).[80] The researchers Betsy Stevenson and Justin Wolfers found that although women's lives have improved and their opportunities have expanded in the previous thirty-five years, their subjective well-being—their happiness—has declined. Conservative commentators such as Douthat suggested that although there may be a feminist explanation, one could look at the study and "see evidence of a revolution gone awry, in which women have been pressured into lifestyles that run counter to their biological imperatives, and men have been liberated to embrace a piggish irresponsibility." To fix it, he suggested "some kind of social stigma" on single motherhood.[81]

But the problem isn't too much feminism; it's not enough. Women have added outside-the-home work hours to their day while still doing more at-home work than men. While men do more work at home than they did thirty-five years ago, they've also dedicated more time to activities they find pleasant, while women have not.[82] Everyone, it seems, is stretched thinner than they used to be, but women are pulled particularly taut.

In response, some families simply go back to the old model of the woman staying at home and the husband working; others stagger shifts (which is also associated with higher rates of marital dissatisfaction and divorce) or cobble together something that doesn't quite work but, if they're lucky, doesn't totally fail. This is routinely couched in the language of "choice," and of course some of it is. I hear married women insist time and again that they made the best choice for their families by staying home because the cost of day care was nearly as much as their salaries—as if paying for child care is the sole job of the mother and not a collective obligation for both parents, and as if leaving the workforce doesn't mean missing out on career advancement and better pay down the road. This is technically a choice. It is also a choice shaped by bad policy, an insufficient safety net, and entrenched stereotypes about men and women. None of which makes it a particularly free choice at all.

In pursuit of a couple that seemed to have "balance," I wound up in Takoma Park, Maryland, at home with Howard Wilkins, MaryBeth Hastings, and their two daughters. At 7 a.m., MaryBeth and Howard were drinking coffee, feeding their youngest daughter Molly, who is eight, breakfast, and talking about the trailer for *Dr. Who* season 9 before Molly went off to camp for the day. Their big brown mutt, Buffy, was splayed out on the ground, her liquid chocolate eyes following MaryBeth and Howard around the kitchen. It was August and the kids were home from school, so the older girl, Sydney, twelve, was sleeping in. Half an hour later, MaryBeth was driving Molly to camp while Howard took Buffy for a walk. Then both parents retreated to their respective corners of the house to work at their consulting jobs, popping out every once in a while to talk about work projects, grab a snack, or decide who's shuttling which kid where and when.

"We entered into a partnership when we got married, and we both saw it that way," Howard said. They do their best to split child care. They both try to be emotionally present for their children. Howard does the dishes and MaryBeth does the laundry. They cocoach the soccer team.

I had set out to meet a couple in which a high-earning husband had scaled back after having children—not someone who simply flipped the traditional script and became a stay-at-home dad, but a man who did what so many women do: made conscious choices to balance work and family.

It proved harder than I thought it would. None of the couples I knew personally fit that mold—relatively few of my friends were partnered with kids in the first place, and the ones who were didn't have husbands who scaled back when they had kids. I had a personal interest, too: I'm ambitious and career focused and don't plan on compromising that; I want a partner who is the same. And although I know lots of "power couples" in which both partners are successful and ambitious, few are parents. It seemed, anecdotally, that couples became quickly imbalanced when children entered the picture, with his star continuing to rise and hers dimming. A mutual acquaintance put me in touch with Howard and MaryBeth, suggesting that theirs was the most feminist marriage in the neighborhood.

That feminist marriage didn't come easy. "One thing we had talked about before we had kids was this kind of made-up plan that I would stay home with the first child and he would stay home with the second child," MaryBeth said. When they had Sydney, MaryBeth, a consultant who works on gender and international women's rights, was in a career transition: the funding for the program she was working on recently cut. So she decided to go to massage school and, when Sydney was small, scaled back her consulting practice and worked three days a week as a masseuse. Howard, also a consultant, worked at a large firm that kept him on the road regularly; he took a month of paternity leave, which was unusual in his field, but then was back at work and often gone for days at a time. "I was traveling a lot and MaryBeth had this quote-unquote flexible schedule, and that was probably as unbalanced as we've been over the course of fifteen years," Howard said. "That was the worst in terms of anything related to the home was falling on her. Because I just wasn't around. I'd show up on the weekends trying to reinsert myself into a set of processes and wasn't all that helpful."

Both of them were professionally unhappy and personally frustrated. When Sydney was two, they were both close to their breaking point. "It's not like Sydney was old enough where she was saying, 'Daddy you're never around,'" Howard said. "But I just started to step back and say, 'Okay, I see where this path leads.' It is a financially very rewarding path. But MaryBeth and I started to talk about and think about what is the family structure we want, what kind of father do I want to be, what kind of a husband do I want to be." The answer: not one who provides financially but not emotionally. So he went on the mommy track.

It's a derisive term, one tossed around to mean jobs that are lower stress and less demanding, and routinely populated by women. We had "mommy track" at my law firm, too, and only women took advantage of them. There, they were technically "part time," which meant you still worked more than forty hours a week, but you could work from home on Fridays (your day off, sort of) and it was more acceptable to leave the office by six. This was in exchange for a pay cut of tens of thousands of dollars; most of the lawyers, including most of the mothers, didn't think it was worth it. But, for Howard, the scaled-back job works. He works from home now and takes alternate Fridays off. MaryBeth works from home too, having scaled back her consulting practice when she was pregnant with Molly, their second daughter, and also takes Fridays off. They eat dinner as a family—she cooks and he does the dishes. She does most of the laundry while he takes care of the dog and the lawn. Her work ebbs and flows while his stays fairly steady. "There are weeks when I'm kind of crazy and I think it's good for the kids to see me crazy sometimes, so they understand their dad is not the only one who works in the household," MaryBeth said. "And then I have weeks like this last week where I haven't had that much and I can help Sydney build her IKEA bed. So I like that intensity and then time off."

Some of it's traditional, and they both agree it's imperfect, but it's more balance than most couples find. Both say their joint decision to continue working while still prioritizing their family has made their marriage better and made them better parents. "It has allowed me to be more present and connected in; there is a comfort level and a connectivity around being around each other more," Howard said. "The other reality is just a very practical one. It puts less pressure on some of the time we have together because we have more time together. There's more freedom for each of us to go do our own thing because it's not like, okay, I have this narrow window of time which is either family time or personal time and that's it, because everything else is taken up with work."

They also both believe it's a good model for their daughters—although that was a secondary concern. "Yes, we are modeling this to our daughters, but we are modeling it because this is how we want to live," Howard said. "I would love to say, yes this was a conscious choice, we're going to walk the walk, and by walking the walk this will send a message to our children, and our daughters specifically, that this is a reasonable expectation to have and this is how they should be thinking about the world and partners and equality in their relationships. But it was more about us feeling like this is who we wanted to be as a couple, and who I wanted to be as a dad, and what MaryBeth had the right to expect as a professional woman herself."

Howard and MaryBeth can find that balance because of a combination of factors, only one of which is personal commitment to egalitarianism. They're both well-educated, white-collar professionals and have job prospects outside of their current roles, which makes negotiating for flexibility that much easier. They make enough to provide a comfortable middle-class life for their children. They have options for balance and flexibility that are simply unavailable to women who are single, or whose jobs are low wage and low status, or for whom missing a paycheck might mean homelessness. Watching Howard and MaryBeth, and hearing about their relationship, was inspiring—it also made me wonder what women do if they aren't a MaryBeth and if they don't have a Howard for a husband.

Individual choices, clearly, are not enough—and yet individual choices still matter, a lot. Men's choices are especially salient here: it's a choice to scale back if you can afford to, or to pick up a broom and dustpan, or to get the kids off to school and not assume it's their mother's responsibility. Social stereotypes about men also shape expectations, behavior, and male happiness. For men, unemployment is devastating—much more so than for women—largely because a fundamental aspect of being a man is providing for a family. It's important to be able to provide for oneself and one's dependents, but casting breadwinning as the mark of a real man is as much of a straightjacket as believing motherhood is the ultimate expression of true womanhood. Greater gender-role flexibility would take some of the burden off of men to provide at all costs, while allowing them to be more loving, open, and present fathers.

When it comes to policy changes, the list of feminist demands is now familiar: parental leave, child care, sick days, flextime. But which policies we implement, and the values they both reflect and entrench, matter. In one study of work-family policies in North America and Europe, social scientists identified four major policy strategies: "The carer strategy (where women are treated primarily as carers and secondarily as earners), the earner strategy (where women are treated primarily as earners and secondarily as carers), the choice strategy (where women are treated as choosing whether they are primarily earners or caregivers, particularly when children are young), and the earner-carer strategy (where women and men are treated as equally involved in both earning and caring)." Countries that embraced the carer strategy focused on generous parental leaves and flextime policies, and make it easier for women to work part time. The presumption was that care remained a woman's job, but the state would make it easier for her to be a caregiver. The earner strategy is what we have in the United States: basically, ignoring the fact that workers have families at all and instead just encouraging employment. The choice strategy seeks to give women freedom to choose between being a worker and a caregiver, offering child care for working women as well as substantial support for women who stay home. Finally, the earner-carer strategy treats both women and men as having both earning duties and care duties, and makes it the role of the state to facilitate both. This is the model in countries like Sweden, Finland, and Norway. Although occupational segregation remains high in those countries and women are still more likely to take time off with a sick child, laws that incentivize time off for new fathers bring a feminist bent to work-life policy.

And it's those feminist-minded laws—that seek to challenge traditional divisions of labor rather than assuming care work is women's work—that are the best for women. The earner-carer countries, the study found, had significantly lower rates of children living in poverty; single mothers fared especially well compared to single mothers in other countries. One of the worst strategies is the earner strategy, which the United States uses: "Without generous benefits, leave policies, or child care, families with children must precariously balance care against employment," the study's authors wrote. "This strategy is associated with the highest levels of poverty, with shockingly high poverty levels for single mothers."[83] And any spending on family benefits reaped large returns: "Women who live in countries with 1 percent higher spending on family benefits are 2.3 percent less likely to fall into poverty, controlling for age, employment, education, partnership, and parental status," the researchers found. For every 1 percent spending increase for child care, women are .5 percent less likely to be impoverished. And although some maternity leave helps women stay in the workforce and keeps their wages higher than women who don't get leave,[84] too much—like the year offered in Germany—can actually have the effect of pushing women out.

While much of the conversation and the research on women and work has focused on mothers and work, significantly less has addressed the experiences and interests of women like me: those who work and like to work hard, but don't want to be worked to death, and who also don't have children. Much of what makes work particularly intolerable does come with having kids, but unpredictable and outsized work hours impact all employees, not just mothers and fathers. There has been something of a creeping acceptance that work simply dictates many of the rhythms of our lives—as if work were some outside thing not created by human beings who are also capable of changing its rules and norms. I don't always look back fondly on my years in corporate America, but the truth is that the firm I worked at was a pretty nice place. I was paid well, and although the work I did wasn't usually existentially rewarding, I got to use my brain every day, and high-quality work was mostly rewarded and recognized. I felt challenged. My coworkers and bosses were largely intelligent, liberal-minded, hardworking people who cared about their jobs and took pride in their work. Still, I couldn't picture a future there. And I couldn't identify a single person working there who had a life I wanted to emulate.

This was Howard's experience, too. As he was contemplating asking for a new role that would decrease his future earning potential but give him more time to live his life, "I had a female partner say to me, 'Howard, you're really good at this, you could be partner. Why would you want to limit yourself like that?'" he told me. Ten years later, he said, "I look at my life and the pictures of the various soccer teams I've coached, and knowing I've been there for these important moments for my kids and in my family's life, and that I've been able to have hobbies, and you look at it and at some point you have to say, no, actually, I figured it out. The rest of the world is actually crazy."

Looking back on my blessedly few years in corporate law from my current position as a freelancer—economically unstable but with a flexibility and freedom that brings a kind of happiness money can't buy—I can relate to Howard's feeling that climbing the corporate ladder at the expense of the life you actually want, if you have the choice not to, is kind of nuts. Unlike my grandmother and my mother, I grew up with a steady whisper of "follow your dreams" in the background of my educational and career choices—the idea that a job was for both financial security and for personal happiness. Until I interviewed my own mother for this book, I hadn't thought about how that emphasis on finding happiness by chasing a passion was borne not only out of love for her kids but also from a childhood of observing its absence.

"Grandma wrote songs," my mom told me about her mother. "And most of her songs were love ballads—'I don't care anymore, it doesn't matter, though my heart may be breaking in two.' Her songs were about heartbreak, and I didn't realize that until I was older and I sat down and started reading the words. She never got to go any further. Perhaps if she didn't have five kids . . . she was a good singer, she cut a record with Al Morgan who was a bigwig back then, he was like the Tony Bennett of Chicago—that was another thing she gave up. Perhaps she could have had a singing or songwriting career. But she didn't have the time or the money or the ability to follow any of her dreams. She didn't have the luck to have dreams."

7

The Edible Woman:
Food, Fat, and Feminism

One cannot think well, love well, sleep well, if one
has not dined well.

—*Virginia Woolf*, A Room of One's Own

T HE MOST PLEASURABLE meal of my life was in a little Greek coastal
town called Legrena, about two hours from Athens, where I lived
for a summer during law school. It was sleepy, tiny—there was a church
and a school, a bakery, a little shop that sold toys and magazines, two
restaurants owned by brothers (the meat restaurant and the fish restaurant), and the European law center at which I worked. I had to hitch
a ride on a tourist bus headed to the Temple of Poseidon to get to the
grocery store some twenty minutes away, so I mostly lived on items that
wouldn't go bad in a week's time—crackers, olives, some cured meats.
There were half a dozen Italian lawyers-in-training also working at the
center that summer, but they all lived in a more bustling university
town an hour away; I stayed in Legrena, in a building I shared with two
unfriendly coworkers from Moldova. Toward the end of the summer,
the boyfriend of one of the Italian girls came to visit. She had a young
Donatella Versace look, all tanned and toned, and he was a bodybuilder
who cut a striking resemblance in both shape and hairstyle to Hulk
Hogan. He also brought several pounds of homemade spaghetti from
Italy. We planned a big dinner to be held at the meat restaurant, which

217

despite its pedigree also served pretty good fish. Michael, the proprietor of the restaurant, went out early in the morning and collected baskets of spiny purple sea urchins from the rocks next to the beach. That night, the Italians sliced dozens of cloves of garlic razor-thin, broke the ur-chins open, glugged in lots of good olive oil, and made a vat of spicy, briny, garlicky, orange-flecked sea urchin spaghetti. It was just before my twenty-third birthday, and I had never had anything like it. It was good in the sense that the taste was nice, but it was also so *different*, a set of flavors I had never experienced. The pleasure was multifold: it was savory, it was novel, and it was interesting. It was also enjoyed at a table of sunburned, wine-drunk, late-July friends, with a kind of summer camp affection: promising we would all stay in touch, under-standing we inevitably wouldn't. I remember the sensation and the taste viscerally and uniquely, the way my skin pricks with the feeling of salt and cold when I think about the first time I swam in the Mediterranean at night, or how the smell of a certain old-fashioned aftershave puts me in my grandfather's Chicago home, playing with the empty glass bottles, all cast into different shapes—a dog, a train, a gun.

Food is no doubt one of the most basic human pleasures. What we eat and how we eat it anchors experiences and memories, shapes and reflects cultures, imbues meaning, and builds social connections. Food can be simply life sustaining, or it can be life changing. It can nourish you and it can kill you. It can expand your universe of experience, offer-ing new sensations, a peek into different ways of living, or it can ground you into the familiar and carry the past into the present. Eating together is a foundation of family and friendship. But around the world, our re-lationships with food are gendered: women are often charged with food preparation but don't get enough of it; professionalized food preparation and consumption remains largely male; denial of food is often a positive female trait; and in eating, many women experience shame and guilt as much as pleasure or satiation.

Food is also heavily moralized, and not just for women. Many reli-gious traditions include strictures around food to be observed daily or during particular holidays: not eating certain animals, not eating par-ticular combinations of food, not drinking alcohol, not eating during certain times of day, eating only animals that have been slaughtered in an approved way, eating only foods that have been deemed accept-able by a religious leader, not cooking if you're menstruating. These rules aren't necessarily punitive—they can also foster a sense of community, mindfulness about how and when one eats, a connection to the past, and deeply embedded memories. But they do speak to how food has long been a cornerstone of both spirituality and morality. The Quran, Hebrew scriptures, and the Bible all warn against gluttony. In the United States, fat people face pervasive discrimination, their bodies stand-ins for negative attributes associated with overconsumption: excess, slovenliness, laziness, lack of self-control. And increasingly, *how* we eat is a moral statement, if not necessarily a religious one—regularly feeding your children fast food or sugary drinks is seen in many parts of the United States as bad parenting; eating locally and buying organic food from a farmer's market, or going fully vegan, reflects not just one's culinary preferences but a broader set of ideals and lifestyle choices.

Most people find pleasure in food. But for many women, that pleasure is more complicated.

Karen Washington loves getting her hands dirty. "When I put my hands in the ground I have a connection," she said. "There is something in my DNA that I feel." The sixty-two-year-old New York native likes to say that "it was a tomato that changed my world": When she moved to the Bronx in 1985, two kids in tow, her new home had a big backyard, and she decided to grow vegetables. She had never gardened or farmed, and, as far as she knew, no one in her family had, either. So she checked out a few books from the public library and got to work. "Once I started to taste the food that I was growing against the food that I was purchasing at the supermarket, the taste was totally different, the freshness was different, the vitality of the food was different, it just had a feel of completeness, and it made my body feel good when I would eat it," she said. "So I got hooked." One afternoon, standing at her kitchen window looking across the street at the kind of vacant lot that is a fixture of many low-income and of-color New York City neighborhoods, she saw a man with a shovel and a pick enter. "I ran across the street and asked him, 'What are you doing?'" Karen said. "And he said, 'I'm thinking about starting a garden.' And I said, 'Can I help?'"

With that, she and Jose Lugo started one of New York's most famous urban gardens. That year, 1988, the city was rolling out a project to invest in urban green spaces, and Karen and Jose's garden was its first project. With a little help from the city and a lot of work from the neighbors, the empty lot became a sprawling collection of green plots, thirty-six of them to date. They call it the Garden of Happiness, which was Jose's idea. "And I'm so glad it's named that," Karen said. "I tell people, if you're not happy now, once you come into that garden, once you leave, you will be happy."

Karen didn't grow up farming, but she did grow up in a family of women who cooked the kind of food they themselves were raised on in the rural South. "I came up in a family where all the cooks were females except for my grandfather," Karen said. "Other than him, until this day, in my family, women are the ones who cook. In the garden, when we had a block party, who was cooking? Women. We were cooking. And I don't think women get enough credit in agriculture. Definitely women are the backbone when it comes to food." You can find Karen's family dynamic in homes across the United States: according to the Bureau of Labor Statistics 2015 Time Use Survey, 70 percent of women did food preparation or cleanup in the course of an average day; just 43 percent of men did the same. The average American man spends just twenty-one minutes a day making food or cleaning up after making food.[1] "Who's in the kitchen and who's in the garden?" Karen asked. "It's women. After the hard work is done, then the men come."

And yet it's almost always male chefs who food writers, media outlets, and restaurants glamorize. In a 2014 Bloomberg analysis of kitchen positions in fifteen major restaurant groups across the United States, of 160 head chefs, only 10 were women. It's not just women who are underrepresented in the upper echelons of the food industry: many cooks who do much of the behind-closed-doors work in professional kitchens are immigrant men, who are also notoriously underpaid and see scant opportunity for promotion. But women remain rare at every level in professional kitchens, from line cooks to head chefs—and it isn't because women can't cook professionally. More than 40 percent of "classic" graduates from the International Culinary School—that is, graduates who studied traditional culinary arts and not pastry, which has long been a more acceptably female option—are women, and have been for a decade. Jean-Georges Vongerichten, an internationally famous chef who as of 2014 owned twenty-four restaurants in the United States, employed exactly zero female head chefs that same year. About one female chef de cuisine working at his New York City restaurant

ABC Kitchen, he told *Bloomberg,* "She's an excellent chef. Very committed. Very pretty girl. She should be a model, not a cook."[2]

When men derive status and money from professionalized cooking but women's kitchen labors are low status and unpaid, that can make cooking and, sometimes, eating a less pleasurable experience for women. I grew up with two working parents who both cooked, but my mom cooked more often. For her, it was a chore to get food on the table for one kid who was a vegetarian, one who wanted to eat only meat, herself, and my dad; for my dad, cooking was often a fun weekend activity, an opportunity to try out a new ingredient or fire up the grill. It was something special to indulge in. As an adult, I love to cook—I find it fun and relaxing. But that's in part because I cook and eat with my partner. We try out new recipes and regularly carve out an hour or two from our demanding jobs to close our laptops, make a meal, and have a long conversation while we share it. For us, that turns food prep into an enjoyable activity, not something we do purely so we don't starve. I imagine it would be less fun if I were primarily tasked with doing it alone or if I were catering to the tastes of a picky toddler day in and day out. And because we're two working professionals, if we're feeling tired or lazy, we can go out or order in without cutting into our rent budget.

But even in my own fairly egalitarian relationship, I make most of the food decisions—I draw up the grocery lists, I pick out new recipes. It's not because my partner won't, but rather because I take the kitchen as my domain and exert a level of control over it that doesn't extend to anywhere else in the house. I came into the relationship with a broader culinary skill set, raised with the understanding that food preparation was a basic skill I needed in life; my partner was not. When we throw dinner parties, we both cook, but his first priority is having fun; mine is making sure the food is perfect, my stomach knotted with dread at the idea that our guests might think I don't cook well. Against my own feminist logic, I tightly internalize the idea that being a bad cook would be a particular kind of feminine failing.

Despite the fact that women prepare most of the food for American families and, like in my home, make most of the food purchasing decisions, men get the lion's share of attention for talking and writing about food. Karen was dubbed "urban farming's grande dame" by the *New York Times*[3] and received a 2014 James Beard Foundation Leadership Award, but she stands out from most prominent people in the modern food movement—men like *The Omnivore's Dilemma* author Michael Pollan or *New York Times* food columnist and cookbook author Mark Bittman, both of whom also received a James Beard award the same year as Karen. "The food movement definitely lacks diversity and voices," Karen said. "I think that my attribute as a woman of color and living in a poor neighborhood is definitely a voice to be reckoned with, to highlight some of the injustices that still persist in the system. Everyone is on board with farm-to-table and healthy eating, but there is part of society that does not have access to food, does not have access to the farm-to-table experience. We still have hunger and poverty. And I think my job, what I try to do, is bring to the forefront that we cannot celebrate the success of this food movement without recognizing that we have a lot of work that still needs to be done, and we have a lot of people that still have no access to the food we talk about and we glamorize."

Unless, like Karen, we are growing our own fruits and vegetables and cooking them ourselves, the food we eat is almost always at least a partial product of someone else's labor: someone else planted the seed, tended the seedling, plucked the fruit, dug up the vegetable, slaughtered the chicken, plucked the egg from the nest, milked the cow, packed it in a box, drove the truck, unloaded it onto a grocery store shelf. Maybe someone boiled the pasta water, grilled the steak, baked the chicken, sautéed the spinach, or steamed the rice before you sat down and ate. If you ate this meal out at a well-regarded restaurant in a city like New York, the kind that gets reviewed in the *Times,* chances are the head chef is a man, and the kitchen staff is mostly male, too—and depending on the restaurant, maybe mostly Hispanic even if the food is French or New American, maybe Japanese if you're having sushi. But peek into the kitchen and it's a proverbial sausage fest. If you ate in an American home, though, your food was probably prepared by a woman, her labor largely invisible.

The international stereotype of the Ugly American hinges on a few characteristics: we are boorish and not particularly worldly or respectful, we are very loud, and we are very large. The big American body has become a metaphor for so much of what is unattractive about this country: our entitlement, greed, gluttony, dominance. Our military is in every corner of the world, and our bodies, the stereotype goes, similarly take up more space than we deserve. Our hypercapitalist culture extends its tentacles around the globe, taking out or perverting local cuisines, customs, clothing. Anti-WTO rioters routinely target not just banks but McDonald's franchises.[4] Cosmopolitan New Yorkers, who tend to see themselves as simultaneously American and not quite American, mock the Middle America tourists who visit a great international city only to dine at the Olive Garden in Times Square.

And, indeed, the way we eat remains particularly unhealthy and often thoughtless, and the way our large food companies expand abroad often predatory and destructive. Nine out of ten Americans say they consume a healthy diet,[5] while almost half of Americans eat fast food at least once a week.[6] Fewer than 3 percent of us meet the most basic requirements for what experts consider a "healthy lifestyle."[7] Nationwide we eat just a single serving of fruit per day, and we're only marginally better when it comes to vegetables.[8]

But it's not just consumption that shapes the America's relationship to food; it's also shame, vice, and denial. While the large American body looms as a symbol of gluttony, many American women spend enormous amounts of time and effort trying to make their bodies smaller. Our bodies aren't universes we alone occupy, they're objects for male aesthetic approval and vehicles for male pleasure. This, of course, extends to food and the gendered ways in which we eat (or don't). Men certainly diet and try to lose weight, but not in nearly the same numbers as women. And for men, denial isn't glorified; consumption is. In the feminist-vegetarian tome *The Sexual Politics of Meat,* author Carol J. Adams made the case that the fates of women and animals are inherently intertwined; some of it is less than convincing, but the argument that continues to ring true even decades after the book's publication is that meat is seen as manly, and women's bodies are often depicted as pieces of meat fit for consumption.[9] Animal protein is tied to strength and virility, which men need; women, whose goodness comes from denial and fragility, are left with the vegetables. Adams gave the example of cookbook Father's Day meals versus those suggested for Mother's Day and found that while many of the Mother's Day options are light vegetarian fare, fathers get hearty pieces of meat, often with potatoes. *The Sexual Politics of Meat* was published in 1990, so I decided to see whether this pattern still holds true more than twenty-five years later. And, indeed, online collections for Mother's Day versus Father's Day recipes are surprisingly unchanged. Celebrity chef Jamie Oliver's Mother's Day recipe collection is mostly cakes, tarts, and a few dishes with salmon or shrimp.[10] The Father's Day collection, by contrast, is a festival of red meat: sausage, burgers, steaks, venison.[11] Martha Stewart's collection of thirty Father's Day options are nearly all meat,[12] whereas of her thirty Mother's Day recipes, only one has meat as a main course, and it's lamb; most of the rest are vegetarian, although a few have a bit of bacon, fish, or chicken.[13] We have cultural images of the vegetarian woman as slim and healthy and of the steak-eating, whiskey-swilling woman as cool and desirable—the first more traditionally feminine, the second respectable because she's doing guy stuff. (The quintessential Cool Girl, wrote *Gone Girl* author Gillian Flynn, "jams hot dogs and hamburgers into her mouth like she's hosting the world's biggest culinary gang bang while somehow maintaining a size 2."[14]) The vegetarian man, though, is kind of a pansy, a stereotype so entrenched that in response, vegan men have taken to branding themselves as ultramasculine "hegans"; one, John Joseph, wrote a book called *Meat Is for Pussies*.

Across countries and cultures, women often deny themselves meat so that their husbands and then children can have it; husbands routinely take more meat than is their fair share. This female sacrifice for others persists today: when I visit Janet in North Carolina, I bring breakfast sandwiches for her and the kids; she's hungry, but she gives the children her sandwich anyway.

The popularity of low-carb, high-protein diets has eroded the men-and-meat stereotypes, at least insofar as women may gravitate more to lean proteins than to grains. But meat and masculinity remain strongly tied. In fact, men eat so much meat—almost twice the recommended daily amount[15]—that in January 2016, the USDA and the Department of Health and Human Services warned them against it in a set of new dietary guidelines. Women's bodies, meanwhile, are often represented as literal meat—the rapper Ludacris about to bite into a woman's leg on the cover of his album *Chicken-n-Beer*, actress and vegetarian Pamela Anderson posing in a PETA ad, dressed in a bikini with meat cuts drawn on to her nearly naked body: leg, round, rump, breast.

How we got here is complex, an interplay between global capitalism, a work-first culture that offers little space for sensory pleasures, endemic poverty, and stark income inequality, and a refusal of policymakers to correct for past errors or create new systems in a changed world. But much of the blame for what *The Omnivore's Dilemma* author Michael Pollan has called "our national eating disorder" has been placed on women. In a 2009 *New York Times Magazine* story, Pollan compared Julia Child to *Feminine Mystique* writer Betty Friedan, saying they both spoke to the same group of women, but Child with less condescension: "[Child] tried to show the sort of women who read *The Feminine Mystique* that, far from oppressing them, the work of cooking approached in the proper spirit offered a kind of fulfillment and deserved an intelligent woman's attention. (A man's too)," Pollan wrote. Simone de Beauvoir's claim that cooking could be oppressive but also a space for female "revelation and creation" was, Pollan wrote, "a bit of wisdom that some American feminists thoughtlessly trampled in their rush to get women out of the kitchen."[16]

In fact, it's systems created mostly by men that have fed America's unhealthy appetites—not kitchens abandoned by women. Industrial food companies, largely owned by men, have made large sums of money by selling convenience foods. These foods are popular in part because American workplaces are still structured to serve a patriarchal family, and most American families remain imbalanced at home—of course a woman who has a job but is still charged with making dinner every night will gravitate toward a quick meal over a process that is intensive in labor, time, or cleanup. Soaking beans for homemade chili or roasting a chicken with vegetables may be a healthy option, but it requires more planning ahead, more chopping, more time in the kitchen, and a heavier washup than microwaving some fish sticks or grabbing fast food or takeout. It's not that feminists threw the pasta out with the boiling water; it's that women en masse entered a professional universe that did not adjust for that new reality. And instead of men stepping up at home or policy changes that would make this new world more tenable—reasonable work hours, parental leave, vacation days, and fair wages for women so low-income mothers wouldn't have to work multiple jobs to stay afloat—corporate food interests swept in to ease the day-to-day burden just a little, and make a lot of money for themselves in the process.

It's also notable that Pollan's timeline is off. Although new workplace norms certainly contribute to the modern-day reliance on processed foods, often to the exclusion of home-cooked, whole-ingredient meals, feminism did not, in fact, lead to their introduction. Processed foods didn't enter the American marketplace along with Friedan's book and second-wave feminism; they predated it, marketed along with new washer-dryers and state-of-the-art vacuum cleaners as conveniences for the modern housewife. Through the 1950s and into the '60s, postwar prosperity and the happy homemaker ideal boosted the profits of the food industry, especially in the realm of convenience foods. A cultural fascination with rapidly shifting technology and futurism, too, made nearly unrecognizable foods strangely appealing—Kool-Aid, Tang, cake from a box. As journalist Michael Moss reports in *Salt Sugar Fat*, his investigation into the processed food industry, food companies recognized that women didn't want to spend all day in the kitchen making everything from scratch, so they met that need by offering increasingly chemical-laden convenience items. They also deployed their own marketing teams, in the form of industry-paid home economics teachers, to counter the movement of women wanting to teach traditional food preparation skills. These instructors, along with fictional housewives like Betty Crocker, showed American women that a good homemaker should have her pantry stocked with a plethora of instant foods, ready to entertain on a moment's notice. And they created new recipes with their processed ingredients, like Jell-O salads and casseroles made with canned Campbell's soup. The homemaker's daily duties were to keep a perfect house and prepare tasty food for a husband and kids—even if the "homemaker" also worked outside the home. Day in and day out, one can see how that turned monotonous, especially for the many women for whom cooking wasn't a joy but simply a task. The food industry claimed to offer a solution: not a new division of household labor, of course, but a way to make cooking faster, with foods increasingly laden with sugar, salt, and fat that were more likely to please even picky kids. By the end of the 1950s, Moss reports, General Foods Corporation was the world's biggest food processor, selling billions of packages of processed food and pulling in more than $1 billion a year on Birds Eye frozen foods alone.[17]

Contrary to Pollan's gauzy vision of women finding purpose and creativity in the kitchen, the housewives of the 1940s and '50s were more or less like women today: some liked to cook and found it a satisfying arena for ingenuity and enjoyment, and some hated it, finding it burdensome and placing it alongside other household drudgery. Today, many men continue to identify the kitchen as a locus of female oppression, a place that symbolically sequesters women off from public space: as a female writer, two of the more common insults lobbed at me are, "Get back in the kitchen," or "Make me a sandwich"—shorthand for "shut up, go away, and serve a man."

In her book *Homeward Bound: Why Women Are Embracing the New Domesticity*, journalist Emily Matchar took aim at what she called "the myth of foodie nostalgia" and pointed out that even back in the good old days when women cooked for their families, "lots of women, it turns out, were simply not so fond of cooking."[18] Two of the most popular cookbooks of the twentieth century, she noted, were *The Can Opener Cookbook* and *The I Hate to Cook Book*. The latter includes a recipe for Skid Row Stroganoff, which instructs women to "add the flour, salt, paprika, and mushrooms, stir, and let it cook five minutes while you light a cigarette and stare sullenly at the sink." Friedan and other feminists didn't convince women that cooking was boring and oppressive; lots of women already found cooking to be boring and oppressive, and market forces responded long before feminism.

Americans are still wildly unhealthy, especially compared to our peer countries in western Europe. But in the past decade, we have moved toward a marginally healthier diet, and this is very much reflective of a political moment. Across class and racial groups people are eating better, although this change seems to be especially pronounced among those with more disposable income to spend on things like organic vegetables. Food today isn't just a thing you eat; it's a moral and political statement. Blogs, mostly written by glowing young white women wielding very expensive cameras, document what Matchar called "the new domesticity": gardening, canning, baking your own bread, making your own baby food, cooking elaborate meals, anything homemade and DIY. Women who post their all-organic recipes and prioritize making food from scratch "are part of our country's burgeoning new food culture, a culture that places an immense amount of faith in the idea of food as a solution for a variety of social ills, from childhood obesity to global warming to broken families to corporate greed," Matchar wrote.[19] "In progressive, middle-class circles these days, there's the overwhelming sense that procuring and cooking the freshest, healthiest, most sustainably sourced food should be a top priority for any thinking person."

I'm skeptical of much of this new food culture, at least insofar as it shows up in saturated Pinterest photos and on judgmental mommy blogs. But at the same time, I recognize myself in Matchar's descriptions. I also buy organic chicken and cage-free eggs, frequent my local farmer's market, make most of my meals from scratch, avoid fast food and soda, and keep my ultraprocessed food consumption minimal. I have a copy of *The Omnivore's Dilemma* on my bookshelf and another on my iPad. As much as I cringe at the veneration of a lifestyle accessible to only a privileged few that is a staple of publications like Gwyneth Paltrow's *GOOP* or the e-newsletter *Well + Good,* I still subscribe. And as I mentally mock the organic-obsessive lifestyle bloggers, I note with some discomfort that I simultaneously take quite seriously the writings of men like Michael Pollan and Mark Bittman—men who have professionalized this DIY food ethos. I doubt I'm the only one who carries this internalized sexism that treats men as the respectable professionals in the world of wholesome at-home eating while writing off the women who are the at-home doers.

If healthier eating patterns reflect both better individual choices and expanded access to a variety of fresh, healthy foods, then recent changes in the American diet are good news. But, just as the blame for convenience food culture was laid at women's feet, the invisible labor behind this healthier shift comes largely from women—and the burden of meeting greater demands for healthy eating within the family falls on women as well.

The food guilt now leveled at women (and on mothers especially) may be obsessed over by the most affluent and educated—the mothers who buy organic string cheese and would just as soon give their child a Happy Meal as arsenic. But the space between the ideal—healthy, nutritious, home-cooked food—and the reality is the widest for women with the fewest resources, and the judgment the harshest.

Take women who rely on food stamps to feed their families. Across the country, obesity rates are highest among women in the poorest communities, and for women and their children, obesity increases with food stamp usage. (Obesity is an imperfect measure of health, but the US government and health researchers use few other measures to track the impact of our food policies on vulnerable populations. I use the terms "obese" and "overweight" here not because I think they're particularly good ones, but because so many studies rely on BMI-determined classifications that it's nearly impossible to find and accurately characterize data and research on weight without using these terms.)[20] That there's a link between poverty and poor health isn't news, and neither are the reasons. The US government subsidizes the production of certain food products, most notably corn, that are in turn used to make very cheap ultraprocessed food items. Because these items are more affordable than fresh fruits, vegetables, and lean meats, it's no surprise that they fill the grocery carts and the bellies of the poorest citizens. On top of affordability is access: there simply aren't grocery stores that sell fresh fruits, vegetables, and meats in many of the poorest areas of the country, especially if those areas are also mostly populated by black and Hispanic residents. This means getting to a store that sells fresh produce requires a car and gas money, or a longer bus trip. And then there is time: time on public transportation, if that transportation even exists, to get to the far-away grocery store; time to wash and chop and prep and cook a meal that your kids may refuse to eat; and time to clean up. Time is already in short supply for many low-income women working multiple jobs at irregular hours. Race interplays with poverty here: contrary to claims that supermarkets will go anywhere there's a market for them, majority black or Hispanic neighborhoods routinely have fewer supermarkets than do white neighborhoods, even when you take income into account.[21]

There are policy solutions, some complicated and some straightforward: subsidizing healthier foods rather than ultraprocessed ones, expanding incentives for grocery stores to open in neighborhoods of color, healthy school lunch programs, requiring reasonable working hours and reliable schedules, a higher minimum wage, more investments in infrastructure and public transport, a more generous food stamp budget to allow families to afford pricier but more nutritious foods.

Instead, politicians have aimed to give people with very little even less, cutting food stamp budgets and concocting rules that would limit what kinds of foods they can buy—no soda or junk food, for example.[22] Advocates for poor families point out that it's hard to draw neat lines around "healthy" and "not healthy"—for example, soda may be nutritionally deficient, highly caloric, and sugary, but so are many flavored fruit drinks or sugary coffee beverages that aren't targeted; candy bars may be packed with sugar, but so are many flavored yogurts. Allowing food stamps to purchase some food items but not others sets recipients—mostly women—up for public humiliation at the checkout line. For all the talk from food experts about the pleasure of eating and the creativity and sense of purpose that comes with cooking, there isn't much of a parallel theory that food should be enjoyable for everyone—including those who have constraints of time and money.

The roster of professional foodies may still be dominated by men, but efforts to better feed those in need have long been the province of women and activists of color. Grassroots efforts to claim for everyone the pleasure of making and eating food, like Karen Washington's garden in the Bronx, are representative: white men may write the books and get much of the recognition, but they aren't typically the ones getting their hands dirty. Many of these food justice efforts have been explicitly political, starting in local communities and moving their way up the national chain. First Lady Michelle Obama has continued this tradition of making food a political centerpiece, although even she was no match for the big food companies. Her suggestions that it was past time to better regulate these companies—and especially the way foods are marketed to children—was met with immense blowback from the food industry, and Obama swiftly turned away from food and toward less controversial programs promoting physical fitness. She had some successes, including the Healthy, Hunger-Free Kids Act, which sought to ensure that school meals are nutritionally sound—a departure from the Ronald Reagan era of cutting funding for hungry kids and the infamous claim that ketchup is a vegetable.[23] The act passed in 2010, and despite its theoretically uncontroversial provisions—more money for school lunches with whole grains, fruits, and vegetables—the backlash was significant, with cafeteria workers complaining that kids were throwing out their healthy food and conservative politicians claiming the program was another government intrusion into the fundamental right of Americans to eat their daily tater tots. In reality, the claims of food waste were overblown, and one Harvard study found that kids were more inclined to eat their food if they were given at least twenty-five minutes to eat instead of rushed through a brief lunch.[24] Which makes sense: lunch is something that's crammed in before recess, the food treated as little more than fuel. It's not a time to savor or enjoy or bond; it's just one more chaotic, slightly gross part of the school day. In this, we train our kids for a lifetime of unhealthy eating. And we train our girls especially.

A few months ago, I was out to dinner with a friend in New York, and the waitress came by to set down a breadbasket. My friend waved her away. "No thanks," she said. "We're trying to be good."

"Good," for women, means saying no: to food, to sex, to temptation, to pleasure. Denial of what one wants is, for women, a morally righteous act. For some women and girls, denial is taken to an extreme through anorexia, bulimia, or other eating disorders. For others, restrictive eating habits that may not qualify as an eating disorder are still filtered through a set of rules, the breaking of which brings guilt, self-loathing, and shame. Sitting down to a meal becomes morally and emotionally fraught: Will I make a "good" choice? What do I want to eat versus what should I be eating? How many calories are in this? Why did I eat the whole thing? If I order a salad, will my date think I'm the kind of calorie-obsessed girl who isn't very fun? If I order a burger will I look like a pig? Amid all this anxiety, the primitive pleasure of eating takes a backseat.

Christy Harrison, now thirty-five, was an anxious eater. She had an eating disorder in college—restricting, starving, binging, exercising like mad to make up for the binging—and her eating eventually transitioned into less of a diagnosable disorder but still an act rife with rules, restrictions, and apprehension. She was a journalist who wrote about food but maintained an uncomfortable relationship with it. A foodie boyfriend in her twenties meant adventurous dinners, vacations centered on eating, and less time at the gym, which loosened her restrictions a bit, but like many women her age, the food anxiety remained. "I missed out on presence," Christy said. "I wasn't present for a lot of my twenties because I was obsessing over food or thinking about how I was going to work off something that I ate or thinking about what I needed to do to prepare for a big meal." It put pressure on her relationships and made dining with friends more difficult. "My neediness around food—maybe not neediness, but my excessive worry—really challenged the people I was with," Christy said. "I went gluten-free, totally overhauled my diet, and suddenly I couldn't go out to normal restaurants or had to make a big deal of it when I did. It was so much energy and work researching what had gluten and what didn't, researching the calories because I was still fairly obsessive about calories. I was going down Google rabbit holes constantly with these things I now see are so unimportant. What interesting things could I have been learning at that time if I hadn't done that?"

The transition to focusing on the pleasure of food rather than seeing it as a menace came, perhaps predictably, over a meal: dinner with her boyfriend at a Russian nightclub in Los Angeles. "There was a dinner, a huge twelve-course meal, and a floor show where they had these dancers in crazy sequin costumes, and a dance party after," Christy said. "A whole affair. Endless vodka. I was so mesmerized by the whole thing. And the food was incredible. I hadn't expected that, because I was like, 'Ugh it'll be weird borscht,' but it was so different. I just remember a dill potato salad that was not what I expected by looking at it—it tasted lighter and fresher than I worried it would. I let myself go for that night, let go of the restrictions I had placed on myself, and was eating bread and really calorie-dense things and lots of carbs, which had been a real fear for me. And it was all in the context of this really fun weird foreign experience. It's the first time I remember letting go around food."

That, and her growing career as a food writer, pushed Christy to open up more about her eating issues in therapy, and then go back to school for a master's degree in public health and a license to work as a nutritionist. She read the book *Intuitive Eating* and "realized I could be a normal eater and I could listen to my body and it would guide me in the right direction. I wasn't going to suddenly double my weight by giving up the remaining restrictions I had. I threw out my scale and deleted the calorie calculators." Christy started a podcast called *Food Psych,* where she talks to people about their relationships with food, and also works as a nutrition counselor, developing a specialty in eating disorders, intuitive eating, and the ethos that people can be healthy at every body size. She wants people to eat what nourishes them and what their bodies need, not to seek to alter the size and shape of their bodies through food. "For women to have a goal to lose weight, it's taking away so much mental energy and creative potential from their lives," Christy said. "It's really a feminist issue for me, to work on helping people to accept their bodies as they are and to do other things with their time and energy than obsess over food and their weight."

Beejoli Shah is one woman who would like to spend less time and energy obsessing over food and weight. Beejoli, now twenty-nine, also had an eating disorder as a young woman, but it came less from a desire to be skinny than a need for control and a simple lack of understanding of how to feed herself. She grew up in Cerritos, California, a largely Asian Los Angeles suburb she called a "model-minority ethno-burb"—an enclave of immigrants and their high-achieving children. As a dancer and cheerleader, restricting food to stay thin was simply the norm among Beejoli's peers, and despite being a naturally skinny kid, as a young teen she joined in to feel part of the group. She read some pro-anorexia, or "pro-ana," websites and chatrooms, but largely disregarded them. When her hips started to fill out in high school, though, her body became more central to her eating habits. And the culture she grew up in meant no one seemed to notice: the emphasis was on doing well in school, and because Beejoli was a good kid with good grades, by her community's measures she was doing great. "There was no institutional support," she said. "Everyone else on these pro-ana forums had stories of hiding stuff from their family because they were all at dinner and they had to hide stuff in their napkin, but that didn't happen to us. It was very self-policing. We were so mature in the sense of the amount of responsibility we got for being good Indian kids that this was not even something on the parental radar to watch out for. Boys were, so were falling calculus grades, but not our food."

It took being hospitalized for dehydration and anemia and passing out twice in one week for teachers and coaches to take notice. Her parents got involved then, too, and Beejoli met with the school nurse, her cheerleading coach, and her high school advisor. But none of these people were particularly well trained in dealing with eating disorders. Her parents, with whom she is close, wanted to help but didn't know how—especially because Beejoli, who was bright and active, had an eating disorder that didn't fit the Lifetime movie image of a skeletal white girl refusing to touch the food on her plate.

When she went off to college, the desire to have fun drinking with friends outweighed the desire to be skinny; ditto when she moved to New York. Both times, she gained both weight and self-loathing. She's in therapy now, and has been on and off for about five years, but food still poses a challenge. This disrupts Beejoli's life beyond the dinner table. Growing up, she said, her mother suspected she had ADHD, and her peers often noted her lack of follow-through. "People just thought I was ditzy or flaky," she said, but her doctor now suspects it came from not having enough nutrients. "I was probably eating 900 or 1,000 calories a day. I got stomach ulcers when I was twenty." Now she frets over preparing food at home for dates or even friends. She forgoes small indulgences, none of which may be a big deal individually but that add up to a toxic pattern of saying no, refusing pleasure, and then feeling shame and guilt at a perceived overindulgence: "I wouldn't eat a frozen pizza when I got stoned with a guy I was dating, because I didn't want him to think I was the kind of person who would do that," she said. "There's a lot of shame around food."

When you don't have enough calories, there's little else you do well—think, write, run, orgasm. When you're busy counting calories or churning over the "mistake" you just made by eating something "bad," it's hard to focus on anything else—work, playing with your kids, paying attention to your partner, reading a book, fighting for social justice. "Naomi Wolf in *The Beauty Myth* made the great point that as women have gotten more power in society and more freedoms, the beauty myth and the diet industry have only tightened their stranglehold on us," Christy said. "It's no coincidence that these things have come about at times of women's greatest social power. Women have gotten more and more power over the past forty to fifty years, and the diet industry has only gotten stronger. Women as a category could do anything, we could do whatever we set our minds to, whether that's advancement in a particular career, or being present in your life or with your kids, or whatever you choose to do. But I think the pleasure and power of it is reduced when so much of your mental energy and your physical energy is taken up with pursuing dieting and weight loss."

The ultimate goal of intuitive eating, Christy said, is to "make choices out of self-care and desire, rather than self-control and denial." In other words, pleasure-centered eating. But when it comes to nourishing ourselves, pleasure gets complicated. There is the immediate sensory pleasure in tasting something good, but if that food item is packed with sugar or salt, it might make your body feel pretty bad later. And some things that make your body feel good later may not feel particularly pleasurable at the time—choosing to eat a vegetable over a piece of candy, getting up and going for a walk instead of watching a TV show. "Self-care" is an increasingly popular term, an important bit of encouragement for the stressed-out and overworked to prioritize their own health and well-being, mental and physical. Self-care is crucial and, as many feminists have pointed out, a radical act in a world that demands women serve others. But self-care isn't just about spa days and chocolate bars; it also includes doing things that are unpleasant or annoying to put you in a better position later: going to the doctor for a checkup, paying your bills on time, and, yes, eating your vegetables. In a culture of female denial and shame, where women are trained to second-guess their intuition, choke down their own desires and cravings, and then encouraged in advertisements to "indulge"—usually by buying something, and often by eating something—self-care gets tricky, especially around food.

In the United States, diet culture is declining. There's less of an emphasis on Weight Watchers or Jenny Craig and more of a focus on health and wellness—that instead of eating prepackaged microwave diet meals, the better choice is whole grains and organic fruits and vegetables. In 1991, more than a third of American women said they were on a diet; that number was down to just over one in five by 2012. That's not because people are satisfied with their bodies—more than half of American adults say they want to lose weight.[25] But, instead of diet culture, we have "wellness" culture. Wellness is in many ways a step in the right direction. Wellness experts encourage people to eat minimally processed foods, to exercise, and to eat well and work out because it feels good, not to make yourself look one way or another. Like in the diet industry, many of these experts are women. The most visible ones with the most valuable brands are white, slim, conventionally attractive, and disproportionately blonde.[26] They're yoga teachers, celebrities who like to cook, and food bloggers with definitional prefixes (paleo, gluten-free, wholesome, mindful).

Notably, the women who seem to have had the most professional success from this move toward the domestic also play on old tropes about femininity and succeed in part because of deep female insecurities. A woman who makes fresh, healthy food for her family is desirable and, importantly, physically attractive—what she's selling isn't just a set of recipes but a set of values and an implicit promise that eating "right" will also make you glowing, virtuous, and slim. One should "eat clean" by avoiding processed foods; to get clean, one can use a low-calorie and highly restrictive "cleanse"—drinking only fresh-pressed juices or eating only dairy-free vegan soups. The new well woman has a list of clean-eating rules to obey, foods to which she should just say no. maybe she's paleo and doesn't eat grains, soy, dairy, refined sugar, or vegetable oil; maybe she's gluten-free and avoids wheat and barley, which means no bread or pasta; maybe she's avoiding bloat and inflammation and so cuts out milk, alcohol other than red wine, and nightshades (tomatoes, eggplant, peppers). The promise of "wellness" and "clean eating" is glowing skin, a stronger body, a longer life, and, perhaps most of all, the moral righteousness that comes with being a healthy person in an unhealthy culture. It's not a diet, which implies temporary restriction; it's a better way of living, a holistic and never-ending lifestyle. The unspoken promise, of course, is that if you are just well enough, you will also be thin.

Few would argue that seeking health and wellness is a bad thing, and certainly most nutritionists would agree that eating more whole grains and vegetables is better than eating a Lean Cuisine meal every night. In the face of a food industry more beholden to shareholder interests than to the well-being of consumers—an industry that increasingly looks like the new tobacco in the extent to which it has fudged the science and done significant harm to the public—a countervailing effort focused on exercise and eating whole foods is a good thing. But there's a specific kind of female perfectionism demanded from clean eating and much of wellness culture—if you fail to eat clean one day, then you're dirty, sullied, contaminated from the inside out. It's easy to see how that contributes to a noxious cycle of eating something "unclean" and then doubling down because you've already made a mistake, only to try to walk it back with extreme restrictions later on. This is particularly pronounced for women, who are already raised in a culture where femininity often means denial and rule following.

This has been Beejoli's experience as she tries to eat healthier. "For me a lot of the food control now comes around shame of not knowing how to be better at it and how to be consistent," she said. "But when I'm sitting here being like, 'You have to be super healthy,' losing weight feels like a secondary victory to having done it 'right.' The victory comes from passing as a healthy person."

America is a country of fat people. If we're basing "fat" on body-mass index (BMI) alone, then more than two-thirds of Americans qualify.[27] Compared to the BMIs of people around the world, Americans are among the largest.[28] If you're an average American reader, that probably sounds like a bad thing—we're used to hearing that fat is unhealthy, unattractive, and bad, and the fact that so many Americans are fat is a national shame. But our perceptions and assumptions about body size don't necessarily match up with the reality of the research about diet, health, and fat. "Fat," at the end of the day, is just a descriptor, and one that fits many Americans, but the word itself conveys judgment, disgust, and shame. Fat isn't just a body type; it's a moral failure. For women, the group long charged with saying no to temptation, it's a particular kind of sin—evidence on the body that a woman has said yes to what she wants.

The fact that our body sizes have changed so rapidly in the past few decades is cause for investigation, research, and potential concern—if in the space of a generation we all got a foot taller, that would be worth looking into, too. That our collective weight gain has also come along with many serious illnesses doesn't necessarily mean that weight gain is causing those illnesses—it could, but it could also indicate that something is causing both our weight gain and our poor health. There remains much we don't know about what makes people unhealthy and what has led to our national uptick in weight, but so far, general consensus among medical experts and scientists is that the "somethings" making us sick at least include our sedentary lifestyles and our food supply; some suggest that the various chemicals and hormones we come into contact with, in our food and elsewhere, also have an impact. We eat in accordance with our cultural values, which in a land of plenty often means more, and in a land of busy often means quickly and without much thought. That makes us very sick. And it makes some of us fatter than we would be. But if the real concern is health, does it make sense to focus primarily on body size?

"We don't have randomized controlled trials that show if you gain weight you end up with these poor health outcomes; all we have is longitudinal data, because it's unethical to make someone gain weight to see whether they'll have negative health outcomes," Christy said. "There is some evidence that weight cycling is linked to poor health outcomes, and weight cycling is more common in heavier people, because heavier people are told they need to lose weight." Many studies also fail to demonstrate that weight loss leads to better health or don't control for the health-supporting activities—eating a more balanced diet, exercising regularly—that we know are good for us and sometimes, but not always, can also lead to weight loss.

The cultural shame and stigma around fatness make it hard to have an honest conversation—let alone conduct reliable research—on the relationship among health, size, food, and movement. People may not report what they actually ate accurately if they fear judgment, or researchers may not believe someone could be both fat and a healthy eater. Researchers and doctors may chalk up to weight health problems that are actually caused by other serious issues, leaving patients vulnerable.

It's also awfully hard to be kind to your body if you are taught to hate it. For women in particular, the message is that we should exist less—or at least that less of us should exist. We should be slender, quiet, delicate, and take up as little space as possible. What we associate with femininity is very much tied to staying small, physically, vocally, professionally. Feminists often mock "manspreading," the habit of many men to sit with their legs wide apart, taking up as much room as they want, even if it impedes on someone else's comfort. The reason we notice it is because women, often unconsciously, do the opposite: we sit with our legs crossed, our elbows in, attempting to make our bodies little and unobtrusive. Being small is polite, feminine, attractive—and fat is the opposite.

I can't remember the first time I understood that fat was bad, but I can remember the moment I decided I was fat, and knew that was bad. I was sitting on the toilet and looked down at my thighs spread out on the seat. They were huge, I decided. And huge, for a girl, was disgusting—it was fat. I remember feeling hot, ashamed, disgusted at myself, and determined that I would make a change. I would eat less. I would run more. I was eight.

In reality, I was a slim kid; I was not then, and have not ever been, "overweight," at least according to my BMI. But regardless of the number on the scale—which has fluctuated by about twenty pounds during my adult life, hitting low points when I am very careful and restrictive about what I eat and the high ones when I'm stressed, drinking excessively, and not exercising or cooking for myself—I have, for twenty-five years, never felt as though my body was good enough. It has been an adversarial relationship, my body insisting on getting larger while I will it, and sometimes force it, to shrink. I've forced that shrinking by denying myself the pleasure of eating what I want and what my body craves.

As a feminist, this is an embarrassing thing to admit. We are supposed to love our bodies, to reject patriarchal and fashion industry ideas about skinny and pretty going together, to agree that all bodies are beautiful. The fat acceptance movement has overlapped with feminism, to the benefit of both movements—size, most feminists now realize, is one vector upon which women are oppressed. Within feminist communities, and increasingly in the United States generally, sizeism is less and less acceptable. This is a good thing. But it can be difficult to have a candid discussion about how we feel about our bodies when speaking ill of your own can sound a lot like judgment of others—when feeling ill about your own comes from internalized bigotry and judgment.

I've seen women I think are beautiful who are all different sizes and women I think are ugly of all different sizes, and I don't think body type determines attractiveness—except when it comes to my own body. This, I suspect, is true for a lot of women. Although some companies have used "real women" in their ads to sell female consumers everything from bras to cellulite cream (and gotten the free advertising of positive press coverage in the process), these images are billed as relatable, not aspirational. That, still, remains the province of the thin.

Despite these small shifts toward "real bodies" in media and advertising, the overwhelming majority of images we see of women in ads, on television, and in magazines represent a narrow segment of the population: conventionally attractive, almost always thin, usually white, often posed to suggest sexual appeal or readiness. By contrast, fat bodies are portrayed as a joke or a warning—Dr. Charlotte Cooper, the author of the book *Fat Activism: A Radical Social Movement,* coined the term "headless fatties" to describe a media dynamic where "every hand-wringing article about the financial cost of obesity, and every speechifying press release about the ticking time bomb of obesity seemed to be accompanied by a photograph of a fat person, seemingly photographed unawares, with their head neatly cropped out of the picture."[29] Coverage of the "obesity epidemic," and the headless fatty photos that illustrate it, emphasizes individual choices—eating too much, not exercising enough—as the primary cause of society-wide weight gain in the United States, rarely digging into the complex and more systematic influences. And the emphasis on the "obesity crisis" gives the processed food industry an easy out: just blame the personal choices of fat folks, and the booming food industry doesn't have to make any changes that could hurt its bottom line. This, already, is an industry strategy.

The individualization of the "obesity epidemic" means more profits for food companies. Some of the biggest profiteers from weight loss programs, which largely target women, are the same companies who make processed, nutritionally deficient, highly caloric foods. Nestlé, for example, owns the weight-loss program Jenny Craig.[30] Weight Watchers was owned by the H. J. Heinz Company until 1999; after it was sold, the new owner hired a former PepsiCo executive as CEO.[31]

Despite the fact that one-third of the American population qualifies as "overweight" and another third as "obese," meaning that a minority of Americans are "normal weight" or "thin," fat people face substantial discrimination and marginalization in American society. It's legal to fire someone for being overweight, and fat women particularly suffer: a "heavy" woman makes an average of $9,000 less per year than an average-weight one, and a "very heavy" woman makes $19,000 less.[32] Thin women, by contrast, are rewarded—"thin" women make an average of $7,000 a year more than average-weight women, and "very thin" women make $22,000 a year more. And weight discrimination is very much a gendered dynamic, with women facing more severe penalties for being fat. Among American CEOs, only 5 percent are obese regardless of gender. But between 45 and 61 percent of male CEOs are overweight—a higher average than in the American population overall. Yet there are fewer overweight female CEOs—between 5 and 22 percent of female CEOs nationwide are above average weight.[33] In other words, while there are very few obese people heading big companies, there are lots of physically large men in charge. But the majority of powerful women are physically smaller than the "average" American woman. And study after study has shown that fat people are perceived as lazy,[34] insecure,[35] unintelligent, and unclean.

This discrimination has real consequences. Fat people are more likely than thin people to live in poverty, earn less, be unemployed, and hold lower-status jobs—and these things of course are cyclical, with poverty also contributing to the stress, eating habits, and lack of time to exercise that for many correlate with weight gain.[36] Fat people achieve lower levels of education than thin people, and fat children experience more bullying and harassment than their thinner peers.[37] Fat women routinely report being harassed and mistreated for having the gall to eat food in public.[38] Male jurors are even more likely to find fat female criminal defendants guilty than thinner ones.[39]

Fat people, and fat women especially, face intense stigma—and stigma is not a great way to lose weight or treat one's body with kindness. While the weight loss industry has been booming for decades because of weight-related stigma, once weight is gained it's extremely difficult to lose. Recent research, though limited, is starting to point to the conclusion that the body fights weight loss at every turn—an individual who reduced their weight has to exercise more to burn the same number of calories as a person who weighs the same without dieting, and even the neurological response of dieters may demonstrate a greater emotional response to food and less of an ability to restrain desire than is observed in the brains of nondieting eaters.[40] Much of this research is new, still evolving, and vastly imperfect, and it would be foolish to rely on a handful of unreplicated studies to come to a definitive conclusion. But the body of evidence appears to point to a few probable truths: people who are deemed obese or overweight are often physically large because of a complex combination of factors, including biology, genetics, food choices, and food access. And an observation of American society points to one more: that our toxic relationship with food, fat, and pleasure means that for many women, eating is less a pleasurable sensory experience than a locus of stress and shame.

The sea urchin spaghetti I ate in Greece remains seared into my memory a decade later in part because it was one of the only days that summer I let myself eat solely for pleasure. I was living off of a small stipend that meant my food expenses had to stay low, so I bought the bare minimum I needed. But more influential was the fact that I was depressed and desperate for something in my life I could control, and food fit the bill. The first year of law school, which my summer in Greece followed, had been demoralizing, in large part because my feminist blogging hobby had come to the attention of a group of men who posted on an online message board popular with law students across the country. They savaged me daily, posting photos of me to dissect my appearance and discussing all the ways I should be shunned, humiliated, and even raped—and a few of them claimed to be my classmates. I started cutting class and stopped making friends, too paranoid that anything I said or did would be posted on the board for public mockery. I spent many hours reading through hundreds of ugly comments, learning all of the ways I was worthless and repulsive. Many of those comments were one iteration on the same theme: I was fat.

I'm ashamed to admit that mean people on the Internet eventually got under my skin, but their comments in combination with the stress of law school made me feel like an insect on display, trapped, cruelly observed, and careening emotionally sideways. I took the job in Greece to get away from it all, and spent most of the summer on a strict regimen: coffee for breakfast, a few crackers for lunch, some olives and a slice or two of salami for dinner, a long run in the blazing heat for as long as I could stand it. By the end of the summer I was thin and tan, and the satisfaction I got from my appearance and my newfound sense of control, I told myself, outweighed any pleasure I could find in food.

Until, of course, it didn't. That end-of-summer meal cracked open a door to a set of sensory experiences I didn't realize I had been craving. I was hungry.

This fear of fat means women miss out on one of the greatest pleasures of being human. The ability to take pleasure in taste is a gift, not a vice or a weakness. Food companies have exploited this natural desire to eat what tastes good, and in turn we've stigmatized people whose bodies we've decided represent gluttony. We've decided it's the bodies that should change, not corporate behavior or the cultural values.

Americans consume a lot of food, but little about how we consume it indicates that we value it. At work and school we rush through meals, and a family dinner is, in too many households, a rare indulgence to be enjoyed only when there's time. This time crunch that so many women face—women who aren't eating sea urchins in Greece but just trying to grab a snack to get them through the night shift—means there are not enough hours in the day to sit and savor food, not enough time to prepare healthy food, and not enough money to afford it even if the time was there. For many women, this lack of time turns food into a chore, a lack of money turns it into a source of stress, and a broader cultural disgust aimed at fat people turns it into a source of fear. When it comes to food, the message is that women are supposed to serve others, not themselves.

"Women," Christy said, paraphrasing a famous quote from John Berger's *Ways of Seeing*, "are followed around by the image of themselves wherever they go. Men don't have that. We could be doing anything, grieving a loved one's loss, accepting an award, getting married, and we're haunted by this image of how we look while doing it. And that's not okay. And it prevents us from achieving everything we are meant to achieve."

"A woman must continually watch herself" is the actual quote from Berger. "She is almost continually accompanied by her own image of herself. Whilst she is walking across a room or whilst she is weeping at the death of her father, she can scarcely avoid envisaging herself walking or weeping. From earliest childhood she has been taught and persuaded to survey herself continually."[41] Women live with this split self—the surveyor and the surveyed, as Berger put it—and navigate our lives through this dual existence, which forces us to see ourselves through the eyes of men, rather than simply living as we are. Women don't just look out of our own eyes; we look back at ourselves and evaluate how we must look from a man's vantage point. Watching yourself instead of existing in the moment makes it awfully hard to enjoy life, whether you're having sex or working out or taking a walk on a nice day—but especially if you're eating. Living in a body that has been deemed bad and unattractive, or living under the threat of being deemed bad and unattractive if you make the wrong choices, makes looking back at that body from a bird's-eye view and with microscopic scrutiny all the more painful. It impedes some of the most basic human pleasures. If eating makes you fat and if fat, for women, is a particular kind of feminine failure worthy of moral condemnation, of course many women have a hard time taking simple pleasure in eating. In a culture that so hinges on female sacrifice, of course women are tasked with making food for others. Women who appear to have taken too much of it for ourselves are punished—socially, yes, but also in the confines of our own minds.

"She has to survey everything she is and everything she does because how she appears to others, and ultimately how she appears to men, is of crucial importance for what is normally thought of as the success of her life," Berger wrote. "Her own sense of being in herself is supplanted by a sense of being appreciated as herself by another."[42] I first read *Ways of Seeing* in college, in an art history class. I remember walking out of class that day, heading back to my dorm, and glancing, as I did every day, in a big reflective café window I passed on my way home. I quickly averted my eyes, both worried someone would catch me looking and think I was a shallow narcissist, and also repelled by my own reflection, my body looking, to me, unpardonably large.

8

The Story of a New Name:
Identity and Female Sacrifice

Interviewer:
> You've mentioned disappearance—it's one of your
> recurring themes.

Elena Ferrante:
> It's a feeling I know well. I think all women know it.
> Whenever a part of you emerges that's not consistent
> with some feminine ideal, it makes everyone nervous,
> and you're supposed to get rid of it in a hurry.

A s I WROTE this book, one of the big questions on my mind was
what it means to be an American woman today. With fewer constraints of traditional femininity and more ways to be female than ever
before, it's hard to pin down exactly what a woman is, what the defining
characteristics of femininity are. For some, being a woman is defined
by being a mother or a potential mother; for others, it's caregiving, or
being sexually attractive to men, or providing for children or other family members. For still others it's about being a source of strength and
nurturing in their communities or for their friends, or using fashion to
be a walking piece of art, or being connected to the earth and the natural world in a way men are not. As I talked to women across the United
States from vastly different backgrounds, they told me about all sorts of

ways they were women. Across their stories, one theme emerged: the female identity hinges on service and sacrifice.

Women give. We give birth, we give life, we give milk created in our own bodies. We give up—food, ambition, money, fun. We sometimes give up our children. When we have sex with men, we're "giving it up." We give up our names. We are told to give until it hurts, and then give more. We are expected to understand that we are not by ourselves complete people; we are partially formed sketches waiting for someone else to draw us into definition.

I kept journals as a kid, and my seventh-grade diary has typical seventh-grade girl doodlings around the margins: hearts with the name of my crush in the middle, spider webs in the corners when I was feeling depressed. And then in loopy script: "Jill Butterfield." Jon Butterfield was my middle school crush, and even at twelve I understood that the ultimate culmination of love was turning into a new person. "Jill Butterfield" sounds like a blonde Wisconsin mom of three who makes really good pancakes; I wanted to be a journalist who lived in New York, or maybe working in politics in DC. But a crush didn't mean fantasizing about who I would be; it meant dreaming about belonging to someone else, folding into a new identity as his. And that meant a new name.

Diary doodling about crushes may be silly, but these young fantasies illustrate a particular kind of girlhood psychology that bleeds into womanhood: you grow up with the understanding that you are not wholly yourself, that your identity is transient. Language is how we move through the world, how we create shortcuts to understanding, how we identify everything; it's how we can tell a friend we bought a new chair, and she conjures up an image of a chair and not a car. The things we name, and those we don't, hint at what we value and what we find culturally significant. Girls and boys both get names when they are born, their surname usually their father's. But it is only women who, after decades of living with their name, traditionally change it when they marry, in one of the more literal incarnations of patriarchal authority. What does this do to girls' sense of self and identity, when the very words they put on themselves are, they know from a young age, bound to disappear? What does it do to their sense of self and identity when that change comes with marriage, and they give up their own name in exchange for a man's—and when that's sold as romantic?

As far as historians can tell, feminist and abolitionist Lucy Stone was the first American woman to keep her last name after she married in 1855 (technically, she changed it when she married, then changed it back a year later).[1] "A wife should no more take her husband's name than he should hers," she wrote. "My name is my identity and must not be lost."[2] Her attitude didn't catch on. Although it was never legally required that a woman take her husband's name in marriage, it was a legal principle that she was folded into his authority and her existence dissolved into his. Once a woman married, she had few rights of her own, and under the law (as in language) she was an appendage of her husband. In some parts of the United States, the failure to take your husband's name meant you couldn't exercise certain rights—some state laws barred married women from keeping their driver's licenses if they retained their birth names, or allowed them to vote only if they shared a last name with their husband.[3] Although many of these laws weren't enforced, some of them also didn't change until the 1970s. And the concept that married women existed under the legal authority of their husbands persisted well into recent history, with married women's rights to own property or have their own credit cards curtailed through the mid-twentieth century and the right to refuse marital sex not recognized in all fifty states until the 1990s. The second-wave feminist movement of the 1960s and '70s brought with it important social upheavals, including emphasizing that marriage shouldn't mean women lose their rights and their identities, and women took note: more women in that period began retaining their names upon marriage, about 17 percent in the 1970s.[4]

In the forty years since, that proportion hasn't changed much. It dipped in the 1980s, and by the 2010s a Google consumer survey estimated that just over 20 percent of women kept their surnames when they married.[5] That's on the high end of estimates: another survey by the wedding website TheKnot.com found that just 8 percent of women kept their names in 2011.[6] Even in an age where women outnumber men in college and nearly all of us have attached a professional reputation to our names by working before we marry, the overwhelming majority of women erase their names when they wed, opting into a tradition that is

a vestige of women becoming legally invisible on their wedding days—
and a modern reality that erases a woman's own history.

I was shocked to see this happening in real time. Once I was no longer a seventh-grade girl, the idea that I would change my name when
I married fell away. It wasn't something that came up in my relationships. I assumed that women getting married in the 2000s and 2010s
would all keep their names, because we were all our own people with
our own accomplishments. Our college degrees were in our names,
and whatever we accomplished before marriage would be in our own
names, and changing your name because you got married seemed so
backward, antifeminist, and regressive. Who takes their husband's
name anymore anyway?

Almost everyone, it turns out. I figured this out in a thoroughly modern way: through Facebook. I would be scrolling through and see an
unfamiliar name, and wonder how I became friends with this random
stranger. I'd click through the photo to defriend them and more often
than not realize it was an old high school classmate—no longer Elena
Jordan, she was now Elena Frankel, a stranger I didn't recognize. Now
that I've been out of high school for fifteen years and some of my classmates married for a decade, there are women on Facebook whose old
names, and old identities, I struggle to recall. There are a lot of "friends"
who, even when I click through and look at their photos, I don't recognize—I know they're high school acquaintances because of our mutual
connections, but being called Courtney doesn't narrow it down if that
first name is paired with a new last one. Their new names have totally
erased any memory I have of who they were.

Writing about this, even in feminist circles, will get you in a lot
of trouble. I've written critically about name changing before, in both
Cosmopolitan and the *Guardian,* and the blowback is always intense.
Criticizing a sexist cultural standard often offends the people who adhere to that standard but who don't like thinking they've made an unfeminist decision. It's mean and it makes people feel bad; don't we have
bigger things to worry about? "It's a choice," the argument goes, "and
aren't feminists all about choice?"

Well, yes and no. No one is trying to make it illegal for women to
change their names, but according to one 2011 study published in the journal *Gender and Society,* half of Americans think it would be a good idea to
legally require a woman to take her husband's name upon marriage.[7] And

Americans aren't so quick to say that men should have a choice when it comes to their last names: in a *Huffington Post* / YouGov survey, more than a third of Americans said they believe men should not be *allowed* to take a woman's last name.[8]

Naming matters. Nowhere is that clearer than for people who change their names for reasons other than marriage. Transgender people routinely change their names to match their gender, sometimes referring to their birth name as their "dead name"—a painful piece of history that never fit, an identifier that identified them wrongly. A small number of people change their names for other reasons—to exorcise the memory of an abusive parent, to take on the last name of a mother who was more involved than a father. But, overwhelmingly, among people whose identities match up with the gender they were assigned at birth, your name stays—unless you're female and you marry.

If there was a real hunger among women to change their name and that had nothing to do with folding their identity into their husband—if it was really because they disliked their last names—then we would see it happening more often outside of marriage. But we don't. And if marital naming conventions were simply a free choice, we would expect to see men making that choice, too—after all, about as many men marry as women, giving them just as many opportunities to change their surnames. Same-sex couples can now legally wed in fifty states, and although it's too early for researchers to have analyzed name-changing data on those couples, anecdotally, most married same-sex couples I know either both kept their own names or both hyphenated. Men, like women, have abusive or absent fathers to whom they don't want to be tied. Men, like, women, have unappealing last names or marry women whose last names are "better" than theirs. But virtually no men change their names when they get married, nor would most consider it. In one survey conducted by *Men's Health* magazine, 96.5 percent of respondents said they would not even consider taking their wife's name. Why not? According to one man who took the survey, "My name is part of who I am."

"Who I am," with or without a husband, is not an identity we've socially cultivated in women. And the same men who said they would never even consider changing their last names largely demanded that their wives take theirs: 63 percent of respondents in that same survey said they would be upset if their wives kept their own names.[9] "It sounds like she's trying to hang onto her 'single person' identity and not identify with the fact that she's married now," said one man. "One family, one name," said another. "If she didn't take my name, I'd seriously question her faith in us lasting as a couple. And I don't want hyphenated kids." And another: "Hyphenation is a direct 'f*ck you' to a man's masculinity . . . it elevates his father-in-law's manhood over his own."

It's hard to read those responses, and men's refusal to change their own names, and not conclude that name changing isn't about love or family; it's about power, and the understanding that a woman's identity is contingent on a man's. If both parties really saw marriage as a union of equals, then it wouldn't be a big deal for each individual to keep their name; if the only reason for name changing was a strong desire for a shared family name, then you would see men take their wives' names as often as women take their husbands' names. But you don't.

Men don't take their wives names because when you change your name upon marriage, something is lost—identity, history, culture, professional accomplishments. When we change that name, we sever our professional histories and make it just a little bit more difficult to show a prospective employer who we are. This is particularly true in the age of Google. If you apply for a job, the person doing the hiring is almost surely going to Google your name. And if your married name is Alicia Waters and your birth name was Alicia Gonzales, all of Alicia Gonzales's accomplishments—the degrees and awards she received, the research she published, where her work was cited, is invisible. Former coworkers with a job opportunity may not be able to find you if they knew you as Jennifer Washington and you're now Jennifer Markofsky on LinkedIn. James Gonzales, though, remains fully detectable online.

My own difficult-to-pronounce last name marks me as Serbian, or at least eastern European; were I to take my partner's last name, it would imply I'm Irish (which as far as I know, I'm not). It would suddenly render unconnected to me a body of work published under my name, an undergraduate and law degree earned in my name, awards for legal services and journalistic accomplishments engraved with my name. Everyone who knew me as a child knew me as Jill Filipovic—I still get occasional e-mails from high school teachers or elementary school friends who read something I wrote and wanted to reach out and say hi. Old contacts sometimes reach out with story ideas or feedback. Were I to start publishing under a name I changed when I got married, that would be gone.

Individually, each of these losses may be small (although losing one's attachment to a decade or so of work is not actually so minor). But they add up. And the pressure is all on women. For a man to take a woman's last name would be emasculating; it would imply that his identity is folded into hers, that he's no longer fully himself. It would be a loss of power and individuality. For women, losing power and individuality in marriage is the expectation. If she wants to challenge that norm, the work is all on her to do—the intellectual inquiry, the emotional effort, the answering questions of why she kept her name. This is time and labor men never have to spend. It is a female-only sacrifice, wrapped in the language of "choice" and romance.

The arguments in favor of marital name changing, and the language around it generally, belies the sexism at the root of the practice. Women have "maiden names" and "married names"; men just have names. In defending the choice to change their names, many women have told me that their last names were their father's anyway. By that logic, though, women never get to have names of their own, and, somehow, having an identity given to you through a naming convention at birth doesn't fully count for women the way it does for men. I have never once heard from a man that his last name is "really" his father's. Women don't think they're taking their husband's father's name (and, by extension, not his name either but his father's and his father's and so on); they say they're taking their *husband's* name, even though it too came down a familial lineage. So why isn't the wife's name just as much hers?

Unsurprisingly, the women with the most social power and the most to lose professionally tend to keep their surnames when they marry. Women with advanced degrees are between five and ten times more likely to reject a marital name change than women without higher education, one 2004 Census Bureau study found; among brides featured in the *New York Times* wedding section, who tend to be highly educated and urban dwelling, about half keep their names, and it's been that way since the mid-1980s.[10] The older a woman is when she marries—the longer she's been living with her name and accruing personal and professional accomplishments under it—the less likely she is to change it. Harvard economist Claudia Goldin found that the top predictor of whether a woman changes her name is how much she had accomplished under that name.[11] Women keep their names, then, when their identities attach primarily to them, their accomplishments, and experiences, as opposed to their partner or their marital status. That the women with the most social power are also the most likely to reject a long-standing sexist tradition and retain their names upon marriage should tell us something about the power in keeping it.

In feminist circles, the idea that a woman should keep her name is only a little controversial, and the pushback seems to come from women who have changed their names and feel like their independence or feminism is being questioned. Anecdotally, most feminist-identified women I know didn't change their names when they got married; this too is born out in the research, which indicates that more liberal, feminist-minded women keep their names when they marry.[12]

But even among feminists, their children almost all have the father's last name; at best they hyphenate (the one exception I can think of is a single mom whose child's father is not involved at all and was not planning to be when the child was born). This seems to be the most stubborn barrier: feminist-friendly men may be fine with their wives not changing their names upon marriage, but the idea of a child taking only the mother's name does not stand. And so, routinely, mom is the family outlier—everyone is a Smith and she's a Johnson—or her last name is effectively the child's middle name, easily hidden or dropped in favor of the father's. I know single mothers whose children have the father's last name, despite the father not being the child's primary caregiver and often not even being particularly involved during the pregnancy. It's a strange custom, given that mothers still overwhelmingly manage children's lives—picking then up from school, attending parent-teacher conferences, taking them to the doctor, ferrying them to sports and activities. For all practical purposes, it makes more sense if a child shares a name with her mother; that rarely happens if a woman's last name is different from her child's father's name.

It makes symbolic sense, too. Women do all the labor of bringing a child into the world: carrying the pregnancy, giving birth, often breast-feeding or at least attempting to. Even the things that could be shared—waking up in the middle of the night, taking time off from work to care for a new baby—almost always fall on the mother. Yet American babies usually get their father's last names. Women are supposed to give, not assert identity over what they create.

Women are also supposed to give until it hurts—or give until it kills us. One of the most physically arduous things the majority of women do is carry a pregnancy and give birth. And yet the disregard, and disrespect, of maternity is stunning. Perhaps nowhere is this more evident than in the American antiabortion movement. The same people who say they value life and love babies seem to have very little regard for just how difficult it is to bring one of those babies into the world. You see this in the regular argument that women who are considering abortion should just give their babies up for adoption—as if carrying a pregnancy is no big deal, as if childbirth is no big deal, as if having a baby and then relinquishing your child is no big deal. As if women should just sacrifice.

Some abortion opponents will say this outright. In a speech republished on dozens of prolife websites, Mother Teresa spoke at the National Prayer Breakfast in 1994 and said about women considering abortion, "We must persuade her with love and we remind ourselves that love means to be willing to give until it hurts. Jesus gave even His life to love us. So, the mother who is thinking of abortion, should be helped to love, that is, to give until it hurts her plans, or her free time, to respect the life of her child."[13]

This is what is required of women: give until it hurts.

That's certainly true in childbirth, which has perhaps never been more micromanaged or politicized, and wherein pain has perhaps never been more fetishized—at least not since it was first meted out as punishment for a curious Eve. Nearly every mother I have spoken with told me that she faced tremendous pressure to have a carefully crafted birth plan that reflected her priorities and values. Are you having a doula or a birth coach? Natural or with painkillers? Epidural or no? Water birth? Hospital birth? Scheduled C-section? You're definitely breast-feeding, right? These aren't merely a list of choices offered up to pregnant women; they are imbued with moral judgment. And in America today, the emphasis is on women making parenting choices that are "natural"—even if "natural" means hurting.

"How often do people really want women to be or do anything 'natural'?" comedian Jenni Klein wrote in an essay, adapted from her book, for the *New York Times*. "It seems to me the answer is almost never. In fact, almost everything natural about women is considered pretty

horrific. Hairy legs and armpits? Please shave, you furry beast. Do you
have hips and cellulite? Please go hide in the very back of your shoe
closet and turn the light off and stay there until someone tells you to
come out. (No one will tell you to come out.) It's interesting that no one
cares very much about women doing anything 'naturally' until it involves
their being in excruciating pain."[14] That's why, she wrote, women should
just get the epidural in childbirth and not feel guilty about it.

"The expectation of sacrifice—regarding sex, childbirth, career, the
caretaking of children and aging parents—is the axis around which so
many women's lives revolve," Klein wrote. "Men, of course, face pressure around standards of masculinity, but there is not the same jeweler's
loupe scrutiny over every bodily centimeter, and every one of their life
decisions." There is no way for women to endure this level of scrutiny
without being miserable. And that requirement of female sacrifice goes
double for mothers, for whom sacrifice is practically part of the job
description. This is where much of the guilt around birth begins: What
kind of mother wouldn't sacrifice her own comfort for her child?

Having never had a baby, I have no dog in the birth fight and more
or less think women should have babies in ways that have been proven
to be medically sound and safe, for both them and their child. Having
an epidural or choosing to forgo it; both seem to fit the bill. But the
reaction to each choice is imbalanced. When I tweeted Klein's piece,
a feminist-identified man tweeted back immediately, and repeatedly,
to lecture me on how epidurals are bad for women and natural birth
with minimal medical intervention is best. Reading his tweets from my
apartment in Kenya, I wondered how many doctors and women in the
developing world, for whom having a baby is a death-defying event and
for whom hospital births remain a great privilege, think "natural" trumps
all else. Naturally, childbirth often kills women.

Which of course doesn't mean women shouldn't have the right to decide for themselves how to give birth, and what interventions they want
to take up and which they prefer to forgo. The developed-world eleva-
tion of natural birth is itself a backlash to the pain and suffering so often
inflicted upon women in the delivery room by disinterested doctors. But
just as the requirements of good motherhood have been ratcheted up,
so too have the requirements for a "good" birth. The hyperintense focus
on women's birth choices is in the service of one goal: a healthy baby. A
healthy woman—a happy woman—is largely a side issue.

Sometimes, this is taken to the extreme, with women who refuse certain medical interventions finding that their doctors just ignore them, or worse. Take Melissa Rowland, a pregnant woman struggling with drug addiction who against the advice of her doctor refused a caesarean section for the twins she was carrying. She was charged with murder when she gave birth to a stillborn boy (her daughter was born alive but with cocaine in her system).[15] A shining example of maternal health she was not, but instead of prebirth or preconception concern for Melissa's health and treatment for her addiction—many addiction treatment programs will not accept pregnant women,[16] leaving them in an impossible spot—she was legally penalized. Melissa ended up accepting a deal to avoid the murder charges and instead pleaded guilty to two counts of child endangerment.[17] Another woman, Rinat Dray, didn't want to deliver by C-section either; her doctor overrode her wishes entirely and forced one upon her.[18] This is the reality for pregnant American women: you can have your body cut open against your will if a doctor (and often a court) decides that their opinion about what's best for your fetus is more important than your opinion about what happens to you.

There are a great many birth traumas less extreme than forced C-sections but that can feel just as violating: women forced to lie on their backs when they are begging to get up, women who have medical procedures foisted upon them without their consent, women who are essentially treated like dumb cows in the delivery room. There are reasons so many people are skeptical, and even hostile, to the medicalized American way of birth. Most of them stem from the fact that pregnant women are treated like vessels, and the baby—and the doctor's comfort—are considered more important than the woman herself. With things in the delivery room (or the home birth room) moving fast and women often physically incapacitated and vulnerable, there is great opportunity for abuse, especially from doctors making decisions without getting the full consent of their patient—or acting as if the fetus is the primary patient and the woman is secondary. A great many women report being traumatized and even suffering from posttraumatic stress disorder as a result of their birth experience.

In the years after giving birth, many women also suffer through painful birth-related injuries, many of which do not abate—back pain, pain during sex, incontinence, horrible pelvic pain.[19] In one 2015 study out of the UK, about a quarter of women reported that sex remained painful a year and a half after childbirth.[20] Another found that more than three-quarters of women still suffered from back pain a year after giving birth, and half from urinary incontinence (40 percent had both).[21] At least a quarter of American women also experience pelvic floor disorders, some of which appear in the aftermath of childbirth and many of which worsen with age, affecting half of women over eighty. These include pelvic organ prolapse, where parts of the uterus, vagina, anus, or bowels may fall out of place, sometimes descending down into the vagina or even out of it; urinary incontinence; and fecal incontinence.[22] "Childbirth is one of nature's most wondrous but biologically brutal feats," wrote journalist Laura Beil in a groundbreaking article on childbirth injuries for Cosmopolitan.com. "For nine months, a woman's muscles and bones bear the increasing weight of a baby that isn't even slightly ergonomically positioned. During a vaginal birth, muscles and other tissues stretch and often tear as something the size of a cantaloupe is forced through an opening that is normally about the size of a carrot. Sometimes, pelvic bones crack under the duress. At the beginning of the last century, as many as 9 in 1,000 American women did not survive the process. And according to a recent spate of studies, a disturbing number of women . . . still quietly endure incontinence, painful sex, back aches, and crippling pelvic pain for years after giving birth because of undiagnosed and untreated childbirth injuries."[23]

This, many doctors tell women, is "normal." It seems that when a woman has a baby, even many in the medical profession believe she signs herself up for years of pain and discomfort. What is being a mother, after all, if not giving until it hurts—even if it keeps hurting?

This disregard for the woman's happiness and well-being does not stop once the baby is born. In a justified backlash to predatory corporations that demonized breast-feeding so they could sell more baby formula, a mother's milk is touted as something close to magic for infants, with breast-feeding advocates asserting that breast milk lowers rates of obesity and diabetes and raises a child's IQ, while the act of breast-feeding itself helps women bond with their babies and even lose weight. The importance of breast-feeding is so widely accepted that, in many hospitals, formula is now kept under lock and key.

But baby formula is not a dangerous narcotic—indeed, it's a sophisticated nutritional supplement and an excellent source of nourishment for babies. Although breast-feeding does bring with it a slew of benefits, those can be offset if it takes a heavy toll on a mother. Some babies don't latch and cry incessantly and heartrendingly because they're starving. Other mothers have to return to work soon after giving birth and may not have the time or the private space to pump every few hours. Others find breast-feeding incredibly painful—they have physical complications or infections, or an infant with teeth coming in practically bites their nipples off. Many mothers find themselves exhausted and short tempered by waking up every two hours to either feed their baby or pump their breasts; instead of enjoying their child's first days or months on earth, they miss it, existing in a fog of fatigue and frustration. Other women love breast-feeding and take immense pleasure in using their bodies to nourish their child but find themselves judged in public—ordered, for example, to go breast-feed in the bathroom instead of at the dinner table—or not accommodated at work. Some women who have been honest about how breast-feeding can be sexually arousing—a fact that shouldn't be surprising, given that many women find nipple stimulation sexually arousing—struggle with feelings of guilt, or at the extremes have gone to jail or had their children taken away.[24] Still others may not like breast-feeding but make a decision to do it anyway, until they no longer can.

But in all of the dialogue around breast-feeding—and everyone, it seems, has an opinion—the comfort, well-being, and just plain experience of mothers doesn't seem to count for much. Unsurprisingly, researchers have found that women who plan to breast-feed but have difficulty doing so are more than twice as likely to develop postpartum depression than women who never intended to breast-feed in the first place.[25]

This demand for maternal sacrifice doesn't just make women sick, sad, and stressed out. Sometimes, it kills us. And when it does, some people applaud.

"Maternal sacrifice during childbirth shows the rightness and the resignation which souls must have in following the natural law," read an article published in a Roman Catholic magazine, which opened with the story of a young mother dying in childbirth. "Mothers today are confronted with a dynamic choice of following their own devices or surrendering to God and their husbands. . . . This human practice of love is shown by your daily surrender to your husband, your God, and even, to an extent, your circumstances. Your consolation is a joyful heart and the peace of knowing that you are doing all you can to sanctify your own soul and get your family to heaven."[26]

It will come as little surprise to learn that the above article was written by a man.

If this were simply a religious theory—that women come second to their children, that maternity is inherently sacrificial—it would be disturbing but at least arguably a personal choice. But it's not—it's been folded into American medical care. One in six US hospital beds is in a Catholic facility, where health care is determined not by scientifically agreed-upon medical standards but by religious morals and ethics.[27] This means women who seek care at Catholic facilities may have trouble getting contraception or sterilization procedures, even if they are done with childbearing or if a previous pregnancy almost killed them. It means Catholic facilities are not supposed to conduct prenatal diagnostic exams if a woman wants to know whether her fetus has a severe abnormality and intends to end the pregnancy if it does. And doctors treating a pregnant woman must treat her fetus as a patient with equal rights and interests—so even if a pregnant woman is seriously ill and having an abortion will help save her life, it's not permissible in a Catholic hospital.

Although Catholic facilities are probably the worst when it comes to treating women like fetal incubators instead of people, this is a pervasive problem in the medical establishment. More than 90 percent of drugs include no safety information for pregnant women, largely because of government regulations forbidding drug testing on vulnerable populations, which includes women carrying pregnancies.[28] As a result, many doctors advise pregnant women not to take a whole slew of pharmaceutical treatments for fear it could harm their fetuses. That often includes medications that treat depression, anxiety, or substance addiction—putting a pregnant woman's physical and mental health behind the health of her fetus. This, wrote Greer Donley in an article for the NYU Review of Law and Social Change, creates a "Catch-22" for pregnant women: "On the one hand, avoiding needed medications during pregnancy can cause negative health consequences for both pregnant women and their fetuses. On the other, given that both pregnant women and their fetuses metabolize drugs differently from other adults, drug consumption during pregnancy can cause adverse reactions in both parties. This dilemma, at best, can cause significant anxiety for pregnant women choosing whether to consume medications; at worst, it can cause blind decision-making, which can lead to physical harm of the pregnant woman and/or fetus."[29]

In insisting women sacrifice for their children, they often end up sacrificing their own health and, sometimes, their lives.

This norm of female sacrifice starts young, and womanhood and girlhood alike are routinely about taking less. One 2012 study found that 80 percent of ten-year-old girls have been on a diet at some point in their short lives.[30] Some 20 million American women have an eating disorder, many of which begin in girlhood.[31] Globally, women are more likely than men to suffer from nutritional deficiencies, both because they often lack access to food and because of cultural norms that entrench female denial.[32]

In some places, the sacrifice is brought on by scarcity—women eating last, or not eating at all, so someone else can consume those calories. In others, food is plentiful, but female denial persists as a moral value. Women don't just give up food but money: weight loss in the United States is a $64 billion industry, most of that coming from women's pockets.[33] In the pursuit of attractiveness, the American woman spends an average of $15,000 on cosmetics in her lifetime.[34] In 2015 alone, Americans spent $13.5 billion on cosmetic procedures, with more than half of that going to surgical procedures.[35] Liposuction, breast augmentations, and tummy tucks top the list. More than 90 percent of cosmetic surgeries are performed on women.

This dedication to attractiveness also takes times and energy. Cosmetic surgery requires recovery hours, if not days or weeks, off work. Your average woman's basic morning routine takes much longer than a man's—add time to shave her legs and underarms in the shower, put on foundation and eye shadow and eyeliner and mascara and blush, brush and blow-dry and perhaps curl or straighten her hair, and you're talking easily an extra hour just to start off the day. For some women, this is not a choice: there are employers that require female employees to wear makeup or skirts, and fire them if they don't. For other women, it's part of looking "professional" or "put together": an employer may not fire you for not wearing makeup or coming to work with hairy armpits, but doing so would send the message that you're slovenly and unserious. For others, these rituals are just part of a female thing—and they're kind of fun. I fall mostly in that last category (perhaps because I work at home and so don't have to even shower most mornings if I don't want to): makeup, high heels, and dresses are things I wear with some regularity. They make me feel attractive. I wear them by choice.

Except when I don't. When I did work in an office, there were plenty of mornings when I would have preferred to roll into work in ill-fitting slacks and a button-down, the way my male colleagues did. But if I had a client meeting or had to drop by to see a partner, I knew I'd better look presentable, and so blow-dried hair and eyeliner it was. This is a minor complaint, and female lawyers having to wear wrinkle-free clothing and brush their hair does not even crack the list of the top 100 feminist concerns. But when your average woman spends fifty-five minutes every morning getting ready,[36] that adds up—to almost two weeks every year. Do that for forty years, and you're talking about a year and a half of your life. If this were fully voluntary—if clothes and makeup really were just wearable art, accoutrements we put on and took off to reflect our tastes and personalities—this would be a different discussion, and we'd also see men spending as much time altering or augmenting their physical appearances with clothes and makeup as women do. Although men do have their own standards of fashion and grooming and many men also diet and spend lots of time at the gym, the bulk of appearance-based pressure remains on women. And the fashion choices women are encouraged to make tend to be more sadistic than those offered to men. I have a closet full of high heels; they're horrible for my feet and back, but I wear them anyway. I have drawers full of makeup and beauty products that are barely regulated by the US Food and Drug Administration; I use them anyway in a daily effort to look younger and prettier. Admit this is the case and you're vain; refuse to partake and you're an unattractive, unfeminine radical feminist.

Makeup and feminine clothing aren't inherently bad, and the world, I think, would be an even more brilliant place if more of us expressed our creative selves through our physical appearance. Human beings have always sought out the aesthetically pleasing, have always dedicated time and money to creating art, have always enjoyed grooming and a bit of vanity. Carrying these values on the body can be wonderful; more beauty in the world and more interesting displays on the body and off it would be delightful.

But when it comes to women and the culture around fashion and beauty, it's not just about art, creativity, expression, and aesthetic appeal. Much of the time, it's about expressing class status, with particular conspicuous brands or a certain look that reflects one's interests and social tribe. Men do this too, of course, but women have the added obligation of doing it *more*—more expensively, in more detail, with more variation, and with the added expectation of being sexually appealing. And it's not nearly as optional for women as for men. In the 2016 Democratic primary, many observers noted that if a candidate like Bernie Sanders had been female, she would have utterly failed on appearance alone—a bedraggled, wild-haired old lady yelling about socialism might not be allowed on a public bus, let alone into the US Senate, and surely wouldn't be a serious candidate for the presidency.

The expectation that women will either wear makeup and dress fashionably or make a statement by opting out is another layer of obligation—of time, of money—laid on women's bodies. At the very least, women are supposed to *try*, and keep trying. Perfection isn't an achievement, and there's no point at which the right face cream or lipstick or pair of shoes is enough. Instead, women are supposed to always be striving to be better: thinner, more toned, brighter skinned, more flatteringly dressed. There's a financial interest here, from the big companies who sell women all these things and make billions. There's also a cultural interest: maintaining women's role as a class of aesthetically pleasing bodies perpetually trying harder to fit ever-changing molds of attractiveness maintains differences between men and women, and ultimately, male power.

When Naomi Wolf wrote on these same themes almost three decades ago in *The Beauty Myth*, she made waves around the world with her suggestion that the time and money women were pushed to spend on beautifying ourselves kept us from other important matters: accruing wealth, negotiating for a raise, starting a rape crisis group. Dieting, she pointed out, kept women mentally pliable and physically weak—it's hard to focus when you're calorie deficient, as anyone who has ever tried a juice cleanse can attest. "A culture fixated on female thinness is not an obsession about female beauty, but an obsession about female obedience," Wolf wrote. "Dieting is the most potent political sedative in women's history; a quietly mad population is a tractable one." When so much of our time and energy is dedicated to striving for beauty—never just *being* beautiful, which would be a determination we made about ourselves and therefore intolerably vain—we begin to see ourselves as objects for male approval, not individuals striving for whatever it is we actually want. And yet, a generation later, we spend more money on beauty than we did when Wolf's book was published in 1990. We continue to go hungry.

This denial serves a political purpose. "A consequence of female self-love is that the woman grows convinced of social worth," Wolf wrote. "Her love for her body will be unqualified, which is the basis of female identification. If a woman loves her own body, she doesn't grudge what other women do with theirs; if she loves femaleness, she champions its rights. It's true what they say about women: Women are insatiable. We are greedy. Our appetites do need to be controlled if things are to stay in place. If the world were ours too, if we believed we could get away with it, we would ask for more love, more sex, more money, more commitment to children, more food, more care. These sexual, emotional, and physical demands would begin to extend to social demands: payment for care of the elderly, parental leave, childcare, etc. The force of female desire would be so great that society would truly have to reckon with what women want, in bed and in the world."

Far better for women to forgo.

For the most part, women are coaxed into sacrifice, socially rewarded for being the most giving, the biggest martyr, the most willing to surrender our own desires to meet someone else's needs. But with that carrot of social reward also comes a stick for the women who refuse, even in small ways, to forgo what they want—that punishment is violence. And with that pervasive threat comes another defining condition of female existence: fear.

Living in a female body means living with the soft hum of fear in the background, and the ingrained sense that our bodies are inherently vulnerable—inherently penetrable—is the white noise scoring our lives. As a result, women give up a lot of enjoyment and are told we should forgo even more. When I started college at NYU, we had a brief orientation session on safety. The basic advice was straightforward: keep cab fare on you (this was in 2001, well before Uber or even credit card machines in taxis), stay with a group of friends, never leave your drink unattended, don't take the subway after dark. These tips, obviously, were geared toward women—the young men on my freshman year floor weren't worried about a little nighttime subway riding, and they could set their beer down on the bar and be reasonably confident that it would remain undrugged if they looked away for a moment. And while many of these tips don't actually relate to much of the best research on how sexual violence operates, they do tell women exactly what they are: vulnerable. They tell us we should be fearful. And the only way to counteract this inherent, definitional female vulnerability is to give up on having too much fun.

The early 2000s were also a high point of chain e-mails, and a popular one that I must have received a dozen times, and that I still see making the rounds fifteen years later, was called "Through a Rapist's Eyes."[37] It includes tips like this:

* The first thing men look for in a potential victim is hairstyle. They are most likely to go after a woman with a ponytail, bun, braid or other hairstyle that can easily be grabbed. They are also likely to go after a woman with long hair. Women with short hair are not common targets. The second thing men look for is clothing. They will look for women whose clothing is easy to remove quickly. Many of them carry scissors around to cut clothing.

* They also look for women using their cell phone, searching through their purse or doing other activities while walking because they are off guard and can be easily overpowered.

* The number one place women are abducted from / attacked at is grocery store parking lots. Number two is office parking lots / garages. Number three is public restrooms.

These are the constraining and often-conflicting rules women are supposed to abide by. Don't wear your hair in a ponytail, braid, bun, or just down and long. Don't wear clothing that can be cut off with scissors. Don't use your phone or do anything else other than walk. Avoid grocery store parking lots, your office parking lot, and bathrooms. Basically, cut your hair short, avoid all non-Kevlar clothing, don't leave the house, and if you *do* leave the house, don't go to the bathroom. And this is just for stranger rape, which is much less common than rape at the hands of someone a woman knows. To avoid acquaintance rape,[38] women—usually in college—are told to avoid drinking, to always stay in a group (but not in a group of men), to watch their drinks carefully, to not accept drinks unless you know exactly what is in it, to not allow others to touch you, to not give out your phone number or other personal information to a stranger, to always drive your own car (but never to drink and drive), and to learn self-defense.[39] All of which may help prevent victimization but also largely prevents socializing and dating. And considering that many rape and abuse survivors are attacked by an intimate, often in their own homes—a boyfriend, a date, a friend, a family member, someone they believe they can trust—the standard rape prevention tips are largely useless.

While I was an undergraduate, the story of a young woman who was kidnapped and raped by a cab driver made headlines in the city's tabloids; why, many male commentators wondered, was she taking a cab by herself so late at night? It was a stark illustration of how, when hindsight is 20/20, women always seem to make the wrong choice: They take cabs, or they don't when they should have. They go home with a man they know, or they walk home alone. They're too assertive in rebutting a man's advances; they don't rebut a man's advances assertively enough. They take any risk whatsoever. They don't take any risks.

The truth is that risks can be fun, and we all take them—no pleasure comes without peril. "Even if you never leave your house, you risk depression due to lack of sun and social interaction (never mind the risk of fire, gas explosion, electric shock, earthquake, falling down stairs, cutting yourself on a kitchen knife, or getting a splinter)," wrote feminist writer and educator Jaclyn Friedman in the anthology *Yes Means Yes: Visions of Sexual Power and a World Without Rape.* "But rape is not a risk inherent in partying or in 'wild' sexual behavior." Consider, Friedman implored, that "it's not a risk for nearly half the population. I've never met a straight man who worried about being raped as he contemplated a night of debauchery."[40]

The threat of rape keeps women fearful, and we learn to live our whole lives around that fear: walking with our keys out in parking garages, taking self-defense classes, thinking about our ponytails as potential rape-handles before we go for a run. It also poisons pleasure: either we avoid all risk by staying home and not going to that party or the bar with our friends, or we do so knowing we're risking not just a hangover but being blamed for any potential assault—after all, the fact that we took the risk in the first place means we'll be treated like it's a little bit our fault. A "risk," in this instance, is going out with other human beings while under the influence of alcohol—a pretty standard part of socializing for all of adulthood. Yes, college students are known to drink more than your average forty-year-old, and binge drinking is a real problem. But that's also how young people figure out their limits, and how many navigate the initial anxiety of being surrounded by all new people in a new place and a new social universe. Rapists know that women are routinely held responsible for whatever choices they made leading up to an assault, which is why men who rape tend to target the most vulnerable of the college herd: first-semester freshmen who are drunk and don't have friends around them. All of the antirape advice in the world won't solve the fact that there will always be a youngest, drunkest girl in the room of any party.

The truth is, people go to parties and get drunk because it's fun; sometimes they go home with each other because that's fun, too. Humans experiment with mind-altering substances; wanting to feel loose and high and uninhibited is about as normal as it gets. So is wanting to experiment sexually, whether that's making out or heavy petting or oral sex or intercourse—and just as normal as wanting to get drunk and hook up is wanting to stop at some point, or draw a boundary, or just get drunk without some guy groping you. These are not options women are told are on the table. Instead, we're told that some of the most pleasurable human experiences are, for us, inherently dangerous, because our status as women makes us inherently vulnerable. And because a small number of (usually) men choose to turn what could be pleasurable experiences like drinking and sex into acts of violation and violence, women as a group are cautioned against just letting go. The right of men to get obliterated and do stupid stuff—the *fun* men have getting obliterated and doing stupid stuff—is so culturally accepted that it's a cornerstone of best man speeches and bro comedies. This is fun that women have, too, but always with a warning hanging over it. The vast majority of times women go out and get drunk, there's no sexual assault. But if there is, a kind of sympathy gap emerges. She should have known better than to prioritize her own pleasure. She should have given up a little bit of that fun, and then, maybe, this wouldn't have happened to her. Never mind that any woman's decision won't make a rapist disappear; had one woman stayed home, it would have happened to someone else. But this is the rule: You can have fun. Just not too much.

Defending the right of young women to party, drink, and have fun may not seem like the most pressing feminist issue. Maybe not. But it's one iteration of the many ways women and girls are constrained and taught to sacrifice our own desires. Fear is so often used to threaten women who would even consider transgressing these rules and doing what we want: fear we'll get raped if we go out and have fun, fear our baby will have a worse outcome if we don't breast-feed or birth the right way, fear we'll be romantically ignored or socially isolated if we flout the rules of feminine beauty. Fear is a pervasive emotion in women's lives, used to keep our worlds smaller and to enforce norms of female sacrifice where it's not given freely.

These two things, fear and sacrifice, come in a pair. They shape female identity and carve out the contours of female experience. This yin-yang of fear-sacrifice tells women to give until it hurts. It promises that if they don't, it'll hurt even more. It tells us, happiness is not yours to pursue.

Goodbye to All That:
A Conclusion (and what comes next)

F OR THIS BOOK, I set out to speak with a cross-section of American women, identifying what was making us unhappy and zeroing in on ideas for a more pleasure-centered public policy, and I found that the more I learned, the more questions I had. The more women I interviewed, the more I wanted to talk to, and the more the missing voices rang out—where were the undocumented immigrants, the retirees, the elderly, the women in rural communities? This book is not exhaustive, nor was it intended to be, and I hope the absent voices whisper into readers' ears as persistently as they do in mine, insisting that this text is a starting point, not an all-inclusive story. One of the goals of this project was to show that there is no one definition of womanhood, no singular experience of pleasure seeking, and no individual thing that will bring happiness for all women, but there are a great many commonalities, and a great many ways to improve the status quo. My hope is that this book offered a little peek into the overlapping struggles of so many women, as well as the many joys—however unsupported and individualized.

When the first inklings of this project swirled in my head, my plan was to emphasize politics and policy; it turns out that is a very boring way to write a book, and so the stories and experiences of a diverse group of women (and some men) became the focal point. But it would be a mistake to read these simply as elucidations of modern American life and its stubborn frustrations and displeasures, its unprecedented wonders and delights. What I took away from all of the conversations I had, all the women and men I met, and all the research that went in to understanding our current way of life is fundamentally political: it doesn't have to be this way.

We live in a country of incredible prosperity and abundance, brought into being with a natal philosophy that promised a privileged few of its citizens the right to pursue happiness—a promise that was, at the time it was made, explicitly political. Two centuries later, it is those same few who remain the most free to pursue pleasure. Our government and our leaders have fallen down on extending that earliest of promises, and indeed Americans have moved away from the idea that the right to seek out happiness isn't just personal and consumptive, but collective and radical, a fundamentally civic-minded goal. In a place of such bounty, we are making a choice to expand opportunities for some while leaving others to struggle in deprivation.

So why not the rest of us? Isn't an interesting, pleasurable, and hopefully happy existence why we're all working so hard in the first place? Even the men that our government has long catered to are not all that well served by our contemporary political landscape. The men I know want many of the same things as women I met: more time to do what they love, meaningful work where they feel respected and useful, the chance to really connect with their friends and neighbors, deep ties with their families and the time it takes to keep those bonds strong, healthy minds and bodies, fulfilling sex lives. To get there, championing gender equality isn't enough (although it's a good start). For many of the problems the women and men I talked to described, there are clear policy solutions that would improve their lives. For other problems, the answers are more complicated. Because people don't live their lives split into neat issue areas, some of the solutions for one challenge may help (or potentially hinder) another, which calls for a more holistic look at how to promote happiness and pleasure.

Fostering Relationships

Those of us who live in nontraditional, nonnuclear arrangements are hungry to see our choices supported—and where they help out the environment or space-constrained cities, rewarded. Many cities and municipalities limit the number of unrelated adults who share a house (and sometimes specifically limit the number of women—an old antibrothel measure). This is fundamentally silly—in an increasingly resource-constrained world, adults like Jennifer Becker who share a home and therefore save space, electricity, gas, and other resources should be applauded, not punished. Nontraditional families are also beginning to challenge traditional ones in terms of sheer numbers, but our tax code, health-care system, and workplaces still assume there are two married parents with children. And especially with an increasing number of single women who rely on their boyfriends or girlfriends for social support, it doesn't make much sense to assume that for unmarried people (and even for some married ones), one's next of kin should be the decision maker if things go wrong.

"I would love a federal system in which every adult gets to name 'their person,'" journalist and *Call Your Girlfriend* cohost Ann Friedman told me. "At points in my adult life when I've been single, I've always been afraid that I would get really sick and my parents—whom I love very much but who have a VERY different worldview from me—would be legally recognized to make decisions about my body. I really wish everyone could designate one primary person for legal/medical purposes. And that we weren't insistent that the primary person be a romantic partner."

The tax breaks on offer to religious institutions could also extend to secular organizations, like Dan's men's group in Seattle, that serve many of the same social and emotional functions. And as progressives push back on the decimation of unions and antiunion "right to work" laws, the valuable social place these collective bargaining institutions hold—and the broader community benefits that come along with them—should be part of our advocacy.

Promoting Sexual Pleasure

Supporting healthy, pleasurable sex lives should be a public policy goal—not just handling the public health challenges that result when sex is treated like a vice. The median age of first marriage in the United States is twenty-eight for men and twenty-six for women, and increasing numbers of people never marry at all. The vast majority of them are sexually active by their early twenties. The public has already decided to have sex for pleasure. The question is whether our politics will enable better, more pleasurable sex or continue with policies that make sex harder for women to enjoy.

When I interviewed Samantha Pugsley and Leah Torres about sex, virginity, and pleasure, I thought about my promise ring—about how glad I am my toe-dip into purity culture didn't end up in a full cannonball. It was also clear to me that the very concept of preserving your virginity until marriage is poisonous. Both Samantha and Leah are open-minded feminists, and both spoke to the value of choice: that staying a virgin until marriage is a valid choice but should be one of many, and not positioned as the only moral option. This is the standard feminist line, and of course it's true—no one needs to outlaw virgin marriage. But why, I wondered as I spoke with both of them, say it is just as valid a choice as any other? Virginity, not being a biological reality, is a social status, something we've agreed means "no sex." But every single reason in favor of preserving virginity until marriage is premised on something sexist. The entire structure of setting marriage as the point at which you should have sex is one divorced from sexual pleasure and readiness and instead tied to a woman's status, her body being claimed by someone else. Sex, too, is for many couples an act that is ideally supposed to happen only within their relationship. Signing up for what is in theory a lifetime of sex with a person whom you've never actually had sex with is a bad plan; having sex for the first time based on the arbitrary deadline of a wedding date instead of when you feel ready and want to equally sets you up for unnecessary stress and pain. This is something feminists, not to mention sexual educators, should speak about honestly.

Conversations about sex should start at home, but for many kids, they start in the classroom. Instead of teaching abstinence, educators should teach students the truth about sex: that it can be really fun, but it's also a responsibility. Some countries, most notably in Scandinavia, already do this. Not only is their sex ed comprehensive, but abortion and birth control are either free or very affordable, and young people hear that sex is normal, fun, and to be treated with respect. These nations are not perfect, but they have low rates of STIs, unintended pregnancies, and abortions, and are consistently rated some of the happiest countries on earth. Sex education should also be inclusive of gay, lesbian, bisexual, and transgender students, emphasizing that not every woman has sex with men, and not every person who is born male or female stays that way their whole lives—and that no gender identity or sexual orientation means forgoing the possibility of a pleasurable and a healthy sex life.

"America is a very sex-negative culture," sexual health educator Twanna Hines told me. "And by that I mean when we teach and talk about sex, in an educational context, we talk about the things that we don't want. Sex education teaches how to not get pregnant or get someone pregnant, how to not get or give someone a sexually transmitted disease or infection, and traditionally we've paid very little attention to achieve the things we do want: healthy sexuality throughout the life course, enthusiastic consent, and other topics that actually improve their lives."

Whether you're married or not, certain skills make for better relationships: communication, maintaining healthy self-esteem in relationships, learning how to please a partner emotionally as well as sexually, learning how to advocate for your own needs emotionally as well as sexually, and figuring out what you like and don't like in other people and relationships in all their forms. Premarital sex, including with partners other than the one you end up marrying, is part of an important and valuable learning process. Yet we currently teach sex—formally and in media—as a thing women have and men are trying to get, a kind of push-pull where women are the temptation and then the brakes, but may eventually give in. That is a recipe for sexual disaster. We know that female sexual autonomy is related to pleasure and happiness, while passivity brings women less pleasure. But we still teach our girls, in ways big and small, to be passive.

"We aren't training individuals to have healthy interpersonal relationships," Twanna said. "The root of it is learning to compromise, learning to be vulnerable, understanding what it means to communicate emotion. These are all skills. And if you can't talk about them and if we're not being trained on them, how do we expect anyone to succeed at them?"

The idea that we should raise girls and boys to have healthy, pleasurable adult sex lives makes a lot of adults uncomfortable. But encouraging girls to feel good, autonomous, and powerful in all ways—including in their bodies and in their sexual selves—would pay dividends in health and happiness. High self-esteem and a sense of self-worth not dependent on relationships—that is, not derived from being a good wife or mother or daughter or sister, but from being a good, smart, kind person in one's own right—breeds self-confident girls who are also more sexually autonomous.

Part of ensuring that women and girls are fully independent is making sure that they are able to prevent and end pregnancies at will. This not only keeps us on the path to success—it can be the life raft that keeps us afloat when we're drowning. And, yes, it lets us have sex for pleasure. That's a good thing, not some dirty secret. Contraception, abortion, and the ability to parent when we choose are unassailable social goods necessary not just for the rights of women but for our happiness, too. They should be easily available and affordable for every woman, regardless of income or location. If the American political conversation around birth control, abortion rights, and parenting started from the premise that sex is fun and healthy and women should have it without shame, the debate over reproductive rights would cease to exist.

Sex as a mutually pleasurable experience should also be reflected in our criminal and civil law. Feminists made great gains in outlawing marital rape and many forms of sexual assault, and establishing rape shield laws so that a rape victim's sexual history cannot be used against her in criminal court. But in many states, the criminal code still defines rape as "forcible" and either says or implies that women have to resist for unwanted sex to really count as a crime. The idea that anything less than mutually agreed-upon sex could be considered a sex crime flabbergasts many moderate legal theorists and armchair commentators. But if I take money out of your wallet when you're not looking, and you don't say no, but you also don't say yes—I'm still a thief. If sex really is, and should be, about mutual pleasure, then it cannot also be a thing women must vociferously refuse in order to avoid being sexually penetrated. That's not protectionist or treating women like delicate flowers; it's treating them like individuals with sexual appetites and autonomy, who get to decide for themselves when they want to have sex.

Pleasurable sex should also be considered a basic health-care right and an integral part of whole-body health and wellness. For doctors and medical professionals, that would mean if a patient has diabetes or hypertension or any other condition, asking whether it's negatively impacting their sex life and assessing ways that impact could be mitigated. For health-care policy, that would mean taking as seriously—and covering as generously—conditions that impact one's sexual health as conditions that impact other aspects of physical well-being. For politicians and advocates, it would mean dedicating public funds to research on sexual pleasure, as well as treatments that focus on alleviating or eliminating sexual dysfunction and negative sexual side effects from common ail-ments or medications. It would also mean finally fully funding research on male birth control—because for all the benefits of women's many birth control options now, many of the most popular methods compro-mise women's sexual desire and enjoyment. Libido shouldn't have to be what one trades for a sex life without the anxiety of pregnancy; cramp-ing, bleeding, and bloating are not minor inconveniences women should simply have to tolerate if we want to avoid getting pregnant.

A good sex life also doesn't just happen; it requires time and com-mitment. And a good sex life isn't a bonus, something you deserve only if you're lucky and have the privileges of spare time and good health and a generous partner. As Americans generally and liberals in particular increasingly agree that "balance" is important (even if we can't agree, politically, how to achieve it in the workplace), sex should be on the list of things we deserve to balance with our work lives, along with family, relationships, exercise, travel, children, and recreation. This is something that should appeal to social conservatives who worry about low rates of marriage and high rates of divorce in low-income, high-stress, overworked communities. After all, to keep relationships strong enough for couples to consider marriage, and to support marriages robust enough to last, you have to give people time together, and that includes time for intimacy.

Time for Pleasure, Time for Parenting, Time for Play

Perhaps the most pervasive and obvious challenge women face is time: nearly every woman I talked to, whether she was a single mother or married coparent or single child-free working woman, said she was con-stantly crunched for time and stressed out because of it. Some of this is simply because many of us work too many hours. Compared to our eco-nomic peers, Americans work more hours per week: an average of 34.4 when you include part-time employees, and 47 for full-time employees. Those of us who work full time, in other words, work six days a week, not five. And almost 40 percent of full-time workers say they work more than 50 hours a week. We have no federally mandated vacation time, and the average American gets just fifteen days off a year. Europeans, by contrast, get an average of twenty-eight days off.

For other women, the crunch comes from not enough working hours, hours that are unpredictable, and schedule changes that mean it's hard to arrange consistent child care. And budgeting is nearly impossible when you get paid by the hour but don't know how many hours you'll work in any given week. These kinds of schedules are the new normal in the United States: 6.5 million Americans worked part time in 2015 but wanted full-time employment. And although women and men are working harder than ever, as evidenced by the century-long rise in pro-ductivity, that hasn't translated into more money: real income for work-ers has stagnated since the 1970s. Part of the reason is that CEOs and other top executives—mostly men—have taken a much larger share of the earnings than they did in past decades, while many of the women who entered the workforce right when real wages leveled out entered low-paying jobs (or jobs that immediately lost prestige and pay when they became female dominated).[1]

The economist Heather Boushey wrote a whole book on the econom-ics of this work-life time crunch, and came up with four general buckets for new policies: Here (policies that make it possible for workers to be at home when need be), There (those that allow workers to have predict-able work schedules and enough working hours in a week), Care (those that make sure people who can't care for themselves—usually the very young and the very old—have their needs met), and Fair (that all of these policies benefit workers at all levels and all genders, not just the most privileged). We also have to look at what lawyer and writer Caro-line Fredrickson called "the whole elephant" that working-class women in particular live: "It wasn't just the wages," she wrote. "It was the lack of benefits and access to credit, child care, paid sick days, and time off, and it was the indignities of harassment and misogyny."[2]

Women first need fair wages. This means a higher minimum wage—no one should work full time and still find their families fall below the poverty line—and penalties for companies that intentionally short-change their workers on hours so they won't have to give them full ben-efits. Those workers end up relying on federal and state governments to make up the difference, while the companies they work for routinely get tax breaks and other windfalls. That's a broken system, and given that it's women (and often single mothers) who head most of the house-holds that fall below the poverty line, a pressing feminist issue. Workers deserve a predictable number of hours and level of compensation each week, and fair pay regardless of their gender or even negotiating skills. That means more wage transparency, with companies required to track and report employee pay across a variety of categories, including race, gender, and time with the company. There may always be pay variations as a result of individual talents and circumstances, but companies (and regulatory bodies) need to know whether there are significant differences based on race, gender, or other aspects of employee identity instead of employee skill.

Employees also deserve to work in a humane environment, which means not being abused or harassed on the job. Regulations punishing sexual harassment and other actions that make for inhospitable workplaces should be tightened, and it should be easier for workers to join together to push back on poor treatment, whether that's sexual harassment or inequitable pay. Recent Supreme Court decisions have made class action cases harder to bring, something that most negatively impacts those with limited resources, who are unlikely to be able to afford to pursue individual legal actions. Congress should take this on and ensure that all Americans can have their day in court if they're mistreated.

Women and men also need the "Here" benefits Boushey recommended. How we structure those benefits makes all the difference. Although the inclination among feminists may be to assume that longer is better for parental leave, the social science research doesn't necessarily bear that out—there is a point at which being out of the workplace becomes too long. It's not clear what the ideal amount of time off is, but it seems it's more than ten weeks (which is what the average American woman takes) but less than a full year.[3] It would need to be paid leave so that having a baby doesn't mean risking bankruptcy (right now, most of the women who take those ten weeks do so without pay). Most crucially, leave has to be structured to incentivize both parents to take it— not just mothers. If only mothers take leave, it sets women back even further in terms of pay and advancement. This means a Swedish-style carrot and a stick: giving both women and men generous leaves when they have children with a little extra for the party who actually birthed the child, but conditioning some of the leave time on a man taking his (for same-sex couples, the same dynamic would give the birthing partner, if there is one, extra leave, and give the couple more total leave if both partners take time off).

Just as important as time off of work is making sure going back is easy. This is perhaps the biggest challenge for the federal government to take on. There are a lot of competing ideas for how this would work, but one of the best—and one that is currently not on the table—is a network of public day-care facilities. "Government-run child care" is no doubt a lightning rod for the political Right, but given that we already have government-run public education for children ranging in age from five to eighteen, and then high-quality public higher education for students eighteen and above, it's not such a stretch to imagine a public care system for the youngest among us, to be run parallel to a private one. Workers at both public facilities and private ones must be qualified and well compensated for their work. As it stands, the day-care system in the United States is terrifyingly underregulated; we should absolutely ratchet up the requirements for day-care employees and the safety of the facilities in which they operate, and compensate child-care workers fairly. If caring for children is in fact "the most important job in the world," we should be paying the people who care for children more than the bare minimum.

The burden of that payment should also be distributed fairly and not put entirely on individual parents. There are a variety of mechanisms to make that happen: large employers and institutions of higher education, particularly community colleges, could be required to either have on-site day care for which they would enjoy a tax benefit, or they could pay into a plan that would partially cover day-care costs for all workers; parents could receive tax breaks and vouchers for child care, whether they place their child in a day-care facility or have a nanny come to their home.

And we need a break: for when we get sick, for when our kids or aging parents get sick, and just because human beings are not machines. Our vacation policies, and our cultural assumption that vacation isn't all that necessary, need a serious revamp. Paid time off isn't just a way to recharge and come back to work reinvigorated and ready to work harder; it's also when there's time to engage in all the other little pleasures that make a life, connect us with those we love, and bring both short-term happiness and longer-lasting satisfaction: going someplace new and experiencing something different; going somewhere familiar and letting yourself be awash in good memories; staying home and enjoying the kind of slow, satisfying meals you may not have time for on busy workdays; having sex with your partner or otherwise intimately reconnecting without worrying about getting up early the next day or having the stress of a big project clouding your mind.

Make Food Feminist

In the health-care and health policy realm, there's also room for big changes in how we talk about fat, weight, food, and health. Many federally funded research efforts and health programs are geared toward obesity prevention and use BMI as the relevant measure rather than actual health measures—rates of diabetes or the ability to walk a mile. One procedure Christy Harrison, the nutritionist, said should definitely go is the obesity-prevention BMI Report Card, wherein "students are weighed in front of their class, given a grade on their BMI, and often shamed in front of the class," she said. "Then they're sent home with this report card that says your child needs to lose weight." That sets kids up for a lifetime of shame about their bodies and a view of food as an off-limits vice, not a normal part of life. Advertising for diet products should also be more tightly regulated—the products should actually have to do what they say they do, and companies should have to prove, and then disclose, their actual efficacy and side effects. "Insurance companies should be required to provide financial assistance to those with eating disorders," said Melissa Fabello, a Philadelphia-based body acceptance activist. "Schools should revamp their health and physical education curricula to reflect that health is not a one-size-fits-all issue—kids should be able to explore their own individual needs and wants and should be assessed from that space."

A better use of resources would be more generous benefits for low-income families, which would allow them to buy healthier foods, and health education programs to help adults and children understand the basics of nutrition without tying health to "good" or "bad" bodies— nutrition education programs, research has shown, save ten dollars in health-care costs for every dollar spent.[4] Nutrition, and the pleasures of eating well, should be part of every student's education—and it should be taught from a place of reverence for the body and with an ethos of meeting its needs, not from a place of pushing deprivation or simply trying to make oneself smaller. School lunches, too, should be about nourishing our children, not simply packing them with food and moving on with the day, and we should give kids time to savor them. And small-scale farmers like Karen Washington should see their efforts supported and fairly remunerated; so too should our government support

sustainable agriculture and reevaluate the degree to which it is beholden
to big food companies and agribusiness.

This, I realize, is quite the laundry list. But it points to just how insufficiently we have met the needs of American women, especially as our social roles have evolved to give us more options, and in many ways more
power, than ever before. That so many of us are so unhappy demon-
strates not an individual failure to seek pleasure but a political failure to
insist that the ability to pursue happiness—to be stable enough to seek
out new experiences, to learn, to evolve, to take a break, to relish the
many pleasures that modern life offers—is a fundamental right and a
bedrock feminist cause.

And of course there's only so much that political change can do; profound and profeminist cultural shifts, particularly but not solely among
men, are also indispensable to the project of women and happiness. At
no point in living memory has this been clearer. For the past decade,
feminists have been forging ahead and making great gains both culturally and politically. And then, riding a wave of largely white, largely male
resentment aimed at women and people of color, Donald Trump won
the election for president of the United States. The chances of feminist
public policy becoming a reality anytime soon look awfully slim. The
chances politicians and pundits will learn all the wrong lessons—that
feminism is the problem, not the solution; that white male anger is
better catered to rather than dismantled; that gender roles are static
characteristics and not constraints to be pried open—look awfully high.

Which is why the stubborn insistence that women deserve happiness—that female happiness will in turn make men's lives better, too—
is more important than ever before.

As I wrapped up my final conversation with Janet, we talked about
what would make her happy. She ran down a predictable and basic list:
enough money to make rent, buy food, clothe herself and her children,
and give her kids the occasional treat; a mold-free house big enough for
her family; recovery from her injury so she could go back to work; a job
that paid her fairly and where she could move up the ladder; and the
ability to work full time and still have a few hours a day at home with her
kids. Where, I asked her, does she hope to be in the future? "I don't know
how, but in ten years I see us in a home," she said. "I want it to be the

home that I'm going to live in the rest of my life." And she sees herself going to work at the domestic violence shelter she plans to open and run. She's even picked out a place—an abandoned warehouse—and a name: Moving Forward. "We don't know where we will get the money yet, but we are going to start. We have big dreams and we are going to accomplish them," she said. "In a couple of more years, you will hear of us."

What Janet craves is the same essential thing so many of us seek: a stable foundation upon which to build a life that feels meaningful. If she can just get to the first stage—a safe, steady base on which to build—Janet is confident she can eventually live the kind of life she wants—a life that will bring her purpose, fulfillment, and, ultimately, happiness. After all, what else is there?

Acknowledgments

From the earliest stages of this project, this book was conceived of, fleshed out, and midwifed into existence by my editor Alessandra Bastagli at Nation Books. Thank you, Alessandra, for keeping me focused and pushing this thing into the world. Carrie Watterson and Collin Tracy at Perseus were also invaluable and careful editors; I am so grateful for their contributions. Chris Juby was an enthusiastic, creative and effective publicist, perpetually pushing me to think bigger and making the craziness of putting out a book feel manageable and even fun. Hannah Brown Gordon at Foundry Media understood this project on a fundamental level and was such an incredible sounding board and advocate when I needed it; I could not have asked for a better agent.

My tireless and innovative research assistant Alexandra Natale made so many contributions that determined what this book would be, and found not only the information I needed to ground my thesis, but added challenging and illuminating little gems that shifted my view and made this entire project more complex and powerful. Christina Filipovic was creative and diligent in her research, and one of the first people with whom I really talked this idea through—her ideas, suggestions, and contributions shaped much of the final product, and her readings and critiques of some chapters were incredibly helpful. Julie Schwietert Collazo made sure every fact was correct—a daunting mission she completed swiftly and conscientiously. Hilary Weaver's administrative assistance made it possible to write this book across four continents and half a dozen states.

A few of my most trusted friends read parts of this manuscript at various stages of the process, and their feedback, critique, and encouragement was key. Diane, Shannon, Julie, Priscilla, Anne, Chrissy, Jess: thank-you thank-you thank-you, for being readers and critics, but also just for being my people. I owe you all so much wine forever and ever.

My parents were kind enough to not ask me, "How's the book coming?" *too* often and didn't give me a hard time when I spent whole days of vacations together, on the few days of the year we see each other, writing and working. Mom, thank you for being the first person to buy a copy (technically five copies), for letting me tell your and grandma's stories, and, well—for everything, a list far too long to write out. Dad, thanks for being a model of what a less traditional father can look like and for being an unflagging source of support.

Thanks Auntie Vicky, for reminding me to eat the wind.

My feminist community was the catalyst for the ideas of this book, and it was with them that I hashed out many of the ideas in this book. Fellow feminist writers, thinkers, and activists have been a great source of mutual support, affirmation, and loving critique. What an incredible group of women (and a few men), and what a great blessing to have found them online and off. There are too many women to name individually, but I hold a special reservoir of appreciation for Lauren Bruce, the founder of *Feministe,* who invited me to write alongside her and launched the rest of my professional life, and the rest of the *Feministe* bloggers, contributors, and commenters, from whom I learned so very much.

I have been extraordinarily privileged to work with many incredibly talented editors, chief among them Joanna Coles, Amy Odell, and Lori Fradkin at *Cosmopolitan;* Rachel Dry at the *New York Times;* and Matt Seaton at the *Guardian* and later the *Times,* who not only made my words better but extended me so many new opportunities and made room for me to grow.

The heart of this book lies with the women and men who let me into their homes, spent hours in conversation, and shared with me some of their most intimate experiences and greatest hopes. To them I am grateful beyond words. Janet, Jennifer, Anna-Brown, John, Dan, Corinne, Ranjit, MaryBeth, Howard, Samantha, Amy, Christie, Beejoli, Karen, Sally, Jade, Amy, Diane, Merle, Tamara, Lucy, Karen, and all the women who responded anonymously to my survey: thank-you for trusting me with your stories; I hope I was able to do them justice. The many experts who talked to me for this project were also indispensable in grounding my reporting and anecdotes: Stephanie Coontz, W. Bradford Wilcox, Leah Torres, Twanna Hines, Christine Heyrman, Amanda Porterfield, Melissa Fabello, and Julie Finger were all absurdly generous with their time and thoughts. And there were several scholars, writers, journalists, and thinkers whose work I relied heavily on and whose research and writings deeply influenced this book: Caroline Fredrickson, Katha Pollitt, Melissa Harris-Perry, Claudia Goldin, Angela Davis, Heather Boushey, Ann-Marie Slaughter, Rebecca Traister, Anna Holmes, Roxane Gay, Gail Collins, Jessica Valenti, Imani Gandy, Kathryn Joyce, Irin Carmon, Mychal Denzel Smith, Patricia Hill Collins, Jaclyn Friedman, Amanda Marcotte, Loretta Ross, Lindy West, Jamil Smith, Peggy Orenstein, Aminatou Sow, Courtney Martin, Michelle Goldberg, Jamelle Bouie, Dorothy Roberts, Samhita Mukhopadhyay, Latoya Peterson, and Ann Friedman, among many many others.

Finally, Ty. Nothing I write can adequately display my bottomless well of gratitude for you. I could not ask for a better partner in love and in life and in work. Thank-you for all the nights you made me dinner so I could write, all the back massages, all the meals we spent only talking about this project, all the times you forced me to go out for walks, all the cups of coffee you brought me in bed. Thank-you, most of all, for reading and editing this entire book from front to back (much of it twice); it would not exist without you. You, and our big, untraditional, adventurous lives, have brought me a kind of happiness I didn't know I could feel. I am the luckiest.

Notes

1. Outrageous Acts and Everyday Rebellions

1. Text of the Massachusetts constitution. Retrieved from http://www.john-adams -heritage.com/text-of-the-massachusetts-constitution/

2. See, e.g., Zagarri, Rosemary (2008). *Revolutionary backlash: Women and politics in the early American republic.* Philadelphia: University of Pennsylvania Press; Berkin, Carol (2006). *Revolutionary mothers: Women in the struggle for America's independence (vintage).* New York: Knopf Doubleday; Hymowitz, Carol, & Weissman, Michaele (1984). *A history of women in America.* New York: Bantam Books.

3. Zagarri, *Revolutionary backlash.*

4. Ibid.

5. Haines, Michael (n.d.). *Fertility and mortality in the United States.* The Economic History Association encyclopedia. Retrieved from https://eh.net/encyclopedia/fertility -and-mortality-in-the-united-states/

6. Acevedo, Z. (1980). Abortion in early America. *Women & Health, 4*(2), 159–67. Retrieved from http://www.ncbi.nlm.nih.gov/pubmed/10297561

7. D'Emilio, John, & Freedman, Estelle (1998, February 28). *Intimate matters: A history of sexuality in America.* Chicago: University of Chicago Press.

8. Brown, Robert C. (1929, February). Breach of promise suits. *University of Pennsylvania Law Review.* Retrieved from http://scholarship.law.upenn.edu/cgi/viewcontent .cgi?article=8342&context=penn_law_review

9. Coontz, Stephanie (1992). *The way we never were: American families and the nostalgia trap.* New York: Basic Books.

10. Ibid.

11. Traister, R. (2016, November 12). Hillary Clinton didn't shatter the glass ceiling: This is what broke instead. *New York Magazine.* Retrieved from http://nymag.com/thecut/ 2016/11/hillary-clinton-didnt-shatter-the-glass-ceiling.html

12. Swarns, R. L., & Kantor, J. (2009, Oct. 7). In First Lady's roots, a complex path from slavery. *New York Times.* Retrieved from http://www.nytimes.com/2009/10/08/us/ politics/08genealogy.html

13. Coontz, *The way we never were.*

14. Ibid.; see also Rothstein, Richard. (2012, October 11). Public housing: Government-sponsored segregation. *American Prospect*. Retrieved from http://prospect.org/article/public-housing-government-sponsored-segregation; PBS (2003). Race—the power of an illusion: Go deeper. Retrieved from http://www.pbs.org/race/000_About/002_06_a-go deeper.htm.

15. Coontz, *The way we never were*.

16. Ibid.

17. Fredrickson, Catherine (2015). *Under the bus: How working women are being run over*. New York: New Press; Collins, Gail (2009). *When everything changed: The amazing journey of American women from 1960 to the present*. New York: Little, Brown.

18. Collins, *When everything changed*; Coontz, *The way we never were*.

19. Stevenson, Betsey, & Wolfers, Justin (2009, August). The paradox of declining female happiness. *American Economic Journal: Economic Policy, American Economic Association, 1*(2), 190–225.

20. Sachs, J., Becchetti, L., & Annett, A. (2016). *World happiness report 2016, special Rome edition*. (Vol. 2). New York: Sustainable Development Solutions Network.

21. Runfola, C. D., Von Holle, A., Trace, S. E., Brownley, K. A., Hofmeier, S. M., Gagne, D. A., & Bulik, C. M. (2012). Body dissatisfaction in women across the lifespan: Results of the UNC-SELF and gender and body image (GABI) studies. *European Eating Disorders Review, 21*(1), 52–59. doi:10.1002/erv.2201

22. PR Web (2013, April 16). Weight loss market in U.S. up 1.7% to $61 billion. Retrieved from http://www.prweb.com/releases/2013/4/prweb10629316.htm

23. Young, Emily A., Clopton, James R., & Bleckley, Kathryn. (2004). Perfectionism, low self-esteem and family factors as predictors of bulimic behavior. *Eating Behaviors, 5*, 273–283.

2. Summer Sisters

1. Traister, Rebecca (2016). *All the single ladies: Unmarried women and the rise of an independent nation*. New York: Simon & Schuster.

2. For more on transgender and queer terminology, see Trans Student Educational Resources, http://www.transstudent.org; other suggested reading: Serano, Julia (2007). *Whipping girl: A transsexual woman on sexism and the scapegoating of femininity*. Berkeley: Seal Press; Mock, Janet (2014). *Redefining realness: My path to womanhood, identity, love & so much more*. New York: Atria Books.

3. Cohn, D., Passel, J. S., Wang, W., & Livingston, G. (2011, December 14). Barely half of U.S. adults are married—a record low. Pew Social Trends. Retrieved from http://www.pewsocialtrends.org/2011/12/14/barely-half-of-u-s-adults-are-married-a-record-low/

4. Sachs, J., Becchetti, L., & Annett, A. (2016). *World happiness report 2016, special Rome edition*. (Vol. 2). New York: Sustainable Development Solutions Network.

5. Blieszner, Rosemary (2014). The worth of friendship: Can friends keep us happy and healthy? American Society on Aging, *Generations, 1*(7), 24–30; Kamen, R. (2012, November 29). A compelling argument about why women need friendships. *Huffington Post*. Retrieved from http://www.huffingtonpost.com/randy-kamen-gredinger-edd/female-friendship_b_2193062.html; Waxler-Morrison, N., Hislop, G. T., Mears, B., & Kan, L. (1991). Effects of social relationships on survival for women with breast cancer: A prospective study. *Social Science & Medicine, 33*(2), 177–183. doi:10.1016/0277-9536(91)90178-F; Hafner, K. (2016, September 9). Researchers confront an epidemic of loneliness. *New York Times*. Retrieved from http://www.nytimes.com/2016/09/06/health/lonliness-aging-health-effects.html; Texas Conference for Women (2010, September 1).

Good friendships: Great health. Retrieved from https://www.txconferenceforwomen.org/good-friendships-great-health

6. Taylor, S. E., Klein, L. C., Lewis, B. P., Gruenewald, T. L., Gurung, R. A., & Updegraff, J. A. (2000). Biobehavioral responses to stress in females: Tend-and-befriend, not fight-or-flight. *Psychological Review, 107*(3), 411; Berkowitz, G. (2008). UCLA study on friendship among women. Retrieved from http://www.raperreliefshelter.bc.ca/sites/default/files/imce/UCLAstudy.pdf

7. June-Friesen, K. (2014). Old friends Elizabeth Cady Stanton and Susan B. Anthony made history together. *Humanities, 35*(4). Retrieved from http://www.neh.gov/humanities/2014/julyaugust/feature/old-friends-elizabeth-cady-stanton-and-susan-b-anthony-made-histo

8. Faderman, Lillian (1999). *To believe in women: What lesbians have done for America —a history*. Retrieved from https://www.nytimes.com/books/first/f/faderman-believe.html

9. Wells, Ida B. Papers. Special Collections Research Center, University of Chicago Library. Retrieved from https://www.lib.uchicago.edu/ead/pdf/ibwells-0008-008-02.pdf

10. Faderman, *To believe in women*.

11. Wallace, Michele (1993). A black feminist's search for sisterhood. *All the women are white, all the blacks are men, but some of us are brave: Black women's studies*. New York: Feminist Press at City University of New York.

12. Combahee River Collective (1986). *The Combahee River Collective statement: Black feminist organizing in the seventies and eighties*. New York: Kitchen Table Press.

13. Rudulph, Heather Wood (2016, October 10). Get that life: How I got my own humor column at the *Washington Post*. *Cosmopolitan*. Retrieved from http://www.cosmopolitan.com/career/a63347/alexandra-petri-washington-post-get-that-life/

3. Playing in the Dark

1. Sanchez, Diana T., Fetterolf, Janell C., & Rudman, Laurie A. (2012). Eroticizing inequality in the United States: The consequences and determinants of traditional gender role adherence in intimate relationships. *Journal of Sex Research, 49*(2–3), 169–183. Retrieved from http://rutgerssocialcognitionlab.weebly.com/uploads/1/3/9/7/13979590/sanchez_fetterolf__rudman_2012.pdf

2. Pronier, C., & Monk-Turner, E. (2013). Factors shaping women's sexual satisfaction: A comparison of medical and social models. *Journal of Gender Studies, 23*(1), 69–80. doi:10.1080/09589236.2012.752347

3. Sanchez, D. T., Moss-Racusin, C. A., Phelan, J. E., & Crocker, J. (2010). Relationship contingency and sexual motivation in women: Implications for sexual satisfaction. *Archives of Sexual Behavior, 40*(1), 99–110. doi:10.1007/s10508-009-9593-4

4. McClelland, S. (2014). "What do you mean when you say that you are sexually satisfied?" A mixed methods study. *Feminism & Psychology, 24*(1). Retrieved from http://www.academia.edu/5121925/_What_Do_You_Mean_When_You_Say_That_You_Are_Sexually_Satisfied_A_Mixed_Methods_Study

5. Mann, S. A., & Patterson, A. S. (2016). *Reading feminist theory. From modernity to postmodernity*. New York: Oxford University Press.

6. Godbeer, R. (2002). *Sexual revolution in early America (gender relations in the American experience)*. Baltimore: Johns Hopkins University Press.

7. Cooke, Nicholas Francis (1892). *Satan in society, a plea for social purity: A discussion of the true rights of woman, marital and social*. Retrieved from http://onlinebooks.library.upenn.edu/webbin/book/lookupid?key=ha002188049 and https://babel.hathitrust.org/cgi/pt?id=mdp.39015020117571;view=1up;seq=9

8. Ibid.

9. Hasday, J. E. (2000). Contest and consent: A legal history of marital rape. *California Law Review*, 88(5). doi:10.15779/Z387Q79

Retrieved from http://scholarship.law.berkeley.edu/cgi/viewcontent.cgi?article=1484 &context=californialawreview

10. Timeline: The Pill (1999). *American Experience. PBS.* Retrieved from http://www.pbs .org/wgbh/amex/pill/timeline/index.html

11. Coontz, *The way we never were.*

12. Eig, Jonathan (2014). *The birth of the Pill: How four crusaders reinvented sex and launched a revolution.* New York: W. W. Norton.

13. Griswold v. Connecticut (June 7, 1965); Eisenstadt v. Baird (March 22, 1972); Roe v. Wade (January 22, 1973).

14. Gurley Brown, Helen (1962). *Sex and the Single Girl.* New York: B. Geis; distributed by Random House.

15. Boston Women's Health Collective (1973). *Our Bodies, Ourselves.* Boston: Touchstone. Retrieved from http://www.ourbodiesourselves.org/history/preface-to-the-1973 -edition-of-our-bodies-ourselves/

16. Fields, S. (1993, December 2). Best lesson elders could teach is the seductive eroticism of sex withheld. *Washington Times.* Retrieved from http://articles.sun-sentinel .com/1993-12-02/news/9311300858_1_arkansas-health-department-joycelyn-elders -comprehensive-health-education

17. Jehl, D. (1994, December 10). Surgeon general forced to resign by White House. *New York Times.* Retrieved from http://www.nytimes.com/1994/12/10/us/surgeon-general -forced-to-resign-by-white-house.html

18. Landor, A. M., & Simons, L. G. (2014). Why virginity pledges succeed or fail: The moderating effect of religious commitment versus religious participation. *Journal of Child and Family Studies,* 26(3). Retrieved from http://www.ncbi.nlm.nih.gov/pmc/articles/ PMC4090803/

19. Culp-Ressler, T. (2014, August 20). How virginity pledges can end up hurting kids. ThinkProgress. Retrieved from http://thinkprogress.org/health/2014/08/20/3473653/ virginity-pledges-sexual-health/

20. Landor & Simons, Why virginity pledges succeed or fail.

21. Girls fragrance & body care. Abercrombie kids. Retrieved from https://www.aber crombiekids.com/shop/wd/girls-fragrance

22. Clothing: Angelina girls bear-jr animal pattern faux thigh high pantyhose. Walmart .com. Retrieved from http://www.walmart.com/ip/Angelina-Girls-Bear-Jr-Cotton-Animal -Pattern-Faux-Thigh-High-Pantyhose/52058518

23. Clothing: 100% cute little girls multi color heart lettering 5 pc panty set small 4–6. Walmart.com. Retrieved from http://www.walmart.com/ip/100-Cute-Little-Girls-Multi -Color-Heart-Lettering-5-Pc-Panty-Set-SMALL-4–6/51751150

24. Girls Hawaiian luau adjustable coconut bra hula bikini top. Walmart.com. Retrieved from http://www.walmart.com/ip/Girls-Hawaiian-Luau-Adjustable-Coconut-Bra -Hula-Bikini-Top-Child-Size/192546581

25. Angelina 6-pack sweets for you and me girl's training bra. Walmart.com. Retrieved from http://www.walmart.com/ip/Angelina-6-Pack-Sweets-for-You-and-Me-Girls-Training -Bra/173665541

26. Abbasi, J. (2012, July 16). Why 6-year-old girls want to be sexy. *Live Science.* Retrieved from http://www.livescience.com/21609-self-sexualization-young-girls.html

27. Pappas, S. (2011, May 20). 30% of girls' clothing is sexualized in major sales trend. *Live Science.* Retrieved from http://www.livescience.com/14249-girls-clothing -sexualized.html

28. Paquette, D. (2015, August 6). Not even a third of speaking roles in popular movies go to women. *Washington Post.* Retrieved from http://www.washingtonpost.com/news/wonkblog/wp/2015/08/06/not-even-a-third-of-speaking-roles-in-popular-movies-go-to-women/

29. De Melker, S. (2013, December 21). Researchers measure increasing sexualization of images in magazines. *PBS NewsHour.* Retrieved from http://www.pbs.org/newshour/updates/social_issues-july-dec13-sexualization

30. Ibid.

31. Levy, Ariel (2005). *Female chauvinist pigs: Women and the rise of raunch culture.* New York: Simon & Schuster.

32. Centers for Disease Control and Prevention (CDC) (2015). *Results from the school health policies and practices study 2014.* Retrieved from http://www.cdc.gov/healthyyouth/data/shpps/pdf/shpps-508-final_101315.pdf

33. Blackman, K., Scotti, S., & Heller, E. (2016). State policies on sex education in schools. National Conference of State Legislatures. Retrieved from http://www.ncsl.org/research/health/state-policies-on-sex-education-in-schools.aspx

34. Sex and HIV education (2016). *Guttmacher Policy Review.* Retrieved from http://www.guttmacher.org/statecenter/spibs/spib_SE.pdf

35. CDC, *Results from the school health policies and practices study 2014.*

36. Darroch, J. E., Singh, S., & Frost, J. J. (2001). Differences in teenage pregnancy rates among five developed countries: The roles of sexual activity and contraceptive use. *Family Planning Perspectives,* 33(6), 244. doi:10.2307/3030191; Sedgh, G., Finer, L. B., Bankole, A., Eilers, M. A., & Singh, S. (2015). Adolescent pregnancy, birth, and abortion rates across countries: Levels and recent trends. *Journal of Adolescent Health,* 56(2), 223–230. doi:10.1016/j.jadohealth.2014.09.007

37. Rosenbaum, J. (2009). Patient teenagers? A comparison of the sexual behavior of virginity pledgers and matched nonpledgers. *Pediatrics,* 123(1). Retrieved from http://www.ncbi.nlm.nih.gov/pubmed/19117832

38. Brathwaite, L. (2016, March 11). Less than 50% of teens identify as straight, new study says. *Out Magazine.* Retrieved from http://www.out.com/news-opinion/2016/3/11/less-50-teens-identify-straight-says-new-study

39. Flournoy, M. (2015, August 18). Under assault, Planned Parenthood blames Jindal for making a "shambles" of health care. *Lens New Orleans.* Retrieved from http://thelensnola.org/2015/08/18/under-assault-planned-parenthood-blames-jindal-for-making-a-shambles-of-state-health-care/

40. Barrow, Bill (2015, July 10). Bobby Jindal touts Louisiana as "most pro-life state." *Associated Press.* Retrieved from http://bigstory.ap.org/article/cef38cf3948c4b78860c8aebd6332a17/bobby-jindal-touts-louisiana-most-pro-life-state

41. State facts about unintended pregnancy: Louisiana (2016, September). Retrieved from https://www.guttmacher.org/statecenter/unintended-pregnancy/LA.html

42. Barrow, Bobby Jindal touts Louisiana as "most pro-life state."

43. Pierce, C. (2015, Sept. 2). While syphilis outbreak rages in New Orleans, Bobby Jindal tries to defund Planned Parenthood. *Esquire.* Retrieved from http://www.esquire.com/news-politics/politics/news/a37572/bobby-jindal/

44. Barrow, Bobby Jindal touts Louisiana as "most pro-life state."

45. American Sociological Association (ASA) (2014, August 17). Virginity pledges for men can lead to sexual confusion, even after the wedding day. *Science Daily.* Retrieved from www.sciencedaily.com/releases/2014/08/140817215854.htm

46. Webb, C. (2014, March 28). I was a virgin on my wedding night—the best and worst thing for my first year of marriage (a guest post). Finding My Virginity. Retrieved from http://www.findingmyvirginity.com/2014/03/i-was-virgin-on-my-wedding-night-best.html

47. Strong, E. (2015, September 17). My husband raped me on our wedding night. Wedding Digest Naija. Retrieved from http://www.weddingdigestnaija.com/my-husband -raped-me-on-our-wedding-night/

48. Shim, E. (2014, June 27). The median age of marriage in every state in the U.S., in two maps. Mic.com. Retrieved from https://mic.com/articles/92361/the-median-age -of-marriage-in-every-state-in-the-u-s-in-two-maps#.OptPRUcxw

49. Jacobson, M. (2015, July 20). U. professor finds new trends between age and divorce rates. *Desert News Utah*. Retrieved from http://www.deseretnews.com/article/ 865632962/U-professor-finds-new-trends-between-age-and-divorce-rates.html

50. Wescott, L. (2016, April 20). Utah becomes first state to declare pornography a public health hazard. *Newsweek*. Retrieved from http://www.newsweek.com/utah-porn -public-health-hazard-450223

51. Conroy, S. (2006, December 19). Premarital sex: Almost everyone's doing it. *Associated Press*. Retrieved from http://www.cbsnews.com/news/premarital-sex-almost-everyones -doing-it/

52. National Sexual Violence Resource Center (2014). *Statistics about sexual violence*. Retrieved from http://www.nsvrc.org/sites/default/files/publications_nsvrc_fact-sheet_media-packet_statistics-about-sexual-violence_0.pdf

53. Cheng, Zhiming, & Smyth, Russell (2015, January 20). Sex and happiness. *Journal of Economic Behavior & Organization, 112*, 26–32.

54. McClelland, "What do you mean when you say that you are sexually satisfied?"; Pronier, C., & Monk-Turner, E. (2013). Factors shaping women's sexual satisfaction: A comparison of medical and social models. *Journal of Gender Studies, 23*(1), 69–80. doi: 10.1080/09589236.2012.752347

55. Mulvey, L. (1975). Visual pleasure and narrative cinema. *Screen, 16*(3), 6–18. doi:10.1093/screen/16.3.6. Retrieved from http://www.columbia.edu/itc/architecture/ ockman/pdfs/feminism/mulvey.pdf

56. Blanchflower, D. G., & Oswald, A. J. (2004). Money, sex and happiness: An empirical study. NBER working paper series. National Bureau of Economic Research. Retrieved from http://www.nber.org/papers/w10499.pdf

57. Wade, L. D., Kremer, E. C., & Brown, J. (2005). The incidental orgasm: The presence of clitoral knowledge and the absence of orgasm for women. *Women & Health, 42*(1), 117–138. doi:10.1300/j013v42n01_07

58. Galinsky, A. M., & Sonenstein, F. L. (2011). The association between developmental assets and sexual enjoyment among emerging adults. *Journal of Adolescent Health, 48*(6), 610–615. doi:10.1016/j.jadohealth.2010.09.008

59. Ibid.

60. Dotinga, R. (2014, August 21). Study: Men, lesbians more likely to have orgasms. *Health Daily*. Retrieved from http://consumer.healthday.com/women-s-health-information -34/abortion-news-2/study-men-lesbians-more-likely-to-have-orgasms-690934.html

61. Armstrong, E. A., England, P., & Fogarty, A. C. K. (2012). Accounting for women's orgasm and sexual enjoyment in college hookups and relationships. *American Sociological Review, 77*(3), 435–462. doi:10.1177/0003122412445802

62. Wade, Kremer, & Brown, The incidental orgasm, 117–138.

63. Orenstein, Peggy (2016). *Girls & sex: Navigating the complicated new landscape*. New York: HarperCollins.

64. Galinsky & Sonenstein, The association between developmental assets and sexual enjoyment among emerging adults, 610–615.

65. Orenstein, *Girls & Sex*.

66. Blanchflower & Oswald, Money, sex and happiness.

67. Cheng & Smyth, *Sex and Happiness.*

68. Fasula, A. M., Carry, M., & Miller, K. S. (2012). A multidimensional framework for the meanings of the sexual double standard and its application for the sexual health of young black women in the U.S. *Journal of Sex Research, 51*(2), 170–183. doi:10.1080 /00224499.2012.716874

69. Fahs & Swank, Social identities as predictors of women's sexual satisfaction and sexual activity. https://www.ncbi.nlm.nih.gov/pubmed/20878224.

70. Eyler, K. (2006). *Women of color network facts & stats: Sexual violence in communities of color—June 2006.* Retrieved from http://www.doj.state.or.us/victims/pdf/women _of_color_network_facts_sexual_violence_2006.pdf

71. Office for Justice Programs Office for Victims of Crimes (2014, June 2). Responding to transgender victims of sexual assault. Retrieved from http://www.ovc.gov/pubs/forge/ sexual_numbers.html

72. LGBT Bar Association (2015). Gay and trans panic defense. Retrieved from http:// lgbtbar.org/what-we-do/programs/gay-and-trans-panic-defense/

73. Republican platform (2012). https://prod-static-ngop-pbl.s3.amazonaws.com/ docs/2012GOPPlatform.pdf

74. Blue, M. (2015, October). Anti-choice organizer: Defund Planned Parenthood because "its sexual ethic is corrupted." Right Wing Watch. Retrieved from http://www .rightwingwatch.org/content/anti-choice-organizer-defund-planned-parenthood-because -its-sexual-ethic-corrupted

75. Schu, W. J. (2016). Contraception and abortion: The underlying link. United States Conference of Catholic Bishops. Retrieved from http://www.usccb.org/issues-and-action/ human-life-and-dignity/contraception/articles-and-publications/contraception-and-abortion -the-underlying-link.cfm

76. Polling: Abortion (2016, May 26). Gallup. Retrieved from http://www.gallup.com/ poll/1576/abortion.aspx

77. Downs, R. (2013, June 10). Abortion as the ultimate rejection of personal responsibility. *Live Action News.* Retrieved from http://liveactionnews.org/abortion-as-the-ultimate -rejection-of-personal-responsibility/

78. Dolan, E. W. (2013). Tea Party speaker: "Well, they want to call me a racist? Go ahead." Raw Story. Retrieved from http://www.rawstory.com/2013/08/tea-party-speaker -well-they-want-to-call-me-a-racist-go-ahead/

4. Life Among the Savages

1. Davis, Angela Y. (1981). *Women, Race and Class.* New York: Random House. Retrieved from https://www.marxists.org/subject/women/authors/davis-angela/housework.htm

2. 4 reasons being a stay at home mom is a damn job. SAHM.org. Retrieved from http://sahm.org/mom/14-reasons-why-being-stay-at-home-mom-is-a-damn-job/

3. Catt, C. (2014). Trapped in the kitchen: How advertising defined women's roles in 1950s America. Honor's thesis, Baylor University, Waco, TX. Retrieved from https:// baylor-ir.tdl.org/baylor-ir/bitstream/handle/2104/8951/Thesis%20Overall%20Format.pdf

4. Glass, J., Simon, R., & Andersson, M. (2016). CCF brief: Parenting and happiness in 22 countries. Council on Contemporary Families. Retrieved from https://contemporary families.org/brief-parenting-happiness/

5. O'Reilly, Bill (2013, July 23). President Obama and the race problem. *Fox News.* Retrieved from http://www.foxnews.com/transcript/2013/07/23/bill-oreilly-president-obama -and-race-problem/

6. Casey, T., & Maldonado, L. (2012, December). *Worst off: Single-parent families in the United States*. Retrieved from http://www.legalmomentum.org/resources/report-worst-%E2%80%93-single-parent-families-united-states

7. Badger, E. (2014, December 18). The unbelievable rise of single motherhood in America over the last 50 years. *Washington Post*. Retrieved from https://www.washingtonpost.com/news/wonk/wp/2014/12/18/the-unbelievable-rise-of-single-motherhood-in-america-over-the-last-50-years/

8. Taylor, P., Funk, C., & Clark, A. (2007, July). Generation gap in values, behaviors: As marriage and parenthood drift apart, public is concerned about social impact. Pew Social Trends. Retrieved from http://www.pewsocialtrends.org/files/2007/07/Pew-Marriage-report-6-28-for-web-display.pdf

9. Badger, The unbelievable rise of single motherhood in America over the last 50 years.

10. Ibid.

11. Kaufmann, G. (2012, Dec.21). This week in poverty: US single mothers—"the worst off." *Nation*. Retrieved from https://www.thenation.com/article/week-poverty-us-single-mothers-worst/

12. Ibid.

13. Vanassche, S., Swicegood, G., & Matthijs, K. (2012). Marriage and children as a key to happiness? Cross-national differences in the effects of marital status and children on well-being. *Journal of Happiness Studies, 14*(2), 501–524. doi:10.1007/s10902-012-9340-8

14. Millennials in adulthood (2014, March). Pew Social Trends. Retrieved from http://www.pewsocialtrends.org/2014/03/07/chapter-3-finances-social-trends-and-technology/

15. Taylor, Funk, & Clark, Generation gap in values, behaviors; see also Jones, S. (2008). Exercising agency, becoming a single mother. *Marriage & Family Review, 42*(4), 35–61. doi:10.1300/j002v42n04_03

16. Shih, G. (2012, February 2). Does being overweight affect your birth control? Bedsider. Retrieved from https://bedsider.org/features/164-does-being-overweight-affect-your-birth-control

17. Reeves, R. V., & Venator, J. (2015). Sex, contraception, or abortion? Explaining class gaps in unintended childbearing. Brookings Institution. Retrieved from https://www.brookings.edu/research/sex-contraception-or-abortion-explaining-class-gaps-in-unintended-childbearing/

18. Christopher, K. (2005). A "pauperization of motherhood"? Single motherhood and women's poverty over time. *Journal of Poverty, 9*(3), 1–23. doi:10.1300/j134v09n03_01; Jones, Exercising agency, becoming a single mother.

19. Badger, The unbelievable rise of single motherhood in America over the last 50 years.

20. Wayne, T. (2015, May 12). No kids for me, thanks. *New York Times*. Retrieved from http://www.nytimes.com/2015/04/05/style/no-kids-for-me-thanks.html

21. Livingston, G. (2015, May). *Childlessness falls, family size grows among highly educated women*. Pew Social Trends. Retrieved from http://www.pewsocialtrends.org/2015/05/07/family-size-among-mothers/

22. Unintended pregnancy in the United States (2016, October 5). Retrieved from https://www.guttmacher.org/fact-sheet/unintended-pregnancy-united-states

23. Livingston, *Childlessness falls, family size grows among highly educated women*.

24. Ibid.

25. Rich, Adrienne (1976, October 1). *Of woman born: Motherhood as experience and institution*. W. W. Norton.

26. Bialik, M. (2011, August 3). No diapers, no potty training, no kidding: The practice of "elimination communication." *Today.* Retrieved from http://www.today.com/parents/no-diapers-no-potty-training-no-kidding-practice-elimination-communication-1C7398317

27. Havrilesky, Heather. (2014, November 8). Our "mommy" problem. *New York Times.* Retrieved from http://www.nytimes.com/2014/11/09/opinion/sunday/our-mommy-problem.html

28. When "mom" becomes her identity (2014, November 17). Letters to the editor. *New York Times.* Retrieved from http://www.nytimes.com/2014/11/17/opinion/when-mom-becomes-her-identity.html

29. Hersch, J. (2013). Opting out among women with elite education: SSRN. *Vanderbilt Law and Economics Research, 11,* 469–506. doi:10.2139/ssrn.2221482

30. Schulte, B. (2015, March 28). Making time for kids? Study says quality trumps quantity. *Washington Post.* Retrieved from https://www.washingtonpost.com/local/making-time-for-kids-study-says-quality-trumps-quantity/2015/03/28/10813192-d378-11e4-8fce-3941fc548f1c_story.html

31. Miller, C. C. (2015, June 9). Mounting evidence of advantages for children of working mothers. *New York Times.* Retrieved from http://www.nytimes.com/2015/05/17/upshot/mounting-evidence-of-some-advantages-for-children-of-working-mothers.html

32. Dew, J., & Wilcox, W. B. (2011). If momma ain't happy: Explaining declines in marital satisfaction among new mothers. *Journal of Marriage and Family, 73*(1), 1–12. doi:10.1111/j.1741-3737.2010.00782.x

33. Why is everyone so busy? (2014, December 20). *Economist.* Retrieved from http://www.economist.com/news/christmas-specials/21636612-time-poverty-problem-partly-perception-and-partly-distribution-why

34. Paltrow, G. Lunch box. GOOP. Retrieved from http://goop.com/lunch-box-2/

35. Bialik, No diapers, no potty training, no kidding.

36. Friedersdorf, C. (2014, July 15). Working mom arrested for letting her 9-year-old play alone at park. *Atlantic.* Retrieved from http://www.theatlantic.com/national/archive/2014/07/arrested-for-letting-a-9-year-old-play-at-the-park-alone/374436/

37. Covert, B. (2014, August 15). Mother arrested for leaving her kids in a park while she went to a food bank. ThinkProgress. Retrieved from https://thinkprogress.org/mother-arrested-for-leaving-her-kids-in-a-park-while-she-went-to-a-food-bank-64f123929663#.jeobjwftk

38. Strasser, A.-R. (2014, March 27). Homeless mother gets job interview but doesn't have childcare, ends up in jail. ThinkProgress. Retrieved from https://thinkprogress.org/homeless-mother-gets-job-interview-but-doesnt-have-childcare-ends-up-in-jail-afa54acba86b#.gza55w94k

39. Douthat, R. (2016, January 2). The birthrate and America's future. *New York Times.* Retrieved from http://www.nytimes.com/2012/12/02/opinion/sunday/douthat-the-birthrate-and-americas-future.html

40. Shulevitz, J. (2012, December 6). The grayest generation. *New Republic.* Retrieved from https://newrepublic.com/article/110861/how-older-parenthood-will-upend-american-society

41. D'Arcy, J. (2012, December 12). What has delaying childbirth wrought? *Washington Post.* Retrieved from https://www.washingtonpost.com/blogs/on-parenting/post/what-hath-delaying-childbirth-wrought/2012/12/11/da44f1e6-43db-11e2-8061-253bccfc7532_blog.html

42. Twenge, J. (2013, July/August). How long can you wait to have a baby? *Atlantic.* Retrieved from http://www.theatlantic.com/magazine/archive/2013/07/how-long-can-you-wait-to-have-a-baby/309374/?single_page=true

43. Common myths about having a child later in life (2012, August 7). *CBS News*. Retrieved from http://www.cbsnews.com/media/common-myths-about-having-a-child-later-in-life

44. Allen, S. (2014, October 17). Don't be fooled by Apple and Facebook, egg freezing is not a benefit. *Daily Beast*. Retrieved from http://www.thedailybeast.com/articles/2014/10/15/don-t-be-fooled-by-apple-and-facebook-egg-freezing-is-not-a-benefit.html

45. McHaney, S., & Jacobson, R. (2014, December 10). 7 things every woman should know before freezing her eggs. *PBS NewsHour*. Retrieved from http://www.pbs.org/newshour/updates/freeze-eggs/

46. Barclay, E. (2015, November 24). More women are freezing their eggs, but will they ever use them? *NPR*. Retrieved from http://www.npr.org/sections/health-shots/2015/11/24/456671203/more-women-are-freezing-their-eggs-but-will-they-ever-use-them

47. Brown, J. (2013, June). Pro-life basics. *Choose Life Magazine*. Retrieved from http://www.clmagazine.org/file.aspx?DocumentId=271

48. Tsigdinos, The sobering facts about egg freezing that no one's talking about.

49. CMV: People who spend thousands of dollars on fertility treatment are selfish and should instead adopt a child already in this world (2015, December 5). Reddit, /r/changemyview. Retrieved from https://www.reddit.com/r/changemyview/comments/3vhod0/cmv_people_who_spend_thousands_of_dollars_on/

50. Joyce, Katherine (2013). *The child catchers: Rescue, trafficking, and the new gospel of adoption*. New York: Public Affairs.

51. PBS (2010, September 7). Off and running. Fact sheet. *POV*. Retrieved from http://www.pbs.org/pov/offandrunning/fact-sheet/

52. Livingston, G., & Cohn, D. (2010, June). Childlessness up among all women; down among women with advanced degrees. Pew Social Trends. Retrieved from http://www.pewsocialtrends.org/2010/06/25/childlessness-up-among-all-women-down-among-women-with-advanced-degrees/

53. Livingston, G. (2014, January). In terms of childlessness, U.S. ranks near the top worldwide. Pew Social Trends. Retrieved from http://www.pewresearch.org/fact-tank/2014/01/03/in-terms-of-childlessness-u-s-ranks-near-the-top-worldwide/

54. Livingston & Cohn, Childlessness up among all women; down among women with advanced degrees.

55. Ibid.

56. Daum, Meghan (2016). *Selfish, shallow, and self-absorbed: Sixteen writers on the decision not to have kids*. New York: Picador.

57. Geiss, L. S., McSeveny, D. R., & Floyd, H. H., Jr. (1983). Parenthood and marital happiness. *International Journal of Sociology of the Family, 13*(1), 159–176.

58. Ibid.

59. Forsyth, C. J. (1999). Perspectives of childless couples. *International Review of Modern Sociology, 29*(2), 59–70.

60. Ibid.

61. Ibid.

62. Saul, H. (2016, July 27). Marina Abramovic had three abortions because children would have been a "disaster" for her art. *Independent*. Retrieved from http://www.independent.co.uk/news/people/marina-abramovic-had-three-abortions-because-children-would-have-been-disaster-for-her-art-a7157566.html

63. Alexander, E. (2014, October 2). Tracey Emin: "There are good artists that have children. They are called men." *Independent*. Retrieved from http://www.independent.

co.uk/news/people/tracey-emin-there-are-good-artists-that-have-children-they-are
-called-men-9771053.html

64. Brooks, K. (2016, April 12). Is parenthood the enemy of creative work? *New York Magazine*. Retrieved from http://nymag.com/thecut/2016/04/portrait-motherhood-creativity
-c-v-r.html

65. Franklin, R. (2016, September 27). The novelist disguised as a housewife. *New York Magazine*. Retrieved from http://nymag.com/thecut/2016/09/shirley-jackson-rather
-haunted-life-c-v-r.html

5. *Wife*

1. Barkhorn, E. (2013, March 15). Getting married later is great for college-educated women. *Atlantic*. Retrieved from http://www.theatlantic.com/sexes/archive/2013/03/getting-married-later-is-great-for-college-educated-women/274040/

2. Taylor, P., Funk, C., & Clark, A. (2007, July). Generation gap in values, behaviors: As marriage and parenthood drift apart, public is concerned about social impact. Pew Social Trends. Retrieved from http://www.pewsocialtrends.org/files/2007/07/Pew-Marriage
-report-6-28-for-web-display.pdf

3. Coontz, S. (2014, August 19). Marriage suits educated women. *New York Times*. Retrieved from http://www.nytimes.com/2012/02/12/opinion/sunday/marriage-suits-educated
-women.html

4. The Shriver report snapshot: An insight into the 21st century man; Groundbreaking new survey cracks old stereotypes of masculinity (2012, February 11). Retrieved from http://www.shrivermedia.com/wp-content/uploads/2016/05/FINAL-Shriver-Report-Snapshot
-Press-Release.pdf

5. Anderson, R. T. (2013, March) *Marriage: What it is, why it matters, and the consequences of redefining it*. Retrieved from http://www.heritage.org/research/reports/2013/03/marriage-what-it-is-why-it-matters-and-the-consequences-of-redefining-it

6. Cady Stanton, E. (1889). *History of woman suffrage*. North Stratford, NH: Ayer.

7. Hasday, J. E. (2000). Contest and consent: A legal history of marital rape. *California Law Review*, 88(5). doi:10.15779/Z387Q79

8. On writ of certiorari to the United States Court of Appeals for the Sixth Circuit brief of historians of marriage and the American historical association as amici curiae in support of petitioners, 14–556 (2015). Retrieved from http://historians.org/Documents/AHA%20Letters/Amici%20Curiae%20on%20Same-Sex%20Marriage%202015.03.06.pdf

9. Voting rights for women: Pro- and anti-suffrage (n.d.). National Endowment for the Humanities. Retrieved from https://edsitement.neh.gov/lesson-plan/voting-rights-women
-pro-and-anti-suffrage

10. Hasday, Contest and consent.

11. Goodwin, H. M., Rev. Prof. (March 1884). Women's suffrage. *New Englander and Yale Review*, 43(179).

12. Hasday, Contest and consent.

13. Allen, S. (2015, June 9). Marital rape is semi-legal in 8 states. *Daily Beast*. Retrieved from http://www.thedailybeast.com/articles/2015/06/09/marital-rape-is-semi-legal
-in-8-states.html

14. Mantyla, K. (2007, March 29). Schlafly: Married women can't be raped by husbands. Right Wing Watch. Retrieved from http://www.rightwingwatch.org/post/schlafly
-married-women-cant-be-raped-by-husbands/

15. Mak, T., & Zadrozny, B. (2015, July 27). Ex-wife: Donald Trump made me feel "violated" during sex. *Daily Beast.* Retrieved from http://www.thedailybeast.com/articles/2015/07/27/ex-wife-donald-trump-made-feel-violated-during-sex.html

16. Baio, J.-A. M. (1982). *Fordham Law Review* loss of consortium: A derivative injury giving rise to a separate cause of action. *Fordham Law Review, 50*(6). Retrieved from http://ir.lawnet.fordham.edu/cgi/viewcontent.cgi?article=2535&context=flr

17. Berkowitz, *The boundaries of desire.*

18. McClain (2012). *Divorce—grounds and procedures: Fault-based divorce.* Retrieved from http://graphics8.nytimes.com/packages/pdf/world/2012/FamilyLaw_Classhandout12_spring2012.pdf

19. Obergefell v. Hodges, 576 U.S. ____ (2015). Retrieved from http://www.supremecourt.gov/opinions/14pdf/14-556_3204.pdf

20. Obergefell v. Hodges. On writ of certiorari to the United States Court of Appeals for the Fifth and Sixth Circuits brief of amici curiae 76 scholars of marriage supporting review and affirmance. Retrieved from http://sblog.s3.amazonaws.com/wp-content/uploads/2014/12/ac76ScholarsOfMarriageOkToPrint.pdf

21. Ibid.

22. Obergefell v. Hodges. Brief of amici curiae North Carolina Values Coalition; Liberty, Life, and Law Foundation; Chaplain Alliance for Religious Liberty; Christian Family Coalition; and Traditional Values Coalition in Support of Respondents. Retrieved from http://sblog.s3.amazonaws.com/wp-content/uploads/2015/04/14-556-562-571-574-bsac-North-Carolina-Values-Coalition.pdf.

23. Schwarzwalder, R. (2013). Complementarity in marriage: What it is and why it matters. Family Research Council. Retrieved from http://downloads.frc.org/EF/EF13J39.pdf

24. Fagan, P. F., Saunders, W. L., & Fragoso, M. A. (2009). How U.N. conventions on women's and children's rights undermine family, religion, and sovereignty. Family Research Council. Retrieved from http://downloads.frc.org/EF/EF09E38.pdf

25. Blase, J. (2008). The power of fathers. Focus on the Family. Retrieved from http://www.focusonthefamily.com/parenting/parenting-roles/the-power-of-fathers/the-power-of-fathers

26. Heffernan, C. (2002). God's design for marriage. Focus on the Family. Retrieved from http://www.focusonthefamily.com/marriage/gods-design-for-marriage/marriage-gods-idea/gods-design-for-marriage

27. Cohen, N. L. (2013, April 24). The national day-care law that wasn't. *New Republic.* Retrieved from http://www.newrepublic.com/article/113009/child-care-america-was-very-close-universal-day-care

28. Author interview with Stephanie Coontz.

29. Whelan, C. B. (2010, October 11). An education for marriage: Pew report confirms a college degree helps relationships succeed. *Psychology Today.* Retrieved from https://www.psychologytoday.com/blog/life-101/201010/education-marriage-pew-report-confirms-college-degree-helps-relationships

30. Springer, S. H. (2012, May 27). Well-educated couples have long had better marriages. *Psychology Today.* Retrieved from https://www.psychologytoday.com/blog/the-joint-adventures-well-educated-couples/201205/well-educated-couples-have-long-had-better

31. Cooper, D. F. (2007, October 16). Feminism and romance go hand in hand. *Science Daily.* Retrieved from http://www.sciencedaily.com/releases/2007/10/071015102856.htm

32. Wilcox, B. W. (2014, Dec. 11). It's (not just) the economy, stupid. *Family Studies.* Retrieved from http://family-studies.org/its-not-just-the-economy-stupid-why-is-the-working-class-family-really-coming-apart/

33. Miller, C. C. (2015, July 30). Millennial men aren't the dads they thought they'd be. *New York Times*. Retrieved from http://www.nytimes.com/2015/07/31/upshot/millennial-men-find-work-and-family-hard-to-balance.html

34. Ibid.

35. Miller, C. C. (2014, November 28). Even among Harvard graduates, women fall short of their work expectations. *New York Times*. Retrieved from http://www.nytimes.com/2014/11/30/upshot/even-among-harvard-graduates-women-fall-short-of-their-work-expectations.html

36. Wilcox, B. W. (2014). It's (not just) the economy, stupid. *Family Studies*. Retrieved from http://family-studies.org/its-not-just-the-economy-stupid-why-is-the-working-class-family-really-coming-apart/

37. Pear, R., & Kirkpatrick, D. (2004, January 14). Bush plans $1.5 billion drive for promotion of marriage. *New York Times*. Retrieved from http://www.nytimes.com/2004/01/14/us/bush-plans-1.5-billion-drive-for-promotion-of-marriage.html

38. Schwartz, M. (2013, January 31). For better or worse: Marriage promotion, cohabitation, and American politics. *Los Angeles Review of Books*. Retrieved from https://lareviewofbooks.org/article/for-better-or-worse-marriage-promotion-cohabitation-and-american-politics/

39. Rector, R., & Pardue, M. (2004, March 26). Understanding the president's healthy marriage initiative. *Heritage Foundation*. Retrieved from http://www.heritage.org/research/reports/2004/03/understanding-the-presidents-healthy-marriage-initiative

40. Glover, G. (2012, May 22). Study finds flaws in marriage interventions. *Binghamton Research*. Retrieved from https://discovere.binghamton.edu/news/marriage-4732.html

41. Trail, T. E., & Karney, B. R. (2012). What's (not) wrong with low-income marriages. *Journal of Marriage and Family*, 74(3), 413–427. doi:10.1111/j.1741-3737.2012.00977.x

42. Wang, W., & Parker, K. (2014, September). Record share of Americans have never married. Pew Social Trends. Retrieved from http://www.pewsocialtrends.org/2014/09/24/record-share-of-americans-have-never-married/

43. Schwartz, For better or worse.

44. Miller, C. C. (2014, December 2). The divorce surge is over but the myth lives on. *New York Times*. Retrieved from http://www.nytimes.com/2014/12/02/upshot/the-divorce-surge-is-over-but-the-myth-lives-on.html

45. Commission on domestic violence (2016). American Bar Association. Retrieved from http://www.americanbar.org/groups/domestic_violence/resources/statistics.html

46. Berkowitz, Eric N. (2015, August 1). *The boundaries of desire: A century of good sex, bad laws, and changing identities*. New York: Counterpoint.

47. Truman, Jennifer L., & Morgan, Rachel E. (April 2014). Nonfatal domestic violence, 2003–2012. US Department of Justice, Bureau of Justice Statistics. Retrieved from https://www.bjs.gov/content/pub/pdf/ndv0312.pdf

48. Modi, Monica N., Palmer, Sheallah, & Armstrong, Alicia (2014, March 1). The role of Violence Against Women Act in addressing intimate partner violence: A public health issue. *Journal of Women's Health*, 23(3). doi:10.1089/jwh.2013.4387

49. Rector & Pardue, Understanding the president's healthy marriage initiative.

50. Graham, J. (2000, June 1). Study finds welfare plan surprise. *Chicago Tribune*. Retrieved from http://articles.chicagotribune.com/2000-06-01/news/0006010213_1_minnesota-family-investment-program-traditional-welfare-manpower-demonstration-research-corp

51. Khazan, O. (2014, June 17). The luxury of waiting for marriage to have kids. *Atlantic*. Retrieved from http://www.theatlantic.com/business/archive/2014/06/why-poor-women-dont-wait-for-marriage-to-give-birth/372890/

52. Coontz, Marriage suits educated women.

53. Noam, S. (2014, February 16). Sexual satisfaction: Highly valued, poorly understood. *Psychology Today*. Retrieved from https://www.psychologytoday.com/blog/insight-therapy/201402/sexual-satisfaction-highly-valued-poorly-understood

54. Wang & Parker, Record share of Americans have never married.

55. Friedman, Howard S. (2012, February 28). *The longevity project: Surprising discoveries for health and long life from the landmark eight-decade study.* New York: Plume.

56. Sachs, J., Becchetti, L., & Annett, A. (2016). *World happiness report 2016, special Rome edition.* (Vol. 2). New York: Sustainable Development Solutions Network.

57. Ibid.

58. McCarthy, Niall. (2016, November 2). A surging American trend: Living with roommates. *Forbes*. Retrieved from http://www.forbes.com/sites/niallmccarthy/2014/11/05/a-surging-american-trend-living-with-roommates-infographic/#43770452bf99

59. Sachs, Becchetti, & Annett, *World happiness report 2016*.

60. Ibid.

61. Livingston, Gretchen. (2014, November 14). Four-in-ten couples are saying 'I do' again. Pew Research Center. Retrieved from http://www.pewsocialtrends.org/2014/11/14/four-in-ten-couples-are-saying-i-do-again/

6. Bossypants

1. Degrees conferred by sex and race (n.d.). National Center for Education Statistics. Retrieved from https://nces.ed.gov/fastfacts/display.asp?id=72

2. Contorno, S. (2014, January 24). Rand Paul says more than half of students at medical, dental and law schools are females. Politifact. Retrieved from http://www.politifact.com/truth-o-meter/statements/2014/jan/28/rand-paul/rand-paul-says-more-half-students-medical-dental-a/

3. Current glance at women in the law (2016, May). American Bar Association. Retrieved from http://www.americanbar.org/content/dam/aba/marketing/women/current_glance_statistics_may2016.authcheckdam.pdf

4. Beasley, M. H., & Gibbons, S. J. (2002). *Taking their place: A documentary history of women and journalism.* (2nd ed.). State College, PA: Strata.

5. Joyce, A. (2014, May 20). Is journalism really a male-dominated field? The numbers say yes. *Washington Post*. Retrieved from https://www.washingtonpost.com/news/style/wp/2014/05/20/is-journalism-really-a-male-dominated-field-the-numbers-say-yes/

6. Fischer, J. A. V., Bjørnskov, C., & Dreher, A. (2007). On gender inequality and life satisfaction: Does discrimination matter? *SSRN Electronic Journal*. University of St. Gallen, Economics Discussion Paper No. 2007-07. doi:10.2139/ssrn.980629

7. Waite, Linda J. (1981, December). *U.S. women at work.* RAND. Retrieved from https://www.rand.org/content/dam/rand/pubs/reports/2008/R2824.pdf

8. Goldin, C. (2006). The quiet revolution that transformed women's employment, education, and family. *American Economic Review, 96*(2), 1–21. doi:10.1257/000282806777212350

9. Waite, *U.S. women at work*.

10. Women in the labor force. (2016). Infoplease. Retrieved from http://www.infoplease.com/ipa/A0104673.html

11. Callahan, M. (2010, March 16). Sorority on E. 63rd St. *Vanity Fair*. Retrieved from http://www.vanityfair.com/culture/2010/04/barbizon-hotel-201004

12. Miller, T. (2012, February 25). The 1927 Barbizon Hotel for women—40 East 63rd street. Daytonian in Manhattan. Retrieved from http://daytoninmanhattan.blogspot .co.ke/2012/02/1927-barbizon-hotel-for-women-140-east.html

13. Callahan, Sorority on E. 63rd St.

14. No men allowed! Inside the glamorous doors of the Barbizon Hotel (2016, March 17). *Bust.* Retrieved from http://bust.com/entertainment/15498-where-the-girls-are.html

15. Wattensburg, B., Caplow, T., & Louis Hicks. The first measured century: An illustrated guide to trends in America, 1900–2000. *PBS.* Retrieved from http://www.pbs.org/ fmc/book/2work8.htm

16. Shank, Susan E. (March 1988). Women and the labor market: The link grows stronger. *Monthly Labor Review.* Retrieved from http://www.bls.gov/opub/mlr/1988/03/ art1full.pdf

17. Wattensburg, Caplow, & Hicks. The first measured century.

18. Coontz, S. (2008). *A strange stirring: "The feminine mystique" and American women at the dawn of the 1960s.* New York: Perseus Books Group.

19. Ibid.

20. Wattensburg, Caplow, & Hicks. The first measured century.

21. Venker, S. (2012, November 26). The war on men. *Fox News.* Retrieved from http://www.foxnews.com/opinion/2012/11/24/war-on-men.html?intcmp=features

22. Sen, B. (2003). Why do women feel the way they do about market work: The role of familial, social and economic factors. *Review of Social Economy, 61*(2), 211–234. doi:10.1080/0034676032000098228

23. Ibid.

24. Bichell, R. E. (2016, January 14). Average age of first-time moms keeps climbing in the U.S. *NPR.* Retrieved from http://www.npr.org/sections/health-shots/2016/ 01/14/462816458/average-age-of-first-time-moms-keeps-climbing-in-the-u-s

25. Barkhorn, Getting married later is great for college-educated women.

26. Sen, Why do women feel the way they do about market work.

27. R. R. Donnelley & Sons Company (n.d.). Encyclopedia.com. Retrieved from http:// www.encyclopedia.com/topic/R.R._Donnelley__Sons_Company.aspx

28. Engemann, K. M., & Owyang, M. T. (2006). Social changes lead married women into labor force. Federal Reserve Bank of St. Louis. Retrieved from https://research.stlouisfed .org/publications/regional/06/04/social_changes.pdf

29. Coontz, *A strange stirring.*

30. Goldin, The quiet revolution that transformed women's employment, education, and family.

31. Ibid.

32. Ibid.

33. Omori, M., & Smith, D. T. (2010). Working and living: The effects of family responsibilities and characteristics on married women's work hours in the USA. *Journal of Comparative Family Studies, 41*(1), 43–55.

34. Trends in labor force participation in the United States (2006). *Monthly Labor Review.* Retrieved from http://www.bls.gov/opub/mlr/2006/10/art3full.pdf

35. Zarya, V. (2016, February 23). Women do twice as much unpaid work as men— here's why that's not okay. *Fortune.* Retrieved from http://fortune.com/2016/02/23/melinda -gates-women-unpaid-work/

36. McLeod, Saul (2007, September 17). Maslow's hierarchy of needs. Simply Psychology. Retrieved from http://www.simplypsychology.org/maslow.html

Notes

37. Aravosis, J. (2013, May 30). *Fox News* mansplains why women should stay at home and have babies. Americablog. Retrieved from http://americablog.com/2013/05/fox-news-is-apoplectic-that-women-are-earning-more-money-nowadays.html

38. Wang, W., Parker, K., & Taylor, P. (2013, May). Breadwinner moms. Pew Social Trends. Retrieved from http://www.pewsocialtrends.org/2013/05/29/breadwinner-moms/

39. Schnittker, J. (2007). Working more and feeling better: Women's health, employment, and family life, 1974–2004. *American Sociological Review, 72*(2), 221–238. doi:10.1177/000312240707200205

40. Nobel, Carmen (2015, May 15). Kids benefit from having a working mom. Harvard Business School. Retrieved from http://hbswk.hbs.edu/item/kids-benefit-from-having-a-working-mom

41. Fisher, A. (2012, August 1). Women: Want a promotion? Find a boss whose wife has a career. *Fortune.* Retrieved from http://fortune.com/2012/08/01/women-want-a-promotion-find-a-boss-whose-wife-has-a-career/

42. Tausig, Mark, & Fenwick, Rudy (2011). *Work and mental health in social context.* New York: Springer-Verlag.

43. Martin, J. (2007, January 1). Gender-related material in the new core curriculum. Stanford Graduate School of Business. Retrieved from https://www.gsb.stanford.edu/stanford-gsb-experience/news-history/gender-related-material-new-core-curriculum

44. Fischer, Bjørnskov, & Dreher, (2007). On gender inequality and life satisfaction.

45. Fullerton, H. N. (1999). Labor force participation: 75 years of change, 1950–98 and 1998–2025. Bureau of Labor Statistics. Retrieved from http://www.bls.gov/mlr/1999/12/art1full.pdf

46. Labor force statistics from the current population survey (2016). Bureau of Labor Statistics. Retrieved from http://www.bls.gov/web/empsit/cpsee_e16.htm

47. Omori & Smith, Working and living.

48. Ibid.

49. Del Río, C., & Alonso-Villar, O. (2015). The evolution of occupational segregation in the United States, 1940–2010: Gains and losses of gender-race/ethnicity groups. *Demography, 52*(3), 967–988. doi:10.1007/s13524-015-0390-5

50. Ibid.

51. The simple truth about the gender pay gap (2016). American Association of University Women. Retrieved from http://www.aauw.org/research/the-simple-truth-about-the-gender-pay-gap/

52. Sommers, C. H. (2014, February 1). No, women don't make less money than men. *Daily Beast.* Retrieved from http://www.thedailybeast.com/articles/2014/02/01/no-women-don-t-make-less-money-than-men.html

53. The simple truth about the gender pay gap.

54. Miller, C. C. (2016, March 18). As women take over a field, the pay drops. *New York Times.* Retrieved from http://www.nytimes.com/2016/03/20/upshot/as-women-take-over-a-male-dominated-field-the-pay-drops.html

55. The simple truth about the gender pay gap.

56. Cohn, D. C., & Caumont, A. (2014, April). 7 key findings about stay-at-home moms. Pew Research Center. Retrieved from http://www.pewresearch.org/fact-tank/2014/04/08/7-key-findings-about-stay-at-home-moms/

57. Ibid.

58. Cohn, D., Livingston, G., & Wang, W. (2014, April). After decades of decline, a rise in stay-at-home mothers. Pew Social Trends. Retrieved from http://www.pewsocialtrends.org/2014/04/08/after-decades-of-decline-a-rise-in-stay-at-home-mothers/

59. Fredrickson, C. (2015). *Under the bus: How working women are being run over.* New York: New Press.

60. Irregular work scheduling and its consequences (2016). Economic Policy Institute. Retrieved from http://www.epi.org/publication/irregular-work-scheduling-and-its-consequences/

61. *Paid family and medical leave: DOL fact sheet* (2015). US Department of Labor. Retrieved from https://www.dol.gov/wb/paidleave/PDF/PaidLeave.pdf

62. *Report on Family Leave* (2014). Council of Economic Advisors. Retrieved from https://www.whitehouse.gov/sites/default/files/docs/leave_report_final.pdf

63. Tausig & Fenwick, *Work and mental health in social context.*

64. Ibid.

65. Ely, R. J., Stone, P., & Ammerman, C. (2014, December). Rethink what you "know" about high-achieving women. *Harvard Business Review.* Retrieved from https://hbr.org/2014/12/rethink-what-you-know-about-high-achieving-women

66. Livingston, G. (2014, June). Growing number of dads home with the kids. Pew Social Trends. Retrieved from http://www.pewsocialtrends.org/2014/06/05/growing-number-of-dads-home-with-the-kids/

67. Burke, L. (2014, January 24). Universal pre-k may not be as good as it sounds. Heritage Foundation. Retrieved from http://www.heritage.org/research/commentary/2014/1/universal-pre-k-may-not-be-as-good-as-it-sounds

68. Board, S.-L. E. (2009, November 6). Don't mess with success: Gov.-elect Chris Christie should catch up on preschool. NewJersey.com. Retrieved from http://blog.nj.com/njv_editorial_page/2009/11/dont_mess_with_success_gov-ele.html

69. Filipovic, J. (2009, Nov. 8). GOP's not-so-hidden agenda on Head Start. *New York Daily News.* Retrieved from http://www.nydailynews.com/opinion/gop-not-good-job-hiding-agenda-head-start-program-article-1.123265

70. North Carolina Work First. Benefits.gov. Retrieved from https://www.benefits.gov/benefits/benefit-details/1219

71. Fredrickson, *Under the bus.*

72. Woolner, David B. (2009, December). Feminomics: Breaking new ground. Roosevelt Forward. Retrieved from http://rooseveltinstitute.org/feminomics-breaking-new-ground-women-and-new-deal/

73. Coontz, S. (1993). *The way we never were: American families and the nostalgia trap.* New York: Basic Books.

74. Fredrickson, *Under the bus.*

75. Policy basics: Where do our federal tax dollars go? (2016, March). Center on Budget and Policy Priorities. Retrieved from http://www.cbpp.org/research/federal-budget/policy-basics-where-do-our-federal-tax-dollars-go

76. OECD. Employment: Time spent in paid and unpaid work, by sex. Retrieved from http://stats.oecd.org/index.aspx?queryid=54757

77. Matos, K., & Galinsky, E. (2014). *2014 National Study of Employers.* Retrieved from http://familiesandwork.org/downloads/2014NationalStudyOfEmployers.pdf

78. Stevenson, Betsey, & Wolfers, Justin (2009, August). The paradox of declining female happiness. *American Economic Journal: Economic Policy, American Economic Association, 1*(2), 190–225. doi:10.1257/pol.1.2.190

79. Douthat, R. (2014, November 10). Liberated and unhappy *New York Times.* Retrieved from http://www.nytimes.com/2009/05/26/opinion/26douthat.html

80. Ehrenreich, B. (2009, October 15). Did feminism make women miserable? *Salon.* Retrieved from http://www.salon.com/2009/10/15/ehrenreich_women_happiness/

81. Douthat, Liberated and unhappy.

82. Stevenson & Wolfers, The paradox of declining female happiness.

83. Misra, J., Moller, S., & Budig, M. J. (2007). Work family policies and poverty for partnered and single women in Europe and North America. *Gender & Society, 21*(6), 804–827. doi:10.1177/0891243207308445

84. Boushey, H. (2008). Family friendly policies: Helping mothers make ends meet. *Review of Social Economy, 66*(1), 51–70. doi:10.1080/00346760701668446

7. The Edible Woman

1. Time use survey (2015). Bureau of Labor Statistics. Retrieved from http://www.bls.gov/tus/

2. Sutton, R. (2014, March 6). Women everywhere in food empires but no head chefs. *Bloomberg*. Retrieved from http://www.bloomberg.com/news/articles/2014-03-06/women-everywhere-in-chang-colicchio-empires-but-no-head-chefs

3. Shaw, D. (2014, Sept. 19). Urban farming's grande dame: Karen Washington. *New York Times*. Retrieved from http://www.nytimes.com/2014/09/21/realestate/urban-farmings-grande-dame-karen-washington.html

4. Friedman, T. L. (2001, July 20). Foreign affairs; evolutionaries. *New York Times*. Retrieved from http://www.nytimes.com/2001/07/20/opinion/foreign-affairs-evolutionaries.html

5. Fox, M. (2015, July 9). You're still not eating enough vegetables. *NBC News*. Retrieved from http://www.nbcnews.com/health/diet-fitness/youre-still-not-eating-enough-vegetables-n389466; Rowan, Karen (2011, January 4). Big fat disconnect: 90% of us think our diets are healthy. *Live Science*. Retrieved from http://www.livescience.com/10389-big-fat-disconnect-90-diets-healthy.html

6. Dugan, A. (2013, August). Fast food still a major part of the American diet. Gallup. Retrieved from http://www.gallup.com/poll/163868/fast-food-major-part-diet.aspx

7. Beck, J. (2016, March 23). Less than 3 percent of Americans live a "healthy lifestyle." *Atlantic*. Retrieved from http://www.theatlantic.com/health/archive/2016/03/less-than-3-percent-of-americans-live-a-healthy-lifestyle/475065/

8. Fox, You're still not eating enough vegetables.

9. Adams, C. J. (1990). *The sexual politics of meat: A feminist-vegetarian critical theory.* (10th ed.). Oxford: Polity Press.

10. Oliver, J. (n.d.). Mother's day recipes. Jamie Oliver. Retrieved from http://www.jamieoliver.com/recipes/category/occasion/mothers-day/

11. Oliver, J. (n.d.). Father's day recipes. Jamie Oliver. Retrieved from http://www.jamieoliver.com/recipes/category/occasion/fathers-day/

12. Stewart, M. (n.d.). Father's day recipes. Martha Stewart. Retrieved from http://www.marthastewart.com/275144/fathers-day-recipes#224183

13. Stewart, M. (n.d.). Mother's day recipes. Martha Stewart. Retrieved from http://www.marthastewart.com/973920/10-most-pinned-mothers-day-brunch-ideas

14. Flynn, Gillian (2012). *Gone Girl*. New York: Crown.

15. Shanker, D. (2016, February 23). Men think they need to eat meat to be manly—and it's making them sick. QZ. Retrieved from http://qz.com/622306/men-think-they-need-to-eat-meat-to-be-manly-and-its-making-them-sick/

16. Pollan, M. (2009, July 29). Out of the kitchen, onto the couch. *New York Times Magazine*. Retrieved from http://www.nytimes.com/2009/08/02/magazine/02cooking-t.html

17. Moss, M. S. (2013). *Salt, sugar, fat: How the food giants hooked us.* New York: Random House.

18. Matchar, E. (2013). *Homeward bound: Why women are embracing the new domesticity.* New York, NY: Simon & Schuster.

19. Ibid.

20. Diet quality of Americans by SNAP participation status: Data from the national health and nutrition examination survey, 2007–2010 (2015, May). US Department of Ag-

riculture. Retrieved from http://www.fns.usda.gov/sites/default/files/ops/NHANES-SNA P07-10.pdf

21. Brooks, K. (2014, Spring). Research shows food deserts more abundant in minority neighborhoods. *Johns Hopkins Magazine.* Retrieved from https://hub.jhu.edu/magazine/ 2014/spring/racial-food-deserts/

22. Saslow, E. (2013, November 9). How the food stamp diet is leaving the Rio Grande valley both hungry and obese. *Washington Post.* Retrieved from http://www.washington post.com/sf/national/2013/11/09/too-much-of-too-little/

23. Nestle, M. (2011, November 15). Ketchup is a vegetable? Again? *Atlantic.* Retrievedfromhttp://www.theatlantic.com/health/archive/2011/11/ketchup-is-a-vegetable -again/248538/

24. Wanjek, C. (2015, October 7). Are healthy school lunch programs a waste? *Live Science.* Retrieved from http://www.livescience.com/52408-healthy-school-lunch -food-waste.html

25. Hellmich, N. (2013, January 7). Fewer people say they're on a diet. *USA Today.* Retrieved from http://www.usatoday.com/story/news/nation/2013/01/07/decrease-dieting -weight/1814305/

26. 12 wellness experts on how they REALLY built their brands online (2015, October 27). mindbodygreen. Retrieved from http://www.mindbodygreen.com/0-22194/12 -wellness-experts-on-how-they-really-built-their-brands-online.html

27. Health statistics (2016, July 27). National Institutes of Health. Retrieved from https://www.niddk.nih.gov/health-information/health-statistics/Pages/overweight-obesity -statistics.aspx

28. Hamblin, J. (2015, January 5). This is the average man's body. *Atlantic.* Retrieved from http://www.theatlantic.com/health/archive/2013/10/this-is-the-average-mans-body/280194/

29. Cooper, C. Headless fatties. Dr. Charlotte Cooper. Retrieved from http://charlotte cooper.net/publishing/digital/headless-fatties-01-07/

30. Moss, *Salt, sugar, fat.*

31. Vardi, N. (2012, September 4). The mystery man behind Weight Watchers and the private equity deal of the century. *Forbes.* Retrieved from http://www.forbes.com/ sites/nathanvardi/2012/09/04/the-mystery-man-behind-weight-watchers-and-the-private -equity-deal-of-the-century/

32. Judge, T. A., & Cable, D. M. (2011). When it comes to pay, do the thin win? The effect of weight on pay for men and women. *Journal of Applied Psychology, 96*(1), 95–112. doi:10.1037/a0020860

33. Weight discrimination could contribute to the glass ceiling effect for women, study finds (2009, April 7). Michigan State University. Retrieved from http://msutoday.msu.edu/ news/2009/weight-discrimination-could-contribute-to-the-glass-ceiling-effect-for-women -study-finds

34. Berry, T., & Spence, J. C. (2009). Automatic activation of exercise and sedentary stereotypes. *Research Quarterly for Exercise and Sport, 80*(3), 633–640. doi:10.1080/027 01367.2009.10599602

35. Phelan, S. M., Burgess, D. J., Yeazel, M. W., Hellerstedt, W. L., Griffin, J. M., & van Ryn, M. (2015). Impact of weight bias and stigma on quality of care and outcomes for patients with obesity. *Obesity Reviews, 16*(4), 319–326. doi:10.1111/obr.12266; Puhl, R., & Brownell, K. D. (2001). Bias, discrimination, and obesity. *Obesity Research, 9*(12), 788–805. doi:10.1038/oby.2001.108; Sikorski, C., Luppa, M., Glaesmer, H., Brähler, E., König, H.-H., & Riedel-Heller, S. G. (2013). Attitudes of health care professionals towards female obese patients. *Obesity Facts, 6*(6), 512–522. doi:10.1159/000356692

36. Drewnowski, A. (2009). Obesity, diets, and social inequalities. *Nutrition Reviews, 67*, S36–S39. doi:10.1111/j.1753-4887.2009.00157.x

37. Lupton, D. (2013, January 2). What does fat discrimination look like? The Conversation. Retrieved from http://theconversation.com/what-does-fat-discrimination-look-like-10247

38. Gray, E. (2014, July 23). Public food-shaming is the insidious type of street harassment no one is talking about. *Huffington Post*. Retrieved from http://www.huffingtonpost.com/2014/07/23/public-food-shaming-women_n_5604185.html

39. Lupkin, S. (2013, January 14). Jurors biased against obese women? *ABC News*. Retrieved from http://abcnews.go.com/blogs/health/2013/01/14/male-jurors-biased-against-obese-women-study-shows/

40. Parker-Pope, T. (2014, September 1). The fat trap. *New York Times Magazine*. Retrieved from http://www.nytimes.com/2012/01/01/magazine/tara-parker-pope-fat-trap.html

41. Berger, J., et al. (1973). *Ways of seeing based on the BBC television series*. London: British Broadcasting Corporation. Retrieved from http://waysofseeingwaysofseeing.com/ways-of-seeing-john-berger-5.7.pdf

42. Ibid.

8. The Story of a New Name

1. Goldin, C., & Shim, M. (2004). Making a name: Women's surnames at marriage and beyond. *Journal of Economic Perspectives, 18*(2), 143–160. doi:10.1257/0895330041371268

2. Lucy Stone, biography (n.d.). Bio. Retrieved from http://www.biography.com/people/lucy-stone-9495976#acclaimed-speaker

3. Goldin & Shim, Making a name.

4. Miller, C. C., & Willis, D. (2015, July 1). Maiden names, on the rise again. *New York Times*. Retrieved from http://www.nytimes.com/2015/06/28/upshot/maiden-names-on-the-rise-again.html

5. Ibid.

6. Angyal, C. (2013, February 11). More women are taking their husbands' last names—sort of. *New York Magazine*. Retrieved from http://nymag.com/thecut/2013/02/more-women-are-taking-husbands-names-sort-of.html?mid=huffpost_weddings-pubexchange_article

7. Hamilton, L., Geist, C., & Powell, B. (2011). Marital name change as a window into gender attitudes. *Gender & Society, 25*(2), 145–175. doi:10.1177/0891243211398653

8. Hallett, S. (2013, April 14). Should a woman take her husband's last name? *Huffington Post*. Retrieved from http://www.huffingtonpost.com/2013/04/14/changing-your-last-name_n_3073125.html

9. Hilmantel, R. (2013, August 8). How men REALLY feel when you keep your last name. *Women's Health Magazine*. Retrieved from http://www.womenshealthmag.com/sex-and-love/how-men-really-feel-when-you-keep-your-last-name

10. Miller & Willis, Maiden names, on the rise again.

11. Hamilton, L., Geist, C., & Powell, B. (2011). Marital name change as a window into gender attitudes. *Gender & Society, 25*(2), 145–175. doi:10.1177/0891243211398653

12. Hamilton, Geist, & Powell, Marital name change as a window into gender attitudes.

13. "Whatsoever you do . . . " (1994, February 3). Speech of Mother Teresa of Calcutta to the National Prayer Breakfast, Washington, DC. Priests for Life. Retrieved from http://www.priestsforlife.org/brochures/mtspeech.html

14. Klein, J. (2016, July 9). Get the epidural. *New York Times.* Retrieved from http://www.nytimes.com/2016/07/10/opinion/sunday/get-the-epidural.html

15. Goodwin, M. (2014, June 13). Who owns your womb? Women can get murder charge for refusing C-sections. *AlterNet.* Retrieved from http://www.alternet.org/civil-liberties/who-owns-your-womb-women-can-get-murder-charge-refusing-c-sections

16. Stone, R., & Lowell, M. (2015). Pregnant women and substance use: Fear, stigma, and barriers to care. *Health & Justice, 3*(1), 2. doi:10.1186/s40352-015-0015-5

17. Goodwin, Who owns your womb?

18. Ibid.

19. Beil, L. (2016, July 18). Millions of women are injured during childbirth: Why aren't doctors diagnosing them? *Cosmopolitan.* Retrieved from http://www.cosmopolitan.com/lifestyle/a59626/birth-injuries-postpartum-pain-untreated/

20. McDonald, E. A., Gartland, D., Small, R., & Brown, S. J. (2015). Dyspareunia and childbirth. *Obstetrical & Gynecological Survey, 70*(5), 319–320. doi:10.1097/01.ogx.0000466340.51108.12

21. Mannion, C. A., Vinturache, A. E., McDonald, S. W., & Tough, S. C. (2015). The influence of back pain and urinary incontinence on daily tasks of mothers at 12 months postpartum. *PLoS One, 10*(6). Retrieved from http://www.ncbi.nlm.nih.gov/pmc/articles/PMC4471341/

22. Memon, H. U., & Handa, V. L. (2013). Vaginal childbirth and pelvic floor disorders. *Women's Health, 9*(3). Retrieved from http://www.ncbi.nlm.nih.gov/pmc/articles/PMC3877300/

23. Beil, Millions of women are injured during childbirth.

24. Hillin, T. (2015, December 16). Many women feel sexually aroused while breastfeeding: So what? Fusion. Retrieved from http://fusion.net/story/240876/sexual-arousal-breastfeeding/

25. Choices, N. (2014, August 21). Is breastfeeding inability causing depression? NHS. Retrieved from http://www.nhs.uk/news/2014/08August/Pages/Failing-to-breastfeed-linked-with-postnatal-depression.aspx

26. Rayes, M. J. (2015, July). The sacrifices of motherhood. Society of St. Pius X. Retrieved from http://sspx.org/en/the-sacrifices-of-motherhood

27. Somashekhar, S., & Zauzmer, J. (2016, May 5). Report: 1 in 6 hospital beds in U.S. is in a Catholic institution, restricting reproductive care. *Washington Post.* Retrieved from https://www.washingtonpost.com/news/acts-of-faith/wp/2016/05/05/report-1-in-6-hospital-beds-in-u-s-is-in-a-catholic-hospital-restricting-reproductive-care/

28. Donley, G. (2015). Encouraging maternal sacrifice: How regulations governing the consumption of pharmaceuticals during pregnancy prioritize fetal safety over maternal health and autonomy. *NYU Review of Law and Social Change.* Retrieved from https://www.ncbi.nlm.nih.gov/pubmed/26793823

29. Ibid.

30. Helfand, C. L. (2012, July 7). Study finds 80 percent of 10-year-old girls have been on diet. *CBS Seattle.* Retrieved from http://seattle.cbslocal.com/2012/07/02/study-finds-80-percent-of-10-year-old-girls-have-been-on-diet/

31. Facts on eating disorders. (n.d.). National Eating Disorders Association. Retrieved from https://www.nationaleatingdisorders.org/get-facts-eating-disorders

32. Ransom, E. I., & Elder, L. K. (2003). Nutrition of women and adolescent girls: Why it matters. Population Reference Bureau. Retrieved from http://www.prb.org/Publications/Articles/2003/NutritionofWomenandAdolescentGirlsWhyItMatters.aspx

33. Kell, J. (2015, May 22). Lean times for the diet industry. *Fortune.* Retrieved from http://fortune.com/2015/05/22/lean-times-for-the-diet-industry/

34. Mychaskiw, M. (2013, April 17). Report: Women spend an average of $15,000 on makeup in their lifetimes. *InStyle.* Retrieved from http://www.instyle.com/beauty/15-under-15-best-bargain-beauty-products

35. Cosmetic surgery national databank statistics (2015). American Society for Aesthetic Plastic Surgery. Retrieved from http://www.surgery.org/sites/default/files/ASAPS-Stats2015.pdf

36. Thapoung, K. (2014, March 3). You'll be shocked by how long women spend on their hair and makeup each day. *Women's Health Magazine.* Retrieved from http://www.womenshealthmag.com/beauty/womens-beauty-routine

37. "THROUGH A RAPIST'S EYES" (PLS TAKE TIME TO READ THIS. It may save a life.) (2016). Facebook. Retrieved from https://www.facebook.com/notes/if-i-knw-wat-is-love-its-bcoz-of-you/through-a-rapists-eyes-pls-take-time-to-read-this-it-may-save-a-life/283308541696821?ref=nf

38. How to prevent date rape (n.d.). WikiHow. Retrieved from http://www.wikihow.com/Prevent-Date-Rape

39. Date rape—avoiding acquaintance rape (2016). Santa Monica Police Department. Retrieved from http://www.santamonicapd.org/Content.aspx?id=2459

40. Friedman, J., & Valenti, J. (2008). *Yes means yes: Visions of female sexual power and a world without rape.* Berkeley: Avalon.

Goodbye to All That

1. Isidore, C., & Luhby, T. (2015, July 9). Turns out Americans work really hard . . . but some want to work harder. *CNN.* Retrieved from http://money.cnn.com/2015/07/09/news/economy/americans-work-bush/

2. Fredrickson, C. (2015). *Under the bus: How working women are being run over.* New York: New Press.

3. Dusenberry, M. (2015, September 16). How America's lack of paid maternity leave worsens inequality. *Pacific Standard Magazine.* Retrieved from https://psmag.com/how-america-s-lack-of-paid-maternity-leave-worsens-inequality-4519f94a3f38

4. Saslow, E. (2013, November 9). How the food stamp diet is leaving the Rio Grande valley both hungry and obese. *Washington Post.* Retrieved from http://www.washingtonpost.com/sf/national/2013/11/09/too-much-of-too-little/

Index

Sandberg, Sheryl, 86, 184
Sanders, Bernie, 261
Sanger, Margaret, 59
Satan in Society: A Plea for Social Purity (Cooke), 57
Schlafly, Phyllis, 147
schooling, 121–122
Schu, Walter J., 88
Schwartz, Madeleine, 154
Schwarzwalder, Ron, 150
second-wave feminist movement, 4, 43–45
self-care, 234
self-made man, 23
self-objectification, 65
servants, 20
sex, 67–68, 78
    anal, 76
    attitudes towards, 82
    with birth control pill, 58
    coercion in, 76
    consent to, 75
    cultural discomfort with, 83
    enjoyment in, 80
    feminism in, 55, 83
    frequency of, 84
    on Internet, 63–64
    with marriage, 19–20, 57–58
    with men, 57–58, 76
    in monogamous relationships, 81
    mutual pleasure in, 272
    norms of, 79
    oral, 81, 83
    orgasms in, 80–81
    to please men, 76
    in politics, 55–56, 63
    in pop culture, 55
    as recreational, 19, 89–90
    reputation from, 20
    sexiness and, 84
    shame in, 66

    See also birth control pill; oral sex; virginity
Sex and the City (television show), 63
Sex and the Single Girl (Gurley Brown), 60, 63
sex industry, 19
Sex Object (Valenti), 90
sexiness, 66, 84
sexism
    of Trump, 30
    of virginity, 270
sexual assault, 85–86
sexual education, 63, 270
    downfalls of, 69–71
    for LGBT people, 67
    negativity in, 271
    state mandates for, 66–67
sexual harassment, 274–275
sexual pleasure, 54
    abortion and, 88–89
    intersectionality in, 86
    masturbation for, 83
    for men, 19, 147
    promotion of, 269–273
    in womanhood, 90
The Sexual Politics of Meat (Adams), 223
sexual privacy, 59–60
sexual revolution, 6, 59
sexual violence, 77
    in pop culture, 78
    toward transgender people, 85
sexuality
    health in, 85, 272–273
    Puritan ethics of, 15
    religion on, 53
    sexiness and, 66
sexualization, 66, 68
sexually transmitted infection (STI), 64

JILL FILIPOVIC is a journalist based in Nairobi and New York City. A contributing opinion writer for the *New York Times,* she is also a regular columnist for Cosmopolitan.com, where she was previously a senior political writer. A former columnist for the *Guardian*, she is also an attorney, and her work on law, politics, gender, and foreign affairs has appeared in the *New York Times,* the *Washington Post, Time,* the *Nation, Foreign Policy,* and others. She was the recipient of a 2014 Newswomen's Club of New York Front Page Award for her global health reporting, and the winner of a Society of Professional Journalists Sigma Delta Chi award for political commentary in 2014 and 2015.

Photo by Kathleen Kamphausen

The Nation Institute

Founded in 2000, **Nation Books** has become a leading voice in American independent publishing. The imprint's mission is to tell stories that inform and empower just as they inspire or entertain readers. We publish award-winning and bestselling journalists, thought leaders, whistleblowers, and truthtellers, and we are also committed to seeking out a new generation of emerging writers, particularly voices from underrepresented communities and writers from diverse backgrounds. As a publisher with a focused list, we work closely with all our authors to ensure that their books have broad and lasting impact. With each of our books we aim to constructively affect and amplify cultural and political discourse and to engender positive social change.

Nation Books is a project of The Nation Institute, a nonprofit media center established to extend the reach of democratic ideals and strengthen the independent press. The Nation Institute is home to a dynamic range of programs: the award-winning Investigative Fund, which supports groundbreaking investigative journalism; the widely read and syndicated website TomDispatch; journalism fellowships that support and cultivate over twenty-five emerging and high-profile reporters each year; and the Victor S. Navasky Internship Program.

For more information on Nation Books and The Nation Institute, please visit:

www.nationbooks.org
www.nationinstitute.org
www.facebook.com/nationbooks.ny
Twitter: @nationbooks